Shooting Stars
of the
Small Screen

ELLEN AND EDWARD RANDALL SERIES

**ENCYCLOPEDIA OF TV WESTERN ACTORS
(1946–PRESENT)**

Douglas Brode

UNIVERSITY OF TEXAS PRESS ⌄⌄ AUSTIN

791.4
Brode
2009

3 1712 01319 9966

Requests for permission to reproduce
material from this work should be
sent to:
    Permissions
    University of Texas Press
    P.O. Box 7819
    Austin, TX 78713-7819
    www.utexas.edu/utpress/about/
    bpermission.html

♾ The paper used in this book meets the
minimum requirements of ANSI/NISO
Z39.48-1992 (R1997) (Permanence of Paper).

Designed by Lindsay Starr

Frontispiece
THE END OF THE TRAIL: Clint Eastwood
(*center*) and the drovers from *Rawhide*'s
final season. Courtesy of CBS.

LIBRARY OF CONGRESS CATALOGING-IN-
PUBLICATION DATA

Brode, Douglas, 1943–
    Shooting stars of the small screen : encyclo-
pedia of TV western actors (1946–present) /
by Douglas Brode ; foreword by Fess Parker.
— 1st ed.
      p. cm.
    Includes indexes.
    ISBN 978-0-292-71849-4 (pbk. : alk. paper)
    1. Western television programs—United
States.   2. Television actors and actresses—
United States—Biography—Dictionaries.
I. Title.
    PN1992.8.W4B76 2009
    791.4502'8092273—dc22
    [B]
                              2008053319

To my grandson
Tyler Reese Brode
Keepin' the legends alive!

TV 6780

FROM CONFRONTATION TO COMMUNICATION: *The Saga of Andy Burnett* starred Jerome Courtland (*left*) and Jeff York. Actress unknown. Courtesy Walt Disney Television/ Buena Vista Releasing.

CONTENTS

KING OF THE WILD FRONTIER: Virtual unknown Fess Parker skyrocketed to superstardom in 1954 as Davy Crockett, the first significant Western hero to be created entirely by the new medium of television. A decade later, Parker produced his own *Daniel Boone* series. Courtesy Walt Disney Television/Buena Vista Releasing.

FOREWORD

FESS PARKER

IN the early 1950s I'd headed to Hollywood in hopes I might find success as an actor. At first I had small (even bit) parts. Even so, I got to work with such luminaries as Gary Cooper, John Wayne, and Randolph Scott. Finally came the big break: Walt Disney picked me to play Davy Crockett during *Disneyland*'s first season on the air (ABC; 1954–1955). All of us knew we were part of something special. I don't think, though, that anyone had a sense while shooting those shows of the immediate impact our three hour-long episodes would have. For they set off a national craze. One year later, it became evident that even if this phenomenon had started to fade, something else had emerged from it.

In addition to two more *Crockett*s for the Disney hour, a trio of non-Disney shows—*Gunsmoke, The Life and Legend of Wyatt Earp*, and *Cheyenne*— premiered, all successful. Within a year, the TV Western had tied situation comedies and game shows as the most popular fare on the air. Though related to theatrical Westerns, particularly of the B order, the TV Western soon emerged as a genre unto itself.

For the next ten years, I concentrated mostly on films for Mr. Disney and other producers. Then in 1964 I returned to TV with *Daniel Boone*, which I also executive-produced. The show ran for six years on NBC. When *Boone* came to an end in 1970, the TV Western was in decline and would shortly all but disappear, owing to changes in the world around us and what an audience looks for in its popular culture. *Bonanza* and a few others did remain in place for a little while longer. Since then, there have always been attempts to revive the Western, from *Centennial* through *Lonesome Dove* to most recently *Deadwood*. Perhaps someday the genre will come back full force, when and if *we* come full circle and once again take pride in our history as the American people.

In the meantime, this volume enshrines and preserves the essence of what the TV Western has always been all about. I take delight in the fact that at long last there will be a permanent record of what we all hoped to achieve, and particular pride in the heady position I've been assigned in the development of the TV Western.

AUTHOR'S NOTE

ALL of the photographs contained in this book were personally delivered, by mail or by hand, to Douglas Brode. They were provided either by the motion-picture producing and distributing company responsible for promoting the TV series or movie; by the TV network that originally aired the show; or by public relations professionals whose duty it was to attract ongoing, positive interest in either a project or a star/actor. All contributors were fully aware of the author's position as a writer of scholarly books, whose intention is to provide a serious record of TV Western actors for educational and academic purposes. The images in this book are included for precisely that objective.

Shooting Stars
of the
Small Screen

Fess Parker as Davy Crockett, 1954.
Courtesy Walt Disney Productions/Buena Vista Releasing.

INTRODUCTION

OUR HEROES HAVE
ALWAYS BEEN
COWBOYS

FOR those of us who constituted the first generation of TV-addicted children, the Western proved to be the most important single influence on our lives. Values promoted by such shows shaped our sensibility, even if we were under the impression that nothing was going on here except for some action-filled fun. But *all* entertainment contains subtexts, whether the people who fashioned the work intended them to be there or not. TV product, like movies, music, and comic books, shapes the mind of the receiver (particularly impressionable children) experiencing them. At the same time, pop culture reflects, if often unconsciously, the world out of which such shows emerge. Or at least a vision of that world held by the individual artisans, and in rare cases true art-

ists, who work within a commercial medium to create what we then blissfully enjoy.

"Cowboys are special," Willie Nelson mournfully sighs in a country-western song. In the twenty-first century, that's true for fewer Americans than was once the case. The very word *cowboy* has become politicized. When journalists speak of "cowboy politics," they aren't being complimentary. Since the election of 1980, the Cowboy Way has ceased to suggest a *universalized* American style of thinking, being, doing; that phrase is associated instead, fairly or unfairly, with a specific agenda. Tragic, perhaps, yet true: The cowboy—an icon from dime novels, TV, and movies as opposed to the hardworking person that term was created to describe more than 200 years ago—is more likely to divide twenty-first-century

Americans according to their sensibilities than to bring us together. Still, for a child of the fifties, as well as most anyone who was young then, cowboys *were* special. To again quote Willie Nelson, they have always been, and will always be, our *heroes*— role models we have aspired to emulate ever since the cowboy (and sometimes cow*girl*) during *that* century became transformed into an ideal; part of our myth pool, a nation's shared imagination, at a time when the daily news was the least-watched thing on TV. Not anymore! We exist in a reality that comes at us from every possible direction via cable news channels; all day, every day.

This is now; that was then.

This book is intended as a source on those actors who defined the TV Western, as well as the shows in which they appeared. Though the volume is as complete as possible, there had to be limits, owing to space. So, then: My first priority was to include every actor ever to receive star billing in a Western series. As to shows with more than one name above the title, all are present here. As it became imperative *not* to repeat information, key details about a series not found under one performer's entry show up in the section on a costar, explaining why the book is carefully cross-indexed.

An obvious example: All four of *Bonanza*'s leads are included, but details on that show are divided between them (as well as key supporting actors), based on which facts seemed most appropriate for a specific player. As to supporting casts, the selection process had to be determined by the impact of any one actor. Glenn Strange, beloved bartender on *Gunsmoke*, has his own entry. Many townspeople who wandered in and out of that show's Dodge are mentioned in passing under James Arness, if they came into contact with "Matt Dillon," or Amanda Blake, the case with various bartenders employed by "Miss Kitty." The same approach holds true for other shows with large ensembles.

My next priority: Include every star who has made his or her reputation by appearing in made-for-TV Western movies/miniseries. For instance, country singers Johnny Cash and Kris Kristofferson so closely associated themselves with Westerns in the eighties that they became essential to this book's concept. On the other hand, there's a difference between acting in a Western and being perceived as a Western actor. People who once or twice appeared in a Western (there are hundreds of them) aren't necessarily thought of as cowboy stars and so aren't included here.

The credits for each entry had to be selective, owing to space considerations. For any one series, dates given are those years in which the show ran. Cast members who left early or joined later are identified by the year span during which they appeared. TV movies are dated by the

THE BAR 20 RIDES AGAIN: In a brilliant financial move, actor William Boyd bought up the rights to his old *Hopalong Cassidy* films and marketed them to individual TV stations. Courtesy William Boyd estate.

size, then, that the form or *genre* covered here is related to theatrical Westerns. Any attempt to totally separate the two conveys a false impression of each. On the other hand, certain key differences should not, and will not, be overlooked.

So, to start at the beginning, during the early days of commercial television (roughly 1946–1951), old movies dominated in tandem with experimental live programming. During afternoon hours, when children constituted the chief audience, Westerns ruled. Because major studios initially feared TV, hesitating to release product, offerings were low-budget quickies from Poverty Row companies such as Mascot, PRC, and Monogram. The best of the lot, shot with more care and craftsmanship than those featuring, say, Whip Wilson, were William Boyd's *Hopalong Cassidy*s. This partly explains the era's "Hoppy Craze" when these were first aired, though the charisma of the man in black with silver hair cannot be overstated. Quickly, TV's immense appetite (showing on a weekly basis movies that had taken the better part of a month to produce circa 1930–1950) created the need for *more*. Producer/star Boyd filmed new *Hoppy*s even as the first season of *The Lone Ranger* commenced.

precise day, month, and year when initially broadcast if such information was available. Likewise, guest appearances, miniseries (two to three nights), and maxi-series (four or more nights) are indicated by the day the show debuted. Another priority was to provide a sourcebook as to which actors have portrayed actual people. Historical names are listed without quotation marks, which indicate a fictional character.

As many performers were also active in movies, theatrical credits are selectively listed to offer a full sense of the actor's screen (big *and* small) iconography: what the career, the image, *meant*. It's necessary to empha-

Shortly, Gene Autry–Roy Rogers "singing cowboy" films showed up as well. By 1951 both big-screen luminaries were, like Boyd, busily producing fresh material. While such shows must be considered descendents of their theatrical precedents, they constitute something other than extensions of them. Rogers and Autry chose thirty-minute formats (twenty-two to twenty-four minutes of film, leaving six to eight minutes for commercials) rather than the fifty-plus minutes of theatrical Bs. Scripts were designed as two-act plays, constructed so ads could be placed after the opening titles, at the midpoint, and as the story concluded but before the final credits rolled. This led to a different and unique narrative form. Hour-long B Westerns, like non-genre pieces produced on a larger budget, naturally fell into a three-act format. In Roy Rogers–Dale Evans movies, the way in which they met, first rubbed each other wrong, fell in love, then came together for a fade-out kiss became a ritual, each movie a variation on that theme. Rogers used his own name, while Evans played a new character in each. On their TV series, Evans, like Rogers, went by her own name. Their relationship, set in cement in the pilot (initial installment), continued from one week to the next.

All of this helps us understand why the TV Western can be considered a form unto itself. The *Hoppy* television films came closest to previous theatrical movies, allowing for an understanding of why, despite their incredible impact then, they're less vividly recalled today than the Rogers or Autry shows. TV *Hoppy*s, however

important as a bridge between what came before and what would follow, represented an attempt to make movies for TV. Autry and Rogers, rather, created the TV Western series, which soon usurped their forerunners' place in public entertainment. Autry originally employed his series to plug upcoming movie releases; within a few years, Autry films were no longer being produced. Little matter the subtle if basic differences between a theatrical film and a TV episode. To the public, it seemed silly to pay for B movies when, at least in the potential audience's conception, they could catch a reasonable facsimile for free. This raises the issue of what a B Western *is*, and the manner in which that term will be employed here.

A certain type of B Western used to be churned out quickly, often without quality control. These featured minor-league names (Eddie Dean), mounted by those aforementioned Poverty Row companies. Such films would be better referred to (as they are here) as C Westerns. A higher level of juvenile film (Rogers, Autry) was produced, often at Republic Studios, by people who *did* care about their reputation. These truly do rate as B items. With a bigger budget for exterior action scenes—rather than stock footage left over from silent-movie days, which the "cheapies" relied on—they rated as B movies at their best. *Don't Fence Me In* (1945) with Roy Rogers, the title song provided by the prestigious Cole Porter,

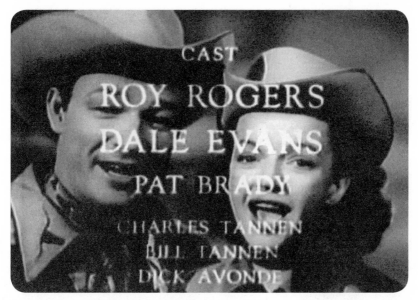

"HAPPY TRAILS TO YOU . . .": Roy Rogers and wife Dale Evans sang the theme song (written by Evans) as the closing credits rolled at the conclusion of each episode. Courtesy the Roy Rogers/Dale Evans estate, NBC.

sits at the top of that heap.

Republic is often referred to as the biggest of the minor studios, sometimes too as the smallest major. On occasion, Republic pushed the limits of B filmmaking by producing what will be referred to here as B+ films. Originally starring John Wayne (1940s), later Sterling Hayden (1950s), many were impressive in their visual approach and ran a full ninety minutes or more. Often they were shot in color, though color at Republic didn't compare with that element at any other studio. Republic color reduced everything to blue-greens and orange-reds, disorienting to newcomers today, charmingly nostalgic for longtime fans. The

true majors, ranging from Columbia and Universal (lowliest at that time) to the big boys over at Warner Bros. and MGM (20th Century-Fox, Paramount, and RKO Radio Pictures existed somewhere in between), likewise turned out Westerns, each company too proud to release junk. Still, they had writers, actors, directors, cinematographers, sound people, etc., under contract, drawing paychecks whether they worked or not. It wouldn't have been cost efficient to allow them to perform only on occasional prestige products.

Such studios regularly made what are (incorrectly) referred to as B movies. These featured the same professionalism as their A movies,

FROM PROGRAM PICTURES TO TV PROGRAMS: Richard Long (*left*) and Audie Murphy, seen here in Universal's *Kansas Raiders* (1950), would each in the 1960s star in a TV Western: *The Big Valley* and *Whispering Smith*, respectively. Courtesy Universal-International.

if with tighter budgets and shorter (seventy-five to eighty minutes) running times, featuring lesser names. B+ items ("bread and butter pictures"), including Westerns, are more properly referred to as *programmers*. Playing double bills, a Universal Audie Murphy might be paired with an Abbott and Costello comedy or the latest sci-fi/horror opus. Along with a cartoon and coming attractions, such a program could fill the bill at local theaters in an off-week, in between releases of that studio's A pictures. At various companies, Randolph Scott, Joel McCrea, George Montgomery, and John Payne were the featured stars.

Such films did continue to appear even after the advent of TV, since television could not yet provide anything comparable on a weekly basis. If you hankered to see such stuff, you had to pay. To ensure that the audience would do precisely that, studio-program pictures inched ever closer to A-movie status. Whereas a relatively early Audie Murphy like *Cast a Long Shadow* would consist of an eighty-two-minute black-and-white item, two years later *Posse from Hell* ran eighty-nine minutes and was shot in color. Some even employed the new widescreen process.

Yet between 1959 and 1961, these films too disappeared, again in reac-

MODES OF REALISM: *The Life and Legend of Wyatt Earp* opted for historical realism via recreations of actual events, including the gunfight at the O.K. Corral. *Top, left to right:* Sheriff John Behan (Steve Brodie), Virgil Earp (John Anderson), Doc Holliday (Douglas V. Fowley), and the title character (Hugh O'Brian). Courtesy Desilu/ABC. *Bottom: Gunsmoke* set the pace for stylistic realism, adapting the film noir style to TV with James Arness as the fictional "Marshal Dillon." Courtesy CBS.

tion to TV. More ambitious shows were now being filmed. Most ran sixty minutes. The half-hour *Gunsmoke* expanded to an hour. Many series, like *The Big Valley*, were shot in color. Again, why would a viewer pay to see what he could catch at home for free? So Hollywood concentrated on A Westerns, starring the likes of Wayne, James Stewart, and Robert Mitchum. When TV dared try a ninety-minute format (begin-

ning with *The Virginian* in 1962), A movies swiftly declined in number. Hollywood now focused on all-star extravaganzas (*How the West Was Won*, 1962), even as European-lensed spaghetti Westerns appeared with *A Fistful of Dollars* (1964), reinventing the movie Western after what had previously constituted precisely that now popped up on TV.

In addition to production values, television had, back in 1955, made the move from juvenile Westerns for Saturday mornings and weekday afternoons to adult oaters for prime-time. The adult Western film had been born early in the decade, following the success of *The Gunfighter* and *Winchester '73* (both 1950), *High Noon* (1952), and *Shane* (1953). Here, the lines between good and bad were purposefully blurred, villains no longer motiveless malignancies but psychologically troubled souls. Heroes gave way to antiheroes. As the most conservative of all mass media, TV waited until such fare had been accepted by the public before venturing into this territory. In fall 1955, *Cheyenne*, *The Life and Legend of Wyatt Earp*, and *Gunsmoke* appeared. Like the juvenile shows preceding them, which continued to be made, such series obeyed essential genre rules: fist- and gunfights, action balanced with romance. The hero never allowed himself to be tied down by any one attractive lady, whether for the fact-based Earp (his wives, two or three depending on differing accounts, were not present) or for the fictional "Matt Dillon" on *Gunsmoke*.

Another key element of the adult variation was a protagonist's need to make a living. In the juveniles, the hero—whether he assumed the name, if nothing else, of an actual person, as with Wild Bill Hickok or Kit Carson, or was entirely fictitious, as on *The Lone Ranger* and *The Range Rider*— had no visible means of support. He merely rode around solving problems for people, likely with a trustworthy sidekick. In an adult TV Western, as with its theatrical counterparts, the hero needed a paycheck; *that* much was true to life. On the other hand, he had no interest in family commitments, or had been married and now lived as a widower (*The Rifleman*, *Bonanza*).

As such, the hero qualified as a male fantasy figure. Suburbanites could come home to what Malvina Reynolds called little houses made of ticky-tacky (and they all looked just the same). And after supper, or better still while consuming a TV dinner, they could escape into a dream west where a man named "Bronco" never did get around to settling down. All that would change during the 1960s as society shifted; shortly, so did the popular culture that reflects our world. The bland conformity of the Eisenhower era abruptly ended. Jack Kennedy's New Frontier (the very term referencing Westerns) became central. During the hippie era, young people were not content to merely *watch* romanticized images of footloose drifters. They *became* just such people, likely in part as a result of earlier absorbing TV's fantasy images and trying to turn that cowboy ideal into a reality. No wonder fringed jackets and Indian beads were part of every dropout's costume!

Such behavior threatened an older America that once took delight in such escapism while remaining tightly locked into a traditional value

THE WARNER BROS. CORRAL: By the late 1950s, one company dominated the TV Western, for better or worse; pictured here are Wayde Preston (*Colt .45*), Ty Hardin (*Bronco*), Jack Kelly (*Maverick*), John Russell (*Lawman*), James Garner (*Maverick*), Peter Brown (*Lawman*), and Will Hutchins (*Sugarfoot*). Courtesy Warner Bros./ABC.

system. The idea that their kids were, for better or worse, actually living out their own bygone dreams of freedom sparked hostility, so no longer did they care for the *kind* of Westerns they'd once enjoyed. At that moment, the loner cowboy disappeared.

There were still loners, only now they were spies, more in tune with the international/ultra-contemporary tenor of the times. Even as *High Noon* led to *Gunsmoke*, the success of *Dr. No* (1962), the first James Bond film,

opened the door for *I Spy*, *The Man from U.N.C.L.E.*, and *Secret Agent/ Danger Man* on TV. Now, Westerns focused on *families*, from *Bonanza*'s always happy Cartwrights in the decade's early years, each male as single as those earlier TV cowboys but bound together in one place by land and blood, to *The High Chaparral*'s ever-arguing Cannons in the late sixties, which included marriage and children as part of the equation. As the once hopeful decade drew to its difficult close, everything from assassinations of national leaders through Vietnam and ghetto burnings to the Watergate hearings conspired to shake the foundations of our society. And with it, our popular culture.

Dennis Hopper, who guest-starred as Billy the Kid on various TV shows in the fifties, now offered an anti-romantic vision of "Billy" as a contemporary drug-dealing motorcyclist. His partner? "Wyatt" (Earp?), played by Peter Fonda, son of the greatest movie Wyatt Earp, Henry, in *Easy Rider* (1969). Hopper stated: "I don't believe in heroes anymore." In an era when "Travis Bickle" (Robert De Niro) in *Taxi Driver* (1976) reflected the alienation of many Americans (notably, he affected the guise of an Indian, the *enemy* of cowboys), the old hero, with his Code of the West, could not exist.

In ever more cynical times, the cowboy would be posited first as a tragic figure (Kirk Douglas in *Lonely Are the Brave*, 1962), then as a perfect fool (Lee Marvin, *Cat Ballou*, 1965), later still as a dangerous nihilist (William Holden, *The Wild Bunch*, 1969). Or, on a lighthearted note, *Butch Cassidy and the Sundance Kid* (1969), as a misplaced sophisticate. That same year, in a far darker incarnation, Holden, one of the stars who a decade earlier had embodied the old myth, now undermined it. "If they move," his bank robber "Pike" instructs his cohorts about the semi-innocent people standing in

their way, "*kill* them!" In due time, TV took up this mantle. Soon small-screen Westerns also were set at the *fin de siècle*, involving old-timers (Richard Boone in *Hec Ramsey*, James Garner in *Nichols*) attempting to adjust to a more scientific world or bad boys who provided role models (*Alias Smith and Jones*) during the Youth Movement.

Not that the family drama ceased to exist. In the second half of the sixties, *Daniel Boone* set the pace for full-family shows (husband, wife, kids) who farmed rather than ranched. That series ended its six-year run in 1970. Similar shows such as *Little House on the Prairie* and *The Waltons* succeeded it. Were they, in fact, Westerns? The former (set on the frontier, if without genre trappings), perhaps. The latter (the thirties, in the Southeast)? Probably not. Then again, was *Daniel Boone* a Western? According to executive producer/star Fess Parker, the show might more correctly be considered an Eastern. Here, then, is yet another paradox: a series that did obey most Western genre rules yet presented them in an earlier farm community rather than a later ranching one.

The very term *Western*, then, is more complex than it appears, most often employed to indicate stories set during the post–Civil War era, up to the turn of the century, with the focus on men who wear what we call cowboy hats. So the term *Western* has often been interchangeable with the

FAMILY VALUES: The TV image of a frontier family radically changed over the decades, less to accurately reflect the way things were than to mirror societal values when any one series was produced. *Top, left to right:* The all-male brotherhood on *Bonanza* (early 1960s) included "Ben" (Lorne Greene), "Hoss" (Dan Blocker), cook "Hop Sing" (Victor Sen Young), "Little Joe" (Michael Landon), and "Adam" (Pernell Roberts). Courtesy NBC. *Bottom: Deadwood*'s dysfunctional unit, the Bullock family, featuring Timothy Olyphant (Seth), Anna Gunn (Martha), and Josh Eriksson ("William"). Courtesy HBO Productions.

sobriquet *cowboy movie/series*. Even in major projects, however, that's more perception than reality. Several important works (obviously Howard Hawks's *Red River*, 1948, and Charles Marquis Warren's *Rawhide*, 1959–1966) *do* deal with men who drove cattle up the trail from Texas. Others, including film and TV versions of Owen Wister's *The Virginian* (1902), dealt with "hands" employed on a ranch. Still, in them, aspects of the gunfighter, a small coterie of perhaps two thousand people compared with the *millions* of young men who actually cowboyed, were grafted onto what in truth is best described as a blue-collar worker on horseback. As a result, we witnessed the creation of a mythic figure, best referred to as (borrowing from critic Robert Warshow) the Westerner.

Most traditional TV Westerns, like movies, deal with such a figure: part cowboy, part Indian fighter, part gunslinger, etc. Certain Western subgenres assume a different tack by focusing on mountain men, the cavalry, townspeople, or miners; sometimes (more recently) the Indian, from his point of view rather than glimpsed as a threat by Anglo heroes; occasionally African Americans and other ethnicities, like the Latino as hero rather than surly villain or silly sidekick; and, particularly since the seventies' feminist movement, women not as the hero's girlfriend but as a central character.

As to time and place, the aforementioned Eastern is set on the first frontiers, before Lewis and Clark, and in time John Charles Fremont and Kit Carson, explored those vast ranges of forest and prairie that lay to the west, as Jane Tompkins has put it, of *everything*. In Easterns, stories concern *la longue carabines*, be they fictional ("Natty Bumppo") or factual (Daniel Boone). Most such stories take place during the French and Indian Wars or the American Revolution. To Boone, living in North Carolina, the dark, bloody, uninhabited (even by Indians) ground called Kan-Tuc-Kee *was* the West. But for David Crockett a generation later, Kentucky, even some portions of Tennessee, represented the *East*. The West consisted of unknown land beyond the Obion

River. And, once that was settled, far-off places . . . Texas. California. Oregon.

Most of what we refer to as the East at one time had been perceived as the West. And the *Far* West at that! To people living in Albany, New York, in 1776, as described in Walter Edmonds's novel *Drums Along the Mohawk* (1936, realized onscreen in John Ford's 1939 film), anything west of their city constituted the frontier, those two terms becoming synonymous in our American lexicon. The West/frontier symbolized a promised land, those seemingly endless unknown territories, a place where no man (at least no Anglo) had walked before; *virgin* land. That conception, however unaware everyone may have then been of the implications, at once suggested religious, political, and sexual implications.

The Western frontier, as Frederick Jackson Turner would posit it in 1890 (when he and the Bureau of the Census announced that the American frontier would shortly cease to exist), could best be thought of as an invisible line on the horizon, dividing civilization just behind the great national march from the savagery that stretched ahead. A frontiersman (the Westerner) may in his early incarnation wear a coonskin cap instead of a Stetson, live not in Dodge City or San Antone but Detroit, or, in the case of a Southern, the swamps of Florida. A Northern? Skagway's frozen landscape.

But since the mid-sixties, most "oaters" (sometimes called Turnerian Westerns) have been set at a moment in time *after* that demarcation point disappeared, when no frontier exists, and, speaking symbolically rather than geographically, no *West*. Such narratives are played out on a post-frontier landscape, the protagonist no longer a man of the moment but an embarrassing anachronism: a once noble figure who now looks a little ridiculous. In literature, here is the end of the American adventure as portrayed in James Fenimore Cooper's *The Pioneers* and *The Prairie*, even as the first frontier had appeared in *The Deerslayer*, *The Pathfinder*, and *The Last of the Mohicans*. At least since Sam Peckinpah's elegiac *Ride the High Country* (1962), films have provided much the same vision. On TV, this conception first appeared with Rod Serling's *The Loner* (1965), each such work indicating that at the moment of its production, the Western had slipped into the sort of decline that "the West" itself had half a century earlier.

As the golden age of Westerns closed, genre pieces came to deal with the end of the West's golden age, real or imagined, helping us understand why, after 1970, a young cowboy became hard to locate on the small screen. Not to worry, though, since those two long-associated terms had split apart: The end of the West did *not* necessarily imply the end of the frontier. We simply had to move in other directions. Norman Mailer, in *Why Are We in Vietnam?* (1967), suggested that America's involvement in Southeast Asia might derive from an unconscious desire to find a new place where we could play cowboys and Indians; this likely posited the first significant debunking of the cowboy icon.

In a totally different vein, we now traveled upward rather than west. Kennedy's New Frontier led to *Star Trek* ("Space: The *Final* Frontier") on TV, as well as *Lost in Space*, and at the movies, *2001: A Space Odyssey* and *Planet of the Apes* (both 1968). When *Star Wars* (1977) opened almost a decade later, viewers noted that the cantina looked like a Western saloon reset on some distant planet; Han Solo, the lone gunman, is Ringo from *The Gunfighter*, challenged by the young punk Greedo. *Battlestar Galactica* then popped up on TV. Its premise? *Wagon Train* in deep space. The star? Lorne Greene, formerly of *Bonanza*. The space opera (as compared to actual science fiction like *Blade Runner*, featuring the same star, Harrison Ford) is the horse opera transferred to that new frontier. Little wonder, then, that Clint Eastwood (of TV's *Rawhide*) eventually directed and starred in a film called *Space Cowboys* (2000) with TV Western veterans James Garner (*Maverick*) and Tommy Lee Jones (*Lonesome Dove*). Apparently, our heroes will always be cowboys, in one form or another, if now heroes to only half of America.

When the traditional cowboy disappeared from large and small screens in the 1970s, other groups of Western people—farmers, Indians, Asians, Latinos, mountain men—previously relegated to the backdrop came into their own: in the movies, *Jeremiah Johnson* (1972); on TV, *Grizzly Adams*. In an age when weekend camping first became a popular pastime and environmentalism went mainstream, the mountain man (who in reality ransacked the wilderness) would be presented and accepted as a symbol of the rare enlightened Anglo who could live at peace with Indians, at one with the natural world. Owing to changes in our social orientation, the mountain man supplanted the cowboy as Western hero, though Hollywood's seventies' version of such trappers had no more in common with his historical predecessor than did the icons of earlier cowboy shows.

Nor should they. History exists in books; on screens, big or small, the mythology of Westerns is derived from Homer, not Herodotus. The cowboy would, incidentally, inch back into our public consciousness. The same year that Ronald Reagan campaigned for and won the presidency in part by posing in front of the Alamo in a Stetson, more Western films (*Long Riders*, *Tom Horn*, *Bronco Billy*, etc.) were released than during the entire previous decade. Simultaneously, the Western made a comeback on TV, if not in series form,

then as made-for-TV movies and miniseries starring a new generation of Western stars (Sam Elliott, Tom Selleck). Most were based on books by Louis L'Amour, favorite author of John Wayne, for whom *Hondo* had been specifically written. These new TV films were self-consciously designed in a traditionalist manner, aware and proud of retro sensibilities. Often they featured old-timers as living homages to that real or imagined "Code," if not of the West itself than of Western TV shows and movies. Yes, the cowboy *was* revived as a hero, though no longer a national one, now more likely revered in red states, reviled in blue ones.

Must that mythic figure now always be divisive? Not necessarily; *Lonesome Dove* (1989), a work of TV narrative genius from Larry McMurtry's superb novel, managed to have it both ways, delighting traditionalists as well as a new generation of viewers hoping for something more realistic and less romanticized. In truth, though, that show appears to be an exception, not the rule. *Deadwood*, the most significant undertaking since *Lonesome Dove* (a period piece, certainly, though hardly a genre piece in any conventional sense), offends traditionalists (mainly older, mostly rural) as much as it delights an emergent urban generation that perceives cowboys less as heroes than as dirty rotten scoundrels.

The answer to my rhetorical question, then? Probably, unless some mir-

THE A-LIST: Some of Hollywood's top movie stars made the transition to the small screen. *From top left:* Henry Fonda brought his fair-and-square persona from *The Ox-Bow Incident* to *The Deputy* (courtesy 20th Century-Fox); Gary Cooper, star of such big pictures as *Vera Cruz*, hosted a memorable special about the historical West (courtesy Flora Productions); Glenn Ford, star of *3:10 to Yuma*, appeared in *Cade's County* (courtesy Columbia Pictures); James Stewart of *Winchester '73* starred in episodes of various anthology series (courtesy Universal).

acle happens and America sets aside the polarization of both our politics *and* our popular culture.

Finally, this encyclopedia is intended as interpretive in addition to informative. While I go to great lengths to include all pertinent details about any one performer and the show (or, in many cases, shows) of which he or she was a part, I present this as a subjective work. Which series I most (or least) admire will be obvious. Larger amounts of space are spent analyzing those shows and stars I believe made the greatest contributions. We are what we watch, though it's often difficult to determine whether the images in our entertain-

A CHILD'S FANTASY OF THE FRONTIER: Every little boy's dream of living with his dog among some wonderful male heroes—and no parents or women—was realized in *The Adventures of Rin Tin Tin*. Clockwise, from bottom left: the title dog, Lee Aaker, James Brown, Rand Brooks, and Joe Sawyer. Courtesy Screen Gems/ABC.

ment imitate reality (an idea traceable back to Sophocles) or if it's the other way around. Most likely a bit of both. The point is, if today's pop culture/ TV allows us a window, however distorted, on our world, then artifacts from yesteryear let us glance into a mirror that reflects the way we were. I hope that this volume will accurately represent that mirror, or at least the element of it called the TV Western.

Lee Aaker

(1943–)

Born in Inglewood, California, to a dance-teacher mom, Aaker began performing at age eight. In *High Noon*, he pretends to be "Marshal Kane" (Gary Cooper) as Hadleyville's children stage the upcoming gunfight. Aaker had been slotted for the role as the Starrett child with Alan Ladd in *Shane* (1953) but was passed over for Brandon De Wilde. The following year Aaker won a similar role in *Hondo*, "John Wayne's *Shane*." He appeared in Screen Gems' *The Adventures of Rin Tin Tin* (1954–1959) as "Corporal Rusty B. Company," an orphan discovered by the cavalry and adopted as the mascot of Fort Apache, Arizona. This was the first TV Western to feature a child protagonist, serving as a surrogate for suburban kids and setting the pace for *Circus Boy, Buckskin*, etc. After *Rin Tin Tin*, Aaker found few acting jobs. He became production assistant (*Route 66*) to Herbert B. Leonard, his *Rin Tin Tin* mentor, then later left acting for carpentry. SEE ALSO: Rand Brooks, James (L.) Brown, Tommy Farrell, Joe Sawyer.

Rudolfo Acosta

(1920–1974)

This Mexican actor was discovered by John Ford while filming The *Fugitive* (1947, Henry Fonda). Regularly cast as Mexican banditos and cold-blooded Apaches such as "Silva," John Wayne's enemy in *Hondo* (1953), Satanta on *The Rebel* (10/18/59), and Bloodshirt in *Rio Conchos* (1964), Acosta played the sympathetic roles of "Chief Gabriel" on *Daniel Boone* (11/25/65 and 10/06/66) and the continuing part of "Chief Vaquero" in *The High Chaparral* (1967–1969). SEE ALSO: Linda Cristal, Henry Darrow, Leif Erickson, Fess Parker.

Nick Adams

(1931–1968)

Raised in a Pennsylvania coal town, Nicholas Adamshock seemed an unlikely candidate to symbolize the Old Confederacy. In 1959 *The Rebel* appeared as part of ABC's Sunday night all-Western lineup along with *Maverick*, *Lawman*, *Colt .45*, and *The Alaskans*. Adams's show proved to be a unique series, beginning with its title sequence: A flaming branding iron burned the silhouette of young "Johnny Yuma" onto a wooden wall while Johnny Cash warbled the theme song. The short, sensitive Yuma employed a sawed-off shotgun to blow away big guys who bullied him, afterward slipping off to write in his journal.

Like his alter-ego, Adams was a writer, collaborating with producer Andrew J. Fenady to create the concept. ABC loved their idea, but execs wondered whether a more handsome actor might play the part, Angrily, Adams replied: "I *am* 'the rebel.'" That was that! Teens saw the show as a Westernized equivalent of the movie that shaped their self-image, *Rebel Without a Cause* (1955), the comparison hardly coincidental. Adams had played one of the LA juvenile delinquents in James Dean's film; like Dean and Dennis Hopper, he perceived himself as a modern-day Billy the Kid, a role Adams played in his second film, *Strange Lady in Town*

TV'S ANGRY YOUNG MAN: On *The Rebel*, character actor Nick Adams helped create and embodied "Johnny Yuma," a restless teenager wandering the post–Civil War West, bearing more than a passing resemblance to one of his pal James Dean's antiheroes. Courtesy ABC.

(1955). Adams conceived "Johnny Yuma" as a combination of the Dean-type troubled teen with those James Cagney and John Garfield tough guys he'd idolized in his youth. Talented directors like Irvin Kershner (*Star Wars: Episode V—The Empire Strikes Back*, 1980) helped Adams and Fenady create a noir mood. Intellectuals claimed the title referenced Albert Camus's existential statement: "The Rebel is the man who says '*No!*'" Not that the Civil War was played down; several episodes referenced our country's blue-gray conflict.

Adams had hitchhiked to California and talked his way into *Mister Roberts* (1955), later claiming to be discovered by John Ford. Adams played small roles in big movies, including the paper boy "Bomber" in *Picnic* (1955) as the first-ever rebellious teen to wear a baseball cap backward. Adams not only acted with Dean in *Rebel Without a Cause*, he also shared a role with that star. Dean had died before dubbing voiceovers for "Jett Rink" in George Stevens's *Giant* (1956), so Adams did the honors. Adams then befriended Dean's Hollywood successor, Elvis Presley, though unaccountably never appeared in any of that star's films.

The Rebel made Adams rich and famous. ABC canceled the show despite high ratings, owing to an ugly dispute between the network and *Rebel's* production company about a proposed follow-up series, *The Yank*, which ABC rejected and Fenady then wanted to take to NBC. *The Rebel* initially did not go into syndication, reappearing on NBC in repeats following *Wagon Train* on Wednesdays. Adams showed up on NBC in fall 1962 as another writer, this time a modern journalist on *Saints and Sinners*. The series flopped, but then came supporting roles in big films: *Twilight of Honor* (1963), for which he won a Best Supporting Actor nomination, and *The Hook*

(also 1963), for which he *should* have been nominated. Adams coproduced and acted in *Young Dillinger* (1965), a grind-house predecessor to *Bonnie and Clyde*. His best friend Robert Conrad costarred; shortly before his death, Adams guest-starred in two episodes of Conrad's *The Wild Wild West*. Adams also played real-life Western outlaw the Apache Kid on *Hondo* (1967). He delivered his best TV performance as the title character in *Rawhide*'s "Corporal Dasovik" (12/4/64) playing a distressed cavalry non-com. Adams was found dead in his apartment early in 1968; the authorities never determined whether his death was intentional, an accidental drug overdose, or murder. SEE ALSO: Robert Conrad, Steve McQueen.

Claude Akins
(1926–1994)
••••••••••••••••••••••••••••••

Georgia born, Akins came naturally to playing small-town lawmen, as his father had been one in real life. A stint at Northwestern University was followed by service in the U.S. Army Signal Corps in WWII. Akins often portrayed rugged types (cruel, decent, indifferent) in major films: *From Here to Eternity* (1953), *The Caine Mutiny* (1954), *The Defiant Ones* (1958), and *Rio Bravo* (1959). His best early TV role came as the rational suburbanite in the *Twilight Zone* classic "The Monsters Are Due on Maple Street"

(3/4/60). He made numerous appearances on *Gunsmoke* (1955–1972) and *Wagon Train* (1957–1961) and appeared as Ben Thompson on *Outlaws* (3/22/62). Akins's first continuing TV roles were as rancher "Joe Hovarth" on *Empire* (1962–1963) and Father Kranz, a real-life priest who witnessed the Massacre at Wounded Knee, on *The Great Adventure* (1963–1964). His Western movies included *A Distant Trumpet* (1964) and *Return of the [Magnificent] Seven* (1966). When Neville Brand jumped ship during the final months of *Laredo* (1967), Akins joined the cast as "Cotton Buckmeister," a no-nonsense Texas Ranger.

During the following decade, truck drivers emerged as the modern equivalent to cowboys. Akins played "Sonny Pruett" on *Movin' On* (1974–1976), the favorite show of President Gerald Ford and his wife, Betty. Akins played "Stonewall Jackson Huff" on *Nashville 99* (1977), a fair-minded lawman in the modern South based on his own father, with Jerry Reed as a deputy. The two were matched again (along with Tom Selleck) in *The Concrete Cowboys* (1979), with Akins as "Woody Stone." Then it was back to truck-drivin', now as the pursuing policeman in *B. J. and the Bear* (1979–1981), with Greg Evigan and Akins mimicking the Burt Reynolds–Jackie Gleason characters from *Smokey and the Bandit*, followed by the spinoff: *The Misadventures of Sheriff Lobo* (1979–1981), broadly

played, fun on that level. His final TV Western role cast Akins as mountain man Tom "Broken Hand" Fitzpatrick in *Dream West* (1986), with Richard Chamberlain as John Charles Fremont and Rip Torn as Kit Carson.
SEE ALSO: Neville Brand, Jerry Reed.

Rex Allen
(1920–1999)
••••••••••••••••••••••••••••••••••

Notable for his Arizona drawl, sweetly masculine singing voice, and low-key personality, between 1950 and 1954 Allen rated as the last of the singin' cowboys, beginning with *Arizona Cowboy* and running through *Phantom Stallion*. The following year, he sang the theme song for the B+ *Rails into Laramie* (1954, John Payne). Allen's series *Frontier Doctor* (1958–1959) was an adult-oriented show, surprising perhaps when considering Allen's film career. He played the soft-spoken "Bill Baxter," living in the Arizona Territory circa 1900. This allowed director William Witney, a B-movie vet, to include news footage from that era. One episode depicted the San Francisco earthquake, so pre-existing celluloid footage of the event was effectively integrated into the show, allowing for an early docudrama approach. Allen later enjoyed a second TV career as the singing storyteller for Walt Disney nature docudramas set in the West: *The Legend of Lobo* (1962) and *Charlie, the Lonesome Cougar* (1967).

Ed Ames

(1927–)

••••••••••••••••••••••••••••••

Along with his brothers Vic, Gene, and Joe, four sons of poor immigrants (original last name Urick), Ed formed the singing group the Ames Brothers. His powerful baritone made the pop group beloved in pre–rock 'n' roll America. Interested in acting, he won the role as "The Narrator" in *The Fantasticks!*, Off-Broadway's longest-running show. Kirk Douglas picked Ames for the role of "The Chief" in the Broadway adaptation of Ken Kesey's *One Flew Over the Cuckoo's Nest* (1963) after Anthony Quinn turned it down. This led to the role of "John Talltree" on *Redigo* (9/24/63), making Ames the perfect candidate for "Mingo" on *Daniel Boone* the following fall. As Fess Parker boasted at the time, "He's the handsomest Jewish Indian since Jeff Chandler" (in *Broken Arrow*, 1950). By accident, Ames ended up becoming central to the best-remembered incident in the history of *The Tonight Show*: Demonstrating frontier-style ax-throwing, he hit his target squarely in the crotch. Always quick with a comeback, Johnny Carson insisted *Boone* ought to be retitled "Frontier Bris."

Ames left the series after four seasons to pursue his reignited singing career ("Try to Remember," "My Cup Runneth Over"). Eventually sensing he had achieved all he could in show business, he dropped out, attended university, and earned a Ph.D. SEE ALSO: Fess Parker.

John Anderson

(1922–1992)

••••••••••••••••••••••••••••••

This tall, stern Lincoln-esque actor is best recalled today for Rod Serling's *The Twilight Zone* (2/24/61) episode "The Odyssey of Flight 33" as a pilot who experiences a strange "bump in the night." One of several actors to play older brother Virgil on *The Life and Legend of Wyatt Earp*, Anderson performed that role during the show's final season (1961) in several episodes leading up to the gunfight at the O. K. Corral. SEE ALSO: Hugh O'Brian.

Michael Anderson, Jr.

(1943–)

••••••••••••••••••••••••••••••

The son of a noted director (*Around the World in Eighty Days*, 1956), Michael Jr. often appeared in Westerns, including the Aussie oater *The Sundowners* (1960) as the son of Robert Mitchum and Deborah Kerr. He played the youngest of the title characters in *The Sons of Katie Elder* (John Wayne, Dean Martin, Earl Holliman) and a youthful cavalryman in *The Glory Guys* and *Major Dundee*, all in 1965. Anderson gained short-lived TV stardom as "Clayt" in *The Monroes* (1966–1967), a show about hippie-like frontier runaway children fending for themselves. SEE ALSO: Barbara Hershey, Ben Johnson.

Richard Dean Anderson

(1950–)
•••••••••••••••••••••••••••••••

Shortly before his hit *MacGyver* (1985–1992), Anderson starred in the modern quasi-Western *Seven Brides for Seven Brothers* (1982–1983), a non-musical version of that film classic, as "Adam McFaddin," with Peter Horton and River Phoenix among his siblings. Before the success of *Stargate SG-1* (1997), which Anderson also produced, he played "Ernest Pratt," a debauched Ned Buntline–type dime novelist, in the brief-lived *Legend* (1995). The plot: Pratt knocks out silly adventure stories about a great frontier lawman who employs futuristic gadgets to beat bad guys. Two lovably crazy scientists, "Bartok" (John de Lancie) and "Ramos" (Mark Adair-Rios), convince Ernest they'll bring those sci-fi curios to life if he'll agree to become a living version of his heroic character.

Stanley Andrews

(1891–1961)
•••••••••••••••••••••••••••••••

The voice of "Daddy Warbucks" on radio's *Little Orphan Annie*, Andrews's over 400 movie/TV credits included many Westerns: *The Texas Rangers* and *The Plainsman* (both 1936), as

well as the Sheriff of Coffeyville in *The Doolins of Oklahoma* (1949). He also played "Mr. Welch" in Frank Capra's classic *It's a Wonderful Life* (1946). Andrews had a recurring role as "Judge Stone" on *The Gene Autry Show* (1950–1954) when he was picked to host *Death Valley Days* during its first decade on the air (1952–1963) as "The Old Ranger," coming across as a savvy codger who served up tales of the frontier. Ronald Reagan eventually replaced Andrews in this role. SEE ALSO: Rosemary DeCamp, Ronald Reagan.

Tod Andrews

(1914–1972)
•••••••••••••••••••••••••••••••

A New Yorker known for low-budget horror films (*Voodoo Man*, 1944; *From Hell It Came*, 1957), Andrews won brief fame as Major (later Colonel) John Singleton Mosby, leader of a Southern ranger outfit, in *The Gray Ghost* (1957–1958). The series had been planned for broadcast on CBS, but during the era's civil rights upheaval, network brass confessed to feeling nervous about the Confederate flag waving over stock footage from *The Birth of a Nation*'s battle scene during the opening credits, explaining why the show was syndicated instead. *The Gray Ghost* proved highly popular, particularly in the South, due to its Western-style action and the "Yellow Rose of Texas" theme. Phil Chambers showed up regularly as "Sergeant Myles Magruder," Sherwood Price as General Jeb Stuart. In a strange coincidence, Andrews played an officer named "Mosby" immediately before this show in the WWII film *Between Heaven and Hell* (1956).

Anna-Lisa

(1933–)

A stunning Ingrid Bergman lookalike and émigrée from Norway, Anna-Lisa initially worked at Warner Bros., where she charmed Will Hutchins on *Sugarfoot*, James Garner on *Maverick*, and Ty Hardin on *Bronco*. She appeared in two feature films, both about spaceflight: *Have Rocket, Will Travel* (1959, Three Stooges) and *12 to the Moon* (1960), as the only woman on board in each. Anna-Lisa was third-billed in *Black Saddle* (1959–1960) as townswoman "Nora Travers," with Peter Breck as "Clay Culhane," gunfighter turned lawyer, and Russell Johnson as "Marshal Gib Scott." Scripts often focused on her attempts to keep the two macho men from killing each other while trying to decide with which she would eventually settle down. Later she would be cast as real-life Scandinavian pioneer Huldah Swanson on *Death Valley Days* (4/7/66). Bored with Hollywood, she returned home and became a renowned stage star, now using her last name, Ruud. SEE ALSO: Peter Breck, Russell Johnson.

Michael Ansara

(1922–)

Syrian by birth, Ansara played Arabic characters in films after his discovery at the Pasadena Playhouse: *The Desert Hawk* (1950) and *Soldiers Three* (1951). His first Native American role was as "Tuscos" in *Only the Valiant* (1951, Gregory Peck); afterward, he became typecast as an Indian. For the 1956 season, 20th Century-Fox transformed *Broken Arrow* (1950, which had starred James Stewart as honest Indian agent Tom Jeffords and Jeff Chandler as Chief Cochise) for TV with John Lupton as Jeffords and Ansara as the legendary Apache. The show enjoyed a healthy two-year ABC run, dealing with the efforts of both men to maintain an uneasy peace between Indians and Anglos in Arizona. Next Ansara was introduced on an episode of *The Rifleman*, "The Indian" (2/17/59), as "Marshal Sam Buckhart," a Harvard-educated lawman. He repeated that role in "The Raid" (6/9/59). The following fall Buckhart became the centerpiece of *Law of the Plainsman*, an NBC one-season wonder in which he teamed with a female equivalent of *The Rifleman*'s "Mark" (Johnny Crawford), orphan "Tess" (Gina Gillespie), for whom Sam Buckhart becomes a father figure.

Supporting parts in big movies included *The Comancheros* (1961, John Wayne) and *Texas Across the River* (1966, Dean Martin). Ansara

A

received much journeyman work on episodic TV as Indians as well as varied other exotics. When the big-budget miniseries *Centennial*, from the James Michener epic, arrived on NBC in 1978, Ansara appeared as "Lame Beaver" (Ray Tracey played him as a child) in segments depicting the relationship of varied nations preceding the coming of the white man. He is best known today for his role as "Kang" in *Star Trek* (1968), *Star Trek: Deep Space* (1994), and *Star Trek: Voyager* (1996). Ansara also replaced Henry Silva as "Kane" on *Buck Rogers in the 25th Century* (1979–1980). He was once married to Barbara Eden; they toured together in a popular version of the musical *The King and I.* SEE ALSO: Chuck Connors, John Lupton.

CHARACTER PEOPLE: One great pleasure of the TV genre is provided by scene-stealing actors, including R. G. Armstrong. Courtesy ABC, NBC, and CBS.

R. G. Armstrong

(1917–   )

••••••••••••••••••••••••••••••

Gruff, grimacing, jowly, and chronically displeased, the Alabama-born Robert Golden Armstrong holds a master's degree in English from the University of North Carolina. Though Armstrong was trained at New York City's Actors Studio, fans perceive him as having more in common with Ben Johnson than with Marlon Brando. He piled up over 200 movie/TV credits, the lion's share in Westerns, including virtually every oater during TV's golden age. Armstrong won recurring roles as "Malone" in *The Californians* (1958) and "Sheriff Fred Tomlinson" on *The Rifleman* (1958). Noticed by one of that show's avatars, Sam Peckinpah, that filmmaker cast Armstrong in his second feature, *Ride the High Country* (1962), as Mariette Hartley's Bible-thumping father, then as a scowling reverend in *Major Dundee* (1965) and deputy Bob Ollinger in *Pat Garrett & Billy the Kid* (1973). In 1972 he appeared as James gang member Clell Miller in Phil Kaufman's *The Great Northfield Minnesota Raid.* Made-for-TV Western movies include *The Legend of the Golden Gun* (4/10/79) and *The Shadow Riders* (9/28/82). Memorable big-screen roles include the tracker in Henry Hathaway's *From Hell to Texas* (1958) and a Western ranch clan leader in Howard Hawks's *El Dorado* (1966). Later parts were

"Alfred Grimes" on *Dynasty* (1982) and the creepy "Lewis Vandredi" in *Friday the 13th* (1987–1989).

James Arness

(1923–)

••••••••••••••••••••••••••••••

At 6'6" towering over longtime friend John Wayne, Arness rates as the tallest TV Western hero ever. Never shy to herald the importance of his mentor, Arness happily credited the Duke with his own stardom. Arness attended Beloit College, served (at Anzio) during WWII, then sought acting jobs upon his return, mostly in B+ movies. His best early parts were as the hulking villain "Floyd Clegg" in Ford's lyrical *Wagon Master* (1950) and the title monster in Hawks's tingly *The Thing from Another World* (1951). Associations with these leading filmmakers put Arness in touch with their favorite star, Wayne, who in turn cast Arness in the red-baiting *Big Jim McLain* (1952), *Island in the Sky* (1953), and *Hondo* (1953). Producer Charles Marquis Warren was even then planning to bring radio's *Gunsmoke* to the new medium and, according to some sources, approached Wayne, asking him to play "Marshal Matt Dillon." Not relishing the grind of a weekly show, Big John suggested they consider Arness: Following its 1955 premiere, the series ran for twenty years.

Gunsmoke raises key issues for TV Westerns, including the oft-misused adjective "realistic." From the beginning, creator John Meston and original writer Sam Peckinpah wanted a clear departure from TV's kiddie oaters. The opening of all early episodes featured Dillon facing a lone gunman (Rodd Redwing) who gets off the first shot only to be killed by the marshal, slower on the draw but more accurate. This sequence had been filmed on the same street that, three years earlier, provided the backdrop for the shootout between Gary Cooper and four villains in *High Noon*, visually keying *Gunsmoke*'s audience to understand that they were far removed from *The Range Rider*, *Roy Rogers*, etc. Dillon emerged as a fine if flawed man, doing the best he could to keep Dodge City peaceful, yet anything but a simple white knight. One memorable early story placed Dillon in the same situation as other TV/movie lawmen: In front of his office, the marshal tries to persuade an angry mob to leave, threatening to blast them with a shotgun if they try to lynch his prisoner. Audiences certain of the outcome (he'd back them down) were stunned when Dillon allowed them to hang the man, telling his deputy "Chester Goode" (Dennis Weaver) he wouldn't shoot his constituents to save a killer. They, not he, would in time regret what happened here.

No wonder critics widely hailed *Gunsmoke* as realistic. Tone, however, is but one aspect of entertainment. Another is historical accuracy, not as to actual people (characters here were fictional) but rather a feel for period. In this sense, *Gunsmoke* rated as the *least* realistic adult Western. During early seasons, Dillon would wander through Boot Hill, musing about being a "U.S. Marshal." He was in fact the town's *deputy* marshal, something else entirely. *Gunsmoke* did not address the issue of a marshal's all-important relationship to the county sheriff; *The Life and Legend of Wyatt Earp* focused on precisely that, with Dodge on the *Earp* show accurately rendered as a Kansas cowtown. Dillon's Dodge had nothing in common with the real place other than the name of the saloon (Longbranch). Despite its "realistic" reputation, *Gunsmoke* posited a fantasy Dodge (if in its opening seasons an unpleasant fantasy), embodying *every* frontier settlement. In some episodes, Dodge appeared to be a cowtown; in others, a mining village. One week Dodge seemed a remote outpost, the next a large, well-settled community. The early seasons were filmed in the dusty streets of Gene Autry's Melody Ranch, but later ones were shot in colorful Old Tucson, Arizona, with gorgeous Southwest settings. The only way to accept this shift was to take *Gunsmoke* as a metaphor, Dodge symbolizing many/varied places with Dillon himself emerging as a larger-than-life symbol of the Western lawman.

In its original form, *Gunsmoke* enjoyed six successful years, often number one in the Nielsen ratings as a late-night Saturday standard. Expanded to an hour beginning in 1961, the show now ran from ten to eleven o'clock EST. The main reason for the changeover of many dramatic series from thirty to sixty minutes was strictly commercial: Producers realized that a rough cut of a weekly half-hour show ran fifty minutes, then had to be trimmed to half that length. If they instead left in all the material, maybe adding a little more padding, the producers could turn out an hour-long drama for the same price. By charging the standard amount for commercial airtime, the network would then double its profits. This sound business decision had a weakening impact on TV dramas. Though there *were* shows that needed a full hour to relate their stories (*Wagon Train* among them), others (*Gunsmoke* in particular) lost the old edge when tales that could have been quickly related dragged on. In 1966, as the price of color TV sets dropped and customers purchased them in larger numbers, all TV programming shifted to color. Some shows, like NBC's *The High Chaparral*, required that element, audiences anxious to see the beauty of on-location shooting. *Gunsmoke* continued (at least initially) to be shot on indoor sets, the color distracting from dramatic impact.

Peckinpah had long since fled, sensing that although the same characters remained on view, everything else now appeared totally different

IN THE STILL OF THE NIGHT: During its first season, James Arness (*right*) as "Marshal Matt Dillon" stealthily made his way through Dodge City's mean streets with "Deputy Chester Goode" (Dennis Weaver) dutifully following. Courtesy CBS.

from his initial concept. Whereas Dillon had originally been at odds with his town, despising people he was paid to serve owing to their greedy and craven ways, now they came off as lovable rubes, and he adored them. This was not so different from Andy Griffith as "Sheriff Andy Taylor" in Mayberry, and, excepting only the occasional (though ever less frequent) gunplay, *Gunsmoke* came to resemble that popular series more and more as the West and the South gradually collapsed into each other during the 1960s. "Doc Adams" (Milburn

Stone) ceased to be an unpleasant curmudgeon and transformed into a lovably crusty character. When Dennis Weaver left, he was replaced not by another Western type but by the countrified "Festus" (Ken Curtis). So many characters appeared that an encyclopedia could be created for them. Most long-lived and best remembered were Kelton Garwood (undertaker "Percy Crump"), Sarah Selby (boardinghouse keeper "Ma Smalley," 1961–1972), Howard Culver (hotel clerk, 1955–1974), Dabbs Greer (store owner "Wilbur

Jonas," 1955–1974), Woody Chambliss (store owner "Woody Lathrop," 1957–1975), James Nusser ("Louie Pheeters," 1956–1970), and Robert Brubaker (stage driver "Jim Buck," 1955–1975).

This total makeover became obvious in the opening sequence. Social violence during the late sixties caused critics to scrutinize TV for a possible cause, that legendary shootout was dropped. Dillon himself tended to be seen ever less as *Gunsmoke* transformed into an ensemble show about a likeable American community. The once hard-bitten drama now served as a predecessor to *Little House on the Prairie* and *The Waltons*, sentimentalizing the lives of those who live close to the earth, with ever more focus on farmers than cowboys. When *Gunsmoke* finally dipped in the Saturday night ratings, CBS shifted the durable hit to early Monday evenings and the show shot back up in popularity, running for several more years. Arness appeared in 233 half-hour and 402 hour-long episodes.

When CBS canceled the series, Arness returned (*sans* supporting cast) for five made-for-TV movies: *Return to Dodge* (9/26/87), *The Last Apache* (3/18/90), *To the Last Man* (1/10/92), *The Long Ride* (5/8/93), and *One Man's Justice* (2/10/94). In homage to his mentor, he played Wayne's role "Tom Dunson" in a 4/10/88 remake of Howard Hawks's *Red River* (1948). A year earlier, Arness incarnated Jim Bowie (the part Wayne originally

hoped to take on in 1960's *The Alamo*, though he eventually played Davy Crockett) on TV's *The Alamo: Thirteen Days to Glory* (1/26/87). Arness returned to the Western series format with *The Macahans* (1/19/76) as mountain man "Zeb," whose brother "Timothy" fights in the Civil War, leaving this rugged loner with a family including lovely, melancholy "Kate" (Eva Marie Saint) and various young people, among them "Seth" (Bruce Boxleitner) and "Laura" (Kathryn Holcomb). This movie of the week proved so popular that ABC spun it off into a pair of miniseries (1977 and 1978, each called *How the West Was Won*), then a weekly show in 1979. To live up to the new title, borrowed from the Oscar-winning 1962 film, Zeb and his family, now including "Molly" (Fionnula Flanagan), began the trek from Virginia to Oregon, settling down in Nebraska. Color photography enhanced an epic scope thanks to on-location work and an emphasis on the grimmer, grittier side of frontier life. Like most Westerns of this era, *The Macahans* placed an emphasis on marriage and family, showing the necessity of a woman (and children) in the rugged hero's life.

Incidentally, the actual spelling of the star's last name is Aurness; he's the brother of actor Peter Graves. SEE ALSO: Amanda Blake; Harry Carey, Jr.; Ken Curtis; Peter Graves; Burt Reynolds; Milburn Stone; Dennis Weaver.

BACK IN THE SADDLE AGAIN: Beloved singing cowboy Gene Autry not only starred in his own series but produced many others under his Flying A Productions banner. Courtesy Gene Autry/Flying A Productions.

Gene Autry

(1907–1998)

• •

The Oklahoma-raised Orvon Autry embodies the American Dream more than any other TV/movie cowboy, with the possible exception of Ronald Reagan. Sensing his own star potential, the young railroad worker/ telegraph operator talked his way into a spot on a Tulsa radio station (1928), then created his own show, often writing Western songs himself. He made his movie debut in a low-budget Ken Maynard serial, then later won the lead in *The Phantom Empire* (1935), an odd cliffhanger with Autry cast as the owner of Radio Ranch (title of the shortened feature version) who discovers an Atlantis-like continent under the prairie, resulting in sci-fi, musical, and contemporary oater all rolled into one. Autry was propelled into status as *the* singing cowboy, a B-movie sub-genre he all but invented, with a huge following in rural areas and popularity with children everywhere. Smiley Burnette played the original sidekick, later replaced by Gabby Hayes. Autry established the concept of an anachronistic West in which cars and airplanes coexisted with cowboys wearing pistols, an approach imitated by competitor Roy Rogers, who played a supporting role in Autry's *The Old Corral* (1936). Fans consider *Melody Ranch* (1940) Autry's best musical, with Jimmy Durante and Ann Miller along for the ride. Autry then volunteered for the Air Transport Command during WWII, returning to find Rogers billed as "King of the Cowboys," which resulted in a lifelong feud.

Autry's wonder horse Champion dominated many features, including *The Strawberry Roan* (1948). Picking up on TV at once, Autry starred in/executive-produced *The Gene Autry Show* (1950–1955), a half hour marked by strong production values, silly stories, at least one song (occasionally written by Autry, including the signature "Back in the Saddle Again") per episode, as well as exciting chases and fights. The show was shot entirely on location at Autry's Melody Ranch, a standing Western set also seen to great advantage in *High Noon* (1952). Pat Buttram played Autry's sidekick for most TV episodes, John Forrest "Fuzzy" Knight the occasional stand-in. Unlike Rogers, who was content with a single TV project, Autry thought big, bigger, biggest. He developed a stock company of players—notably Gail Davis and Dickie Jones—who eventually spun off to their own series, *Annie Oakley* and *Buffalo Bill, Jr.*, from his own Flying A Productions. The Autry shows set the tone for TV oaters during the first half of the 1950s, with *The Adventures of Champion, The Range Rider*, and other offerings making Autry so incredibly rich that, after his series ended (at least the new episodes, though a long syndication run followed), acting could no longer be considered financially viable. Instead, he oversaw the company's productions and invested in real estate, sports teams, etc. Best of all, in life Gene Autry always proved to be the mellow figure he portrayed onscreen. SEE ALSO: Pat Buttram, Gail Davis, Dick Jones, Jock (Jack) Mahoney.

Scott Bairstow

(1970–)

••••••••••••••••••••••••••••••

Bairstow assumed the role made famous by Rick Schroder in the *Lonesome Dove* miniseries, playing "Newt" (now going by his last name, "Call") in two TV shows. First came *Lonesome Dove: The Series* (1994–1995), in which Newt settled down in the small town of Curtis Wells, Montana, and competed with town boss "Clay Mosby" (Eric McCormack) for the hand of beautiful "Hannah Peale" (Christianne Hirt). The love triangle ended after the girl died soon after marrying the hero (shades of *Bonanza*'s final season), and the hero headed off to drink, fight, etc. The following fall, he was back at work in *Lonesome Dove: The Outlaw Years*; despite the misleading title, this show failed to chronicle Newt living on the edge. Instead, he returned to Curtis Wells, this time competing with Mosby for *two* beauties, the mysterious "Amanda Carpenter" (Tracy Scoggins) and the hardworking "Mattie Shaw" (Kelly Rowan). This marked quite a departure from Larry McMurtry's original, the franchise appealing now less to *Dove* buffs than to casual viewers. Bairstow also played Kris Kristofferson's pal in *Two for Texas* (1/18/98), about fictional bandits who become heroes at San Jacinto some two months after the fall of the Alamo. SEE ALSO: Kris Kristofferson, Rick Schroder.

Stephen Baldwin

(1966–)

••••••••••••••••••••••••••••••

The youngest of four acting brothers (Alec, Daniel, Billy), Stephen Baldwin played William Frederic Cody (Buffalo Bill) in *The Young Riders* (ABC, 1989–1992). Baldwin was twenty-three years old when this series began, making him nine years older than Cody himself was when he rode for the Pony Express (1860–1861). Still, this was the first time the youthfulness of the riders had been stressed; in 1953's *Pony Express* film, Charlton Heston played Cody as the seasoned scout he later became. Baldwin's only other association with the Western was as the single Anglo hero in Mario Van Peebles's black ensemble Western *Posse* (1993). SEE ALSO: Josh Brolin, Ty Miller.

Jim Bannon

(1911–1984)
••••••••••••••••••••••••••••••

A college athlete turned stuntman and then actor, Bannon played "Jack Packard" in the brief-lived *I Love a Mystery* B-film series. Then it was on to "Red Ryder" in a quartet of low-budgeters, *Roll, Thunder, Roll!* (1949) the most memorable. Bannon was billed as himself in several Whip Wilson/Fuzzy Knight flicks, then played Bob Ford in *The Great Jesse James Raid* (1953), shooting Willard Parker in the back. He replaced Allan "Rocky" Lane in TV's *Red Ryder* (1956) and was later picked up by Flying A Productions as "Sandy North" in *The Adventures of Champion* (1955–1956), the title referring to Gene Autry's famed horse. In this show, Sandy owned a ranch in the 1880s Southwest and cared for young nephew "Ricky" (Barry Curtis). When outlaws showed up, that mystery stallion roared down from the nearby hills to save them in the nick of time. SEE ALSO: Gene Autry, Allan "Rocky" Lane.

Roy Barcroft

(1902–1969)
••••••••••••••••••••••••••••••

"Everything I know about being a bad guy," Barcroft once confided to close friend Clayton Moore, "I learned from Harry Woods": i.e., by closely watching the legendary character actor who made "being bad" his stock in trade. Also, by *listening* to Woods: Moore claimed that in person Barcroft spoke in an entirely different tone than the cool, cruel croak he "borrowed" and employed in over 350 movies/TV shows. Born Howard Ravenscroft, Barcroft became to villains what Gabby Hayes was to comic sidekicks, playing in tandem with Roy Rogers, Gene Autry, William Boyd, and virtually every other genre star. Initially Barcroft shifted from one Poverty Row studio to the next, until executives at Republic sensed his appeal (kids loved to watch Barcroft being bad) and signed him to an exclusive ten-year contract. Barcroft did play a hero once, which was also his only historical character, Colonel George Custer (back when Custer was still a hero) in *The Oregon Trail* (1939).

On rare occasions, he showed up in A films (*Santa Fe Trail*, 1940; *They Died with Their Boots On*, 1941), Warner Bros. epics starring Errol Flynn. He also had a part in the classic Western musical movie *Oklahoma!* (1955). His first TV appearance was on *Cowboy G-Men* (4/4/53); Barcroft then appeared as a bad guy on *every* kiddie Western, suitably cast as an overweight villain who made clear with his eyes, voice, and body language that he was not to be taken lightly. All this changed when Disney came to TV. Always a fan of reverse typecasting, Walt gave Barcroft a new lease on his career via the *Spin and Marty* series (1955–1956), a serial that appeared in the late-afternoon Monday–Friday daytime slot on *The Mickey Mouse Club* and was followed by two sequels. The cliffhanger dealt with kids (Tim Considine, David Stollery) attending a summer camp/ranch in the modern West, with Barcroft effective as the brusque but understanding owner, "Colonel Jim Logan," who achieved a delicate balance for the boys between Western-style individualism (letting each discover himself as a unique person) and community responsibility (ensuring they did get along). After that, Barcroft returned to his old evil ways. In the opening episode of *Johnny Ringo* (10/1/59), Barcroft played an insensitive father who goads his teenage son into a gun duel with the title character (Don Durant). SEE ALSO: Harry Carey, Jr.; Don Durant; Russell Hayden.

Trevor Bardette

(1902–1977)

••••••••••••••••••••••••••••••

Stern-faced with unrelenting eyes, a drooping mustache, and that softly menacing voice, Bardette perfectly played outlaws in many a B Western, including Sam Bass in *Wild Bill Hickok Rides* (1942). He created sparks as two Texas heroes, Davy Crockett in *The Man from the Alamo* (1953) and Sam Houston on TV's *Frontier* (2/19/56). He played Newman Haynes "Old Man" Clanton during the final seasons of *The Life and Legend of Wyatt Earp* (1959–1961), a role essayed on film by Walter Brennan in Ford's *My Darling Clementine* (1946) as evil incarnate. Bardette's Clanton, though mean-spirited, hardly rated as a simplistic villain. While Earp (Hugh O'Brian) and Clanton despised each other, the hero sensed that however horrible Old Man may have been, he remained a voice of reason who kept the gang's warring factions in check. The famed gunfight happened only after Old Man Clanton was killed by Mexican rivals (5/30/61). SEE ALSO: Walter Brennan, Hugh O'Brian.

Gene Barry

(1919–)

••••••••••••••••••••••••••••••

Born Eugene Klass in Manhattan, Barry emerged as a child musical prodigy, then moved on to vaudeville and finally Broadway, costarring with Mae West in the 1944 play *Catherine Was Great*. In Hollywood, he had a mostly negligible career with two exceptions: *The War of the Worlds* (1953) and *Thunder Road* (1958). Barry sang in *Red Garters* (1954), a semi-surreal musical Western, and played a variation of Morgan Earp ("Wes Bonnell") in Sam Fuller's Freudian *Forty Guns* (1957). On TV, Barry starred in *Bat Masterson* (1958–1961). The problem was, much of William Barclay's career had already been covered in the first three seasons of *The Life and Legend of Wyatt Earp* (1955–1958). So the writers readapted stories from Bat's early days, already dramatized on *Earp* (which opened in the mid-1870s), resetting them ten years later, Bat now a mature man. The first two dealt with Bat's famed killing of the notorious Sergeant King in an argument over saloon hostess Molly Brennan. In "Double Showdown" (10/8/58), the characters' names were changed, with Robert Middleton as "Big Keel Roberts" and Jean Willes as "Lucy Slater." Willes had earlier played Molly under the fictional name "Amy Pelton" in "Bat Masterson Again" (4/17/56), the *Earp* episode concerning this incident with Alan Dinehart's Bat portrayed historically accurate as a teen, never before in a gunfight. On *Bat Masterson*, the hero was already a seasoned gunfighter. The following week, that story was retold again in "Two Graves for Swan Valley" (10/15/58), with Broderick Crawford as "Sergeant Foley" and Marcia Henderson as "Molly Doyle." This episode proved notable in that, for the only time on any TV Western, *two* endings were offered, one in which Molly is killed in crossfire (also dramatized in such movies as *Gunfight at Dodge City*, 1959), another in which she survives, a historical possibility if a notably unlikely one.

Producer Frederick W. Ziv made the decision to play Bat as a frontier dandy. The historical figure, whose birth name was Bartholomew, did once pose for a photograph in fine clothes, grasping a cane and wearing his derby. The TV *Bat Masterson* company either did not know that most Westerners dressed to the hilt when photographed or realized this but opted for a simplified version. Their Bat *always* wore elegant suits, a notion as bizarre as it is incorrect. And, essentially, a reverse of the approach in kiddie Westerns like *Wild Bill Hickok* that had the marshal always in buckskins, even when in town. While that might be forgiven in such a juvenile show, *Bat Masterson* was aimed at adults. In numerous episodes, Barry would ride on a cattle drive or fight Indians in suit and tie, other frontiersmen around him all in rugged trail clothes, which is what the historical Masterson wore on such occasions.

Barry intensified the problem by playing Bat with an affected "sophisticated" voice while spinning his cane (the real Bat carried one not for elegant theatrics but because he had been wounded in the leg by King). The Masterson of history had been a no-nonsense lawman/gambler who transformed into a sophisticate years *later*, when he left the West to work as a New York City sportswriter. The best episodes provided some insight into this emergent personality, including "The Fighter" (11/5/58), which chronicled Bat's first experience with boxing, a sport he would become an enthusiast of, and "Incident in Leadville" (3/18/59), which offered a realistic portrait of Bat's initial journalistic effort. The finest episode is generally considered "The Pied Piper of Dodge City" (1/7/60), which portrayed the 1880s reunion of various law officers from the wild early days of Dodge. Bat, Wyatt Earp (Ron Hayes), Charles Bassett (Tom Montgomery), and others came to the aid of friend Luke Short (Don "Red" Barry) after corrupt legal attempts to close down Luke's saloon. The group called themselves the "Dodge City Peace Commission" and posed for a legendary photo. That incident was again dramatized a year later on *Death Valley Days* as "Extra Guns" (11/20/60), with Guy Madison cast as Luke Short.

Other real-life friends/enemies who appeared at least once were King Fisher (Jack Lambert), Ben Thompson (Robert Swam), Green River Tom Smith (Don Kelly), and "hanging" Judge Isaac Parker (Harvey Stephens). In *The Gambler Returns: The Luck of the Draw* (11/3/91) with Kenny Rogers, Barry revived Bat, riding alongside Hugh O'Brian as Wyatt though the two actors never appeared together in the 1950s, their shows produced by competing companies. Barry's other series included *Burke's Law* (1963–1966), *The Name of the Game* (1968–1971), and *The Adventurer* (1972–1973). He received a Best Actor Tony nomination for his role in the Broadway musical *La Cage aux Folles* (1984). SEE ALSO: (Mason) Alan Dinehart (III), Ron Hayes, Guy Madison, Jody McCrea, Hugh O'Brian.

Charles Bateman

(19??–????)

••••••••••••••••••••••••••••••••••

TV actor Bateman's first role was on a Western as cousin "Jeff" on *Maverick* (1958). Originally planned as a recurring role, the character was dropped to accommodate Jack Kelly as Bret's brother "Bart." Two years later, Bateman played lead(s) on the offbeat syndicated series *Two Faces West* (1960–1961) as identical twins: rugged, nasty Marshal "Ben January" and gentle Dr. "Rick January." Set in Gunnison, Colorado, the show dealt with the constant confusion between them. Chief among the residents were lovely "Stacy" (Joyce Meadows), "Sheriff Maddox" (Francis De Sales), and "Deputy Johnny Evans" (Paul Comi). Following the show's cancellation, Bateman worked on the soap operas *Days of Our Lives* (1980–1981) and *Santa Barbara* (1984–1986).

Elizabeth Baur

(1947–)

••••••••••••••••••••••••••••••

Baur was cast on _Lancer_ (1968–1970) as "Teresa O'Brien," the gorgeous twenty-one-year-old daughter of a ranch hand murdered by outlaws. She became a ward to "Murdoch Lancer" (Andrew Duggan) and his two attractive sons, all the men pretending they had only familial interest in her. She later played "Fran Belding" on _Ironside_ (1975) with Raymond Burr. SEE ALSO: Andrew Duggan, Wayne Maunder, James Stacy.

Adam Beach

(1972–)

••••••••••••••••••••••••••••••

A member of the Salteaux (Manitoba) tribe and part of the Ojibwa Nation, Beach has been associated with non-stereotypical roles since _Spirit Rider_ (1993). He won the lead in Disney's _Squanto: A Warrior's Tale_ (1994), about the _Mayflower_'s impact on the native lifestyle that existed before the 1620 Anglo invasion. Beach starred in the Canadian TV series _North of 60_ (1993–1995) as the youthful "Nevada," forging his identity in a world dominated by whites. He played strong parts on American TV in an episode of _Walker, Texas Ranger_ (3/11/95) entitled "On Sacred Ground" as "Tommy Bright Hawk" and on the _CBS Schoolbreak Special_ "My Indian Summer" (10/24/95), about Anglo "tweens" learning to appreciate native culture.

Beach created the role of "Frank Fencepost" in the theatrical film _Dance Me Outside_ (1995), a part that was played by Darrell Dennis in a TV series follow-up, _The Rez_ (1996–1997), with Beach now recast as "Charlie." Guest spots include "Red Crow" in _Lonesome Dove: The Outlaw Years_ (5/2/96) and "Tom Shadow Wolf" in the "Medicine Man" episode of _Dead Man's Gun_ (9/10/97). Beach had the lead in _Smoke Signals_ (1998) and the second lead (to Nicolas Cage) in _Windtalkers_ (2002), an account of Navajo servicemen employing their language as an impenetrable code during WWII. Two superior TV-movie Western thrillers (contemporary) followed, _Skinwalkers_ (11/24/02) and _Coyote Waits_ (11/16/03). Beach also played the title role in _Cowboys and Indians: The J. J. Harper Story_ (10/5/03; Canada only), about a Native American gunned down by an Anglo cop; Ira Hayes in Clint Eastwood's _Flags of Our Fathers_ (2006), a part earlier essayed by Tony Curtis in _The Outsider_ (1961) and earlier still by Hayes himself (_Sands of Iwo Jima_, 1949); and Charles Eastman in _Bury My Heart at Wounded Knee_ (5/27/07), from the seminal Dee Brown book that kicked off the revisionist study of the American West. This was followed by a fictional part in _Comanche Moon_ (1/13/08) by Larry McMurtry.

Bonnie Bedelia

(1948–)

••••••••••••••••••••••••••••••

This gifted actress continuously searched for the right role to propel her into the big leagues (Glenn Close, Meryl Streep, Jessica Lange); sadly, she has never found it. As "Alice Harper" on *Bonanza* ("Forever," 9/12/72), Bedelia married "Joe" (Michael Landon) only to die later in that very episode. She next starred in *The New Land* (1974), based on Jan Troell's magnificent films about Scandinavians in America, *Utvandarna* (1971) and *Nybyggarna* (1972). Her "Anna Larsen" survives extremes of heat and cold with brothers "Bo" (Kurt Russell) and "Tuliff" (Todd Lookinland). The series steered away from the prettiness/sweetness of Landon's *Little House on the Prairie* in hopes of (like the movies, hits on the art-house circuit if not with the mainstream) providing something authentic. The public wanted sentimentality; the show was canceled after only a few episodes. Her best film work appears in *Heart Like a Wheel* (1983). Pop-culture claim to fame: Bedelia played Bruce Willis's estranged wife in *Die Hard* (1988). SEE ALSO: Michael Landon, Kurt Russell.

Noah Beery, Jr.

(1913–1994)

••••••••••••••••••••••••••••••

Son of the beloved silent-movie star (though projecting a notably different persona from his father, who had been typecast as a villain), Noah Jr., playing an amiable Westerner, took the lead in a dozen little films like *Devil's Canyon* (1935), while also working as a supporting player in epics such as *Of Mice and Men* (1939) as a good-natured ranch hand. He was picked up by Howard Hawks for *Only Angels Have Wings* (1939, Cary Grant), *Sgt. York* (1941, Gary Cooper), and *Red River* (1948, John Wayne). Beery played Ben Dalton in *The Daltons Ride Again* (1945, with Lon Chaney, Jr.), then Bob Dalton in *The Cimarron Kid* (1952, Audie Murphy). He won a recurring role in *Circus Boy* (1956–1957) as "Uncle Joey," a beloved clown. Beery joined *Riverboat* (1960–1961) when Burt Reynolds, unable to work with Darren McGavin, exited. As "Bill Blake," Beery got along great with the star. Next he played "Buffalo Baker," an old frontier scout created by Ward Bond in John Wayne's *Hondo* (1953), on TV (1967); then "Rocky," the charming old codger/dad to James Garner on the long-run hit *The Rockford Files* (1974–1980). Few recall that Beery didn't originate that character, replacing Robert Donley. SEE ALSO: Micky Dolenz, James Garner, Ralph Taeger, Guinn "Big Boy" Williams.

William Bendix

(1906–1964)

••••••••••••••••••••••••••••••

A gifted character actor recalled for his primitive face, heavyset build, and Brooklyn accent (though in fact Bendix was born in New York City), Bendix proved to be so perfectly cast as the silly soldier "Aloysius" in the WWII classic *Wake Island* (1942) that he received an Oscar nomination for Best Supporting Actor. He then played the role again (with a different last name) in *Guadalcanal Diary* (1943), once more accompanied by a pet dog, even though his character died in the first film! Bendix's best movie year was 1944, during which he played the lead in a superb film adapted from Eugene O'Neill's *The Hairy Ape* plus a scene-stealing part in Hitchcock's *Lifeboat*. Bendix incarnated the blue-collar American working stiff in *The Life of Riley* (1949) and eventually replaced Jackie Gleason in the TV sitcom version (1953–1958), then found himself typecast. He hoped a TV Western might salvage his stalled career. Bendix appeared as "Captain Cobb" on the first episode of *Wagon Train's* second season, "Around the Horn" (10/1/58), as the rugged owner of a clipper ship raising his small daughter, "Pat" (Sandy Descher), aboard, a pilot for a *Sea Train* series that never emerged. He did star as "Fred Kelly" in *Overland Trail* (1960) as a lovable veteran stage-line driver accompanied by a young whippersnapper shotgun rider (Doug McClure). Bendix's final Western role came by way of a cameo as a blacksmith in the Rory Calhoun B oater *Young Fury* (1965). SEE ALSO: Ward Bond, Doug McClure.

Tom Berenger

(1949–)

••••••••••••••••••••••••••••••

A journalism major at the University of Missouri, Berenger became intrigued by acting and set off to New York City for lessons. Soon, Hollywood hyped him as a modern sex symbol (*Looking for Mr. Goodbar*, 1977; *In Praise of Older Women*, 1978) of the Richard Gere variety. Berenger shifted to Westerns (*Butch and Sundance: The Early Days*, 1979) as the former, William Katt playing the Kid). Berenger embodied the dark side of war in Oliver Stone's stunning *Platoon* (1986). More history, of which he's a devotee, followed: General James Longstreet (*Gettysburg*, 1993), General Theodore Roosevelt (*Rough Riders*, 7/20/97), and Colonel J. Chivington (*Into the West*, 6/10/05). His most deeply personal role came in *One Man's Hero* (1999) as John Riley, leader of St. Patrick's Brigade, the Irish American soldiers who switched sides and fought for Mexico during the 1840s war owing to Catholic loyalty and ethnic prejudice in the American military; this was a role John Wayne had once considered playing. On TV, *Johnson*

County War (8/24/02) covered the same range war that earlier inspired *Shane*, *The Virginian*, and *Heaven's Gate*. Berenger became a series star as lawman "Jared Stone" on *Peacemakers* (2003), a short-lived TV Western covering the same ground (if less effectively) as *Hec Ramsey* had three decades earlier, focusing on an old marshal trying to adapt to the emergent scientific crime-solving techniques. Berenger lost interest in acting as films turned from personal dramas to special effects extravaganzas. SEE ALSO: Richard Boone.

James Best

(1926–)

Kentucky-born, Indiana-raised (by foster parents) character actor Best's heritage and upbringing led to the unique twang that in time proved his ticket to fame. His second film was also his first Western: *Comanche Territory* (1950), followed by varied parts including historical characters Cole Younger in *Kansas Raiders* (1950), Bitter Creek Dalton (a collapsing of Grat Dalton and Bitter Creek Newcomb) in *The Cimarron Kid* (1952), and Jason (son of John) Brown in *Seven Angry Men* (1955). He always proved most satisfying as an ornery, swaggering cowboy who gets his comeuppance in the end, notably in *Ride Lonesome* (1959), a first-rate Randolph Scott/Budd Boetticher vehicle. Best won a rare lead as a naïve G.I.

in Samuel Fuller's *Verboten!* (1959). He played "Gotch" on *Temple Houston* (1963–1964), then the role of a lifetime as blustery "Sheriff Rosco P. Coltrane" in *The Dukes of Hazzard* (1979–1985), a countrified variation on the outlaw theme. Best has also been a producer (*The End*, 1978), writer (*Death Mask*, 1988), and director (several *Dukes* episodes, 1981–1984). SEE ALSO: John Schneider.

Charles Bickford

(1891–1967)

Craggy looks and a harsh New England demeanor caused Bickford to come across as the obsessed Ahab in Melville's *Moby Dick* by way of a strict Puritan schoolmaster. Burlesque and Broadway preceded Hollywood. Bickford's best roles in Westerns were "Slim" (*Of Mice and Men*, 1939), Pat Garrett (*Four Faces West*, 1948), "Major Terrill" (*The Big Country*, 1958), and "Zeb Rawlins" (*The Unforgiven*, 1960). His first TV Western role was in "The Daniel Barrister Story" (*Wagon Train*, 4/16/58). Bickford joined *The Virginian* at the beginning of its fifth (1966) season as "John Grainger," the third (after Lee Cobb and John Dehner) owner of the Shiloh Ranch. Bickford's stern, steely-eyed persona proved more in line with Owen Wister's conception of "Judge Henry" than had those previous performers. He passed away after filming half a season's episodes, soon to be replaced by John McIntire as John's brother "Clay." SEE ALSO: Lee J. Cobb, John Dehner, Stewart Granger, John McIntire.

Michael Biehn

(1956–)

••••••••••••••••••••••••••••••

Biehn is yet another actor who should have become a star but didn't, owing to poor timing and terrible choices, though certainly no lack of talent/charisma. After dropping out of the University of Arizona's drama department for Hollywood, Biehn was discovered by director James Cameron, who cast him in *The Terminator* (1984), *Aliens* (1986), and *The Abyss* (1989). These big films received fine reviews, yet everything went wrong after Cameron's failure to get *Spiderman* into production, which would have starred Biehn as "Peter Parker." *Alien 3* didn't include him as "Hicks." Half a dozen failed projects were interrupted by one success: Johnny Ringo in *Tombstone* (1993), the most accurate portrait of that gunfighter ever on film or TV, catapulting Biehn into the *Magnificent Seven* (1998–2000) series. The TV-movie premiere (1/3/98) garnered huge ratings, but the numbers dropped each week. As with the earlier *Seven* films, viewers waited to see which of the antiheroes would live or die. For a series, none was ever going to bite the dust. The cast also failed to support Biehn in a comparable way

to the classic 1960 film, in which top-billed Yul Brynner struggled to hold his own against six gifted scene-stealers. Biehn's group included Eric Close ("Vin"), Andrew Kavovit ("J. D."), Dale Midkiff ("Buck"), Anthony Starke ("Ezra"), Rick Worthy ("Jackson"), and Ron Perlman ("Sanchez"), with Laurie Holden as "Mary." Later, Biehn drifted into routine shows like *Adventure, Inc. (2002–2003)*. SEE ALSO: Robert Vaughn.

Patricia Blair

(1931–)

••••••••••••••••••••••••••••••

A fiery-looking redhead from Texas in the Maureen O'Hara tradition, Blair experienced the same sort of relationships with Chuck Connors and Fess Parker on TV that her predecessor had with John Wayne and James Stewart on the big screen. A teen model, Blair was signed to studio contracts in the 1950s, first by Warner's, then MGM, leading to minor film roles. Joan Taylor, who had been added to *The Rifleman* as "Milly," the love interest for "Lucas McCain," left in 1962; the following fall, Blair stepped in as "Lou Mallory." That show concluded in 1963; one year later, Blair won the role of Rebecca Bryan Boone on *Daniel Boone*. Early episodes had her cleaning the cabin and watching over children Jemima (Veronica Cartwright) and Israel (Darby Hinton). As the years wore on (this was the era in which feminism emerged), Blair's role grew in range and intensity. In "The Imposter" (1/18/68), she temporarily became a femme fatale/female spy on the order of a "Bond girl," though at the story's end Rebecca returned to the Boone cabin. This episode's dramatic situation was not historical, perhaps, but it revealed some previously hidden dimensions to a seemingly conventional "housewife." SEE ALSO: Amanda Blake, Veronica Cartwright, Fess Parker.

Amanda Blake

(1929–1989)

••••••••••••••••••••••••••••••

Born Beverly Louise Neill, Blake left her New York job as a telephone operator to conquer Hollywood. This stunning, svelte, statuesque redhead was immediately compared to Greer Garson and Rita Hayworth. She slipped into minor films (*Miss Robin Crusoe* and *Adventures of Hajji Baba*, both 1954), occasionally winning second leads in big ones (*A Star Is Born*, 1954; *High Society*, 1955). Then came *Gunsmoke* and "Miss Kitty," part of the same foursome of characters that had proven so popular on radio. That name suggested more a cliché than a true character: the reliable saloon girl who patiently waits while "Marshal Dillon" does what a man's got to do, then heads to the Longbranch for a drink and . . . perhaps . . . who knew for sure what happened *after* the final credits rolled?

Soon all involved sensed they could play that formula only so many times before viewers became bored. Each character had to be fully developed, including Blake as the female lead. Initially it had been unclear whether Kitty owned the saloon, managed the place for someone, or merely worked there. Before long, Kitty *was* the Longbranch, giving orders to men including a long line of bartenders. Blake's Kitty set the tone for the way cowboys had to behave with her "working girls." As in *The Best Little Whorehouse in Texas* (1982), there was nothin' dirty goin' on here, even if those "hostesses" did appear to have duties beyond beer and sympathy.

During *Gunsmoke*'s black-and-white years, Blake provided the focus for an ever-increasing number of episodes: "Tap Day for Kitty" (3/24/56), "Kitty's Outlaw" (10/5/57), "Kitty's Rebellion" (2/7/59), "Kitty's Injury" (9/19/59), "Kitty's Killing" (2/20/60), "Kitty Shot" (2/11/61), "Miss Kitty" (10/14/61), "Kitty Cornered" (4/18/64), and "Help Me, Kitty" (11/7/64). The very sequence of those titles reveals what no one may have intended yet what clearly did emerge: a proto-feminist progression as the original two-dimensional "whore with a heart of gold" became the most three-dimensional female on TV. Equally important in rounding Kitty out were romances with men other than Matt. Likewise, she created a haven for abused girls needing jobs while gradually revealing more about her personal history as she always takes on the troubles of the town. In time there was no question that, profession (chosen or forced upon her) aside, here was a woman of substance. Importantly, Blake had the acting chops, as well as the good looks, to deliver what this demanding part now called for.

Kitty may have been fictional; likely, though, in later stages the role was modeled on Dora Hand, a real-life Dodge prostitute who sang in the church chorus on Sundays, tending to the emotional as well as the sexual needs of townsmen and wandering cowboys. This character development continued when the series shifted to color and moved to Tuesdays as a family-oriented show (any hints of Kitty's true profession now removed from scripts). Despite the changes, Blake gradually tired of it all. Why? Series veterans tell conflicting stories: She wanted more money, lived in Arizona and hated the commute, did not respect the man now producing, or was aware that ratings were dropping and wanted off what soon would be a sinking ship. Relatively wealthy, Blake desired some time for herself after more than a decade and a half of hard, rewarding work.

Her final episode (4/1/74) featured the first serious quarrel between Kitty and Matt, after which she was gone. Fran Ryan then appeared as "Miss Hannah" (1974–1975). In truth, why did she (Kitty, not Blake) leave? An earlier episode, "The Badge" (2/2/70), revealed that Kitty had seen Matt wounded once too often. If he would not quit as a lawman, she would leave him, necessitating a move from Dodge. Scenes from that episode were incorporated into *Gunsmoke: Return to Dodge* (9/26/87), a TV-movie follow-up, in which Kitty and Matt reunited after fifteen years. In the script, they were to finally get together permanently. But that would have ended the successful string of Arness TV movies, so commerciality won out and he remained the loner. In the final scene, Kitty watches Matt ride out of town, and out of her life, as a single tear passes down Blake's still pretty cheek.

Blake thoroughly enjoyed her free time, working for many charities, in particular deeply dedicated to ending the abuse of animals. Her happiness would not last. A series of difficult operations for oral cancer left Blake exhausted. Then she learned her fourth husband, Mark Spaeth, had infected her with the AIDS virus. Blake shortly became the first celebrity woman to die of the disease. One year after her passing, the next TV movie, *Gunsmoke: The Last Apache* (1990), was dedicated to the memory of "Miss Amanda Blake." SEE ALSO: James Arness, Milburn Stone, Dennis Weaver.

THE ENSEMBLE: One reason *Gunsmoke* remained high in the ratings was its strong ensemble cast, including James Arness (*left*) and, *clockwise,* Milburn Stone as "Doc Adams," Amanda Blake as "Miss Kitty," Ken Curtis as "Festus," and Burt Reynolds as "Quint." Courtesy CBS.

Mari Blanchard

(1927–1970)

••••••••••••••••••••••••••••••••

Mary Blanchard (her real name) overcame polio as a child to work as a dark-haired B-movie vamp in *Destry* (1954), opposite Audie Murphy playing "Brandy" (a variation on Marlene Dietrich as "Frenchy" in the 1939 version). She won a similar TV role as "Kathy O'Hara," a charming bad girl during the gold rush, in *Klondike* (1960). SEE ALSO: James Coburn, Joi Lansing, Ralph Taeger.

Dan Blocker

(1928–1972)

••••••••••••••••••••••••••••••••

Born and buried in Texas, this rotund actor's notable girth and chiseled face had him playing heavies on *Colt .45*, *Tales of Wells Fargo*, and *Cheyenne* (all 1957). His first sympathetic part was as "Tiny Budinger," a law-abiding townsman on *Cimarron City* (1958–1959). When that show died, NBC recycled Blocker, casting him as "Hoss Cartwright" in their new Saturday evening Western *Bonanza*, a show about a father and three sons ranching near Virginia City at the time of the Comstock Lode. Robert Altman, who would establish himself as one of the great movie directors, shot many of the "Hoss episodes." The two became close friends; when Blocker died before shooting commenced on *The Long Goodbye* (1973),

Altman recast that part with Sterling Hayden, then dedicated the movie to the memory of Blocker, whose death hastened the end of *Bonanza*'s run. SEE ALSO: David Canary, Lorne Greene, Michael Landon, George Montgomery, Pernell Roberts.

Dirk Blocker

(1957–)

••••••••••••••••••••••••••••••••

One of actor Dan Blocker's sons, Dirk attempted to follow in his father's footsteps via two made-for-TV movies intended to bring back the Ponderosa. In *Bonanza: The Return* (11/28/93) and *Bonanza: Under Attack* (1/15/95), he played a cowboy working on the newly refurbished ranch, his character *not* biologically related to "Hoss." Other connections to TV Westerns include a 1974 appearance on *Little House on the Prairie* with his dad's onetime costar Michael Landon, the role of mountain man Joe Meek in *Bridger* (9/10/76), a livery stable worker named "Grady" in the first *Desperado* TV film (4/27/87), and a guest spot on *Deadwood* (4/18/04). SEE ALSO: Dan Blocker, John Ireland, Ben Johnson, Michael Landon, Jr.

Ward Bond

(1903–1960)

••••••••••••••••••••••••••••••••

Bond was arguably the finest character in Hollywood history to have

"WAGONS, HO!": Movie veteran Ward Bond, a member of John Ford's stock company, brought his considerable presence to NBC's prestigious *Wagon Train* series as "Major Seth Adams." Courtesy NBC.

Lincoln, a lovable pioneer in *Drums Along the Mohawk* (both 1939), and Morgan Earp in *My Darling Clementine* (1946). Bond then played a thinly disguised version of the director in *The Wings of Eagles* (1957). His greatest roles for Ford were as "Sergeant O'Rourke" in *Fort Apache* (1948) and "Captain Clayton" in *The Searchers* (1956). It is unlikely that Bond appreciated Nicholas Ray's irony when that director cast him as "John McIvers" (a Westernized Joe McCarthy) in *Johnny Guitar* (1954), in which Bond's vicious character induces frightened people to "name names."

In 1950, Bond played "Elder Wiggs," title character in Ford's *Wagon Master*, about a Mormon caravan headed west. Seven years later, with the religious element dropped, *Wagon Train* premiered, Bond cast as "Major Seth Adams." Each week, the show took a close look into the lives of one or more pilgrims traveling with his outfit, the series more a dramatic anthology set in the West than a typical genre piece. Usually, big-name guest stars dominated while the major and his helpers, trail boss Bill Hawks (Terry Wilson) and cook Charlie Wooster (Frank McGrath), provided a framing device. On several occasions they took center stage, most notably in stories that flashed back to the Civil War. Toward the end of season one, the two-parter "The Major Adams Story" (4/23/58–4/30/58) revealed Seth's loneliness after the death of his beloved

never been nominated for (much less won) an Oscar as Best Supporting Actor. That may have had to do with Bond's abrasive personality; during the Communist witch-hunting of the 1950s, he became so passionate (some said obsessive) with rooting out anyone he believed to be less than patriotic that even close friend John Wayne, a rock-ribbed Republican, admitted to being taken aback. Duke had helped Bond break into movies when both were members of the USC football team, telling his teammate how easy it was to make money doing extra work for director John Ford. Shortly, they were inseparable. Ford cast Bond in three Henry Fonda films: the bad guy in *Young Mr.*

"Rainie" (Virginia Grey), revealing how pals Adams and Hawks (who ran a lumber business before the war) met Wooster, the world's worst soldier. Three years later came the most memorable episode, "The Colter Craven Story" (11/23/60), a personal victory for Bond: *he* starred, with Wayne, billed as Michael Morris, in a supporting part (General Sherman) with Ford directing. Outdoor footage from *Wagon Master* created a striking verisimilitude while the cast included a Who's Who of Ford's stock company: Willis Bouchey, John Carradine, Ken Curtis, Anna Lee, Hank Worden, Mae Marsh, Jack Pennick, and Chuck Roberson. The storyline was pure Ford: The title character, an alcoholic doctor (Carleton Young), finds himself unable to perform a delicate operation because he had inadvertently taken a life years earlier owing to his drinking problem. Adams tells Craven about his own friendship with "Sam Grant" (Paul Birch), onetime disgraced drunk turned national hero, raising the Catholic redemption theme. "Few men get a second chance," Adams insists. "What are you going to do with *yours*?" Save a child's life, of course! On November 5, 1960, Bond attended a football game in California, telling friends to be sure to watch the following week. They tuned in, but he couldn't: Bond died of a heart attack later that night, following the sporting event. SEE ALSO: John McIntire, John Wayne, Terry Wilson, Frank McGrath.

Randy Boone
(1942–)

This North Carolina–born country singer/actor was briefly pushed for stardom by NBC/Universal. Boone's first series had been the long-forgotten/highly likeable *It's a Man's World* (1962), about aging boys (including Glenn Corbett and Michael Burns) sharing a houseboat. Boone earned the title role in "The David Garner Story" on *Wagon Train* (5/8/63), then was added to the cast of *The Virginian* at the start of its second season as "Randy," a singing cowboy. He remained on board for four seasons and later played frontier photographer "Francis Wilde" on *Cimarron Strip* (1967–1968). SEE ALSO: Michael Burns, Glenn Corbett, Roberta Shore, Stuart Whitman.

Richard Boone
(1917–1981)

Like his cousin Pat the singer, Boone claimed direct lineage from Daniel himself. As a WWII vet (navy), he employed G.I. Bill benefits to head for New York and study at Lee Strasberg's Actors Studio, where Boone and fellow student Marlon Brando worked on the Method style, eventually costarring in *The Night of the Following Day* (1968). He also performed the classics on Broadway, including *Medea*. A studio contract at

"PALADIN, PALADIN, WHERE DO YOU ROAM?": Richard Boone proved to be one of television's finest actors as well as a memorable Western star thanks to his Man in Black on *Have Gun—Will Travel*. Courtesy CBS.

Fox led to small roles in big movies (*Halls of Montezuma*, 1950) and big roles in better-than-average B films (*I Bury the Living*, 1958). Boone made a huge impression as the scene-stealing, edgy, cynically comical villain in first-rate Westerns, a role he would play excellently and often, in *Ten Wanted Men* (1955, Randolph Scott), *Man Without a Star* (1955, Kirk Douglas), *Rio Conchos* (1964, Stuart Whitman), *Hombre* (1967, Paul Newman), *Big Jake* (1971), and *The Shootist* (1977),

the final two with close friend John Wayne. His movie career high point came with *The Tall T* (1957), made for the best of the B+ Western directors, Budd Boetticher; the low point was *Diamante Lobo*, aka *God's Gun* (1976), the worst-ever spaghetti Western, with Lee Van Cleef and Jack Palance. TV anthologies offered historical roles from Abraham Lincoln (*General Electric Theater*, 2/1/55) to John Wesley Hardin (*Studio One*, 1/28/57); he also played Sam Houston in Wayne's *The Alamo* (1960). Boone's first series, *Medic* (1954–1956), a little-seen docudrama, depicted real problems in modern hospitals.

TV superstardom arrived with *Have Gun—Will Travel* (1957–1963), the first adult oater to break the mold of a conventionally handsome soft-spoken star. "Paladin," a West Point grad, worked as a professional gun based in San Francisco. Paladin loved the good life at the Carlton Hotel, though he proved equally at home in the dreariest frontier backwaters. A black outfit and fancy business card helped qualify this as a one-of-a-kind show, often lauded for originality though some did deride the approach as overly gimmicky. In the Frisco sequences, Kam Tong played hotel worker "Kim 'Hey Boy' Chan"; when he left to costar as "Kam Chang" in *Mr. Garlund* (1960–1961), Hey Boy was temporarily replaced by Lisa Lu as "Hey Girl"; Tong came back for *Have Gun*'s final season.

Boone returned to the TV Western a generation later with *Hec Ramsey* (1972–1974), a rotating element within NBC's Sunday night mystery movie anthology. This new show was perfectly timed for an era when movie Westerns focused on the closing of the frontier. Boone played a crusty, aged lawman saddled with a well-meaning but naïve young deputy (Rick Lenz) who brought scientific police methods to their transitional practice. SEE ALSO: Dennis Weaver.

Powers Boothe

(1948–)

••••••••••••••••••••••••••••••••

A native Texan, part Native American, Boothe's work includes both movies (*The Emerald Forest*, 1985) and TV (*Philip Marlowe, Private Eye*, 1983–1986; the voice of "Gorilla Grodd" on *Justice League*, 2002–2006; and "Vice-President Noah Daniels" in *24*, 2007). Boothe made a powerful impact as Curly Bill Brocious in *Tombstone* (1993), likewise as "Cy Tolliver," the nasty whoremaster on *Deadwood* (2004–2006). SEE ALSO: Ian McShane, Timothy Olyphant.

Ernest Borgnine

(1917–)

••••••••••••••••••••••••••••••••

A scene-stealing villain (*From Here to Eternity*, 1953) and Oscar-winning character lead (*Marty*, 1955), Borgnine appeared in several big Westerns

(*Johnny Guitar, Vera Cruz, The Bounty Hunter*, 1954; *The Last Command*, 1955; *Jubal*, 1956; *The Wild Bunch*, 1969). On TV, he brought legitimacy to the Western genre by guest-starring in the first-ever *Wagon Train*, "The Willy Moran Story" (9/18/57), as an alcoholic, establishing adult themes that would be present from then on, making it easier for producer Frederick Shorr to nab other top actors and, in the process, forever changing the status of the TV oater. Borgnine shared screen time with Sammy Davis, Jr., in the memorable TV movie *The Trackers* (12/14/71). *Sam Hill: Who Killed Mr. Foster?* (2/1/71), a virtual redux of "Willy Moran," introduced a title character loosely based on Western legend Samuel Hall. SEE ALSO: Ward Bond, Sammy Davis, Jr.

Bruce Boxleitner

(1950–)

••••••••••••••••••••••••••••••••

The Illinois-born Boxleitner appeared in *Gunsmoke*'s final episode (3/31/75), "The Sharecroppers," kicking off a long working relationship with James Arness. They costarred in *The Macahans* (1/19/76), a big-scale TV oater that initiated various *How the West Was Won* series during the late 1970s, with Boxleitner cast as "Luke," a foster son to Arness's "Zeb." Afterward, Boxleitner carried the banner of the traditional Western on TV, appearing as "Tyree" in *Wild Times*

(1/24/80) with Sam Elliott, "Billy Montana" in *The Gambler* (4/8/80, Kenny Rogers), and four sequels. Non-Westerns include the role of Frank Buck in *Bring 'Em Back Alive* (1982–1983), and *Scarecrow and Mrs. King* (1983–1987). In *I Married Wyatt Earp* (1/10/83), he played one of the two title characters, with Marie Osmond as Josephine Marcus. Boxleitner then starred as "Collins" in *Down the Long Hills* (11/15/86), a Louis L'Amour TV adaptation, and shortly thereafter reunited with Arness in *Red River* (4/10/88), playing "Matthew Garth" and "Tom Dunson," another foster father-son team originally enacted by Monty Clift and John Wayne in Howard Hawks's 1948 classic. Boxleitner and Arness teamed again in *One Man's Justice* (2/10/94), a TV *Gunsmoke* movie, as "Davis Healy," a vengeance-bent young man mentored by venerable "Matt Dillon." Later roles included "Sam," sheriff of Cochise, in *Wyatt Earp: Return to Tombstone* (7/1/94), with Hugh O'Brian reviving Wyatt Earp; James Longstreet in *Gods and Generals* (2003); and a former TV cowboy turned Wild West show owner/star in *Mystery Woman: Wild West Mystery* (3/18/06) with Nina Siemaszko. More recently associated with sci-fi as "John J. Sheridan" in *Babylon 5* (2007), Boxleitner combined his love of horse operas and space operas as author of the novel *Frontier Earth*. SEE ALSO: James Arness, Kenny Rogers.

William Boyd
(1895–1972)

Following the death of both his parents, the orphaned Boyd drifted to LA searching for work, picking up "extra" jobs. Cecil B. DeMille spotted Boyd and cast him in *Volga Boatman* (1926). Boyd quickly emerged as a major-league silent star. Then, in 1929, the stock-market crash wiped out his fortune, the advent of sound opened the door for new young stars, and false newspaper reports that he had acted badly in public (that had been another actor, William Stage Boyd) damaged Boyd's reputation. Down and out, he took what work he could find. Who said there are no second acts in American lives? Boyd proved them wrong. Producer Harry Sherman acquired the rights to Clarence E. Mulford's *Hopalong Cassidy* books about a mean-spirited coot with a menial job on a ranch, limping around and pestering everyone. Mulford believed that character actor James Gleason would be perfect for the films, but Sherman approached Boyd, who agreed to do a B-movie series if "Hoppy" were cleaned up and turned into a black-clad hero. At the time, author Mulford expressed anger, resentment, and bitterness at what he saw. The public, however, loved it.

Boyd played the part in more than fifty films between 1935 and 1943, initially at $5,000 a shot, a comedown for a star who had earned

$100,000 in 1927. The best was the third, *Bar 20 Rides Again* (1935), featuring lots of action and chases. The series formula called for an aged sidekick (Gabby Hayes, Andy Clyde) and a cocky young pal (James Ellison, Russell Hayden), the *Hoppy* series setting the pace for imitations like *Three Mesquiteers* (1936) and *Rough Riders*. Sherman bowed out, so Boyd produced the next dozen himself; the series concluded in 1948, even as TV emerged. An inspiration caused Boyd to mortgage his home and go into debt to buy all TV rights. He turned down network offers to run *Hoppy*s, choosing instead to contact stations around the country himself and eliminate the middlemen, thereby increasing his profits. On TV, *Hoppy* proved bigger than ever; B Westerns flooded the airwaves, but Boyd's (particularly the early ones) had the most impressive production values. Merchandising (guns, costumes, lunchboxes) proved television's emergent power, particularly with suburban children. Boyd then executive-produced (with Toby Auguist handling the grunt work) over forty TV films, released between 1952 and 1954, rebooting the craze. Though comic "Red Connors" (Edgar Buchanan) kicked Boyd's side, there would be no juvenile second lead for TV. Boyd agreed to only one appearance on TV other than his own series: *The Jackie Gleason Show* (9/29/56). Earlier, he did a cameo as himself in onetime mentor DeMille's *The Greatest Show on Earth*

(1952). If the legend is to be believed, DeMille offered Boyd the role of Moses in *The Ten Commandments* (1956); Boyd turned it down because he believed himself too old for the early youthful sequences. He rode off into the sunset to live a quiet, dignified life with his fourth wife, Grace Bradley. SEE ALSO: Edgar Buchanan, Russell Hayden.

Ray Boyle
(1925–)

This movie character actor assumed the alternative name "Dirk London" on TV Westerns, such roles including younger brother Morgan in episodes (1956–1961) of *The Life and Legend of Wyatt Earp*. SEE ALSO: Hugh O'Brian.

Pat Brady
(1914–1972)

Brady served with distinction in the Fourth Armored Division as a tank crew member during WWII, including the Battle of the Bulge. Afterward, he joined the musical group the Sons of the Pioneers and stuck with band member Roy Rogers when he became a B-movie star at Republic Pictures, appearing in three dozen "sticks pix," as Western musicals were tagged by *Variety*. Brady played mostly characters who shared his own first name, though toward the end of the run in the early 1950s he was called "Sparrow Biffle." When Rogers brought the act to TV, Brady tagged along, using his own name once again. Just as *The Roy Rogers Show* (1951–1957) featured Westerners with holstered Colts in a setting that appeared more modern hillbilly, Brady drove a jeep, "Nellybelle." He was with Roy Rogers and Dale Evans when they returned to TV in 1962 on a brief-lived sixty-minute family musical format. Brady also starred with Marty Robbins in a busted pilot called *30 Minutes at Gunsight* (1963), a failed attempt to revive the golden age of the singing cowboy; Russell "Lucky" Hayden directed that curio. SEE ALSO: Dale Evans, Russell Hayden, Roy Rogers.

Scott Brady
(1924–1985)
••••••••••••••••••••••••••••••

Born Gerald Kenneth Tierney in Brooklyn to a policeman father, Brady was the younger brother of troublesome actor Lawrence Tierney. A gifted boxer during his service years, he headed for Hollywood and B movies, mostly Westerns: Bill Anderson in *Kansas Raiders* (1950), Bob Dalton in *Montana Belle* (1952), Billy Bonney in *The Law vs. Billy the Kid* (1954), and the Sundance Kid in *Maverick Queen* (1956). At Republic, he won supporting roles in big films (*Johnny Guitar*, 1954) and leads in their less prestigious output (*The Vanishing American*, 1955). Weight problems, early balding, and a narcotics charge (1957) derailed Brady's career. TV might have provided a comeback, but "Johnny Nighthawk" (5/2/60) didn't get beyond the pilot stage. Then came *Shotgun Slade* (1959–1961) a highly popular syndicated show nicknamed "*Peter Gunn* on the Frontier." That contemporary detective series featured a hip-talking womanizing hero, jazz music, and offbeat guest stars. So did *Slade*: lots of beautiful women, an arrogant lead, plus that anachronistic bluesy score. In addition to cult comic Ernie Kovacs playing a straight role as a bearded old-timer in the first episode, many other offbeat guests appeared. "Slade" employed a sawed-off shotgun to blow his opponents away; there were no wounded on this series! Brady later turned down the role of "Archie Bunker" on *All in the Family* (1971). He did play "Vinnie" on *Police Story* (1973–1976).

Neville Brand
(1920–1992)
••••••••••••••••••••••••••••••

A highly decorated WWII vet, Brand was asked to appear in a training film and found himself hooked on acting. Always on the lookout for the role that would lift him out of the thug stereotype (which Brand first played in *D.O.A.*, 1949) and transform him into a Wallace Beery–type lovable tough guy, he more often found work as a nasty Viking (*Prince Valiant*, 1954) or Indian (*Mohawk*, 1956). In time, he played the sympathetic lead in the little-known *Riot in Cell Block 11* (1954), Don Siegel's top B movie about a prison revolt. On golden-age live TV, Brand assumed Broderick Crawford's role from *All the King's Men* (5/14/58). He showed up as Butch Cassidy twice (*The Three Outlaws*, 1956; and *Badman's Country*, 1958), King Fisher (*The Lonely Man*, 1957), John Wesley Hardin (*Death Valley Days*, 2/1/62), as well as a cruel Civil War vet menacing Elvis Presley in *Love Me Tender* (1956). Brand's strongest roles were as the mean but patriotic POW in *Stalag 17* (1953, William Holden) and the kindly prison guard in *Birdman of Alcatraz* (1962, Burt Lancaster). He enacted Al Capone in *The Untouchables* (1961) and *The George Raft Story* (1961) and played a rangy mountain man in "The Zebedee Titus Story" (*Wagon Train*, 4/20/64). At last, the role of a lifetime appeared: the boisterous, fair-minded Texas Ranger "Reese Bennett" in *Laredo* (1965–1967). Brand made the most of his larger-than-life character until the announcement of the show's impending cancellation halfway through the second season. Bitter, he jumped ship and was replaced by Claude Akins. The best of Brand's later Westerns featured him as a dedicated Native American tracker in *Cahill U.S. Marshall* (1973) with John Wayne. SEE ALSO: Claude Akins, Peter Brown, Philip Carey, William Smith.

X. Brands

(1927–2000)

Work as a professional stuntman led to bit parts on producer/star Russell Hayden's *Cowboy G-Men* (1954), then bigger roles on *Judge Roy Bean* (1956), *The Adventures of Kit Carson* (1954–1955), and *Rin Tin Tin* (1954). Autry picked Brands up for the shows he produced, occasionally casting him as an Indian owing to a tall frame and darkly handsome/menacing appearance. His best part ever came as "Pahoo-Ka-Ta-Wah," Pahoo for short, the mysterious pal of Jock Mahoney on *Yancy Derringer* (1958–1959). Afterward, Brands played Native American roles on *Rawhide*, *Wagon Train*, *Bonanza*, and even the spy spoof *The Man from U.N.C.L.E.* The best of the lot was "Nock-Ay-Del" on *The High Chaparral* (1967). Brand essayed his final Western role in *Bridger* (9/10/76), with James Wainwright as the title hero, as (what else?) a Native American. SEE ALSO: Gene Autry, Russell Hayden, Jock Mahoney.

Robert Bray

(1917–1983)

RKO signed this big, broad-shouldered former U.S. Marine, but the contract led nowhere. Soon he found himself playing in Tim Holt B Westerns, *Guns of Hate* (1948) the best of a mediocre lot. Bray moved up to B+ oaters as James gang member Charlie Pitts in *The Great Missouri Raid* (1951), then Wyatt Earp on the O. K. Corral segment of *You Are There* (11/6/55). A year earlier, he had been Emmett Dalton on *Stories of the Century* (3/18/54). He played the lead on *Stagecoach West* (1960–1961) as line owner "Simon Kane." By then, the airwaves were glutted with Westerns; this one got lost in the shuffle. Bray enjoyed a long run on *Lassie* (1964–1968) as park ranger "Corey Stuart" but eventually retired to enjoy fly fishing, duck carving, and forest-oriented sports. His best-remembered role was as the driver in *Bus Stop* (1956) with Marilyn Monroe. SEE ALSO: Richard Eyer, Wayne Rogers.

Peter Breck

(1929–)

A strapping leading man, perfect for John Wayne–type roles, Breck won episodic work on Western shows, including the Sundance Kid in the "Sundown at Bitter Creek" episode of *Zane Grey Theater* (2/14/58), a good fit. Breck proved less adequate as the thoughtful Theodore Roosevelt in "Yankee Tornado" (*Bronco*, 3/13/61). His first series, *Black Saddle*, cast Breck as "Clay Culhane," a frontier lawyer, with the shorter, soft-spoken Russell Johnson as "Marshal Gib Scott"; their roles ought to have been reversed. Breck played Doc Holliday

(again, in a role that called for a more intense performer) on *Maverick's* 1961–1962 season. He proved precisely right as "Nick Barkley" on *The Big Valley* (1965–1969), playing the oldest of the brothers. Breck's last important part was in the sci-fi Western series *The Secret Empire* (1979) as "Jesse Keller," a frontier marshal drawn into a hidden alternate world in this throwback to Gene Autry in *Radio Ranch* and other Saturday morning serials of yore, presented as part of the NBC package *Cliffhangers*. SEE ALSO: Anna-Lisa, Charles Briles, Russell Johnson, Richard Long, Lee Majors, Barbara Stanwyck.

Walter Brennan

(1894–1974)

A truly great character actor, Brennan was the first ever to receive a Best Supporting Actor award (for Howard Hawks/William Wyler's *Come and Get It*, 1936) and the only one (so far) to win three times, including a statuette for Judge Roy Bean in *The Westerner* (1940), directed by Wyler. Hawks cast Brennan as Wayne's lovable sidekick in *Red River* (1948) and *Rio Bravo* (1959). Ford employed Brennan only once, for the villainous Old Man Clanton in *My Darling Clementine* (1946). A traditionalist regarding patriotic values, Ford rated as an outspoken progressive on civil rights and, as such, did not cotton to Brennan's frequent outbursts against blacks/Jews/Catholics. The public bought Brennan's faux image of a tolerant country patriarch in the long-running ABC sitcom _The Real McCoys_ (1957–1963). He later returned with _The Guns of Will Sonnett_ (1967–1969) as an old cavalry scout searching for a missing son/father with his grandson. Though Brennan despised the era's Youth Movement (he damned Nixon because of that president's support for civil rights), _Will Sonnett_ offered in its Western setting the perfect paradigm for precisely that: A teenager finds solace with an elderly man after becoming disillusioned with his dad (the generation gap). Those on the set recall Brennan's anguish over the country's direction, relieved twice as he cheered (and purportedly danced a spontaneous jig) after hearing of the assassinations of Martin Luther King, Jr., and Robert Kennedy. SEE ALSO: Jason Evers, Dack Rambo.

Beau Bridges
(1941–)

Like his father an activist on environmental issues, Lloyd's oldest son has been no stranger to Westerns, beginning with his TV premiere in "Image of a Drawn Sword" on _Zane Grey Theater_ (5/11/61). His best movie roles were in _Norma Rae_ (1979) and _The Hotel New Hampshire_ (1984). The TV series _Harts of the West_ (1993–1994) resembled sibling Jeff's film _Hearts of the West_ (1975) in theme. Beau played Chicago-bound working stiff "Dave Hart," living in a fantasy world derived from old TV/movie Westerns. To the consternation of his wife "Alison" (Harley Jane Kozak), he insisted on naming their kids after frontier figures: "L'Amour Hart" (Meghann Haldeman), "Zane Grey Hart" (Sean Murray), and "Duke Hart" (Nathan Watt). After a near fatal heart attack, Dave decides to live out his dream, quits his job, and moves the family west onto a ranch. A sharp distinction between romantic notions and harsh reality led to memorable moments in this short-lived show. Bridges later played pioneer "Stephen Hoxie" in Steven Spielberg's _Into the West_ (2005). He is best known today for the continuing role of "Major General Hank Landry" in the sci-fi _Stargate_ franchise. SEE ALSO: Lloyd Bridges.

Lloyd Bridges
(1913–1998)

Coming from a stage background, on and off Broadway, Bridges entered movies in 1936 and, despite his liberal politics, survived the McCarthy blacklist. Never a huge star, Bridges always found work, including what may be the best WWII movie ever, _A Walk in the Sun_ (1945), featuring John Ireland, who would also emerge as a TV Western star. They were together again in _Little Big Horn_ (1951), a superior B Western; Bridges then played supporting roles in A movies, notably "Deputy Harvey Pell" in *High Noon* (1952). He projected the sense of a tall, handsome, yet inwardly weak man, not unlike Forrest Tucker and Peter Graves. On TV Bridges won more heroic roles, beginning with "Mike Nelson" on the syndicated *Sea Hunt* (1958–1961), and was forever after associated with underwater diving. In "Image of a Drawn Sword" on *Zane Grey Theater* (5/11/61), Bridges played a troubled cavalry officer in a pilot that did not sell. His role as James Butler Hickok in "Wild Bill Hickok—The Legend and the Man" on *The Great Adventure* (1/3/64) marked the first time that Hickok's impending blindness (1876) was portrayed onscreen. Bridges acted in one Western series: *The Loner* (1965–1966), as "William Colton," a post–Civil War drifter like those from a decade earlier, though all similarity ended there. The show was written by Rod Serling who, after *The Twilight Zone*, hoped to do for Westerns what he had done for sci-fi, creating an existential drama about one man's search for meaning in life while also touching on key issues of the era in which the series was produced, notably civil rights. Bridges later played Confederate President Jefferson Davis in *North and South, Book II* (1986) and became a regular on son Beau's contemporary Western *Harts of the West* (1993–1994) as ranch hand "Jake Tyrell." Beginning with *Airplane* (1980), he revealed a gift

for comedy, spoofing his own earlier action/adventure roles. SEE ALSO: Beau Bridges, John Ireland.

Charles Briles

(1945–)

Briles played the youngest Barkley son, thoughtful "Eugene," on the first eight episodes of *The Big Valley* (1965), then was either drafted and forced to leave or dropped from the cast and *then* drafted, depending on whose version you hear. Eugene headed east for college, never to be mentioned again. Briles shortly dropped out of showbiz. SEE ALSO: Peter Breck, Lee Majors, Barbara Stanwyck.

Wilford Brimley

(1934–)

Was this gentleman *born* looking old? Following various turns as a rodeo circuit rider, farmer, U.S. Marine, blacksmith, and bodyguard (to Howard Hughes, no less), Brimley finally took on character roles later in life. His first part was a bit in *True Grit* (1969). Brimley played pioneer "Ludlow" in the TV movie and subsequent weekly series *The Oregon Trail* (1/10/76), crusty "Horace" on *The Waltons* (1974–1977), and "Sheriff Daniels" on *How the West Was Won* (1979). Memorable non-Western films include *Absence of Malice*

(1981), *The Thing* (1982), and *Cocoon* (1985). His Western film appearances include *The Electric Horseman* (1979), *Borderline* (1980), *Tender Mercies* (1983), and *Country* (1984). Brimley played the historical characters President Grover Cleveland (*The Wild Wild West Revisited*, 5/9/79) and Governor Lew Wallace (*Billy the Kid*, 5/10/89). He starred in his own series, *The Boys of Twilight* (1992), as "Bill Huntoon," a contemporary throwback to old-fashioned lawmen. Oscar winner Louise Fletcher (*One Flew Over the Cuckoo's Nest*) played his lady friend, Richard Farnsworth the other "boy." Brimley won strong roles in made-for-TV Westerns *The Good Old Boys* (3/5/95, Tommy Lee Jones), *Louis L'Amour's Crossfire Trail* (1/21/01, Tom Selleck), and *The Ballad of Lucy Whipple* (2/18/01, Glenn Close). SEE ALSO: Richard Farnsworth, Rod Taylor.

Paul Brinegar

(1917–1995)

●●●●●●●●●●●●●●●●●●●●●●●●●●●●●●●●

Wiry, quick-tempered, and cuddly as a puppy in a coarse kind of way, this character actor established himself as a Western regular beginning with his first film, *Abilene Town* (1946, Randolph Scott). Plenty of small parts on episodic TV Westerns followed, usually as an ornery older man, leading to the dream casting as Mayor John "Dog" Kelly of Dodge City on

The Life and Legend of Wyatt Earp. The nickname occurred in real life when Colonel Custer left his beloved dogs to his friend Kelly in his will. After Little Big Horn (6/25/1876), Kelly and the pups were inseparable. Though the nickname was retained for the show, those animals were rarely seen. Pompous yet lovable, Brinegar's Kelly (always operating on the edge of legality, despite his lofty position) could make things rough for Hugh O'Brian's Earp. Still, he supported the marshal when the chips were down. Brinegar's best acting came in episodes dealing with his courtship of Dora Hand (Margaret Hayes), a saloon girl who also sang in church on Sundays. Their relationship developed during the first third of the second season, allowing Brinegar to reveal a romantic side in the initial stories, then a great depth of despair following Dora's death. During a break from filming, he appeared in *Cattle Empire* (1958), about a perilous long drive, for Charles Marquis Warren. That filmmaker soon developed the concept into a TV series and, after initially casting Robert Carricart as "Wishbone" the cook for an unaired pilot, then convinced Brinegar to play the part on *Rawhide* (1959–1966). In an hour-long show, Brinegar would be integral rather than an occasional character; he could not pass up the opportunity. (Ralph Sanford took over as Kelly on *Earp*.) Afterward, Brinegar found plenty of TV work, most notably as ranch foreman "Lamar Pettybone" on *Matt Houston* (1982–1983). In the Kenny Rogers vehicle *The Gambler Returns: The Luck of the Draw* (11/3/91), he showed up as "Cookie," owing to legal questions regarding ownership of the "Wishbone" moniker. SEE ALSO: Clint Eastwood, James Murdock, Hugh O'Brian.

Steve Brodie
(1919–1992)

Solid in appearance, stolid in demeanor, this reliable if unremarkable character actor took the name of a once legendary man who on July 23, 1886, purportedly jumped off the Brooklyn Bridge. Initial appearances in WWII films (*A Walk in the Sun*, 1945), film noir (*Out Of the Past*, 1947), and Westerns (*Winchester '73*, 1950) led to roles as historical figures Bob Dalton (*Badman's Territory*, 1946), Cole Younger (*Return of the Bad Men*, 1948), Harry Tracy (*Stories of the Century*, 5/27/54), and Butch Cassidy (*Bronco*, 12/18/61). Brodie won the regular part of Sheriff John Behan (replacing Lash La Rue) on *The Life and Legend of Wyatt Earp* (1960–1961). He later played continuing roles as "Benson" (*Everglades*, 1961–1962) and "Macy" (*Bonanza*, 1963–1968). SEE ALSO: Ron Hayes, Michael Landon, Hugh O'Brian.

Josh Brolin
(1968–)

Brolin was one of only two actors on *The Young Riders* (1989–1992) to play a historical character, James Butler Hickok (the other was Stephen Baldwin as William Cody). During season three, as the riders appeared ever less young and while Hickok and Cody emerged as living legends, the nickname "Wild Bill" was explained as a dime novelist's confusion of the two friends' names. Brolin later played mountain man turned Indian scout Jedediah Smith on Steven Spielberg's miniseries *Into the West* (6/10/05) and, in due time, President George W. Bush in Oliver Stone's *W* (2008). SEE ALSO: Stephen Baldwin, Ty Miller.

John Bromfield
(1922–2005)

Reminiscent of both Scott Brady and Rory Calhoun, though not as well remembered, Farron McClain Bromfield enjoyed the rare distinction of playing the same character in two series. Earlier, he had made a try for movie stardom as the little-known outlaw Tulsa Jack in *The Cimarron Kid* (1952) with Audie Murphy. Bromfield was briefly married to Gallic star Corinne Calvet and won top billing in two horror flicks, including one of the 1950s' best (*Revenge of the Creature*, 1955) and one of the worst (*Curucu, Beast of the Amazon*, 1956). He was picked by Desilu to play "Frank Morgan" in their contemporary oater <u>*Sheriff of Cochise*</u> (1956–1958), which was syndicated after CBS turned it down. In an intriguing episode, "Wyatt Earp" (6/7/57), Frank had to contend with a deranged man believing himself to be the reincarnation of that famed lawman, cross-referencing one of TV's most popular Westerns, not coincidentally produced by Desilu. *Sheriff* was dropped after two seasons, but the public outcry proved so strong that Desilu brought it back, retitled as <u>*U.S. Marshal*</u> (1958–1960), with the hero promoted and now patrolling the entire state of Arizona. Bromfield, who had never really perceived himself as an actor, left Hollywood and made a solid living as a commercial fisherman. SEE ALSO: James Griffith, Stan Jones, Hugh O'Brian.

Charles Bronson

(1921–2003)

••••••••••••••••••••••••••••••

Writer/director Quentin Tarantino dedicated *Kill Bill: Vol. 2* (2004) to Charles Bronson; in his first major film, *Reservoir Dogs* (1992), Tarantino included a long string of references to that actor/icon who had, in the 1960s, been worshipped by movie lovers in Third World countries as Il Brutto: The ugly one. Along with Sterling Hayden and Lee Marvin, Bronson rated as one of the deceased performers Tarantino would have most loved to work with. Unlike either, this star likely would have turned Q. T. down. He did just that to Sergio Leone, who all but begged Bronson to play "The Man with No Name" in the three spaghetti Westerns that transformed Clint Eastwood into a superstar, this at a time when Bronson was appearing in big roles in miniscule films, supporting parts in big pictures, and episodic TV just to pay the bills. As for TV, in time he would say "no" to two great roles: "Pasquinel," the mountain man in the opening episodes of *Centennial* (1978), and "Woodrow Call," former Texas Ranger in *Lonesome Dove* (1989). (Those roles would be filled by Robert Conrad and Tommy Lee Jones.) John Carpenter dreamed (in vain) of casting Bronson as "Snake Plissken" in *Escape from New York* (1981). Bronson did say "yes" to *Death Wish* (1974), about a New York liberal turned urban vigilante, after Henry Fonda, for whom the role was created, turned it down flat. Had Sam Peckinpah directed, that film might have offered a meditation on retro violence on the order of *Straw Dogs* (1971). Instead, a talentless director, Michael Winner, accepted the job, as he would on endless sequels, each a little more awful than the last. Such projects briefly posited Bronson as a hero figure to the reactionary fringe but went unseen by the American mainstream, causing Bronson to slip

MEANEST MEN IN THE WEST: Often, the villains were far more memorable than the heroes. Charles Bronson. Courtesy CBS/ United Artists Films.

out of the public consciousness, his death barely mentioned in the press when he passed away—such a terrible waste, for the Bronson potential had been as awesome as his taste was terrible.

The son of poverty-stricken Lithuanian immigrants (Buchinsky) living in Pennsylvania, teenager Charlie followed his father's footsteps down into the coal mines. Escape from this blue-collar nightmare came when he was drafted in 1943, serving as a tail-gunner on a B-29 bomber, flying twenty-five missions and receiving the Purple Heart. On his return, the G.I. Bill allowed Bronson to study art, his great passion; *The Sandpiper* (1965) with Elizabeth Taylor and Richard Burton may have been an embarrassing flop for the top-billed stars, but Bronson adored his support-

ing role as a sensitive artist/poet, precisely how he wanted to be perceived in real life.

First discovered at the Pasadena Playhouse, Bronson found work as monstrous figures, notable "Igor," a revival of the crazed hunchback role Bela Lugosi had played in the 1930s, in *House of Wax* (1953). His great potential as a Western badman was first realized in "The Killer" (5/26/56), one of the last (and best) first-season *Gunsmoke*s. In the unforgettable opening, a man sits by a campfire as Bronson, playing the title character, carries on a conversation, gradually losing control. Without warning, he shoots the other man in what may be the most nihilistic moment in the entire history of TV Westerns. The killer then arrives in Dodge, goading decent men into death matches.

"I look like a rock quarry someone has decimated," Bronson once quipped. That was putting it mildly. Nonetheless, he won the part of a heroic photojournalist in *Man with a Camera* (1958–1960), then the lovably brutish antiheroes in John Sturges's *The Magnificent Seven* (1960) and Robert Aldrich's *The Dirty Dozen* (1967), as well as menacing thugs for Aldrich in *Vera Cruz* (1954) and *4 for Texas* (1963). Strong supporting roles as Native Americans, some historical, included Hondo in *Apache*, Captain Jack in *Drum Beat* (both 1954), and best of all, the sympathetic "Blue Buffalo" in Sam Fuller's *Run of the Arrow*

B

(1957). Leads in small indie productions *Showdown at Boot Hill* (Gene Fowler, Jr.) and *Machine-Gun Kelly* (Roger Corman), both in 1958, had Bronson playing psychologically troubled yet strangely appealing killers. In the 1960s, he often joined the cast of floundering TV Westerns to beef up the action quotient, playing the tough but fair cowboy "Paul Moreno" (a role reminiscent of his pal to Glenn Ford in *Jubal*, 1956) in *Empire* (1963) and the rugged wagon master "Linc Murdock" in *The Travels of Jaimie McPheeters* (1963–1964). Historical roles included Butch Cassidy on *Tales of Wells Fargo* (10/13/58) and Wild Bill Hickok in *The White Buffalo* (1977), the latter after becoming a worldwide sensation owing to his stark, craggy presence, fully utilized only once, when Bronson *finally* gave in to Sergio Leone and played the role he was born for: The Man with No Name in Leone's *Once Upon a Time in the West* (1968), now carrying a harmonica.

In time, too many bad choices caught up with Bronson, even as his personal life took a terrible toll owing to the slow death of his wife/costar Jill Ireland from breast cancer. After that ordeal ended, he suffered from the gradual onset of Alzheimer's. Today, Bronson is recalled by Western buffs as a tragic figure, his full potential to become one of the great film/TV stars ultimately unrealized. SEE ALSO: Richard Egan, Jill Ireland, Dan O'Herlihy, Kurt Russell.

Rand Brooks

(1918–2003)

This perennially youthful actor appeared in several dozen films without making an impression, including as "Charles Hamilton" in *Gone with the Wind* (1939) and the young romantic lead opposite Marilyn Monroe in a B effort, *Ladies of the Chorus* (1948). He played Emmet Dalton in *The Cimarron Kid* (1952) and "Lucky" in the *Hopalong Cassidy* features after Russ Hayden dropped out. TV provided grunt work, Brooks eventually becoming a regular on *Rocky Jones, Space Ranger* (1954) as "Andrews." Later that year, he joined *The Adventures of Rin Tin Tin* as "Corporal Randy Boone," always in a friendly conflict with the tough but likeable "Sergeant Biff O'Hara" (Joe Sawyer). When that cavalry series left the air, Brooks moved into another, the far more adult *Mackenzie's Raiders* (1959), in a similar part, "Corporal Brown." Hoping to make his own B movies, Brooks wrote, produced, directed, and self-financed *Legend of the Northwest* (1964), the result so terrible that the film couldn't be released. He left the biz but became wealthy after opening the LA Professional Ambulance Service. SEE ALSO: Lee Aaker, James (L.) Brown, Tommy Farrell, Joe Sawyer, Richard Carlson.

James (L.) Brown

(1920–1992)

••••••••••••••••••••••••••••••••

Tall, handsome, rugged, genial Jim Brown (often confused with the football star turned actor) had good news in 1952. Working in films for a decade, he had never landed the right role to turn him into a star. Now, producer Stanley Kramer announced that the native Texan would become the next great Western hero after *High Noon* was released, with Brown cast in the second lead: a deputy out on the plains whose story parallels Gary Cooper's "Will Kane" in Hadleyville. Would this character arrive in time to help the marshal? When the finished film screened at a preview, Kramer and company were shocked when everyone in the audience hated it. "Too long," people complained, so it was back to the editing room. With the paring-down process complete, Brown had become the proverbial face on the cutting-room floor. As *High Noon* became a huge hit, Brown sensed that while he could always find work, he would never become a big-screen Western star.

Yet he did enjoy considerable small-screen success on ABC for five years as "Lieutenant Rip(ley) Masters" on *The Adventures of Rin Tin Tin*. (The title character, incidentally, was performed by Flame, Jr.) In the initial episode, Masters and members of the "Fighting Blue Devils," a cavalry command stationed at Fort Apache, Arizona (the series was filmed on ultra-realistic structures built for Ford's epic *Fort Apache*, 1948), found a baby boy and his pup at the site of a wagon train massacre. They raised the child, "Rusty" (Lee Aaker), and the pet. In 166 episodes, Brown's character played father figure to the growing boy with an approach combining discipline and sensitivity. Brown also cut a hit record two years into the show's run. In "The White Buffalo" (10/14/55), he sang the title song (written by Alan Bergman) about a mythical bison only the brave can see. This installment proved so popular with kids that ABC reran it constantly. Each episode, incidentally, aired early on Friday evening, then was repeated on most ABC stations Saturday morning. During the off-season, Brown turned "Rip" into a lucrative cottage industry by appearing at rodeos across the country. Typecast in the part, he found few roles in later years, though he did costar in one TV Western, *The Rounders* (1966), and played "Detective Harry McSween" on *Dallas* (1979–1986). His best later role came as a conservative father in the cult classic *Targets* (1968), the debut film for writer/director Peter Bogdanovich. Brown eventually retired from acting to run a successful athletic equipment firm. Early in his career and despite a generally heroic demeanor, he had played two notorious real-life outlaws: Bob Younger in *The Younger Brothers* (1949) and Frank James in *Woman They Almost Lynched* (1953). SEE ALSO: Lee Aaker, Rand Brooks, Tommy Farrell, Joe Sawyer.

Johnny Mack Brown
(1904–1974)
••••••••••••••••••••••••••••••

This likeable, good-looking college football star (halfback) headed for Hollywood, landing the lead in a major MGM Western. Brown played William Bonney in MGM's *Billy the Kid* (1930) with Wallace Beery as Pat Garrett. But his big-time career would prove short-lived; Brown soon slipped into B Westerns for Mascot and Monogram, both on his own as "Johnny" and as one of the constantly changing *Rough Riders* trio. On TV, he showed up as "Sheriff Eaton" during the 1958 season of *Tales of Wells Fargo*. SEE ALSO: Clu Gulager, Dale Robertson.

Peter Brown
(1935–)
••••••••••••••••••••••••••••••

Stationed in Alaska with the Second Infantry, a bored Peter Brown talked other soldiers into staging shows. Back stateside, he pumped gas for a customer in California who turned out to be Jack L. Warner, who signed the stunned youth to a studio contract. After lots of films and episodic TV, Brown finally won the second

lead (to John Russell as "Marshal Dan Troop") on *Lawman* (1958–1962) as dedicated deputy "Johnny McKay" in a notably strong variation on the old professional/young protégé relationship. As the series wore on, Johnny got to head out on his own missions. The ever-young-looking actor then picked up a similar part on *Laredo* (1965–1967) as "Chad Cooper," one of a trio of Texas Rangers (William Smith, Neville Brand) keeping law and order in the title border town for Universal/NBC. Pop-culture claim to fame: Brown was castrated by Pam Grier and her cohorts at the end of *Foxy Brown* (1974), a legendary black exploitation flick. In later years Brown became a soap-opera staple, appearing on *One Life to Live* (1986–1987) and *The Bold and the Beautiful* (1991–1992). He recently returned to Westerns in *Three Bad Men* and *Hell to Pay*, both in 2005. SEE ALSO: Neville Brand, John Russell, William Smith.

Edgar Buchanan
(1903–1979)
••••••••••••••••••••••••••••••

A dentist in Oregon, Buchanan moved his practice to California and began appearing at the Pasadena Community Playhouse for fun, became hooked, closed down his office, and entered the movie business. He often appeared in Westerns, beginning with his seventh film as "Old Timer" (though only thirty-sev-

en) in *When the Daltons Rode* (1940).
He could be nice (sad-faced sodbuster
in *Shane*, 1953) or mean (corrupt
town boss in *Wichita*, 1955) but was
always at his best as a combination
of the two: Curly Bill Brocious in
*Tombstone: The Town Too Tough to
Die* (1942). On TV, Buchanan played
sidekick "Red Connors" to Bill Boyd
in the new *Hopalong Cassidy* episodes
(1952–1954). He next was picked by
producer Russ Hayden for *Judge Roy
Bean* (1956), an exceptional syndicated series shot in color on Hayden's
own Western set. A Sons of the
Pioneers–like chorus sang "Take me
home to the land of the Pecos" over
the opening titles as weary Texas
Rangers slowly rode toward Vinaga-
roon (aka Langtry), Texas, by moonlight; everything about this show projected an elegiac, sentimental, Fordian
tone. Best of all, this Bean came close
to his historical counterpart: neither
a "hang 'em high!" type like Walter
Brennan in *The Westerner* (1940) nor
a roughneck hero like Paul Newman
in *The Life and Times of Judge Roy
Bean* (1972), just a small-town offi-
cial who slapped cowhands on their
wrists for spittin' on his boardwalk.
Buchanan's next TV parts were as the
reformed gunman "Bob Dawson" on
Tales of Wells Fargo and simultaneously the sawbones "Doc Burrage" on
The Rifleman. In the 1960s, Buchanan
switched from cowboy to country as
the lovable old "Uncle Joe Carson"
on three shows: *Beverly Hillbillies*,
Green Acres, and *Petticoat Junction*.

When Westerns returned, Buchanan
was ready, willing, and able, playing
in *The Over-the-Hill Gang* (10/7/69)
with Brennan, Chill Wills, Andy
Devine, and Jack Elam, and a sequel,
The Over-the-Hill Gang Rides Again
(11/17/70). Buchanan was reunited
with Glenn Ford (they had done a
dozen films together at Columbia)
for *Cade's County* (1971–1972), a
modern-day Western, playing deputy
"J. J. Jackson." SEE ALSO: Jack Buetel,
Chuck Connors, Glenn Ford, Russell
Hayden, Jackie Loughery, Dale Robertson.

Jack Buetel
(1915–1989)

Warren Higgens from Dallas, Texas,
was awarded his new moniker by
Howard Hughes, who cast the then
twenty-two-year-old unknown as
Billy the Kid in *The Outlaw*. Ready
for release in 1943, the frankly sexual
(for its time) Western (Billy engages
in a sadomasochistic affair with Jane
Russell's "Rio") wasn't okayed by
the Hays/Breen censorship office
until three years later. In 1948, Howard Hawks (who had unofficially
co-directed Buetel's earlier film)
considered him for the part of John
Wayne's adopted son in *Red River*,
wisely opting for Monty Clift instead.
Buetel didn't work again until 1951,
then found himself cast as outlaw
Bob Younger in *Best of the Badmen*.
He also played Frank James three

years later in *Jesse James' Women*. Buetel portrayed good guys on TV, first as Texas Ranger "Jeff Taggert" on *Judge Roy Bean* (1956), then as Arizona Ranger "Johnny Whitecloud" on *26 Men* (1958), both for producer Russ Hayden. Buetel later found employment as an insurance clerk. SEE ALSO: Edgar Buchanan, Tristram Coffin, Russell Hayden, Kelo Henderson.

the show, removing the tough, gritty feel of its early years to make *Train* user-friendly for Sunday evening family audiences. The new approach included off-the-rack clothes, neat new hats rather than worn outfits, etc., all of which destroyed the series' original appeal. As for Burns, he eventually abandoned acting for academia. SEE ALSO: Robert Fuller, John McIntire, Denny (Scott) Miller.

Don Burnett
(19??–)
••••••••••••••••••••••••••••••

Blandly handsome, Burnett won some small parts in several big pictures: *Tea and Sympathy* (1956) and *Raintree County* (1957). He played "Ensign Langdon Towne" in *Northwest Passage* (1958–1959), MGM's series based on the epic movie about Rogers's Rangers in the French and Indian Wars, in the role that Robert Young played (far more memorably) in the movie. Burnett's biggest film role was as the second lead in *Damon and Pythias (1962)* to Guy (*Zorro*) Williams. SEE ALSO: Buddy Ebsen, Keith Larson, Guy Williams.

Ellen Burstyn
(1932–)
••••••••••••••••••••••••••••••

One of America's great film, stage, and TV actors, Burstyn is best remembered for her remarkable Broadway roles (*Same Time, Next Year*; Tony winner, repeating her part in the 1978 movie), and then films: *The Last Picture Show* (1971), *The Exorcist* (1973), *Alice Doesn't Live Here Anymore* (1974, Oscar winner). Early on, Burstyn made several contributions to the genre, as "Sister Jacob" on *The Big Valley* in "Days of Grace" (4/17/67) and in a continuing role as "Julie Parsons," manager of a frontier general store on *The Iron Horse* (1967–1968). SEE ALSO: Peter Breck, Dale Robertson.

Michael Burns
(1947–)
••••••••••••••••••••••••••••••

Added to the *Wagon Train* cast in 1963 as "Barnaby West," an orphan cared for by the pilgrims, Burns functioned as part of a plan to overhaul

Pat Buttram
(1915–1994)
••••••••••••••••••••••••••••••

Alabama-born Buttram journeyed up to Chicago to see the 1933 World's Fair firsthand, only to find himself interviewed by a local radio station that wanted a rube's-eye view of events. Buttram offered such a surprisingly laconic wit (along with that syrupy voice) that they hired him on the spot to provide a good ol' boy's commentaries on the changing American scene. He hooked up with the National Barn Dance radio program and met singin' cowboy Gene Autry. The two hit it off, and when Autry returned from WWII, he hired Buttram as the new sidekick for B oaters beginning with *The Strawberry Roan* (1948), then sixteen more. Buttram was billed as "Smokey," "Chuckwalla," "Shadrach," "Pecos," "Scat," "Panhandle," "Rawhide," and finally "Pat." He signed on to play that role for *The Gene Autry Show* (1950–1955) as an amiable, dumb-like-a-fox sidekick, more or less Will Rogers as a supporting player. On the TV show and movies like *Mule Train* (1950), gorgeous blonde Sheila Ryan giggled at Buttram, romanced Autry. In real life, she fell for the cagey comic; they were married in 1951. After Autry, Buttram found work as a serious character actor, including two films with Elvis: *Wild in the Country* (1961) and *Roustabout* (1964). He later costarred in Don Siegel's *The Hanged Man* (11/18/64), an early made-for-TV oater, with another vet, Robert Culp (*Trackdown*). Buttram signed on for *The Real McCoys'* 1962–1963 season as a "semi-regular," then as "Charlie Paradise" on *The Cara Williams Show* (1965) and "Jake/Pa Turner"

on *Pistols 'n' Petticoats* (1966–1967). He struck later-life gold as "Eustace Charleton Haney" on *Green Acres* (1965–1971), the country bumpkin to Eddie Albert and Eva Gabor's recently arrived city slickers. Buttram provided the voice of "Cactus Jake" for the animated *Garfield and Friends* (1989–1991). When Robert Zemeckis needed a "typical" figure for his Old West saloon in *Back to the Future Part III* (1990), who better than Buttram? In 1982, the veteran actor helped to create the Golden Boot award to honor veterans of TV/movie Westerns. SEE ALSO: Gene Autry, Robert Culp, John Forrest "Fuzzy" Knight.

Spring Byington
(1886–1971)
••••••••••••••••••••••••••••••••

Following the termination of her relationship with her husband in 1924, Byington became inseparable from best friend/constant companion Marjorie Main, another top-notch character actress. Between 1930 and 1950, Byington appeared in nearly 100 films, receiving an Oscar nomination as Best Supporting Actress for *You Can't Take It with You* (1938). She played Dolly Madison in *The Buccaneer* (1938) and went Western for *Devil's Doorway* (1950), an effective Indian rights mini-epic. Emmy nominated (1959) for her TV sitcom *December Bride,* on *Laramie* (1961–1963) Byington played "Daisy Cooper," a busybody who looked after the male characters on the Sherman Ranch much as Aunt Harriet did the boys on the later *Batman*. Her sweet whine of a voice caused some viewers to question the "orientation" of *Laramie*'s young single men. SEE ALSO: Hoagy Carmichael; Robert Crawford, Jr.; Robert Fuller; John Smith.

Robert Cabal

(19??–????)

Virtually no information exists today on this energetic, likeable Latino actor. After making his debut in Robert Montgomery's noir *Ride the Pink Horse* (1947) as a small Mexican child in a border town, Cabal received plenty of work as Spanish/Indian characters (*Border Incident*, 1949). He portrayed outlaw Joaquin Murietta in his youth in *The Man Behind the Gun* (1953, Randolph Scott), and worked in TV on *The Cisco Kid* (1952), *Annie Oakley* (1956), etc. Eventually he won the role of "Hey Soos," a Hispanic cowboy on the cattle drive in *Rawhide* (1959–1965). In early episodes, the character appeared to be little more than a caricature of a gleeful young vaquero, but as the show progressed, the writers fleshed out Cabal's role, with Hey Soos becoming ever more understandable as a unique person who could be counted on by other drovers to come through in a pinch. Cabal played one other notable TV role, on the "Winner Lose All" episode of *The Big Valley* (10/27/65). SEE ALSO: Clint Eastwood, Robert Loggia, Duncan Renaldo.

Rory Calhoun

(1922–1999)

Born Francis Timothy McCown, Calhoun's troubled youth included car theft, leading to a three-year reformatory stay. Purportedly discovered by Alan Ladd's wife, he appeared in varied movies, including the comedy *How to Marry a Millionaire* (1953), before settling in as a B+ Western star. Calhoun projected a surly, arrogant image, along with a glib way of delivering dialogue that made him perfect for slick, sleazy villains, notably as the mean-spirited lover of Marilyn Monroe in *River of No Return* (1954). In addition to supporting work in Fox's A movies, Calhoun produced B Westerns starring himself in the late 1950s. His protagonists were antiheroes, true also of his role on TV's *The Texan* (1958–1960). In this Monday night CBS adult oater, Calhoun portrayed Bill Longley as a moody loner who fought for the right. This outraged historians; if they had complained about Earp, Masterson, Hickok, et al., being whitewashed for TV, that situation went over the edge here. Longley had been a cold-blooded killer, most of his victims black, the result of post–Civil War hatred there of freed former slaves. In the late 1960s, Calhoun starred in B Westerns (*Black Spurs*, 1965; *Apache Uprising*, 1966) for director R. G. Springsteen during his one-man crusade to bring back the low-budget theatrical oater. SEE ALSO: Rod Cameron, John Payne, Dale Robertson.

Rod Cameron

(1910–1983)
• •

Growing up in Alberta, young Nathan Cox dreamed of becoming a Mountie. A friend suggested he would do better to play one in the movies. Cameron did precisely that in DeMille's *North West Mounted Police* (1940), though his first Hollywood job had been as stunt double for Buck Jones, which led to acting gigs. He played Jesse James in *Remarkable Andrew* (1942), Cameron's sole historical role, though only the beginning for his Westerns, including a full dozen low-budgeters for Republic, the best among them *Beyond the Pecos* (1945), with Fuzzy Knight as his sidekick "Barnacle." First, though, came a pair of WWII serials as "Rex Bennett": *G-Men vs. the Black Dragon* and *Secret Service in Darkest Africa,* both in 1943. In the 1950s, he often played a good guy matched against badman Forrest Tucker (*Ride the Man Down*, 1952; *San Antone*, 1953). Cameron played the hero in *Southwest Passage* (1954, John Ireland), then the heavy in *Santa Fe Passage* (1955, John Payne).

Fawcett comics offered him a monthly publication, *Rod Cameron Western*. His first TV series was a noir, *City Detective* (1953–1955). Cameron's contemporary oater was introduced on *Star Stage* (2/3/56) with the pilot "Killer on Horseback"; this was followed by three successful years on *State Trooper* (1956–1959). The show might have been titled "*Country* Detective," essentially resetting that previous show's premise in today's West, with "Rod Blake" zipping around in an unmarked car. His third series, *COronado 9* (1959–1961), brought Cameron back to big-city police work, the title referring to his telephone exchange. He starred in one German Western as "Old Firehand" in *Thunder at the Border* (1966), from a Karl May novel. Cameron later appeared in two throwbacks to the 1950s Bs: *The Gun Hawk* (1963) and *The Bounty Killer* (1965). Cameron played the actor playing Pat Garrett in the "death of Billy the Kid" sequence in star/director Dennis Hopper's *The Last Movie* (1971). Dubious claim to fame: In 1960, he divorced his wife of ten years, Angela Alves-Lio, to marry her mother, Dorothy. SEE ALSO: Jim Davis, Forrest Tucker.

Bruce Campbell
(1958–)

This cult actor works in purposefully broad strokes and has emerged as the current king of B movies. The Michigan native met aspiring filmmaker Sam Raimi in a high-school drama class. The two at once began work on a series of Super 8 movies. In time, they raised $350,000 and shot *The Evil Dead* (1981), kicking off a new wave of gratuitously violent horror flicks. The sequel (1987) featured ten times the budget, and the third installment (1992) was backed by Universal. Thereafter Campbell starred in *The Adventures of Brisco County Jr.* (1993–1994), a worthy attempt to revive long-faded TV Westerns by adding wise-guy humor and strong doses of science fiction. His title

character roamed the west, looking for the "Bly" gang, killers of his gunfighter father. Campbell even rode a wonder horse, "Comet." But what were those strange "golden orbs" that kept descending from space? Costars included Kelly Rutherford as dancehall girl "Dixie Cousins," Julius Carry as rival bounty hunter "Lord Bowler," and Christian Clemenson as lawyer "Socrates Poole." If properly promoted, *Brisco* might have scored big with hip young audiences; sadly, the show was allowed to die after a single season. But a good season it was, with self-conscious nods to an earlier era thanks to appearances by TV veterans Paul Brinegar (*The Life and Legend of Wyatt Earp*, *Rawhide*), Robert Fuller (*Laramie*, *Wagon Train*), and James Drury (*The Virginian*).

David Canary
(1938–)

In his first film, 1967's *Hombre*, Canary played a nasty youth who gets his comeuppance from Paul Newman. He scored a regular role as ranch hand "Candy Canady" on *Bonanza* in eighty-four episodes between 1967 and 1973 in one of several semi-successful attempts to fill the void left by Pernell Roberts. He later starred in the soap opera *All My Children*, essentially a one-note actor. SEE ALSO: Dan Blocker, Lorne Greene, Pernell Roberts.

Harry Carey, Jr.

(1921–)

Son of a legendary Western star who was also John Ford's original leading man, Harry Jr. transformed himself from supporting player to symbol of the Old West. His nickname, "Dobe," came from his reddish hair, which was the same color as the soil on his parents' ranch. In 1953 director Joe Kane suggested changing the name of Carey's character in the *San Antone* script to "Dobe," the only time he was ever called that onscreen. He initially hoped to be an opera singer; his beautiful voice can be heard briefly in Hawks's *Red River* (1948) as "Dan Latimer" sings to cattle, then more fully in Ford's *3 Godfathers* (1948) and

AN AMERICAN ICON: Harry Carey (Jr.) has enjoyed the longest run of any movie/TV cowboy star, ranging from boyish roles to cantankerous older characters. Courtesy Marilyn and Harry Carey collection.

Wagon Master (1950). In the latter and *Rio Grande* (1950), Dobe played with Ben Johnson as "Sandy Boone" and "Travis Tyree," respectively. His mother, Olive Carey, played his mom in *The Searchers* (1956); Dobe was the third title character with John Wayne and Jeff Hunter. One of his first films had been one of his dad's last, though they never appear together: In the aforementioned *Red River*, Dobe's drover is killed in a stampede, while Harry Sr. appears as the Abilene cattle buyer at the end. Harry Sr. had by this time become an iconic figure, his presence in small roles representing the genre itself, a status Dobe would also assume.

Meanwhile, *Red River* implied a passing of the torch, as did Ford's *3 Godfathers* (1948). Here, Dobe

enacted the "Abilene Kid," with John Wayne and Pedro Armendáriz the outlaws who become "wise men" in Ford's haunting allegorical fable, filmed earlier with Harry Sr. Though Dobe had appeared in six previous films, he's "introduced" in this movie dedicated to his dad, who had passed away the previous year. He had never played a historical Westerner until Marshal Fred White in *Tombstone* (1993), though he did enact future President Dwight D. Eisenhower in Ford's *The Long Gray Line* (1955).

TV beckoned. Walt Disney cast Dobe as "Bill Burnett," camp counselor at the Triple R Ranch on *The Adventures of Spin and Marty* (1955) and two *Mickey Mouse Club* sequels. Then came *Texas John Slaughter* (1958–1961), with Tom Tryon as that real-life Westerner, and Dobe cast as "Ben Jenkins," his fictional sidekick. Carey received constant work on *Gunsmoke, Wagon Train,* etc., and may be the only actor to receive prominent billing in a big Western he's not in: he is listed in the credits of *Rio Bravo* (1959), though his role as a townsman ended up on the cutting-room floor. Dobe always kept busy, effectively adjusting to changing styles: In 1975, he appeared in *Take a Hard Ride*, a bizarre combination of a Lee Van Cleef spaghetti Western and a Fred Williamson black exploitation flick. Gradually Dobe became as associated with the Western landscape as Monument Valley itself. Cameos in films as diverse as *The Long Riders* (1980, as a one-time Johnny Reb, "George Arthur," now a stage passenger) and *Back to the Future III* (1990, as an old-timer in the saloon) added to his movie-metaphor status, and Dobe's presence was always welcome. He appeared in *Once Upon a Texas Train* (1/3/88, with Willie Nelson), *Wyatt Earp: Return to Tombstone* (7/1/94, Hugh O'Brian), and *Last Stand at Saber River* (1/19/97, Tom Selleck). SEE ALSO: Roy Barcroft, Ben Johnson, Stan Jones, Tom Tryon.

Philip Carey
(1925–)
....

A soft-spoken, impressive performer, Carey's first major Western role was as a gentleman psycho who kidnaps Donna Reed in Raoul Walsh's *Gun Fury* (1953). He won supporting parts in John Ford's non-Westerns *The Long Gray Line* and *Mister Roberts* (both 1955), though unaccountably this didn't lead to his becoming part of Ford's stock company. Carey starred in TV's *Tales of the 77th Bengal Lancers* (1956–1957) with Warren Stevens as a Gary Cooper–Franchot Tone type team, and in *Philip Marlowe* (1959–1960) as the Raymond Chandler gumshoe. Carey rode to the Little Big Horn twice, as Captain Myles Keogh in *Tonka* (aka *A Horse Called Comanche*, 1958), then as Colonel Custer himself in *The Great Sioux Massacre* (1965). He played

Cole Younger on *Cheyenne* (2/12/62) and was fourth-billed (behind Neville Brand, Peter Brown, and Will Smith) on *Laredo* (1965–1967) as "Captain Edward Parmalee," the older/mustachioed Texas Ranger. Carey later played "Asa Buchanan" on the afternoon soap *One Life to Live*. SEE ALSO: Neville Brand, Peter Brown, William Smith.

Richard Carlson
(1912–1977)
....

Originally an English teacher at the University of Minnesota (his home state) who hoped to become a playwright, Carlson found success as an actor after service in WWII. He appeared in scores of films, in pretty much every genre *except* Westerns, doing only one at this time, *Seminole* (1953). Most of his films were negligible, but Carlson did costar in two classics: MGM's lavish action epic *King Solomon's Mines* (1950) and the era's best B monster movie, *Creature from the Black Lagoon* (1954). He has the dubious distinction of starring in TV's tribute to Joe McCarthy witchhunting, *I Led 3 Lives* (1953–1956), as real-life anti-Commie agent Herbert A. Philbrick. He appeared in another Western, this time as Alamo commander William Barrett Travis, in *The Last Command* (1955), then starred in the syndicated *Mackenzie's Raiders* (1958–1959) as Colonel Ranald S. Mackenzie, commander of the Fourth Cavalry stationed at Fort Clark, Texas. This series dramatized his difficult assignment, since the law clearly stated that American troops could not cross into Mexico to pursue Apaches, even though word from above unofficially ordered Mackenzie to do precisely that to halt raiding parties. He understood that, should he be discovered by Mexican border patrols, the higher-ups would disavow any knowledge. Unfortunately, this intriguing show is virtually impossible to locate today. Afterward, Carlson appeared in B movies/episodic TV, also directing some filmed episodes and one feature in which Carlson also appeared with Don Murray, *Kid Rodelo* (1966), based on a Louis L'Amour story. SEE ALSO: Don Murray.

Hoagy Carmichael

(1899–1981)

· ·

When producer Mike Todd put together the list of potential guest stars who would make cameo appearances in his extravaganza *Around the World in Eighty Days* (1956), he noted that for the nonspeaking role of the pianist in a Wild West saloon there were only two options: Frank Sinatra or Hoagy Carmichael. When the former agreed, that was that. The Indiana University grad had created the classics "Stardust" and "Georgia on My Mind," collaborating with such jazz greats as Frank Loesser and

CHARACTER PEOPLE: One great pleasure of the TV genre is provided by scene-stealing actors, including Hoagy Carmichael. Courtesy ABC, NBC, and CBS.

Ned Washington, Carmichael's influence on the direction of American music rates as immense and positive, furthering the assimilation of blues into big band, afterward transforming them into modern pop. He played the musician "Cricket" in Howard Hawks's *To Have and Have Not* (1944), earlier serving as a working model for "Sam" in Michael Curtiz's *Casablanca* (1942), though the role went to Dooley Wilson. (Carmichael did play Sam in a TV restaging on 3/3/55.) No stranger to Westerns, he became the singing sidekick to Dana Andrews in *Canyon Passage* (1946), crooning "Ole Buttermilk Sky," for which he received an Oscar nomination (Best Song). On the first season of *Laramie* (1959–1960), he took on a similar role as "Jonesy," a lovably laconic figure who does odd jobs on the Sherman Ranch while singing his

C

tunes. *Laramie* rates as an example of those shows that originally offered something different but were reduced to a formula for commercial reasons. In the second season, supporting characters were dropped to focus on the friendship of blonde "Slim Sherman" (John Smith) and darkly dangerous bad boy "Jess Harper" (Robert Fuller). SEE ALSO: Spring Byington, Robert Crawford, Jr.

Matt Carmody

(1968–   )

Carmody played Adam, the brooding Cartwright brother on *Ponderosa* (2001–2002). SEE ALSO: Jared Daperis, Daniel Hugh Kelly, Drew Powell.

David Carradine

(1936–2009)

This son of screen legend John Carradine studied music at San Francisco State College, then joined a Shakespeare rep company. After a service hitch, David briefly entered the commercial art world. His Broadway role as Atahualpa in *The Royal Hunt of the Sun* (1965) opposite Christopher Plummer as Pizaro led to movie jobs, often cast as Indians or half-breeds. His best early role is as the Utah Kid on *The Virginian* (3/4/64). He was awarded the lead in a belated *Shane* series (1966) though he bore no resemblance to Alan Ladd in appear-

ance. One critic quipped that Carradine came off like a cross between Mick Jagger and John Barrymore. The supporting cast included Jill Ireland as "Marian Starrett," this time around *not* a married woman but a widow, caring for "Little Joey" (Christopher Shea) with the help of her father-in-law (Tom Tully), purposefully eliminating the tense sexual chemistry of the 1953 classic. Production values were high, and the acting often dazzling, but a deadly time slot opposite Jackie Gleason on Saturday evenings spelled doom. Following the series' cancellation, Carradine appeared in forgettable oaters (*Young Billy Young*, 1969; *The McMasters*, 1970) and one bona fide cult film: Martin Scorsese's *Boxcar Bertha* (1972), with Barbara Hershey in the title role. She became Carradine's longtime lover, though not one of his five wives.

The early 1970s witnessed an absorption of Eastern culture into the American mainstream; martial arts and transcendental meditation became highly popular as a result of the late 1960s youth culture. Superstar Bruce Lee had briefly been considered for ABC's *Kung Fu*, though he was eventually rejected as "too Asian" (!?); the writers then transformed "Kwai Chang Caine" into a mixed racial character, with Carradine playing the lead in the TV movie (2/22/72) and subsequent series. Thanks to the producing/directing team of Jerry Thorpe and Alex Beaton, *Kung Fu* did not crassly

EAST IS EAST AND WEST IS WEST: During the 1970s, as a new American consciousness came into being, David Carradine played the Asian spiritual-journeyman "Caine" on *Kung Fu*. Courtesy ABC.

able in *Death Race 2000* (1975) and *Lone Wolf McQuade* (1983, in which he lost an epic martial arts match to Chuck Norris). Carradine endured constant problems with the IRS over his financing for indie film *Americana* (1983), which he wrote, produced, directed, and starred in. His career surged again with *Kung Fu: The Legend Continues*, which he also produced (1993–1997), returning as Caine. Chris Potter played his long-missing son "Peter," and they united to fight crime. Carradine played the title character in Quentin Tarantino's *Kill Bill: Vol. 1* (2003) and *Vol. 2* (2004), sealing his action-icon status.

SEE ALSO: John Carradine, Keith Carradine, Robert "Bobby" Carradine, Jill Ireland.

exploit the craze but rather explored it in depth, Carradine abetted by Philip Ahn as "Kan" and Keye Luke as "Po," masters of martial arts; Radames Pera as "Young Caine"; and David's brother Keith as "teenage Caine."

David played the title character, Tom, in *Mr. Horn* (2/1/79), a first-rate miniseries penned by William Goldman about the man who captured Geronimo then turned outlaw, with Richard Widmark as mentor Al Sieber and Jack Starrett (also director) as General George Crook. Carradine's roles as Woody Guthrie (*Bound for Glory*, 1976) and Cole Younger (*The Long Riders*, 1980) were among his finest later work. He was also enjoy-

John Carradine

(1906–1988)

••••••••••••••••••••••••••••••••••••

A wandering artist from upstate New York, Carradine bummed his way through rural America, ended up in Hollywood, and tried to convince Cecil B. DeMille to hire him as a scenic designer. Instead, the famed director pronounced that the young man had the greatest voice he had ever heard and must become an actor; in time, DeMille cast Carradine as Aaron to Charlton Heston's Moses in *The Ten Commandments* (1956). Carradine's over 400 movie/TV credits (not counting stage, which he considered his true calling) ranged from the heights of cinema (John Ford's *The Grapes of Wrath*, 1940, with Henry Fonda and Jane Darwell) to the lows (Albert Zugsmith's *Sex Kittens Go to College*, 1960, with Mamie Van Doren and Conway Twitty). Carradine became a member of Ford's stock company for both Westerns (*Drums Along the Mohawk*, 1939) and non-Westerns (*The Last Hurrah*, 1958). His greatest role ever was arguably that of "Hatfield," a Doc Holliday type, in Ford's *Stagecoach* (1939). Historical personages ranged from good (Bret Harte in *The Adventures of Mark Twain*, 1944, Fredric March) to the hero's archenemy Simon Girty in *Daniel Boone* (1936, George O'Brien). He played Bob Ford twice, in *Jesse James* (1939) and *The Return of Frank James* (1940). Carradine surpassed Bela Lugosi as Dracula in *House of Frankenstein* (1944) and had a lifelong friendly competition with John Barrymore, his only equal as the era's top actor. He appeared in almost every TV Western series and had regular roles in three: "Elmer Dodson," mentor to would-be writer "Johnny Yuma" (Nick Adams) on *The Rebel* (1959–1961); "General Josh McCord," father to Chuck Connors on *Branded* (1965–1966); and "Reverend Serenity Johnson" on *Kung Fu* (starring son David, 1972–1975). His final words before expiring in Italy were "Milan, what a beautiful place to die!" SEE ALSO: Nick Adams, David Carradine, Keith Carradine, Robert "Bobby" Carradine, Chuck Connors.

Keith Carradine

(1949–)

Keith Carradine is son to John, half-brother to David, and brother to Bobby. He played the lead in many films and TV shows and was a character actor in others; his roles were always first rate, with strong ties to the Western. His first cowboy movie roles were as teenage gunfighters in Robert Altman's *McCabe & Mrs. Miller* (Warren Beatty) and Lamont Johnson's *A Gunfight* (Kirk Douglas), both in 1971. On big brother David's *Kung Fu*, he played "Caine" as a teenager in flashbacks (1972–1973). He won an Oscar (Best Song) for Altman's ensemble piece *Nashville* ("I'm Easy") and played Jim Younger in Walter Hill's *The Long Riders* (1980) with David as "Cole," Bobby as "Bob." Carradine narrated "Annie Oakley" for a Rabbit Ears children's theater production (1992). He was cast by Hill as William Frederic Cody, close friend to the title character (Jeff Bridges) in *Wild Bill* (1995), then played Hickok on *Deadwood*'s five-parter about the death of that famed gunfighter, with Garret Dillahunt as back-shooter Jack McCall (2004). Keith Carradine played Texas Ranger Bigfoot Wallace in *Dead Man's Walk* (5/12/96), based on Larry McMurtry's prequel to *Lonesome Dove*, with David Arquette as "Augustus McCrae" and Jonny Lee Miller as "Woodrow Call," younger incarnations of characters made famous by Robert Duvall and Tommy Lee Jones. Keith costarred with Tom Selleck in two above-par TV oaters, *Last Stand at Saber River* (1/19/97) and *Monte Walsh* (1/17/03), from the fine Elmore Leonard and Jack Schaefer novels, respectively. He played "Captain Richard Pratt" in the Steven Spielberg–produced TV epic *Into the West* (2005). SEE ALSO: David Carradine, Robert Carradine, Tom Selleck, Robin Weigert.

Robert "Bobby" Carradine
(1954–)

The youngest acting son of legendary character actor John Carradine made his TV debut as a cocky, arrogant, boastful Billy the Kid–type in *Bonanza* (12/19/71), playing a similar role ("Slim") in *The Cowboys* (1972) and its series spinoff (1974). He gave a similar performance in *The Long Riders* (1980) as Bob Younger. His best movie role was as the character "Zab," based on Sam Fuller, in that writer/ director's *The Big Red One* (1980), a fitting tribute to the famed WWII fighting outfit. Carradine settled into a solid career doing supporting parts, including "Sam" in *Lizzie McGuire* (2001–2004). He returned to oaters as "the Kid" in Chris Coppola's *Gunfighter* (1998). Pop-culture claim to fame: Carradine played the geeky "Lewis" in *Revenge of the Nerds* (1984). SEE ALSO: David Carradine, Keith Carradine, Moses Gunn.

Leo Carrillo
(1881–1961)

Slobbering, low-born characters of dubious morality were what this Hispanic actor embodied onscreen, incarnating clichés that people of Latino ethnicity find offensive today. In real life, Carrillo claimed lineage from California's Spanish aristocracy. A gifted political cartoonist, he had both a state park and a beach named after him. He first played the sidekick "Pancho" in *Riders of Death Valley* (1941), a big-budget Universal serial with Dick Foran. When Duncan Renaldo was cast as the latest Cisco Kid, Carillo came aboard as Pancho. *Valiant Hombre* (1948) proved a hit, so follow-ups were inevitable. In 1950, Cisco and Pancho shifted intact to TV in episodes broadcast in black-and-white though shot in color. Stories were mostly mundane, but action scenes were well staged. Social activists argue as to whether having an unbelievably idealized star and an ever hungry, shifty-eyed sidekick who stole everything in sight should be considered better than benign neglect or worse than no Hispanic heroes at all. SEE ALSO: Robert Loggia, Duncan Renaldo, Guy Williams.

Veronica Cartwright

(1949–)

....

This durable, versatile actress is best remembered today by sci-fi buffs as a "scream queen" thanks to roles in two classics: as Rod Taylor's little sister "Cathy" in Alfred Hitchcock's *The Birds* (1963) and as the doomed astronaut "Lambert" in Ridley Scott's *Alien* (1979). Like her younger sister Angela (*The Danny Thomas Show*), she rated as a first-rate child star with big Keane eyes, a sensitive face, and a sweetly sad voice, causing the British-born girl to come off as a younger Julie Harris. Her first TV Western was "The Lone Woman" (10/8/59) on *Zane Grey Theater*, the pilot for a proposed Barbara Stanwyck series as a strong pioneer woman/daughter combo. It did not sell, though *Daniel Boone* did; Veronica played Jemima during the first two seasons. The character initially farmed alongside Patricia Blair and said "Yes, Mom" a lot but came into her own during the second season, particularly in "The First Beau" (11/9/65), in which Mima fell for a bad boy (Fabian Forte). Leaving to go freelance, she played roles in movies (*Invasion of the Body Snatchers*, 1978; *The Witches of Eastwick*, 1987) and on TV, including *The X Files* ("Cassandra," 1998–1999) and *Invasion* ("Valerie," 2005–2006). SEE ALSO: Patricia Blair, Darby Hinton, Fess Parker.

Allen Case

(1934–1986)

....

An Off-Broadway musical veteran (*Once Upon a Mattress*), Case played the second lead in two TV Westerns. In *The Deputy* (1959–1961), he had the title role as "Clay McCord" assisting "Marshal Fry" (Henry Fonda). Case was next cast in a part Fonda had done in two films: Frank James, older brother to the title character, in *The Legend of Jesse James* (1965–1966). He also played Sheriff Pat Garrett in the "Billy the Kid" episode of the sci-fi series *The Time Tunnel* (1967). SEE ALSO: Henry Fonda, Wallace Ford, Betty Lou Keim.

Johnny Cash

(1932–2003)

....

Like Elvis Presley, a colleague at Sam Phillips's Sun Records in Memphis, Tennessee, J. R. Cash secretly hoped to parlay success as a singer into an acting career in Westerns. Arkansas born, his twangy renditions of "Ring of Fire" and "I Walk the Line" proved to be perfectly timed as the public turned away from pop covers of country songs to the real thing. Cash's first TV exposure came on the superior Western *The Rebel* (1959–1961). He recorded the title song ("Johnny Yuma was a rebel, he roamed through the West") and joined star Nick Adams for the

FROM COUNTRY-WESTERN SINGER TO TV COWBOY: Johnny Cash (*right*) was one of many legendary performers who in the 1980s brought their musical "outlaw" images to movie-of-the-week projects, including the remake of *Stagecoach*; John Schneider sits beside Cash. Courtesy ABC.

1/3/60 episode. Depression and drugs took a terrible toll, and Cash hit a career low as a singing serial killer (*Door-to-Door Maniac*, 1961) glibly threatening young women with a cryptic ballad: "You got five more minutes to *live!*" Cash desperately wanted his own series, but *The Night Rider* (pilot aired 6/1/62) was not picked up. He persevered and became the stoic Man in Black, developing a cult following. Cash returned to cowboy ballads with "Ride This Train," as well as other albums and TV specials for ABC. Then a weekly musical show costarring new wife

June Carter Cash (with Bob Dylan as a memorable guest) finally turned Cash into a full-fledged superstar. Kirk Douglas (a fan) picked him to costar in *A Gunfight* (1971), which led to great success in TV Westerns: *Thaddeus Rose and Eddie* (with Bo Hopkins, 2/24/78), *Murder in Coweta County* (2/15/83), and John Brown in *North and South* (11/3/85). A cultural conservative/social liberal, he decried porn and defended civil rights activism for all ethnicities, with a particularly strong commitment to Native Americans. Cash starred as Cherokee leader John Ross, who had been forced to move his people west to hostile land, in NET Playhouse's *Trail of Tears* (4/8/71, with Jack Palance as a notably villainous President Andrew Jackson). He teamed with Kris Kristofferson for *The Last Days of Frank and Jesse James* (2/17/86), chronicling events following the disastrous raid on Northfield, Minnesota. The two put together the supergroup the Highwaymen, including Waylon Jennings and Willie Nelson, performing world-class outlaw-country songs. They all costarred in a remake of Ford's *Stagecoach* (5/18/86), with Cash as the tough/fair marshal "Curly." At one point, that TV film was planned as a country-rock opera with the quartet singing all their lines, though that concept was thankfully dropped. When the post–Walt Disney company decided to revive *Davy Crockett* in the late eighties and Fess Parker turned down the role as an older, reflective Crockett, Cash did it in *Rainbow in the Thunder* (11/20/88). His last Western role came in a recurring part as tired gunfighter "Kid Cole" (1993–1994) on *Dr. Quinn, Medicine Woman* with Jane Seymour. SEE ALSO: Waylon Jennings, Kris Kristofferson, Willie Nelson.

Mary Castle
(1931–1998)
••••••••••••••••••••••••••••••••

The "Road Company Rita Hayworth," the press dubbed Castle, due to a strik-

ing physical resemblance to that A-list star. Born Mary Ann Noblett, Mary was no relation to *Lawman*'s Peggie Castle. Unable to rise above B Westerns (*When the Redskins Rode*, 1951; *Gunsmoke*, 1953), she played Jim Davis's partner "Frankie Adams" in the first twenty-six episodes of *Stories of the Century* (1954), as a smart/sexy/sassy railroad detective able to charm or outthink villains. SEE ALSO: Jim Davis, Kristine Miller.

Peggie Castle
(1927–1973)
••••••••••••••••••••••••••••••••

This tall, statuesque blonde yearned for big-scale Hollywood stardom but found herself stuck in B Westerns: *Jesse James' Women* (Don "Red" Barry), *Overland Pacific* (Jock Mahoney), *The Yellow Tomahawk* (Rory Calhoun), all in 1954. At Warner Bros., execs decided "Marshal Dan Troop" on *Lawman* needed a "Miss Kitty" figure, so Castle joined the cast (10/4/59) as "Lily Merrill," new owner of a saloon, creating sparks with star John Russell. Her approach proved more overtly sexual than Amanda Blake's on *Gunsmoke*, closer to Angie Dickinson as "Feathers" in *Rio Bravo* (1959). Castle's final TV role before retiring was on *The Virginian* (2/9/66). Chronic alcohol addiction led to cirrhosis of the liver and an early death. SEE ALSO: Amanda Blake, John Russell.

Lon Chaney, Jr.

(1906–1973)

Son of the silent era's "Man of a Thousand Faces," Lon worked under his real name (Creighton Chaney) for five years, playing everything from leads to supporting roles to bits, often involved in several film projects simultaneously. He took his new moniker on advice from an agent to ensure commercial success, later regretting such reliance on his dad's name and fame. Closely associated with horror roles, Chaney was the only actor to play all four icons: Dracula, the Mummy, Frankenstein's monster, and the Wolf Man. He was the *only* performer at Universal to enact the last. Good-looking in his youth, Chaney appeared a natural for Westerns, among countless other projects, including the lead in the 1932 chapter play *The Last Frontier* (not to be confused with the 1955 Anthony Mann film of the same title). Alcohol abuse contributed to a growing weight problem. Chaney slipped into smaller roles, often as a heavy, beginning with *Billy the Kid* (1941). His greatest critical accolades came with the role of "Lennie" in the film version of John Steinbeck's *Of Mice and Men* (1939).

Chaney played two real-life outlaws—Jack McCall (*Badlands of Dakota*, 1941) and Grat Dalton (*The Daltons Ride Again*, 1945)—and later enacted Louis Rose, deserter from the Alamo (the character's name altered to "Louis Roque"), on *Wagon Train* (10/26/60). His first Native American role was as the title figure in *Battles of Chief Pontiac* (1952); a low-budget indie, the film stuck surprisingly close to history. Though Chaney did continue to do Anglo parts (notably as the forlorn old lawman in *High Noon*, 1952), a sad-eyed Native American elder statesmen became Chaney's great cottage industry. He played the Shawnee chief Blackfish in *Daniel Boone, Trail Blazer* (1956). In his first TV series, Chaney portrayed James Fenimore Cooper's "Chingachgook" in *Hawkeye and the Last of the Mohicans* (1957). Nearly ten years later, he showed up as "Chief Eagle Shadow" on the comedy-western *Pistols 'n' Petticoats* (1966–1967). The caricature he had become recalled Cooper's "John Mohican," a melancholy shadow of the great chief that Chingachgook had once been ("The Sagamore"), in *The Pioneers* (1823). SEE ALSO: John Hart, Ann Sheridan.

Harry Cheshire

(1891–1968)

Somehow managing to appear genial and grumpy at the same time, Cheshire performed in over 100 films, mostly in small roles, including the minister who marries James Stewart and Donna Reed in Frank Capra's *It's a Wonderful Life* (1946). He was born to play a small-town judge, first in Gene Autry's *Sioux City*

Sue (1946), followed by similar parts in many B films, including *The Fabulous Texan* (1947, "Wild Bill" Elliott), and one A film, *Carbine Williams* (1952, James Stewart). On TV, he did the judge bit on *The Gene Autry Show* (1950), *The Lone Ranger* (1952), and *Annie Oakley* (1955), the first and third produced by Autry, who gave Cheshire the go-ahead to portray "Judge Ben Riley," nicknamed "Fair and Square," on *Buffalo Bill, Jr.* (1955–1956), a fictionalized version of Judge Roy Bean, the character's name an anagram for that figure. Kindly but firm, he rode roughshod over the hero (Dick Jones) and his little sister, "Calamity" (Nancy Gilbert). No sooner had the series ended than Cheshire was picked by Warner Bros. to play virtually the same role with another name, "Judge Trager," on the more adult-oriented *Lawman* (1958–1962). SEE ALSO: Gene Autry, Peter Brown, Dick Jones, John Russell.

Gary Clarke
(1936–)
••••••••••••••••••••••••••••••

Graduating from teen horror flicks (*How to Make a Monster*, 1958) to TV Westerns, Clarke was cast as the genial "Steve," friend to the title character in *The Virginian* (1962–1964). Too low-key, in fact, for his own good, the producers gradually eased Clarke out to make room for Clu Gulager, Lee Majors, etc. Clarke

showed up as "Captain Richards," an inexperienced young cavalry officer hoping to subdue hostile Apaches, on the brief-lived *Hondo* (1967). He later moved to Arizona and appeared in TV and theatrical Westerns filmed there, including *The Young Riders* (1990–1991) and *Tombstone* (1993). SEE ALSO: James Drury, Doug McClure, Ralph Taeger.

Andy Clyde
(1892–1967)
••••••••••••••••••••••••••••••

A veteran of Scotland's music halls, Clyde headed for Hollywood to find work with Mack Sennett in silent comedies, then starred in his own series of "Andy Wilson" shorts in the early sound era as the archetype rube. His over 400 film/TV credits included sidekick "California Carlson" to William Boyd's "Hopalong Cassidy" between 1941 and 1948. With his rangy, messy, garrulous, tobacco-chewing, unshaven, temperamental manner, Clyde would have been a natural to play Hoppy if the character had remained true to Clarence Mulford's original. He later portrayed "Winks," saddle pal to the long-forgotten Whip Wilson, and was a semi-regular on numerous TV series, including "Colonel Jack" (*Circus Boy*, 1956–1957), "Homer Tubbs" (*The Adventures of Rin Tin Tin*, 1955–1958), "Old Timer" (*Fury*, 1956–1959), "Scatterbrain Gibbs" (*Colt .45*, 1959), "Andy Miles" (*The*

Texan, 1960), "Pa McBean" (*The Tall Man*, 1960–1962), and "Cully Wilson" (*Lassie*, 1959–1964). SEE ALSO: Lee Aaker; Noah Beery, Jr.; Peter Graves; Barry Sullivan.

Lee J. Cobb
(1911–1976)
••••••••••••••••••••••••••••

Burly, blustery, and undeniably powerful, if somewhat overrated, this character actor achieved fame in the original Broadway production of Arthur Miller's *Death of a Salesman* (1949). He lost the role in the movie to Fredric March but did play "Willy Loman" on a TV restaging (NBC, 5/8/66). Cobb's early films included B Westerns and *Rustler's Valley* (1937), billed as "Lee Colt" (real name Leo Jacoby). A member of the left-leaning Group Theater (1930s), Cobb escaped the 1950s blacklist by appearing before the House Committee as a "friendly witness," naming names. His best film roles were as "Johnny Friendly" in *On the Waterfront* (1954) and "Third Juror" in *12 Angry Men* (1957). Cobb's most famous movie Western role was as the evil patriarch in Anthony Mann's *Man of the West* (1958). Playing a rugged lawman in *How the West Was Won* (1962) established Cobb as a genre star; he transferred to TV as the top-billed performer on *The Virginian* (1962–1966), "Judge Henry Garth," owner of the Shiloh Ranch. In Owen Wister's novel, "Judge Henry" had

been hard-bitten, likely modeled on Judge Isaac Parker, the famed "hanging judge." For family-hour TV, he became a crusty, charming codger raising adoptive daughter "Betsy" (Roberta Shore). Cobb left after the fourth season, eventually starring in *The Young Lawyers* (1970–1971) as mentor to the title heroes. His best TV Western role came as "Josiah Johnson" in "The Colonel" (*Gunsmoke*, 12/16/74). Later movie Westerns included *Mackenna's Gold* (1969) and *Lawman* (1971). SEE ALSO: Charles Bickford, James Drury, Stewart Granger, Doug McClure, John McIntire, Roberta Shore.

James Coburn
(1928–2002)
••••••••••••••••••••••••••••

Early on, Coburn found work in TV/movie Westerns, as a guest on episodic series in the mid-fifties and the semi-regular role of "Anthony Wayne" of San Francisco in the ensemble show *The Californians* (1959). His performance as the Man Without a Name on *Tombstone Territory* (10/16/59) likely provided Sergio Leone's inspiration for his antihero in the famed spaghetti Western trilogy; Leone offered that role to Coburn, who turned it down. Real-life characters include Buckskin Frank Leslie (*The Life and Legend of Wyatt Earp*, 11/24/59) and Jesse James (*Bronco*, 1/12/60). John Sturges picked Coburn for the role of the Man with the Knife ("Britt") in *The Magnificent Seven* (1960). In his second series, *Klondike* (1960–1961), Coburn played "Jeff Durain," a shady/charming con man in Alaska during the 1897 gold rush. Sam Peckinpah directed most episodes and, remembering Coburn's charisma, cast him in a supporting role (*Major Dundee*, 1965) and later as the lead in *Pat Garrett & Billy the Kid* (1973). Coburn shined on TV in the title role in "Culley" (*Outlaws*, 23/16/61), playing a young thief transformed by friendship with a blind old-timer (Henry Hull). He became close friends with *Seven* costar Steve McQueen; they worked together again in the WWII epics *Hell Is for Heroes* (1962) and *The Great Escape* (1963). Set to play Jeff Hunter's sidekick in *Temple Houston*, Coburn shot the pilot, released theatrically as *The Man from Galveston* (1963), then bailed to do movies, the series role going to Jack Elam. He costarred with Kirk Douglas in the TV Western *Draw!* (1984) when Burt Lancaster fell ill. Coburn eventually grew into corrupt cattle-baron roles: John Chisum in *Young Guns II* (1990), and a similar fictional part in *The Cherokee Kid* (12/14/96). He served as the narrator for *Texas Rangers* (2001) and received an Oscar (Best Supporting Actor) for his role in the non-Western *Affliction* (1997). SEE ALSO: Mari Blanchard, Clint Eastwood, Adam Kennedy, Joi Lansing, Nan Leslie, Sean McClory, Ralph Taeger.

Iron Eyes Cody

(1907–1999)

••••••••••••••••••••••••••••••••••

An icon in American advertising, Iron Eyes Cody appeared between 1971 and 1981 in a public-service announcement for the "Keep America Beautiful" campaign. A car full of vacationing suburbanites passes through a breathtaking forest; the passengers toss garbage out the window. An elderly Native American (the Noble Savage incarnate) stares down from a high mountain, witnesses the small but all-too-typical act, then turns to face the camera as a single tear drifts down his right cheek. Most viewers vaguely recognized the actor from endless Western movies and TV shows. While they likely did not know his name, on some level all grasped that here was the real deal, a true Indian working in our modern media to represent everything best and beautiful about his race. There was only one problem: the man had not one drop of Native American blood in his veins, though this fraud would not be unmasked until after Cody's death.

Espera DeCorti had been born to Italian parents who immigrated to America and settled in rural Louisiana. He left home, drifted around the country, and eventually married a Native American, Bertha Parker (arguably) a descendant of Chief Quanah Parker. The couple adopted two Indian sons, at which point

THE GREAT PRETENDER: For nearly half a century, Iron Eyes Cody embodied the Native American spirit in films and on TV; eventually, he would be unmasked as a well-intentioned fraud who had no Indian blood running through his veins. Courtesy United Artists.

DeCorti changed his name to Cody. Heading for Hollywood, he convinced Raoul Walsh he was indeed a Native American and that the director should hire him for an upcoming film, the first sound-era epic (and initial starring role for John Wayne), *The Big Trail* (1930), a notable box-office flop. The Duke retreated to B Westerns for a decade, but Cody had no trouble finding work. He was billed in over fifty early films as, simply, "an Indian." In time, Cody appeared in more than 150 movies (big and small) plus TV shows, playing real-life figures Geronimo (*Train to Alcatraz*, 1948), Wovoka (*Indian Agent*, 1948), Mangas Coloradas (*The Last Outpost*, aka *Cavalry Charge*, 1951), Chief Rain-in-the-Face (*Meet Me at the Fair*, 1953), Crazy Horse (*Sitting Bull*, 1954), and Sitting Bull (*The Great Sioux Massacre*, 1965). The latter employed stock footage from the 1954 film; Cody, playing the elderly "Bull" in the second movie, can also be glimpsed as young "Horse" in the Little Big Horn battle sequence! Cody often played a medicine man, as in *A Man Called Horse* (1970), a quirky nouveau Western in which Cody oversaw the (historically inaccurate) Sun Dance ceremony. Another medicine man, "Mad Wolf," proved to be the only continuing role he played on a TV series; in Disney's *The Saga of Andy Burnett* (1957–1958), Cody must decide if six mountain men who wandered into Blackfoot country should be allowed to live as blood brothers or massacred as unwanted intruders.

Today, most Native Americans are so impressed by Cody's love for their people and the positive image he forwarded that they graciously forgive, if not forget, the great hoax. SEE ALSO: Jerome Courtland, Andrew Duggan, Slim Pickens, John Wayne, Jeff York.

Tristram Coffin
(1909–1990)

This veteran performer labored in numerous B movies, particularly serials, including the title role in *King of the Rocket Men* (1949). That same year, he played "Captain Dan Reid (Sr.)" of the Texas Rangers in the first-ever episode of *The Lone Ranger* (9/15/49); the character's death (along with four others) inspired young brother "John Reid" (Clayton Moore), the only survivor, to become the title hero. Coffin played a similar (though longer-lived and historical) figure on *26 Men* (1957–1958), Captain Thomas Rynning, the hard-bitten commander of understaffed Arizona Rangers circa 1900. He later essayed another actual figure, early Western explorer Major Henry, in the "Hugh Glass Meets the Bear" episode of *Death Valley Days* (3/24/66). Though forgotten today, Coffin had an enormous impact on TV. On 10/7/54, he enacted a corpse on the live TV show *Climax!* When actor Dick Powell, who had been sitting beside "the body," paused in his speech, Coffin incorrectly assumed the scene was over, rose from beneath his sheet and, to the shock of Powell (and millions of viewers), stomped off the set. This won the appropriately named Coffin the sobriquet "dead man walking," convincing the networks to abandon live TV in favor of pre-filmed (and later taped) shows. SEE ALSO: Kelo Henderson, Clayton Moore, Jay Silverheels.

Robert Colbert

(1931–)

••••••••••••••••••••••••••••••••

This broad-shouldered young performer, signed to a studio contract by Warner Bros. in the mid-1950s, immediately went to work in that studio's popular Westerns (*Sugarfoot*, *Cheyenne*, *Lawman*, *Bronco*) and detective shows (*Hawaiian Eye*, *Bourbon Street Beat*, *Surfside 6*) with the understanding that he would eventually star in one of his own. During *Maverick*'s fourth season, Roger Moore quit in mid-season. Jack Kelly needed a new costar; Colbert was introduced in spring 1961 as yet *another* brother, "Brent," wearing the same costume James Garner had sported in the first season. For fans, this silly contrivance proved to be one Maverick too many. Colbert was dropped after three episodes but later reemerged on 20th Century-Fox's science-fiction show *The Time Tunnel* (1966–1967) as "Doug Phillips," costarring James Darren. SEE ALSO: James Garner, Jack Kelly, Roger Moore.

Dennis Cole

(1940–)

••••••••••••••••••••••••••••••••

A male model turned lackluster young TV hunk, Cole was briefly married to Jaclyn Smith (1978–1981). He played "Johnny Reach," soldier of fortune, first in *Powderkeg* (4/16/71),

then in the brief-lived *Bearcats!* series starring Rod Taylor. SEE ALSO: Rod Taylor.

Don Pedro Colley

(1938–)

••••••••••••••••••••••••••••••••

This athlete turned actor joined the *Daniel Boone* cast as "Gideon" in 1968, forwarding that show's civil rights theme. Later projects ranged from live-action Disney comedies (*The World's Greatest Athlete*, 1973) to black exploitation flicks (*Sugar Hill*, 1974). Colley later played "Ongaro" in the *Planet of the Apes* films and "Sheriff Little" on *The Dukes of Hazzard* (1981–1984). SEE ALSO: Roosevelt Grier, Fess Parker.

Don Collier

(1928–)

••••••••••••••••••••••••••••••••

Associated with Westerns from his second film, *Seven Ways from Sundown* (1960, Audie Murphy), Collier had a regular role on *Outlaws* (1960–1962), performing in the original second lead as "Deputy Will Foreman" to old-timer Barton MacLane's marshal. When the series returned the following fall, Will emerged as the central character, promoted to full marshal, with Slim Pickens the new sidekick. Collier's real-life Westerners included Frank Dalton on *Death Valley Days* (12/10/64), repeating that part in *The Last Ride of the Dalton Gang*

(11/20/79), looking no older. He also played Wyatt Earp on *Wagon Train* (4/25/65) and appeared in many movies starring his friend John Wayne: *El Dorado* (1966), *War Wagon* (1967), and *The Undefeated* (1969). Next came "Sam Butler," the foreman who ran the title ranch for owner "Big John Cannon" (Leif Erickson) on *The High Chaparral* (1967–1971). The hands working for Collier included "Joe Butler" (Robert F. Hoy), "Pedro" (Roberto Contreras), and "Reno" (Ted Markland). Collier slipped out of the saddle (albeit briefly) as the quietly persuasive townsman "William Tompkins" for *The Young Riders* (1989–1992). Eventually he embodied a no-nonsense but fair/square lawman in nostalgic TV movies: *Gunsmoke: To the Last Man* (1/10/92), *Gunsmoke: One Man's Justice* (2/10/94), and *Bonanza: Under Attack* (1/15/95). Collier is warmly remembered by Gen X'ers as the "Gum Fighter," parodying his own image on 1980s Hubba Bubba bubble-gum TV commercials. SEE ALSO: Linda Cristal, Leif Erickson, Jock Gaynor, Barton MacLane, Slim Pickens, Bruce Yarnell.

Chris Connelly
(1941–1988)

Fame came early on to Connelly as "Norman Harrington" on *Peyton Place* (1964–1966), then a decade later as "Moses Pray" in TV's *Paper Moon* (1974), in which he and Jodie Foster assumed the roles Ryan and Tatum O'Neal had played in the film. Connelly played the lead in the Disney miniseries *Kit Carson and the Mountain Men* (1977), with Robert Reed as Captain John Fremont and Gregg Palmer in the role of Jim Bridger. Sadly, the show did not live up to its title: No other real-life mountain men were presented, nor did the brief-lived series capture their lifestyle. Worse still, the many Fremont-Carson expeditions were, as in the 1940 film with Dana Andrews and Jon Hall, telescoped into a single trek, with pioneer families shown heading west alongside soldiers/surveyors when such pilgrims actually traveled later, *after* Fremont returned with maps. At least someone finally played Carson as the extremely short man he was in real life. The best-ever TV/movie treatment of these events would be in *Dream West* (1986), featuring Rip Torn as an offbeat Carson and Richard Chamberlain a perfect Fremont. SEE ALSO: Bill Williams.

Chuck Connors
(1921–1992)

Connors provided TV's answer to Charlton Heston, thanks to his similar strapping build and granite jaw. The Brooklyn-born pro-ball player (Boston Celtics/Brooklyn Dodgers/ Chicago Cubs) was spotted during a game by a talent scout and signed to an MGM contract. He played small parts in big pictures (*Pat and Mike*, 1952) and big roles in small ones (*Hot Rod Girl*, 1956). Connors drifted into Westerns, playing "Button Smith," the charming stage driver who turns out to be a cold-blooded killer, in the initial episode of *Tales of Wells Fargo* (3/18/57); he returned as real-life robber Sam Bass (6/10/57). Connors won a recurring role as the rogue "Cephas K. Ham" on Desilu's *The Adventures of Jim Bowie* (1958). After being spotted by Dick Powell, Connors won the role of "Lucas McCain" in *Zane Grey Theater*'s "The Sharp-shooter" (3/17/58). Meanwhile, he showed up in two major films, as a decent-minded cowhand in Disney's *Old Yeller* (1957) and a despicable redneck in William Wyler's *The Big Country* (1958). Farmer Lucas and his son "Mark" (Johnny Crawford) returned that fall for *The Rifleman* (ABC; 1958–1963), a half-hour series about a peace-loving farmer who knows how to fire a Winchester .73 as fast as any gunfighter does his .45. Other cast members included Bill Quinn as "Sweeney," the beloved bartender in North Fork; and Joe Higgins as "Nils Swenson," a Scandi-navian immigrant farmer. Five actors played sawbones "Doc Burrage": Ralph Moody, Edgar Buchanan, Rhys Williams, Jack Kruschen, and Fay Roope. Always some woman hung around, hoping to land handsome widower McCain, Hope Summers as "Hattie" (1958–1960) the first. *The Rifleman* featured a low-key noir

quality yet in its own unique way emerged as a beloved family show. The strangest aspect was that, though sequences on the McCain Ranch were all shot on location for an authentic prairie look, the town itself clearly stood on a soundstage with embar-rassingly obvious painted backdrops.

Connors starred in various the-atrical films between TV series: in *Geronimo* (1962) he proved effec-tive as the stern Apache leader with then-wife Kamala Devi, Indian-born beauty, as his woman "Teela"; he also performed in *Ride Beyond Vengeance* (1966), a notably sadistic revenge tale with nominal stars in support-ing roles. His second Western show could have been something special when iconoclastic writer/creator Larry Cohen came up with *Branded*, in which cavalry officer "Jason McCord" is wrongfully thrown out of the service for supposed cow-ardice, then wanders the West like a Flying Dutchman. Cohen's idea was to have the character physically branded on his face with a hot iron; NBC, planning this as a Sunday eve-ning show following Disney, nixed that idea fast. So McCord was only *emotionally* branded, resulting in a compromised series (1965–1966). The cast of characters included two real military men, General (now President) Ulysses S. Grant (William Bryant) and General Philip Sheridan (John Pickard), plus two fictional ones, "Court Martial Colonel" (John Howard) and "General Josh McCord"

BLOOD BROTHERS: Positive cooperation between Anglos and Indians was promoted on such Dick Powell "Four Star" shows as *The Rifleman*; here, "Lucas McCain" (Chuck Connors, *left*) hits the trail with best friend "Sam Buckhart" (Michael Ansara). The latter spun off to his own series, *Law of the Plainsman*. Courtesy ABC/Four Star.

(John Carradine). Also around on an occasional basis for some romantic interest was the stunning "Laurette" (Devi). A writer as well as an actor, Connors contributed several scripts to this series; he had previously written some for *The Rifleman*.

Branded had been preceded by a one-season run on *Arrest and Trial* (1963–1964), an experimental ninety-minute drama with Connors as a defense lawyer in the second half, Ben Gazzara the arresting cop in the first, qualifying this as an unsuccessful precedent to *Law and Order* (1990–). Meanwhile, Hugh O'Brian, who had played the lead in *Africa: Texas Style* (1967) for Ivan Tors, chose not to do the series. Connors accepted the part for *Cowboy in Africa* (1967–1968), a one-season ABC show, as "Jim Sinclair," a rodeo cowboy hired by "Commander Hayes" (Ronald Howard) to visit the dark continent and work as game-keeper on Hayes's sprawling ranch. Tom Nardini came along for the ride as "John Henry," the hero's Native American blood brother; and Gerald Edwards as "Samson," an orphaned child who idolizes Jim. Gorgeous photography of lions, elephants, etc., led to an admirable environmental-ist sensibility. Connors later played "Tom Moore" in *Roots* (1977), then a supporting part in *The Capture of Grizzly Adams* (2/21/82). Much forgettable film/TV work followed, including the most violent of all European-lensed Westerns, *Kill Them All and Come Back Alone* (1968).

SEE ALSO: Patricia Blair, John Carradine, Johnny Crawford, Paul Fix, John Pickard.

Robert Conrad

(1935–)

Born Konrad Robert Falkowski, this future actor excelled as a high-school athlete, then found jobs as a dock worker, milkman, jazz drummer, and pro boxer. Then came a phone call from best pal Nicholas Adamshock (actor Nick Adams) insisting that Conrad *must* join him in Hollywood. Adams, having already broken in, helped arrange small parts in B movies (*Juvenile Jungle* and *Thundering Jets*, both 1958). Conrad's first TV Western role was as the Native American "Juanito" on *Bat Masterson* (1/21/59). A WB contract, high-profile/low-paying, led to guest stints on *Maverick*, *Lawman*, and Billy the Kid on *Colt .45* ("Amnesty," 5/24/59). He became a series regular as "Tom Lopaka" on *Hawaiian Eye* (1959–1963), played Pretty Boy Floyd in Adams's *Young Dillinger* (1965), and eventually enacted Dillinger himself in *The Lady in Red* (1979). As conventional Westerns floundered and spy shows flourished (*I Spy*, *Mission: Impossible*), Conrad played "Agent James T. West" in *The Wild Wild West* (1965–1969), James Bond anachronistically reset on a cartoonish frontier that had more in common with the world of *Batman* than *Bonanza*. West partnered with "Artemus Gordon" (Ross Martin). The show featured gimmicky guns, dazzling Bond-like girls, megalomaniac Dr. No–type super-villains (most memorable among them Michael Dunn as the diminutive "Dr. Loveless"), and occasionally guest star Nick Adams as a smarmy European count. The tongue-in-cheek tone, appropriate for the mid-sixties camp mentality, caught on big.

Later shows—*The D.A.* (1971), *Adventures of Nick Carter* (1972), and *Assignment Vienna* (1972–1973)—proved less successful. A WWII actioner, *Baa Baa Black Sheep* (1976–1978), won higher ratings than the others, featuring the deceased Nick's son Jeb Adams as a cast member. Then came *The Duke* (as a boxer, 1979) and *A Man Called Sloane* (1979), with more spy stuff, but too little, too late for that craze. Conrad occasionally returned to Westerns, notably in the important role of French Canadian mountain man "Pasquinel" on *Centennial* (1978) after Charles Bronson turned it down. He played Bob Dalton in *The Last Day* (2/15/75), which depicted the Coffeyville Raid; after that came two TV movies, *The Wild Wild West Revisited* (5/9/79) and *More Wild Wild West* (10/7/80), acceptable for fans though neither film recaptured the spark of the series. Conrad played

in two similarly themed contemporary Westerns: *High Mountain Rangers* (1988) as "Jesse Hawkes," with sons Christian and Shane Conrad aboard; and *High Sierra Search and Rescue* (1995) as "Tooter Campbell." SEE ALSO: Nick Adams, Ross Martin.

Pat Conway

(1931–1981)

• •

The grandson of silent-screen legend Francis X. Bushman, Conway played "Sheriff Clay Hollister" on *Tombstone Territory* (1957–1960). Noted for tight body language, pursed lips, emotionless eyes, and clipped delivery, recalling Jack Webb on *Dragnet*, Conway was occasionally accompanied by Gilman Rankin as "Deputy Charlie Riggs." Bob Foulk appeared several times as real-life gunman Curly Bill Brocious. Stories tended toward the routine, with no notable characterization, the focus on hard-riding and rough action. The best element was the theme song, better remembered than the show: "Whistle me up a memory, whistle back where I want to be, whistle a tune that will carry me to . . . " Incidentally, Tombstone is *not* a territory but a town in Cochise County, then part of the Arizona Territory. Conway later had a small role as an inhumane cavalry officer in *Geronimo* (1962). SEE ALSO: Chuck Connors, Richard Eastham.

Jackie Coogan

(1914–1984)

••••••••••••••••••••••••••••••

One of the first child stars to realize he would no longer be the apple of America's eye once he matured, young John Coogan had been discovered by Charles Chaplin while performing in vaudeville with his parents, then cast as the title character in *The Kid* (1921), a truly heartbreaking film. His short-lived superstardom ended after playing Tom Sawyer in a pair of films during the early 1930s. Those youthful good looks quickly faded, leaving Coogan nondescript in appearance. He never had trouble finding work, if often small roles in lesser films. In the 1952–1953 TV season, Jackie costarred in fourteen episodes of *Cowboy G-Men*, playing "Stoney" and then "Stanley Crockett," sidekick to series star Russell Hayden. This was, as the title indicated, a kiddie Western, broadly played, highly entertaining on that level. SEE ALSO: Russell Hayden.

Richard Coogan

(1914–)

••••••••••••••••••••••••••••••

Coogan owns a unique piece of TV history, creating the first-ever kiddie-oriented hero on live television. In 1949, the original fourth network, DuMont, picked up *Captain Video*, originally a local New York program, for national broadcast (if in limited cities). Coogan is not, however, the actor audiences recall in that role. Moonlighting on TV while pursuing a serious Broadway career, Coogan realized early on he could not keep up the pace and dropped out; Al Hodge took over as the intergalactic space traveler. When the more lucrative venue of filmed TV opened up, Coogan traveled west. On 3/11/58, he premiered as "Marshal Matt Wayne" (any resemblance to Matt Dillon intentional) on *The Californians*. SEE ALSO: Adam Kennedy, Nan Leslie, Sean McClory.

Gary Cooper

(1901–1961)

••••••••••••••••••••••••••••••

Though only twenty of the star's 107 films were Westerns, Cooper became more iconic of the genre than any other actor, with the possible exception only of John Wayne, perhaps because so many of Coop's oaters were true classics: *The Virginian* (1929), *The Plainsman* (1936, as Wild Bill Hickok), *The Westerner* (1940, playing a combination of Cole Younger and John Wesley Hardin called "Cole Hardin"), *High Noon* (1952), and *Man of the West* (1958). Born the son of a Helena, Montana, rancher, in Hollywood Frank James Cooper (possibly named after outlaw Frank James) proved equally at home as everything from rubes (*Sergeant York*, 1941) to sophisticates (*Love in the Afternoon*, 1957) to Hemingway heroes (*For Whom the Bell Tolls*, 1943). His TV Western career consisted of a posthumous one-shot. Shortly before Coop's death from cancer (5/13/61), he hosted a TV special unlike anything previously produced—*The Real West* (3/29/60), in an hour-long format that featured photographs taken during the final frontier days, re-shot with a moving camera able to push in, pull out, and travel across the image, lending existing images a sense of movement. Coop appeared briefly at the beginning and end, looking terribly worn and obviously ill and wearing his signature cowboy hat. He also provided a voiceover commentary, pointing out the *un*romantic quality of pioneer life in sharp contradiction to idealized images then offered on TV. Numerous specials/series would later employ such an approach on cable TV outlets such as the History Channel. Mourning his passing even as they watched, audiences felt as if a ghost from our collective past had returned to set the record straight. The show ran at 7:30 (Eastern) on Wednesday, the only time during a five-year period that *Wagon Train* did not appear in its expected time slot.

Glenn Corbett

(1930–1993)

••••••••••••••••••••••••••••••••

Early on, Corbett posed for men's physique magazines, which led to his being discovered by Sam Fuller.

The lead in his first film, *The Crimson Kimono* (1959), was followed by supporting roles as clean-cut soldiers in *The Mountain Road* (James Stewart) and *All the Young Men* (Alan Ladd), both in 1960. Corbett's first series was the innovative dramedy *It's a Man's World* (1962), costarring Randy Boone; they reunited on *The Virginian* (10/13/65), with Boone a regular and Corbett guest-starring as fiancé of "Betsy" (Roberta Shore). Corbett replaced George Maharis as Marty Milner's Corvette-traveling partner in *Route 66* (1963–1964) and later played an airborne lieutenant in *12 O'Clock High* (1964–1965). He played "Chance," a mysterious rider who joins the pilgrims, in *The Road West* (1966–1967). His movies include *Shenandoah* (1965) with Stewart, Pat Garrett in *Chisum* (1970), and an outlaw in *Big Jake* (1971), both of the latter with John Wayne. His final series role was as "Paul Morgan" on *Dallas* (1983–1988). Corbett succumbed to lung cancer after retiring to San Antonio, Texas. SEE ALSO: Randy Boone, Roberta Shore, Barry Sullivan.

Bill Cord

(19??–????)

••••••••••••••••••••••••••••••••

Little is known about this obscure actor, who had appeared in only one B thriller (*She Gods of Shark Reef*, 1958) before being cast as "Tom Clyde" in the syndicated *Pony Express* (1959–1960). As in *Tales of Wells*

Fargo with Dale Robertson, this show had precious little to do with the title company. Tom played not a mail rider but a fast gun hired to troubleshoot. Dick Jones of *The Range Rider* and *Buffalo Bill, Jr.*, fame was occasionally around as his young sidekick. Other actors who showed up regularly were Don Dorrell ("Donovan"), Robert Ivers ("McGrew"), and Grant Sullivan ("Brett"). SEE ALSO: Dick Jones, Dale Robertson.

Lloyd Corrigan
(1900–1969)
••••••••••••••••••••••••••••••

Pleasingly plump and always eager to flatter all those around him: These were characteristics Corrigan brought to over 150 movie/TV roles. His Westerns included *Corky and White Shadow* (1956), a *Mickey Mouse Club* serial, with Corrigan as "Uncle Dan," an aging child of nature who forsakes the town where Buddy Ebsen is sheriff for a shack in the woods, communing with (and singing to, with Darlene Gillespie) the animals. As Ned Buntline on *The Life and Legend of Wyatt Earp* (1957–1958), he hoped to turn the title character into a showman even as he had William F. Cody, providing Wyatt with his trademark weapon, a .45 with an extended barrel called the Buntline Special. Only the lead had one on the series; according to some historians, Buntline delivered five to Earp, Bat Masterson, Charles Bassett, Bill Tilghman, and Luke

Short. The role of Buntline has been played on film by Thomas Mitchell (*Buffalo Bill*, 1944) and Burt Lancaster (*Buffalo Bill and the Indians*, 1976). Corrigan also appeared as "Hank Johnson" on *The Real McCoys* (1958–1959). SEE ALSO: Hugh O'Brian.

Ray "Crash" Corrigan
(1902–1976)
••••••••••••••••••••••••••••••

A good-natured athlete turned actor (if in the loosest sense of the term), Corrigan headed for Hollywood to work as one of the original physical-fitness trainers to the stars, then found stunt work in films. In time he won promotion to a B-movie hero. While filming *Tarzan the Ape Man* (1932) and *Flash Gordon* (1936), Corrigan volunteered to perform smashing "gags" that earned him his nickname. His first major screen role was as the gorilla in *Tarzan and His Mate* (1934), a bit he would return to in due time. His first lead (under his own name) came as the hero of the action-packed sci-fi serial *Undersea Kingdom* (1936), which included a memorable wrestling/punching match with Lon Chaney, Jr. Corrigan played "Tucson Smith" in two dozen installments of *The Three Mesquiteers* (1936–1939), later using his own name in almost as many B Westerns in the spinoff *The Range Busters* (1940–1943). His days of stardom over, Corrigan slipped back into that monkey suit for *White Gorilla* and

White Pongo (both 1945) and, most memorably, the so-bad-it's-good cult classic *Bela Lugosi Meets a Brooklyn Gorilla* (1952). He rates as one of the first B Western stars to try television, with *Crash Corrigan's Ranch* (1950), presenting cowboy-style variety acts for a juvenile audience. The title was no lie, the show performed not on some standing set but in "Corrigan-ville," an actual cowtown/working ranch he had built near Chatsworth, California. During the week, this provided a location for shooting TV/movie Westerns. On weekends, Corriganville served as a predecessor to Disneyland's Frontierland. Families came by to watch stuntmen shoot it out in the streets and perform falls from buildings. One difference from the later Disney theme park: in Corrigan's saloon, parents could enjoy a beer while watching the show.

Genevieve Cortese

(1981–)

This raven-haired Tisch school graduate made her TV debut in a starring role on *Wildfire* (2005–2008) as "Kris Furillo," a juvenile con given a second chance at life by "going west." Foreman "Pablo Betart" (Greg Serrano) convinces "Pete Ritter" (Joe Lando) to invite the fiery girl to their ranch so she can reinvent herself in majestic surroundings while forming a deep relationship with the title horse. SEE ALSO: Joe Lando.

Jerome Courtland

(1926–)

A native Tennessean, the tall, thin Courtland resembled Tony Perkins, if more traditionally masculine. He found work in B+ Westerns, including *The Man from Colorado* (1948) and *Santa Fe* (1951); Courtland also played the title character in *The Barefoot Mailman* (1951) as Florida's first postal-delivery boy in the swamps. Courtland became better known for his marriage (albeit brief) to the popular singer/actress Polly Bergen (1954–1955) until cast in *The Saga of Andy Burnett* (1957–1958). Walt Disney had been a fan of author Stewart Edward White's historical novels about a fictional hero who inherits Tic-Licker, the fabled gun of Daniel Boone. The original idea was to create a maxi-series, six shows per season over a four-year stretch so that, like the interrelated novels, *Burnett* would carry the title character from youth to old age. But *Burnett* premiered on ABC shortly after *Wagon Train* arrived on NBC, winning away many potential viewers. With ratings not what they should have been, only the initial miniseries was filmed, focusing on Andy's early adventures with the mountain men, including his best friend, the fictional "Joe Crane" (Jeff York). The show included two real-life characters, Jack Kelly (Andrew Duggan) and Old Bill Williams (Slim Pickens). An unintended irony: Those were also the names of contemporary actors then starring on *Maverick* and *Kit Carson*.

Burnett is remembered for many fine elements, chief among them an attempt to realistically portray the lifestyle of those "hivernants" who trapped the Rocky Mountains between (roughly) 1825 and 1840, blazing trails into the Spanish-held Southwest. The best-loved bit turned out to be an accurate depiction of wrestling, mountain-man style: Opponents stretch out on the ground beside each other, head to foot; they lock legs, trying to break the other man's back. Yet the series, though scripted by Tom Blackburn (who had done the *Crockett* shows), tended to be overly talky, with mountain men chatting inside a log cabin about the business of trapping, which disappointed viewers did not get to see. As with all Disney Westerns, *Burnett* sensitively dealt with attempts to cut across cultural barriers between Anglos and Indians. Courtland then appeared in Disney's *Tonka* (1958) as Seventh Cavalry officer Lieutenant Henry Nowlan and starred in *Tales of the Vikings* (1959) for Kirk Douglas's Bryna Productions.

Courtland later produced *Pete's Dragon* (1977) for Disney and directed episodic TV ranging from *The Flying Nun* (1968–1970) to *Knots Landing* (1979). Eventually he left the movie business to join the faculty of Columbia College in Chicago, teaching film animation. SEE ALSO: Philip Carey, Andrew Duggan, Slim Pickens, Jeff York.

Chuck Courtney
(1930–2000)
••••••••••••••••••••••••••••••••

This sometime stuntman/aspiring actor played William H. Bonney twice, in a historical manner on *Buffalo Bill, Jr.* (3/1/55), and eleven years later in the drive-in exploitation film *Billy the Kid Meets Dracula*, which matched Courtney against John Carradine's Count. His most significant contribution to TV Westerns came when he played "Dan Reid, Jr.," nephew to "John Reid" (aka the Lone Ranger); Courtney appeared as the heroic teenager in more than two dozen episodes (1950–1955). Next came the "Nevada Kid," a Billy Bonney type, on the Walt Disney afternoon serial *Corky and White Shadow* (1956), followed by various cowhands on the Shiloh Ranch in *The Virginian* (1964–1969). Small roles in A-budget John Wayne/Howard Hawks Westerns include *El Dorado* (1966) and *Rio Lobo* (1970). Incidentally, Dan's horse was named Victor, as any fan of *A Christmas Story* can tell you. SEE ALSO: James Drury, Lee J. Cobb, Tristram Coffin, Stewart Granger, Robert "Buzz" Henry, Clayton Moore, Jay Silverheels.

Walter Coy

(1909–1974)

••••••••••••••••••••••••••••••••

Had Walter Coy become a salesman, he could have talked anyone
into buying anything with a self-
assured but never abrasive voice. Coy
owns a piece of radio history as the
first actor to play the "Lone Wolf."
His most famous role in a Western
came as John Wayne's ill-fated older
brother, "Aaron Edwards," in *The
Searchers* (1956). That same year,
Coy headlined the Sunday evening
NBC broadcast *Frontier,* created by
Worthington Miner, an esteemed
director/producer/writer for *Studio
One* during the golden age of live
TV. Sensing change in the air, Miner
hoped to offer a mature Western
best described as the antithesis of the
highly popular *Death Valley Days.*
Whereas that anthology highlighted
glorious moments from our pioneer
past, *Frontier* focused on things we
would rather forget. Typical of the
tone was "The Texicans" (1/8/56),
which focused on Louis Rose (Paul
Richards), the Alamo's only *deserter.*
The public did not take such debunking lightly; not surprisingly, the show
lasted only one season, during which
Coy served as off-screen narrator and
occasional star. His opening ("This is
the way it happened; movin' west!")
and closing ("That's the way it happened; movin' west!") remain legendary. One of the few actors to play a
historical figure both in movies and
on TV, Coy took over as rowdy Westerner Ben Thompson from Denver
Pyle on *The Life and Legend of Wyatt
Earp*, playing the same character (his
name altered to "Ben Townsend") in
Gunfight in Dodge City (1959). His last
strong Western role came as Chief
Blackfish of the Shawnees on *Daniel
Boone* (1967–1970). SEE ALSO: Hugh
O'Brian, Fess Parker.

Peter Coyote

(1941–)

••••••••••••••••••••••••••••••••

Born Peter Cohon, this actor assumed
his last name as a holdover from a
hippie-era identity. He is best known
for modern films and advertising
voiceovers. Coyote's TV Western
credits include the narrator of Ken
Burns's acclaimed PBS miniseries *The
West* (1996), Jim Bowie in *Two for
Texas* (1/18/98), and General George
Crook in *Deadwood* (6/13/04).

Johnny Crawford

(1946–)

••••••••••••••••••••••••••••••••

The younger brother of Robert Crawford, Jr., Johnny became one of the
original Mouseketeers on *The Mickey
Mouse Club* (1955–1956), followed
by the role of "Mark McCain," son
of Chuck Connors's "Lucas" on *The
Rifleman* (1958–1963). Unaffected
and natural in front of a camera,
Crawford expressed sadness, joy, and
other diverse emotions with seeming

effortlessness. The windup to many an installment had Lucas blowing away half a dozen baddies, afterward engaging in a heart-to-heart with Mark to explain why nonviolence was a better way to go. Crawford later guest-starred with Connors on *Branded* (1/24/65). He had the leads in two little films with big impact: *Indian Paint* (1965), an appealing story of Native Americans from their own point of view, and *Resurrection of Broncho Billy* (1970), an ode to the bygone way of ranch life as city slickers dream of the wide open spaces. John Wayne shot down Crawford twice, in *El Dorado* (1965) and *The Shootist* (1976), the latter repeating the earlier scene as a flashback. Crawford remains active in musical theater/nightclub performances today. SEE ALSO: Chuck Connors; Robert Crawford, Jr.; Andrew Prine.

Robert Crawford, Jr.
(1944–)
....

Son of a Hollywood film editor, Crawford won the role of a troubled youth in *Playhouse 90*'s "Child of Our Time," receiving an Emmy nomination. When NBC needed an actor for "Andy," kid brother of "Slim Sherman" on *Laramie* (1959–1961), Crawford was the obvious choice, helping that series stand out among routine buddy-buddy Westerns. Sadly, that's what the show became during its second season, when the diverse

supporting cast was eliminated. He guest-starred on ABC's *The Rifleman* as a friend of "Mark McCain," played by his younger brother, Johnny. SEE ALSO: Johnny Crawford, Robert Fuller, John Smith.

Linda Cristal
(1934–)
....

The Argentinean-born Cristal starred in low-budget Mexican films during the 1950s. She made her Hollywood premiere in *Comanche* (1956), with Kent Smith as Chief Quanah Parker, and played Cleopatra in *Legions of the Nile* (1960), an above-par sword-and-sandals epic. As "Flaca" in *The Alamo* (1960), Cristal starred opposite John Wayne, embodying an aristocratic

WESTWARD THE WOMEN: Linda Cristal embodied the proud Latina woman on *The High Chaparral* as well as in feature films, including *The Alamo* (courtesy John Wayne estate).

Spanish woman as a figure of intellectual and emotional substance as well as great beauty. Next came *Two Rode Together* (1961) for Ford, after which Cristal won the female lead in *The High Chaparral* (1967–1971), the most ambitious Western of the late sixties. Producer/director William F. Claxton chose Cristal for "Victoria," a Flaca-like woman, the dignified daughter of "Don Sebastian Montoya" (Frank Silvera) and as such heir to a great Mexican ranch. Victoria entered into a loveless marriage to "Big John Cannon" (Leif Erickson), a gruff older Anglo rancher, to maintain peace between the previously feuding factions. Thankfully, Cristal was encouraged to develop Victoria as a well-rounded woman, gradually learning to like and respect her husband if frustrated by the age difference, also possessing a mind of her own that reflected the burgeoning feminist movement of the era during which this show was produced. Cristal returned to her native country to star in the TV soap opera *Rossé* (1985), afterward retiring. SEE ALSO: Leif Erickson, Cameron Mitchell, Frank Silvera.

Brett Cullen

(1956–   )

• •

A veteran of the Houston Shakespeare Festival, Cullen employed his native Texas twang to good advantage in two TV Westerns: *The Chis-*

holms (1980) as "Gideon," a member of a family headed west, and *The Young Riders* (1989–1990) as "Sam Cain," a marshal who befriends the title characters. He took a turn as the Sundance Kid (alongside Scott Paulin as Butch Cassidy) in the TV movie *The Gambler V: Playing for Keeps* (1994) but is better known for non-Western roles: "Dan Fixx" (*Falcon Crest*, 1986–1988), "Detective Burnett" (*Desperate Housewives*, 2004–2005), and "Governor Sullivan" (*The West Wing*, 2005–2006). SEE ALSO: Stephen Baldwin, Don Collier, Robert Preston.

Robert Culp

(1930–   )

• •

Culp appeared in the *Zane Grey Theater* episode "Badge of Honor" (5/3/57) as "Hoby Gilman," a frontier Texas Ranger who employed a modern psychological approach to suspects. Gary Merrill played his commanding officer, though when this metamorphosed into *Trackdown* (1957–1959) Culp performed solo apart from Ellen Corby, a generation before she became "Grandma Walton," as the goodhearted "Henrietta Porter." Sam Peckinpah directed several episodes and also oversaw some of the writing, leading to a grim, often superior show. Following its cancellation, Culp wrote the pilot for a proposed series, "Summer Soldiers," which he hoped to do with Peckinpah though a pilot never materialized. Several of his scripts were produced on *The Rifleman*. Culp was next cast as Sam Houston on *The Great Adventure* (1/31/64), with Victor Jory as Andrew Jackson. He starred in *I Spy* (1965–1968) with Bill Cosby, which was followed by *Bob & Carol & Ted & Alice* (1969). Culp finally returned to the Western as "Cornelius Farnsworth," a dusty old-timer, on *Lonesome Dove: The Series* (1994). He has been well known more recently as "Warren," father to "Debra," on *Everybody Loves Raymond* (1996–2004).

Ji-Tu Cumbaka

(1942–)

This imposing African American actor, whose first name means "giant man" in Swahili, made a major impression on *Daniel Boone* (2/19/70) as "Linus Hunter," the last of a long line of escaped slaves to show up in Boonesborough. The Martin Luther King, Jr., vision of civil rights (equality and inclusion) always provided the essence of that show, but the upcoming decade would see black culture in America take a notably different turn via the Black Panthers and multiculturalism. Not surprisingly, then, when Cumbaka costarred in the short-lived *Young Dan'l Boone* (1977), he played an angrier, more independent character, "Hawk." His best later roles were as "Slim" in *Bound for*

Glory (1976, with David Carradine as Woody Guthrie) and "The Wrestler" on *Roots* (1977). SEE ALSO: Rick Moses, Fess Parker.

Susan Cummings

(1930–)

Born in Bavaria as Suzanne Ta Fel, this pretty blonde made her biggest impression as a scheming former Nazi who marries a naïve soldier (James Best) in writer/director Sam Fuller's *Verboten!* (1959). On TV, she played "Georgia," the female lead in *Union Pacific* (1958–1959). A Miss Kitty type, Georgia ran the Golden Nugget, a kind of Longbranch saloon on wheels; that is, a railroad train car with a bar aboard, carried along the tracks so that the working men had a place to relax after hours. SEE ALSO: James Best, Amanda Blake, Jeff Morrow.

Ken Curtis

(1916–1991)

Son of a Colorado sheriff, Curtis would base his famous "Festus Haggen" on old-timer "Cedar Jack," often a "guest" in the local jail. Before Westerns, Curtis's perfect voice had allowed him to replace Frank Sinatra with Tommy Dorsey's Big Band. This led to a gig with the Sons of the Pioneers, and that in turn to a brief star turn in singin' cowboy pics, beginning with *Rhythm Round-Up* (1945), followed by ten more, mostly as "Curt," with a different last name in each. John Ford picked Curtis for *Rio Grande* (1950), playing a singing soldier in that A oater. Many Ford films followed, as well as marriage (1952–1964) to the director's daughter Barbara. Curtis played Ranger "Charlie McCorry," Jeff Hunter's rival for Vera Miles, in *The Searchers* (1956). He enacted Festus-like characters (though mean) on *Gunsmoke* ("Jayhawkers," 1/31/59) and *Wagon Train* ("The Colter Craven Story," 11/23/60), with Ford directing the latter. Though these roles were all scruffy rubes, he also turned in a fine performance as the charming, soft-spoken, intelligent Captain Almeron Dickinson in *The Alamo* (1960).

Festus, out for revenge following his brother's death, first appeared on *Gunsmoke* on 12/8/62 in "Us Haggens," Dennis Weaver then still onboard as "Chester." Festus would not be seen again until "Prairie Wolfer" (1/18/64); his role grew larger (and the character kinder) with "Once a Haggen" (2/1/64), and he assumed his continuing part in "Deputy Festus" (1/16/65), part of an overall changeover of *Gunsmoke* from brutal adult Western in the *High Noon* tradition to a countrified family show. Curtis appeared in the film *How the West Was Won* (1962), then guest-starred on the TV version as "Sheriff Gant" (2/26/79), with former costar James Arness in the lead. He played the old cowhand "Hoyt Coryell" on *The Yellow Rose* (1983), a primetime soap set in Texas, and made two appearances with Dan Haggerty as "Grizzly Adams," first on TV ("Once Upon a Starry Night," 12/19/78), then in the theatrical feature *Legend of the Wild* (1981). His final Western appearance was in *Conagher* (7/1/91). SEE ALSO: James Arness, Sam Elliott, Katharine Ross, Dennis Weaver.

Michael Dante

(1931–   )

Darkly handsome Italian American Ralph Vitti, from Connecticut, found himself typecast as Indians for TV/movies. A WB contract led to (non-Indian) roles on *Cheyenne* (1957), *Sugarfoot* (1957–1958), *Colt .45* (1957–1958), and as "Jack McCall" on *Lawman* (1/11/59). Dante picked up a recurring role as the young gunfighter "Steve Chambers" on the non–Warner Bros. Western *The Texan* (1959). His best movie role came as the upscale sleazeball murdered by Constance Towers in Sam Fuller's cult classic *The Naked Kiss* (1964). That same year, Dante played his first Native American in *Apache Rifles* with Audie Murphy, then became a series regular as Chief Crazy Horse on *Custer* (1967). Though that show did lionize the title character, this was not done at the expense of the Lakota, there portrayed as victims of corrupt government policy; Crazy Horse and Custer were forced to fight each other though they would rather be friends. Dante later took the lead in Charles B. Pierce's revisionist Western *Winterhawk* (1975). He currently hosts *On Deck*, a syndicated radio talk show. Pop-culture claim to fame: Dante played "Maab" on the much-loved "Friday's Child" episode of *Star Trek* (12/1/67). SEE ALSO: Rory Calhoun, Wayne Maunder, Slim Pickens.

Ray Danton

(1931–1992)

An edgily good-looking leading man, Danton projected an off-putting screen persona that implied a dubious morality. He proved most effective as a rapist in *The Beat Generation* (1959) and as the title gangster in *The Rise and Fall of Legs Diamond* (1960). Danton's first screen appearance was as Little Big Man, an Indian who helped kill the Native American hero played by Victor Mature in *Chief*

Crazy Horse (1955). (A character of the same name is portrayed as a white man raised by the Cheyenne in the novel and film *Little Big Man*.) His best TV work came as another, more sympathetic Indian, in "The Four Thumbs Story" on *Empire* (1/8/63), similar to the later film *Tell Them Willie Boy Is Here* (1969). Danton played "Nifty Cronin" on *The Alaskans* (1959–1960), a cardsharp out to steal from honest miners during the gold rush. He was married to actress Julie Adams for many years and also directed minor films (*Psychic Killer*, 1975). SEE ALSO: Roger Moore, Dorothy Provine, Jeff York.

Jared Daperis

(1990–)

••••••••••••••••••••••••••••••

Daperis played the youngest Cartwright brother, "Little Joe," on *Ponderosa* (2001–2002) and was later seen as "Ralph" on *Holly's Heroes* (2005). SEE ALSO: Daniel Hugh Kelly, Drew Powell, Matt Carmody.

Henry Darrow

(1933–)

••••••••••••••••••••••••••••••

Born in New York City, raised in Puerto Rico, Henry Delgado returned to the United States for a Pasadena Playhouse acting scholarship. Constant TV work led to a role on *The High Chaparral* as "Manolito Montoya," son of Spanish nobleman "Don Sebastian" (Frank Silvera) and brother to "Victoria" (Linda Cristal), who was now married to the Anglo "John Cannon" (Leif Erickson). Manolito moved at will back and forth across the border, spending time on his father's hacienda and the Cannon Ranch, bridging the two cultures. This represented an important step forward in terms of expanding the range of Latino characters, for "Mano" embodied neither a stereotypical Mexican brigand nor the model of integrity of his father. He appeared particularly well matched with Big John's ne'er-do-well brother "Buck" (Cameron Mitchell), the drinking pals creating a bridge between cultures. Darrow later played "Alvarez" in *Centennial* (1978–1979) and Don Erasmo (father to title character Juan, played by A. Martinez) in *Seguin* (1/26/82), an ambitious PBS film. Often associated with Zorro, Darrow provided the voice of masked avenger/Don Diego on the animated *New Adventures of Zorro* (1981) and played the aged hero in *Zorro and Son* (with Paul Regina as the other title character, "Don Carlos") after Guy Williams proved too ill to return when Disney revived the concept in 1983. Darrow replaced Efrem Zimbalist, Jr., as "Don Alejandro," father to Zorro, in a newer version of the old story starring Duncan Regehr (1990–1993). SEE ALSO: Linda Cristal, A. Martinez, Cameron Mitchell, Duncan Regehr, Frank Silvera, Guy Williams.

Richard Davalos

(1935–)

Davalos made his film premiere as "Aron," brother to "Cal" (James Dean), in Elia Kazan's *East of Eden* (1955). His performance holds up wonderfully, some argue even better than Dean's. Yet his career went nowhere, partly owing to his "troublesome" rep. Davalos took second billing (to Darryl Hickman) on *The Americans* (1961), NBC's short-lived Monday night series about two brothers fighting on opposite sides during the Civil War, playing the graycoat "Jeff." He received sporadic film/TV work afterward, most notably as the emotionally disturbed sniper in *Kelly's Heroes* (1970). SEE ALSO: Darryl Hickman, John McIntire.

Gail Davis

(1925–1997)

Born near Little Rock, Arkansas, Betty Jeanne Grayson, TV's most famous country girl, attended the exclusive Bryn Mawr school for young ladies before heading for the University of Texas. She married Bob Davis and took his name when they traveled to Hollywood so that the talented young woman (who had been singing, dancing, and acting in her hometown since childhood) could "break in." A mainstream movie career (including *If You Knew Susie*

and director Nicholas Ray's premiere film, the noir classic *They Live by Night*, both 1948) never really took off. She turned to B Westerns, then the magic happened as Davis costarred in quick succession with Roy Rogers (*The Far Frontier*, 1948), Allan "Rocky" Lane (*Frontier Investigator*, 1949), Monte Hall (*Law of the Golden West*, 1949), Jimmy Wakely (*Brand of Fear*, 1949), Charles Starrett (*Trail of the Rustlers*, 1950), Johnny Mack Brown (*West of Wyoming*, 1950), and Gene Autry (*Sons of New Mexico*, 1949, in the first of over a dozen films with the man who would become her mentor and close friend for life). Autry used his own name in each film, with Davis cast as a different female character, much like Roy Rogers and Dale Evans in their feature films. They, as a real-life married couple, more or less played themselves on their long-run TV series; Autry and Davis, each married to another, did not do a TV show together, though they filmed an unaired pilot in 1957, *Melody Ranch*, which was not picked up. Perhaps the networks feared gossip about two such highly attractive people playing a couple when that was not the case in real life. At least not officially.

In the early 1950s, Davis shifted (at Autry's suggestion) to TV, establishing herself as an in-demand female guest star. She made numerous appearances on *The Range Rider* (two), *The Cisco Kid* (five), *The Lone Ranger* (four), *The Adventures of*

YOU CAN GET A MAN WITH A GUN!: Gail Davis (*center*) won the West as well as the hearts of its men, including "Deputy Lofty Craig" (Brad Johnson) and kid brother "Tagg" (Jimmy Hawkins) as the title character on *Annie Oakley*. Courtesy Gene Autry/ Flying A Productions.

Kit Carson (two), *Death Valley Days* (two), and a whopping fifteen on *The Gene Autry Show* (1950–1955). Davis often played a lovable cowgirl, though on several occasions she showed up as a mystery lady with a dark hidden agenda, proving herself capable of moving beyond the girl-next-door typecasting when given the opportunity to be duplicitous.

Producer Autry cast Davis in the syndicated *Annie Oakley* (1954–1957), a kiddie-oriented show, which had nothing whatsoever to do with the life of the real woman who bore that name and served as the subject of the movies *Annie Oakley* (1935, Barbara Stanwyck), *Annie Get Your Gun* (1950, Betty Hutton), and *Buffalo Bill and the Indians* (1976, Geraldine

Chaplin). Those films concentrated on Oakley's career as a performer with Cody's Wild West show and her difficult marriage to costar Frank Butler. On TV, Annie lived in a small town called Diablo with her younger brother "Tagg" (Jimmy Hawkins), solving crimes that easygoing deputy marshal "Lofty Craig" (Brad Johnson) could not handle. If the eighty-one-episode series had no historical value, it did rate as the only juvenile Western to provide young girls with a bright, innovative, courageous, moral, no-nonsense role model of the type boys found on pretty much every other series.

Another intriguing aspect was the handling of Davis's gender. Her fictionalized Annie Oakley recalled the early silent film career of Mary Pickford, who had played young girls of indeterminate age even after reaching thirty; here, Annie wore her hair in pigtails and acted like a proverbial tomboy, yet Davis's potent sex appeal shined through. Young boys watching could not decide if they wanted Annie for their girlfriend or big sister. Lofty, more an overgrown boy than a man, apparently felt the same way, making for a charmingly suggestive pairing. At each episode's end, Annie always showed him up, not in a bravura manner but simply because she was the superior Westerner.

Davis had, during filming, become an expert rider, roper, and trick shot, subsequently touring the country with Autry's rodeo. In 1959, she revived the Annie character for Bob Hope's comedy Western *Alias Jesse James*. SEE ALSO: Gene Autry, Dale Evans, Jimmy Hawkins, Brad Johnson, Roy Rogers, Barbara Stanwyck.

Jim Davis
(1909–1981)
••••••••••••••••••••••••••••••

After kicking around movies for several years without luck, James Davis finally won the role that was supposed to make this laconic Missouri-bred actor a major star: playing a returning vet opposite Bette Davis, queen of Warner Bros., in the romantic drama *Winter Meeting* (1948). Critics savaged the film, which was ignored by the public; when Jim's name was then romantically linked with Joan Crawford, queen of MGM and Bette's worst enemy, Bette dropped him, as did mainstream Hollywood. It was off to Republic Pictures and lots of B Westerns, including back-to-back roles in *Hellfire* and *Brimstone*, both in 1949. Davis often played small parts in films starring Rod Cameron and Forrest Tucker. He did show up in one big film, as "Streak," the dirty-dealing fur trader, in Howard Hawks's *The Big Sky* (1952). Davis played real Westerners Sam Bass (*The Fabulous Texan*, 1947), Cole Younger (*Woman They Almost Lynched*, 1953), Johnny Ringo (*Toughest Gun in Tombstone*, 1958), and Jim Bowie on TV's *The Time Tunnel* ("The Alamo," 12/9/66).

In the mid-fifties, a faltering Republic decided to try TV, hoping their long-popular, now fading formula would work on the small screen. Their first attempt would be *Stories of the Century* (1954–1955), in which Davis played the fictional "Matt Clark," a railroad detective on the trail of outlaws who had come into conflict with the company. Always in his company was a great-looking proto-feminist female partner who could outthink baddies better than Matt: Mary Castle as "Frankie," then Kristine Miller as "Jonesy," their names suggesting an ahead-of-its-time anti–gender bias approach. All stories were based on fact as different Wild West outlaws (Johnny Ringo, Harry Tracy, etc.) were chronicled.

Owing to Matt's profession, it was necessary to somehow draw the railroads into each tale, causing much fabrication. "Doc Holliday" (3/25/54, with Kim Spalding in the title role), about the infamous Benson stage robbery, in which Doc may have teamed up with Ike Clanton, had Holliday and that outlaw (Frank Richards) instead wreck and rob a train so Matt would be contacted. This allowed Republic to employ a spectacular sequence from an old film (an approach employed throughout this series), resulting in a tightly budgeted show that projected the illusion of a huge budget. To be true to history, Matt (the only TV Western hero who got beat up by the bad guy every week rather than the other way

around) couldn't "be there" for the finale. So, in the Doc show, he was sent off by Wyatt (James Craven) to round up men, arriving just *after* the O. K. Corral gunfight. This approach would later be imitated by *Colt .45* and *Wells Fargo* in their final seasons.

Stories of the Century proved to be so well done (winning the Emmy for Best Western/Adventure Series in 1955) that, later in the decade, it was rereleased under the title *Fast Guns of the West*. Davis shot a pilot that aired on *Cavalier Theatre* (9/27/55), "The Texas Rangers," but it did not sell. He returned to roles big and small in Republic features, most memorably as an Alamo defender in *The Last Command* (1955). He was also impressive as the male lead ("The Sheriff") in one of the rare Westerns mounted by *Playhouse 90*: "Four Women in Black" (4/27/57) with Helen Hayes, Katy Jurado, Janice Rule, and Narda Onyx as the title nuns. Davis starred in *Rescue 8* (1958–1960), predecessor to *Emergency!*, and had a recurring role as gunman Bob Orringer on *The Tall Man* (1960). He was hired by Hawks for small roles in the big John Wayne Westerns *El Dorado* (1966) and *Rio Lobo* (1970). His career low point must be considered a tie between *Jesse James Meets Frankenstein's Daughter* (1966) and *Border Lust* (1967), but he enjoyed a career upswing with strong parts in two of the best Westerns of the early 1970s, *Monte Walsh* (1970) and *Bad Company* (1972).

Then came another series, *The Cowboys* (1974), in a role supplanting the one Wayne had played in the film. At last people began to see Davis as a Duke-like figure, so long overdue success seemed just around the corner. Producers of the upcoming *Dallas* had Big John in mind for the role of "John Ross 'Jock' Ewing," a larger-than-life Texan. But Wayne was seriously ill at the time, so they were looking for a suitable substitute. Davis found himself the centerpiece of a huge hit, playing the role from 1978 to 1981. Tragically, Davis died shortly thereafter. He had become fascinated with costar Victoria Principal, a ringer for his own daughter who had died in an automobile accident at age sixteen (1970), and so took a paternalistic interest in Victoria's well-being. When he passed away, photos of both girls were found on his person. No one could tell them apart. SEE ALSO: Rod Cameron, Mary Castle, Moses Gunn, A. Martinez, Kristine Miller, Forrest Tucker.

Roger Davis

(1939–)

••••••••••••••••••••••••••••••

A WB contract player, Davis found work in an unsuccessful World War II series, *The Gallant Men* (1962–1963), as "Trooper Gibson." He played a dual role on the cult-classic vampire soap opera *Dark Shadows* (1968–1970) as "Jeff Clark" and "Charles Delaware Tate." Roy Hug-

gins, former *Maverick* producer, cast Davis as "Stephen Foster Moody" in *The Young Country* (3/17/70), a youth-oriented post-Woodstock TV Western that was supposed to become a series but did not. He costarred with Joan Hackett who played "Clementine Hale," a charming con woman not unlike "Samantha Crawford" on *Maverick* a decade earlier. Davis did the opening narration for Huggins's *Alias Smith and Jones* in 1971. When top-billed star Pete Duel committed suicide, Davis took over his role. "Clementine Carter" now regularly showed up on this series, played by future Oscar winner Sally Field. SEE ALSO: Pete Duel, James Garner, Ben Murphy, John Russell.

Sammy Davis, Jr.

(1925–1990)

••••••••••••••••••••••••••••••

A show-business legend and Rat Pack member, this African American superstar remained a lifelong fan of the Old West, demonstrating his fast draw on a memorable *Person to Person* live-TV interview with Edward R. Murrow in 1960. Davis paved the way for the portrayal of black Westerners on TV with landmark roles in "The Mission" (11/12/59), as a buffalo soldier who must earn the respect of white cavalrymen on *Zane Grey Theater*, and "Blue Boss and Willie Shay" (3/12/61), as a persecuted cowboy driven to violence on *Lawman*. Davis was also the first African Amer-

THE AFRICAN AMERICAN COWBOY: Though most of TV's Western heroes were Anglo, Sammy Davis, Jr. (seen here practicing his rodeo skills), was among the first black actors to break the color barrier and dramatize the fact that one in every five real-life cowboys had been black. Courtesy Sammy Davis estate; Ted Allan, photographer.

ican to be top-billed in a TV Western movie: *The Trackers* (12/14/71). SEE ALSO: James Edwards, Danny Glover.

Eddie Dean
(1907–1999)
••••••••••••••••••••••••••••••

The older brother of country-western singer turned sausage king Jimmy Dean brought an appealing voice to his role as a singin' cowboy but not much else. He was stiff, sour looking, and uncharismatic, which no one could ever say about Roy Rogers or Gene Autry. Even Dean's sidekick, Roscoe Ates as "Soapy Jones," seemed second rate in comparison to "Gabby" or "Smiley." Like his better-known, better-loved contemporaries, this B-movie star also tried TV, albeit briefly, in 1950. *The Marshal of Gunsight Pass* premiered with Russell "Lucky" Hayden as the title character. He bailed to do *Cowboy G-Men*, and Dean took over. The show, low on action, mild in impact, lasted only a few weeks more. Dean also appeared in *The Night Rider* (6/1/62), a busted pilot with Johnny Cash. SEE ALSO: Jimmy Dean, Russell Hayden.

Jimmy Dean
(1928–)
••••••••••••••••••••••••••••••

A cowboy star and country singer, Jimmy Dean perfectly incarnated the image of a good ol' Texas boy. As mellow pop of the early 1950s gave

way to country/cowboy-tinged rock 'n' roll, Dean toured with the band the Texas Wildcats. Like Bill Haley and the Comets, they exerted a major influence in adding the Big Beat to traditional Western melodies, resulting in cowboy bebop. Like Conway Twitty, Dean swung back to pure country when in the early sixties the Beatles, Motown, and the West Coast surf sound conspired to take rock in new directions. His biggest hits were "Big Bad John" (1961) and "P. T. 109" (1962). Dean appeared on *Daniel Boone* for the first time as the title character in "Delo Jones" (3/2/67) and made such a strong impression that he was invited back as a regular ("Jeremiah") when Robert Logan ("Jericho") left the series. Dean sang country-western songs on the show, a bit anachronistic for the actual Kentucky frontier, though this helped shift the series ever further from a pioneer adventure show to a family-oriented (both in appeal and focus) drama with a country setting, creating the paradigm for *The Waltons* and *Little House on the Prairie* during the next decade. SEE ALSO: Michael Landon, Robert Logan, Fess Parker.

Rosemary DeCamp
(1910–2001)
••••••••••••••••••••••••••••••

Perfectly cast as a simple, positive-thinking, all-American woman following her early success as the mother of George M. Cohan (James

Cagney) in *Yankee Doodle Dandy* (1942), on *Death Valley Days* (1952–1965) DeCamp served as commercial spokesperson for Boraxo, which sponsored the show originally set entirely in the area where mining of that product took place. An early Borax transport wagon crawled across the foreboding frontier in the opening shot, Stanley Andrews initially the series host. But when Ronald Reagan assumed that position and then decided to run for governor of California, a fairness doctrine restricted any appearances on TV during the election. At that point, DeCamp subbed for her friend, qualifying her as the only female host in that show's long run. Her other TV credits include "Peg" on *The Life of Riley* (1949), opposite Jackie Gleason; DeCamp was replaced by Marjorie Reynolds when William Bendix assumed the role. DeCamp also played the big sister to Bob Cummings on *Love That Bob!* (1955–1959), then Mom to Marlo Thomas on *That Girl* (1966–1970). SEE ALSO: Stanley Andrews, Ronald Reagan.

John Dehner

(1915–1992)

••••••••••••••••••••••••••••••

A former Disney animator, this radio disc jockey turned actor, noted for his sonorous voice, regal bearing, melancholy eyes, and drooping mustache, projected the overall persona

of a humbug loser desperately hoping people will believe he's a success. His over 300 movie/TV roles include one of bad-guy Broderick Crawford's henchmen (the other, Noah Beery, Jr.) in *The Fastest Gun Alive* (1956), with Glenn Ford as the title hero, and Sheriff Pat Garrett in *The Left Handed Gun* (1958), a Gore Vidal/Arthur Penn collaboration starring Paul Newman as Billy the Kid. His best series role came as "Burgundy Smith," a corrupt yet charming con man matched against Brian Keith in *The Westerner* (1960). Dehner's other roles include "Soapy Smith" on *The Alaskans* (1959–1960), "Wade Cather" (*Tales of Wells Fargo*, 1959–1961), "Morgan Star" (*The Virginian*, 1963–1969), "Bishop Benjamin" (*How the West Was Won*, 1977), "Marshal Edge Troy" (*Young Maverick*, 1979), and "High Spade Johnny Dean" in the TV remake of *Winchester '73* (3/14/67). SEE ALSO: James Drury, Brian Keith, Roger Moore, Dale Robertson.

Terence De Marney

(1908–1971)

••••••••••••••••••••••••••••••

This British stage, radio, theater, and film veteran played "Case Thomas," the peaceful store owner who provides Don Durant with his special pistol (a single shotgun shell in place for backup after the six chambers were empty), on *Johnny Ringo* (1959). SEE ALSO: Don Durant, Mark Goddard.

Bob Denver

(1935–2005)

••••••••••••••••••••••••••••••••

Though a Texas native, comedy star Denver hardly seemed right for Westerns; yet in his final TV series, he did play an inept frontier scout, _Dusty's Trail_ (1973–1974), a syndicated spoof, had Denver's "Dusty" managing to get a single Conestoga wagon separated from the caravan, causing himself and half a dozen pioneers to become stranded on the prairie. Among them were the gruff wagon master "Callahan" (Forrest Tucker), two pretty girls (Lori Saunders and Jeannine Riley), an older couple (Ivor Francis and Lynn Wood), and a thoughtful pilgrim (William Cort). This situation revived the _Gilligan's Island_ (1964–1967) formula, here reset on the frontier. On that earlier show, the relationship of Gilligan to "The Skipper" (Alan Hale, Jr.) had been modeled on the classic antics of Laurel and Hardy, the case here with the Dusty-Callahan love-hate partnering. SEE ALSO: Alan Hale, Jr.; Forrest Tucker.

John Derek

(1926–1998)

••••••••••••••••••••••••••••••••

Derek first spoke on the screen in _I'll Be Seeing You_ (1944) as a young lieutenant in a sentimental World War II love story, followed by two bona fide classics: _Knock on Any Door_ (1949, Humphrey Bogart) and _All the King's Men_ (1949, Broderick Crawford). Derek was then reduced to juvenile costume mini-epics (_Mask of the Avenger_, 1951; _Adventures of Hajji Baba_, 1954). He played in occasional Westerns: _The Last Posse_ (1953), with Crawford; an interesting civil rights oater, _The Outcast_ (1954); Nicholas Ray's _Run for Cover_ (1955, James Cagney); and John Wilkes Booth in _Prince of Players_ (1955), with Richard Burton as his less volatile brother, Edwin. On TV, Derek starred in _Massacre at Sand Creek_ (12/27/56), an important predecessor to later made-for-TV Western movies; broadcast on _Playhouse 90_, this marked the first time that esteemed series had presented a filmed rather than a live drama. The piece also kicked off revisionism, as the title slaughter referred to the killing of peaceful Indians by Colonel Chivington (Everett Sloane), renamed "Templeton" for the show. Derek played a fictional lieutenant trying to avoid the catastrophe. He next won strong supporting roles in Cecil B. DeMille's _The Ten Commandments_ (1956) and Otto Preminger's _Exodus_ (1960), yet they failed to revive a sliding career. Derek opted for the TV series _Frontier Circus_ (1961–1962), a sixty-minute "traveling" Western (others included _Wagon Train_ and _Rawhide_), with elephants, giraffes, etc., along for the ride. Derek played trail boss "Ben Travis." He later produced/directed low-budget actioners with then-wife Ursula Andress (_Nightmare in the Sun_, 1965), then elegant eroticism with his fourth (final) wife, Bo Derek (*Tarzan, the Ape Man*, 1981). In between, he married Linda Evans of *The Big Valley*. SEE ALSO: Linda Evans, Richard Jaeckel, J. Pat O'Malley, Chill Wills.

Bruce Dern

(1936–)

This hulking, over-the-top heavy's wild hair, mad eyes, slouched shoulders, and lurching gait were undercut by an incongruously feminine voice. Dern made his first impact in 1964 as Bette Davis's murdered lover "John" in *Hush . . . Hush, Sweet Charlotte* (1964); he next played the maniac who terrorizes farmers Pat Buttram and Teresa Wright on the "Lonely Place" episode of *The Alfred Hitchcock Hour* (11/16/64). Dern won a regular spot on *Stoney Burke* (1962–1963) as rodeo rider "E. J. Stocker," thorn in the side of the title character (Jack Lord). On film, he embodied deranged characters in the excellent *Coming Home* (1978; Oscar nomination, Best Supporting Actor) and the reprehensible *Tattoo* (1981). Dern played memorable villains opposite Charlton Heston (*Will Penny*, 1968), James Garner (*Support Your Local Sheriff*, 1969), John Wayne (*The Cowboys*, 1972), and Kirk Douglas (*Posse*, 1975). SEE ALSO: Jack Lord, Warren Oates.

Andy Devine

(1905–1971)

A first-rate Shakespearean clown, Devine played "Peter" in MGM's *Romeo and Juliet* (1936). John Ford cast him as "Buck," the driver in *Stagecoach* (1939). Devine then found himself forever after typecast as the plump sidekick in oaters major and minor, in movies and on TV, most memorably as "Jingles P. Jones," fictional pal to a whitewashed James Butler Hickok, in *Adventures of Wild Bill Hickok* (1951–1958, Guy Madison). The show, which provided lots of fun on a juvenile level, had nothing to do with history. Devine simultaneously replaced the late Smilin' Ed McConnell on Saturday mornings for a retitled *Andy's Gang* (1955–1960), hosting "Gunga Ram" mini-epics, telling the co-host puppet "Plunk your magic twanger, Froggy!," and listening to black cat Midnight purr "*Niiiice!*" Then he drifted back to A Westerns for Ford in *Two Rode Together* (1961), *The Man Who Shot Liberty Valance* (1962), and *How the West Was Won* (1962). More TV roles included "Judge Amos Polk" in *The Over-the-Hill Gang* (10/7/69) and *The Over-the-Hill Gang Rides Again* (11/17/70). Devine provided the voice of "Friar Tuck" in Disney's animated *Robin Hood* (1973) and delivered a charming appearance in *The American West of John Ford* (1971), a TV special featuring that director, John Wayne, James Stewart, Henry Fonda, as well as Devine, all enjoying a bittersweet reunion in Monument Valley. SEE ALSO: Guy Madison.

Brandon De Wilde

(1942–1972)

••••••••••••••••••••••••••••••

Gifted child star De Wilde appeared on Broadway at age nine in Carson McCullers's *The Member of the Wedding*, then repeated the role in the 1952 film. His second movie, *Shane* (1953), created an iconic image of a child ("Little Joe") who worships a lone Westerner (Alan Ladd); that concept would be deconstructed a decade later in *Hud* (1963) with Paul Newman as the cynical cowboy young "Lon" must reject. De Wilde won the lead role as "Jim Tevis" in a Disney miniseries, *The Tenderfoot* (1964), costarring Brian Keith and James Whitmore. He reteamed with Keith for *Those Calloways* (1965), a powerful environmental quasi-Western. De Wilde died in a bizarre camping accident. SEE ALSO: Brian Keith.

Bobby Diamond

(1943–)

••••••••••••••••••••••••••••••

This ultra-natural child star began his career in the TV Western *Fury* (1955–1960), in which "Joey Newton," a ranch-bound boy, befriends the title horse. Peter Graves played Joey's father, "Jim." Diamond then portrayed "Buddy" on *The Nanette Fabray Show* (1961) and the title character in "In Praise of Pip," a memorable *Twilight Zone* episode (9/27/63) as well as the first TV drama to acknowledge the Vietnam War. Where are they now? Today Diamond enjoys a successful career as a lawyer in Los Angeles. SEE ALSO: Lee Aaker, Johnny Crawford, Peter Graves, Darby Hinton, Johnny Washbrook.

Don Diamond

(1921–)

••••••••••••••••••••••••••••••

Of Russian heritage, Diamond became such a master of dialects, in particular Spanish, that he was immediately typecast in Latino roles, much to the delight of pre–political correctness audiences. He began acting in 1951 and was second-billed as "El Toro," pal to the title hero (Bill Williams), in *The Adventures of Kit Carson* (1950–1955), a non-historical kiddie Western. Diamond's role, though over the top, embodied less of a stereotype than Leo Carrillo as "Pancho" on *The Cisco Kid*. Next he enacted skinny "Corporal Reyes" to Henry Calvin's "Sergeant Garcia," played as a Spanish Abbott-and-Costello team on Disney's *Zorro* (1957–1959). He also portrayed one Irish character, John Shanessy, the real-life Wild West saloon keeper who introduced Wyatt Earp (Hugh O'Brian) to Doc Holliday (Douglas Fowley) on *The Life* and *Legend of Wyatt Earp* (4/23/57). Then it was back to the vaquero, with "Arturo," a somewhat less clichéd Hispanic ranch hand, on *Empire* and *Redigo* (1963), both starring Richard Egan. Diamond appeared in more comic oaters as "Crazy Cat," a wacko Indian, with Frank DeKova as "Chief Wild Eagle," in a Laurel-and-Hardy teaming on *F Troop* (1965–1967). Later he played "Chief Galindo" on *The Flying Nun* (1967–1970). For the animated *New Adventures of Zorro* (1981), Diamond provided the voice of "Sergeant Gonzales." SEE ALSO: Richard Egan, Forrest Tucker, Bill Williams, Guy Williams.

(Mason) Alan Dinehart (III)

(1936–)

••••••••••••••••••••••••••••••••

Dinehart is the son of popular character actor Alan Dinehart, Jr., and wife Mozelle Britton and the half-brother of Alan Dinehart, Jr., director of animation for Hanna-Barbera projects. Dinehart was best known for his fine performance as Bat Masterson on *The Life and Legend of Wyatt Earp*, a role so identified with Dinehart that, when Gene Barry played the character on NBC (1958–1961), many viewers had serious problems adjusting to another actor in that role. In fact, Dinehart had been offered a spinoff show by ABC but turned it down to leave acting for the business world, first with Bank of America,

today the head of FEND, as a Securities Expert Witness in Arbitration.

A Desilu *Bat* series likely would have three-dimensionally developed the Old West's most fascinating figure. During the first three seasons of *Earp*, viewers were treated to a dynamic portrayal; Bat was, early on, a reckless teenager who gradually proved his maturity, convincing "Mr. Earp" he could be deputy, earning his star early in season two. One memorable episode, "Bat Masterson Again," had Earp mentoring Masterson on the proper use of a pistol (4/17/56), the most accurate portrayal of gun-fighting techniques in TV Western history. Masterson's personal growth next included a run for sheriff of Ford County, Kansas, when Bill Tilghman, an ally of Wyatt and Bat, was denied the right to run again for political reasons and the death of Bat's brother Ed (Brad Johnson) in a random shooting by drunken cowboys. The overgrown child had finally transformed into a coolheaded lawman, as such treated as an equal by Earp during the third season. The manner in which an appointed town marshal and elected county sheriff worked in tandem, deputizing each other when out of their respective jurisdictions, received an accurate portrayal here, setting up a vivid contrast when Wyatt later moved to Tombstone, where he lacked just such a healthy working relationship with Sheriff John Behan.

In Dinehart's final appearance on the show, "Dodge Is Civilized"

(4/28/59), Bat, now a gambler in black suit/derby hat, insisted he would shortly see Wyatt "in the Arizona territory." Sadly, no such appearance ever occurred, as Dinehart was by then out of acting for good and no one else could handle the part he had defined so well. Historically, Masterson did visit, serving as Earp's deputy when the marshal tracked down stage robbers following the famed Benson stage robbery, so Western fans can only dream about what Dinehart's Masterson show would have been. Desilu likely would have taken the character ever closer to the sophisticated New York sportswriter Bat in time became; his hat served as inspiration for the Brown Derby in Hollywood. Bat would also become the model for "Sky" Masterson in Damon Runyon's *Guys and Dolls*. Trivia: Dinehart's first role had been as the infant "Clark Kent" in the 1948 version of *Superman*. SEE ALSO: Gene Barry, Jody McCrea, Hugh O'Brian.

Micky Dolenz

(1945–)

••••••••••••••••••••••••••••••

This part Native American child actor played "Corky" as a kid raised by Big Top performers; Bimbo the Baby Elephant was his beloved pet in *Circus Boy* (1956–1957). He later starred as a wild and crazy drummer on *The Monkees* (1966–1968). SEE ALSO: Noah Beery, Jr.; Andy Clyde; Robert Lowery.

Kirk Douglas

(1916–)

••••••••••••••••••••••••••••••

Like his pal Burt Lancaster, Douglas (real name Issur Danielovitch Demsky) balanced a career as a "serious" actor with his Western star status, playing in *The Big Sky* (1952), *Man Without a Star* and *The Indian Fighter* (both 1955), Doc Holliday in *Gunfight at the O. K. Corral* (1957, with Lancaster as Wyatt Earp), *Last Train from Gun Hill* (1959), *The Last Sunset* (1961), *Lonely Are the Brave* (1962), and *The War Wagon* (1967, John Wayne). Douglas starred in the first-ever made-for-cable Western, *Draw!* (7/15/84), as old-timer "Handsome Harry Holland." Lancaster was all set to play his old nemesis "Sam Starret," but when he became too ill to work, he was replaced by James Coburn. SEE ALSO: James Coburn.

Joanne Dru

(1922–1996)

••••••••••••••••••••••••••••••

This West Virginia–born druggist's daughter worked as a model in New York City, met and married singer Dick Haymes, then traveled west with him when Hollywood beckoned, enjoying greater success than her husband. Dru made two classic Westerns: Howard Hawks's *Red River* (1948) and John Ford's *She Wore a Yellow Ribbon* (1949), both with John Wayne. She ditched Haymes to marry

Red River costar John Ireland; they appeared together often, mostly in B oaters, most interesting among them *Hannah Lee* (1953), aka *Outlaw Territory* (co-directed by Ireland), which features a stunning twist ending. Her TV work included the lead in *Guestward Ho!* (1960–1961) as Babs Hooten, based on that real writer's book (with Patrick Dennis) about herself and husband Bill (Mark Miller) leaving the big-city life behind to run a New Mexico dude ranch. Also in the cast was J. Carrol Naish as "Chief Hawkeye." As to her status as a movie/TV queen of the West, Dru later reflected that "I always hated horses." SEE ALSO: John Ireland.

James Drury

(1934–)

••••••••••••••••••••••••••••••

Tall, dark, and handsome, with a dangerous glint in his eye, Drury played small parts in Westerns *Love Me Tender* (Elvis Presley) and *The Last Wagon* (Richard Widmark), both released in 1956. An obvious candidate for TV stardom, Drury played "The Virginian" for the first time in a pilot (7/6/58) on the *Decision* anthology, with Robert Burton as "Judge Henry" and Stephen Joyce as the soft-spoken sidekick "Steve." A gimmicky approach featuring a dude-like hero did not go over well. Drury also played Jesse James, Jr., in the *Playhouse 90* (8/7/58) production

of "Bitter Heritage," an ultra-adult oater with Franchot Tone as Uncle Frank. He appeared as "Deputy Joe Monroe" in *Elfego Baca, Attorney at Law* (1959), and Walter (younger brother of John Wesley) Powell in *Ten Who Dared* (1960), a film about the mapping of the Colorado River, both for Walt Disney. Drury attracted attention as Mariette Hartley's hot-tempered fiancé in Sam Peckinpah's *Ride the High Country* (1962). *The Virginian* was then revamped as TV's first ninety-minute color epic, replacing *Wagon Train* on NBC on Wednesday evenings (1962–1971). Despite the show's hit status, the black-clad Drury actually appeared to be playing "Trampas" from the Owen Wister novel rather than that easygoing but formidable cowpoke enacted onscreen by Gary Cooper (1929) and Joel McCrea (1946). Audiences appreciated the show due to its lavish on-location filming and an ambitious desire to present the equivalent of a B+ theatrical film every week. Drury's next show, *Firehouse* (1974) with Richard Jaeckel, flopped. Drury later played the old-timer "Ethan Emerson" on several episodes of *The Adventures of Brisco County Jr.* (1993–1994). He made a cameo appearance in *The Virginian* (1/9/00) with Bill Pullman, a true-to-Wister Turner TV movie. SEE ALSO: Gary Clarke, Lee J. Cobb, Richard Jaeckel, Doug McClure.

Pete Duel

(1940–1971)

••••••••••••••••••••••••••••••

An upstate New York native, Duel (born Deuel) won roles in touring stage companies before heading for California, soon landing the male lead opposite Sally Field in *Gidget* (1965–1966). After the success of *Butch Cassidy and the Sundance Kid* (1969), he saddled up for the quietly sexy "Hannibal Heyes" in an enjoyable TV-movie rip-off, *Alias Smith and Jones* (1/5/71), costarring Ben Murphy. The hit TV movie soon turned into a weekly series, likewise garnering a huge following. As the second season began, Duel took his own life, owing to a longstanding depression augmented by alcohol abuse. He was the older brother (by three years) of Geoffrey Deuel, who made his film debut as Billy Bonney in the John Wayne Western *Chisum* (1970). SEE ALSO: Roger Davis, Ben Murphy.

Andrew Duggan

(1923–1988)

••••••••••••••••••••••••••••••

This Indiana University grad and golden-age TV veteran projected a slightly pompous aura of strained gentility that recalled Joseph Cotten. Duggan scored in Westerns as slimy authority figures (a corrupt lawman in *Decision at Sundown*, 1957, Randolph Scott) and serious-minded citizens ("Padre" in *The Bravados*, 1958, Gregory Peck). His first TV Western series role came as Jack Kelly, real-life mountain man, in Disney's *The Saga of Andy Burnett* (1957–1958), followed by Arizonan "Kirk Stevens" on *Tombstone Territory* (1958). Duggan became a Warner's contract player, guest-starring on many of their Westerns (*Cheyenne, The Dakotas, Lawman*, etc.), as well as playing the lead as southern detective "Cal Calhoun" in *Bourbon Street Beat* (1959–1960). He embodied a thinly disguised Custer ("Fred McCabe") in the B+ feature film *The Glory Guys* (1965), then played a Western series lead as family patriarch "Murdoch" in *Lancer* (1968–1970), a *Bonanza* clone set in California's San Joaquin Valley. Pop-culture claim to fame: Duggan was TV's original "John Walton" in *The Homecoming: A Christmas Story* (12/19/71), opposite Patricia Neal as "Olivia" and Edgar Bergen as "Grandpa Walton." SEE ALSO: Elizabeth Baur, Jerome Courtland, Wayne Maunder, James Stacy.

Tim Dunigan

(1955–)

••••••••••••••••••••••••••••••

Born the year that the Davy Crockett craze gripped America, Dunigan played that frontier hero when the post–Walt Disney company revived Crockett for three made-for-TV movies: *Rainbow in the Thunder* (11/20/88), *A Natural Man* (12/18/88), and *Guardian Spirit*

(1/13/89). Somehow each managed to be worse than the previous one. Earlier Dunigan had been the original "Face" on *The A-Team* (1983), dropped after two episodes in favor of Dirk Benedict. He played the lead in the Saturday morning serial *Captain Power and the Soldiers of the Future* (1987–1988). SEE ALSO: Buddy Ebsen, Gary Grubbs, Fess Parker.

Don Durant

(1932–2005)

••••••••••••••••••••••••••••••

The former Donald Allison Durae alternated a career as a pop singer with roles in episodic TV/low-budget films, including the male lead in Roger Corman's *She Gods of Shark Reef* (1958). He starred in the *Zane Grey Theater* episode "Man Alone" (3/5/59), the pilot for *Johnny Ringo*. The writer/producer assigned to the project, Aaron Spelling, retooled the piece, then with some sequences intact and others altered ran it as the premiere episode, now called "The Arrival" (10/1/59). The opening sequence (identical in both versions) played off Henry King's *The Gun-fighter* (1950), in which the antihero (played by Gregory Peck in the film, referred to there as *"Jimmy* Ringo") reluctantly kills a young punk out to make his reputation. Whereas that movie had ended with Ringo's death (at the hands of yet *another* punk), Durant's Ringo drifted into Velardi,

Arizona, settling down as the sheriff. Though the real Ringo (actual last name Ringgold) was better known as a cold-blooded killer, he did briefly serve in such a capacity. Durant wrote the show's catchy theme song. Disappointed with roles offered him afterward, he ventured into real estate and financial management, becoming wealthy. SEE ALSO: Terence De Marney, Mark Goddard, Karen Sharpe (Kramer).

Dan Duryea

(1907–1968)

••••••••••••••••••••••••••••••

Had Richard Widmark been born a B-movie whiner instead of an A-picture snarler, he would have been Dan Duryea. Sneering, mean, and lily-livered, Duryea played well-etched villains, initially in film noir (*Scarlet Street*, 1945), then beginning with his portrait of Charles E. Boles in *Black Bart* (1948), in several B+ Westerns over the decades, matched against heroes from James Stewart through Audie Murphy to Tony Young. On TV, he played a contemporary adventurer on *China Smith* (1954–1955). Duryea's Western pilot, "Knight of the Sun," aired on *Zane Grey Theater* (3/9/61) but was not picked up. Nonetheless, he exerted a great impact on the genre owing to his unforgettable guest shots: "Roy Budinger" (father of Dan Blocker's hero) on *Cimarron City* (10/18/58), shootist Dan Trask on *Texas John*

Johnnie Dean"; in the eventual TV remake (3/14/67), he enacted "Bart McAdam," the oft-mentioned but never seen father to the hero in the original film. Duryea's final TV Western role embodied another town drunk in *Stranger on the Run*, the first made-for-TV Western movie (10/31/67). SEE ALSO: Dan Blocker, Henry Fonda, Tom Tryon.

MEANEST MEN IN THE WEST: Often, the villains were far more memorable than the heroes. Dan Duryea. Courtesy CBS/United Artists Films.

Slaughter (1/23/59), an alcoholic marshal in "Mr. Denton on Dooms-day" (*The Twilight Zone*, 10/16/59), and the mysterious killer known as "Executioner" (*Rawhide*, 1/23/59). In a feat of reverse typecasting, Duryea played sympathetic, vulnerable "Josh Gilliam" on *Wagon Train* (3/30/60), part of a father/son team (the teen-ager played by his own son Peter) on *Daniel Boone* (2/11/65), and many other roles. Westerns included *Winchester '73* (1950), with Duryea well cast as the crazed gunslick "Waco

Robert Duvall

(1931–)

••••••••••••••••••••••••••••••••••••

Duvall made his film debut as "Boo Radley" in the classic *To Kill a Mockingbird* (1962). He had studied in New York City alongside friends/roommates Gene Hackman and Dustin Hoffman, winning stage roles and attracting the attention of then-young/gifted directors who cast Duvall in offbeat films: Arthur Penn (*The Chase*, 1966), Robert Altman (*Countdown*, 1968), and Francis Ford Coppola (*The Rain People*, 1969). Duvall played Western roles including outlaw "Ned Pepper" in *True Grit* (1969), Jesse James in *The Great Northfield Minnesota Raid* (1972), and the archenemy of Clint Eastwood in *Joe Kidd* (1972). For Coppola, he enacted consigliore "Tom Hagen" in the *Godfather* films (1972/1974). Duvall won an Oscar for his excellent portrayal of a washed-up country singer in *Tender Mercies* (1983). Duvall's best-remembered screen line ever is "How I love the smell of

A NEW FACE FOR THE OLD WEST: Oscar winner Robert Duvall (*Tender Mercies*, 1983) redefined our idea of the cowboy in such films as *Open Range* and TV's most popular Western miniseries, *Lonesome Dove*. Courtesy United Artists.

Napalm in the morning" (*Apocalypse Now*, 1979), delivered as a wild-eyed Vietnam officer. He proved just as effective as gentle General Eisenhower on a TV miniseries the same year. Duvall's definitive TV performance came as "Gus McCrae," a Texas Ranger turned cattleman, in the renowned miniseries from Larry McMurtry's novel *Lonesome Dove* (2/5/89), driving a herd to Montana and stopping in Nebraska to see "Clara Allen" (Anjelica Huston). The role of *young* Gus would be played in *Dead Man's Walk* (5/12/96) (derived from Larry McMurtry's prequel) by David Arquette. Duvall later took on similar, equally strong parts as "Boss Spearman" in Kevin Costner's *Open Range* (2003) and "Prentice Ritter" in Walter Hill's *Broken Trail* (6/25/06), a film notable for its enlightened, anti-cliché treatment of Chinese immigrants in the Old West. SEE ALSO: Danny Glover, Tommy Lee Jones, Rick Schroder.

Richard Eastham

(1916–2005)

••••••••••••••••••••••••••••••

When ABC decided one show about the Town Too Tough to Die (where *The Life and Legend of Wyatt Earp* was set during its final two seasons) was not enough, they added another: *Tombstone Territory* (1957–1960), with this American Theatre Wing/Broadway musical stage vet as "Harris Claibourne," narrator/editor of the *Epitaph*. This approach proved unique, as shows focusing on tough lawmen mostly succeeded, while those about newspapers (*Man Without a Gun*, *Jefferson Drum*) did not. With Eastham balanced by Pat Conway ("Sheriff Clay Hollister"), this oater had it both ways: A solid sense of how journalism impacted the townspeople alternated with lots of action. In real life, Mayor John Clum edited the pro-Earp paper of that name, while another publication, the *Nugget*, sided with John Behan and the Clantons. Eastham later played "General Phil Blankenship" on *Wonder Woman* (1976–1977). SEE ALSO: Pat Conway, Andrew Duggan.

Clint Eastwood

(1930–   )

••••••••••••••••••••••••••••••

Of all the TV actors who hoped to use small-screen popularity as a springboard to lofty status as a Western movie star, Eastwood rates as the only person to fully achieve that crossover. The great irony: He almost lost the part that catapulted him not only to iconic status on the level of John Wayne but also to become the most acclaimed director of Westerns since John Ford. In 1963, Eastwood finished up his fifth season as "Rowdy

Yates" on *Rawhide*. In Europe, aspiring filmmaker Sergio Leone was even then looking for someone to play the lead in a tightly budgeted Western remake of Akira Kurosawa's *Yojimbo* (1961), hoping to pick up where Hollywood's John Sturges had left off with *The Magnificent Seven* (1960), a remake of *The Seven Samurai* (1954), which acknowledged the key connections between the swords-for-hire of Japan and their American counterpart, the gunfighters. Leone originally hoped to convince superstar Henry Fonda to play the Man with No Name. The small paycheck he could proffer rendered that impossible, so Leone lowered expectations and tried for B star Audie Murphy, who failed to grasp the potential and passed on the project that became *A Fistful of Dollars* (1964). Leone considered the young American actor James Coburn (*The Magnificent Seven*), but Coburn wanted what was then the standard salary for a minor-league name to headline an Italian-lensed "spaghetti Western": $25,000. However fair the request was, Leone's budget remained so tight that to pay this sum would cut into funds the filmmaker planned to use in creating his film's unique aura. The final possible choice turned out to be Clint Eastwood, who grasped that working for anything less than $25,000 was insulting yet sensed that, as *Rawhide* had neared the end of its run, it might not be a bad idea to pick up some loose change. Eastwood swallowed hard and agreed to $15,000. Ten years later a beer company offered Eastwood a cool million if, in a TV commercial, he would walk into a bar and order their brand. Eastwood turned them down; the commercial was then shot with a second choice, James Coburn, who had since become a star. Eastwood? A *super*star, thanks to *A Fistful of Dollars!*

A U.S. Army veteran (Korea), Eastwood planned on a business career but was encouraged by two friends from his old Army company, David Janssen and Martin Milner, to, like them, try LA. Signed by Universal as a contract player, Eastwood won bit parts in lesser movies (*Tarantula*, 1955). He and another contract player, Burt Reynolds, were dumped on the same day and met while exiting the studio gates. Eastwood asked Reynolds why he had been let go; Reynolds replied that the brass had told him it was because he could not act. Reynolds asked why Eastwood had been dropped. His reply was that studio bosses had decided Eastwood's Adam's apple was too large for him to ever become a big star. Reynolds considered this, then told Eastwood: "You're in big trouble." Eastwood: "Why?" Reynolds: "Well, I can go out and learn to act. But you're *never* gonna get rid of that Adam's apple!" A few years later, both were on highly rated TV Westerns: *Rawhide* and *Gunsmoke*, respectively. They tied as top box-office stars in the 1970s but teamed only once, in the disappointing *City Heat* (1984).

"KEEP THOSE DOGGIES ROLLIN'!": Clint Eastwood (*left*) first achieved attention as second-billed "Rowdy Yates" on *Rawhide*, in time becoming the last great theatrical Western star as well as a two-time Oscar-winning director; he is seen here with his original costar Eric Fleming. Courtesy CBS.

Everything came together for Eastwood with *Rawhide*, a memorable show and the brainchild of Charles Marquis Warren, producer/director of B+ movies featuring a tough, unsentimental edge. From *Little Big Horn* (1951) through *Trooper Hook* (1957) to *Cattle Empire* (1958), the "Warren Western" featured a hard-bitten quality in place of any romanticization of frontier life, as well as a low-key tone not unlike the noir style for then-modern thrillers. The last of these oaters featured Joel McCrea as a trail boss struggling to get his herd from Texas to Kansas, with Paul Brinegar along for the ride. Warren re-imagined the film as a TV series, with McCrea the obvious choice for the lead. But he had begun work on a series dear to his heart, *Wichita Town* (1959–1960). Warren then cast Eric Fleming as "Gil Favor," and Brinegar as the cook "Wishbone."

Warren still required a second lead. Eastwood meanwhile eked out a living digging holes for swimming pools and, when lucky, picked up bit parts. Feeling sorry for him, a friend enjoying better luck invited Eastwood over to the CBS commissary for lunch. As luck/fate would have it, Warren happened by, spotted Eastwood, and sensed this was the perfect person for the Ramrod (assistant trail boss) role. CBS originally toyed with calling the show *Cattle Drive* to make clear this would be to long drives what NBC's *Wagon Train* was to Conestogas. From the moment the series debuted in its original Friday night slot, *Rawhide* scored in the top twenty Nielsen ratings, often in the top ten. *Rawhide* was one of the few supposed "cowboy" shows to deal, on a weekly basis, with the daily work of a cowhand rather than gunfighters and/or lawman. Warren insisted on authenticity; Indian problems were occasionally on view (as in real life), though more often scripts focused on what had truly been the most pressing issues: anthrax epidemics, prairie fires, droughts, and legal problems encountered when the herd had to pass over privately owned land.

Like *Wagon Train* an "adult Western," *Rawhide* lured top guest stars (Dan Duryea, Barbara Stanwyck, etc.) through strong scripts, allowing them to play varied people who came into contact with the drive. Characters were, particularly in the early seasons, well developed, and the relationships between the regulars proved complex. Attention to realistic detail also rated as impressive: A horse slips on a rim, a cowboy is injured, so every-

thing stops while he is attended to. A "doggie" gets caught in mud; viewers watch as, for ten minutes, drovers debate the best way to extricate him. Adding to the power was a still well-remembered/hell-bent-for-leather song, composed by Dimitri Tiomkin (with Ned Washington); he had created title tunes for such A movies as *Gunfight at the O.K. Corral* (1957). Frankie Laine, who had done the honors on that film, sang the ballad.

After Eric Fleming left (1965), Rowdy found himself promoted to trail boss. Now Eastwood had the opportunity to develop the style of performance that would see him through Leone's Westerns and those he would later perform in for Don Siegel: "My old drama coach used to say, 'Don't just *do* something, *stand* there,'" Eastwood explained. "Gary Cooper wasn't afraid to do nothing." Eastwood loved the Western because, like jazz/blues, "there are not too many American art forms that are *original*." Once that first spaghetti Western (the poncho had been Eastwood's idea) premiered and he had acquired an international audience, Eastwood returned to America as an in-demand star, often in Westerns (*Hang 'Em High*, 1968). Like Wayne, Eastwood also proved effective in World War II action films (*Where Eagles Dare*, 1968; *Kelly's Heroes*, 1970). Fans always wonder, particularly after Eastwood could pick/direct his own projects, why he and Wayne never joined forces. In fact, he'd contacted Wayne with an idea for a film casting them as older/younger cowboys. The Duke sent back a negative response. He had seen *High Plains Drifter* (1973) and did not approve of the way Eastwood played with (i.e., deconstructed) long-established Western mythology. When asked his favorite old Western, Eastwood cited *The Ox-Bow Incident* (1943), which Wayne never cared for owing to what Duke considered its anti-American implications. Eastwood's favorite Ford film was not a Wayne Western but *How Green Was My Valley* (1941).

Though Eastwood is generally thought of as the greatest conservative star since Wayne, the two are dissimilar. Like Wayne a registered Republican, Eastwood does *not* think of himself as conservative. Though the left lambasted *Dirty Harry* (1971) as a call for police vigilantism, Eastwood (in a role Wayne turned down) and director Don Siegel considered it a demand for gun control, as a wacko murderer (Andy Robinson) finds it all too easy to purchase weapons without restriction. Years later, *Unforgiven* (1992), which won Eastwood his first Best Director Oscar, had been intended as "an indictment" of rather than a celebration of violence. "I've always considered myself too individualistic to be right-wing or left-wing," Eastwood claims. When George H. W. Bush requested that Eastwood campaign for him, he refused. "I think what the ultra-right-wing conserva-

tives did to the Republicans is really self-destructive, absolutely stupid." He voted for Ross Perot that year.

Eastwood most despises any form of extremism, the two polar sides always in the end mouthing the same thing: "When you go far enough to the right, you meet the same idiots coming around from the left." Eastwood had become a Republican because he admired the moderation of Eisenhower. Today he says, "I like the libertarian view, which is to leave everyone alone. Even as a kid, I was annoyed by people who wanted to tell everyone how to live."

As a director, Eastwood's big-scale Westerns have been a mixed bag, ranging from terrible (*Pale Rider*, 1985) through mediocre (*The Outlaw Josey Wales*, 1976) to brilliant (*Unforgiven*, 1992). His personal relationship with talentless, unappealing actress Sondra Locke, cast in six Eastwood films that would have been better served by stronger performers, did not help. Imagine *Bronco Billy* (1980) with Eastwood and Goldie Hawn! During the Oscar ceremony in which Eastwood won his second Best Director award (for *Million Dollar Baby*, 2004), actress Hilary Swank unmasked the tough guy, revealing him as sensitive and nonviolent, a deeply caring civil rights progressive, if with traditionalist views on the need for a strong, vigilant, defensive military. SEE ALSO: James Coburn, Eric Fleming, Audie Murphy.

Buddy Ebsen

(1908–2003)

••••••••••••••••••••••••••••••

Ebsen's father owned a dance studio in Florida where Buddy and his sister learned their steps. Broadway, vaudeville, and MGM musical movies followed, including a memorable pairing with Shirley Temple in *Captain January* (1936). All set to play the Tin Man in *The Wizard of Oz* (1939), Ebsen had to be hospitalized owing to aluminum powder makeup, so Jack Haley stepped in. Louis B. Mayer wanted to sign Ebsen to an exclusive contract, but the star refused. Mayer's reaction: "You'll never work in this town again!" Blacklisted (for nonpolitical reasons), Ebsen found work where he could, occasionally in B Westerns as the sidekick ("Homer," "Happy") to genial Rex Allen. Walt Disney, who decades earlier had employed Ebsen to dance while the film crew recorded him so that animators could model Mickey's steps on Ebsen's, was even then searching for the right actor to play Davy Crockett. He considered Ebsen but, after discovering Fess Parker, cast Buddy instead as "Georgie Russel," a quasi-historical character based on George Russell, son of Major Russell of the Choctaw-Creek Indian War of 1813. In reality, Russell and Crockett were friends only briefly; in the series, "Georgie" became the singin' sidekick whose ballad served as a transitional device and shortly as the centerpiece of the Crockett craze. Ebsen even got to dance in the second installment (1/26/55). When Crockett (played as a complex human being attempting to live up to his heroic image rather than as a perfect hero) found himself in danger of becoming seduced by corrupt Jacksonian politics, Georgie turned into a Jiminy Cricket–like conscience, warning the starry-eyed hero in the nick of time. Midway through the third episode (2/23/55), their friendship would be sorely tested at the Alamo when Crockett failed to share bad news of the situation with his best friend, though they were reunited in time for a last stand. Ebsen's final words were "Give 'em what *fer*, Davy!," his refrain throughout the three original shows.

The two stars reunited for a pair of fable-like episodes the following year involving riverman Mike Fink (Jeff York). In 1956 Ebsen also played "Sheriff Matt Brady," father to Darlene Gillespie, in Disney's daytime serial *Corky and White Shadow*. Ebsen revived his Georgie image for the *Northwest Passage* series (1958–1959, his character called "Hunk Mariner" after Walter Brennan's role in the 1940 film). Earlier, Ebsen had been notable in *Red Garters* (1954), a semi-surreal Western musical; he later played in *Attack* (1956), Robert Aldrich's ultra-realistic depiction of the Battle of the Bulge, and *Breakfast at Tiffany's* (1961), as a self-effacing farmer married to Audrey Hepburn's sophisticate/decadent. About to retire, Ebsen was offered the role of "Jed Clampett," the dumb-like-a-fox backwoods patriarch on *The Beverly Hillbillies* (1962–1971). In 1965 he reunited with Fess Parker on a memorable *Danny Kaye Show*. After that came two exceptional TV Westerns, one a comedy (*The Daughters of Joshua Cabe*, 9/13/72), the other a serious drama (*Fire on the Mountain*, 11/23/81). One final hit came as the lead on *Barnaby Jones* (1973–1980). In *The Beverly Hillbillies* film (1993), Ebsen provided a cameo as Barnaby. He had one more late-in-life success: His first novel (*Kelly's Quest*, 1993) became a bestseller. Earlier, Ebsen had penned plays, including *Honest John* (1948). SEE ALSO: Don Burnett, Keith Larsen, Fess Parker.

James Edwards

(1918–1970)

••••••••••••••••••••••••••••••••

This handsome, gifted actor appeared to be in the right place at the right time when producer Stanley Kramer cast him in *Home of the Brave* (1949), the first post–World War II civil rights film. Positive response to his role as an African American soldier joining an all-white squad in the South Pacific after President Truman's edict that the armed forces be integrated hinted that this gifted performer would become the first black superstar, a status that eventually went to Sidney Poitier. Edwards fell victim to the McCarthy blacklist and

had trouble finding work until 1960, when Walt Disney cast him as Batt, a real-life cowboy on the Arizona ranch owned by the title character on *Texas John Slaughter*. In the first-ever attempt on a continuing show to accurately depict the role of blacks on the frontier, Disney encouraged Edwards to play against stereotype, resulting in a complex, well-rounded role model. In the 1960s, when other TV producers followed Disney's lead, Edwards guest-starred on *Death Valley Days* (10/8/64) and *The Virginian* (12/4/68). He played a member of Frank Sinatra's squad in *The Manchurian Candidate* (1962). Days after completing his role as George C. Scott's valet in *Patton* (1970), Edwards died of a heart attack. SEE ALSO: Tom Tryon.

Penny Edwards

(1928–1998)

••••••••••••••••••••••••••••••••

An adorably tomboyish starlet, Edwards, briefly under contract to Warner Bros. in the late 1940s, was underused in minor roles. She instead headed for small-time Republic and B-movie stardom. When Dale Evans became pregnant in 1950, then requested time off to be with her child, Edwards replaced her in the Roy Rogers series, making five films opposite the King of the Cowboys. She also appeared with Rex Allen and Allan "Rocky" Lane and rates as the *only* female at Republic to star in her own oaters, *Missing Women* and *Million Dollar Pursuit*, both 1951. Edwards hit the big time once, opposite Tyrone Power in *Pony Soldier* (1952), a Fox A Western. In 1957 she played one of *The Dalton Girls*, the all-female (and all-fictional) answer to the boys of that name. Her final role came as the real-life Two Gun Nan, who replaced Annie Oakley with Cody's Wild West show, on *Death Valley Days* (2/27/58). SEE ALSO: Gale Davis, Dale Evans, Roy Rogers, Gloria Winters.

Richard Egan

(1921–1987)

A Fox contract performer, Egan during the 1950s developed from bit player to supporting actor to mid-level star, best remembered today for *Love Me Tender* (1956) as Vance Reno, older brother of Elvis Presley. By decade's end, Egan had headlined several big films: action epic (*The 300 Spartans*, 1962), soap opera (*A Summer Place*, 1959), and family fare (*Pollyanna*, 1960). During the 1960s, a whole new Hollywood emerged, distinguished by extravaganzas starring Heston, Wayne, and Lancaster, as well as low-budget flicks for the youth audience via Roger Corman, leaving people like Egan, Jeff Hunter, and Bob Wagner out in the cold. Their best bet was to land TV series. Egan's was NBC's *Empire* (1962–1963) as "Jim Redigo," man-

ager of a huge ranch owned by the Garret family, with matriarch "Lucia" (Anne Seymour), sex-kitten daughter "Constance" (Terry Moore), spoiled son "Tal" (Ryan O'Neal), plus the vaquero "Arturo" (Don Diamond). Set in the modern West, *Empire* resembled the upcoming *Peyton Place* in everything except locale and success. Despite a large budget and sixty-minute format, the show failed to click. NBC spun Egan off into the half-hour *Redigo* in fall 1963, with rugged Jim now on his own small spread and Diamond the only other holdover; Roger Davis signed on as ranch hand "Mike," with Elena Verdugo (of *Meet Millie* fame) on hand as their housekeeper/cook. Ratings plummeted, causing the new show to be canceled at midseason. Egan later played Colonel Carrington in "Massacre at Fort Phil Kearney" (10/26/66) on *Bob Hope Presents the Chrysler Theatre*. After that, he appeared mainly in inexpensive European exploitation flicks. SEE ALSO: Charles Bronson, Terry Moore, Ryan O'Neal.

Jack Elam

(1918–2003)

The Arizona-born Elam got into a fight with another kid at the age of twelve and ended up with a pencil puncture in his left eye. This seeming misfortune *made* him a fortune as a bad-guy actor. Originally laboring as an accountant, Elan talked financially strapped writer/producer Alan Le May (who would pen *The Searchers*) into letting him do all the bookwork for nothing on upcoming projects if only Elam could also act. He was shortly on a career path to menacing many a hero, including Jimmy Stewart in six films. Elan played several real-life outlaws on TV and in movies: Black Jack Ketchum (*Stories of the Century*, 6/24/54), Tom McLowery (*Gunfight at the O. K. Corral*, 1957), Turkey Creek Jack Johnson (*Rawhide*, 3/2/62), and John Wesley Hardin (*Dirty Dingus Magee*, 1970). On occasion he appeared as non-menacing characters, including the amiable town drunk near the end of *High Noon* (1952). Elam did not go for psychologically motivated villains: "When I robbed a bank, it was because I wanted the *money*." He played the baddie "Gomez" on the 1958 season of Disney's *Zorro*; and "Toothy Thompson" irregularly on *Sugarfoot* and *Bronco* in 1958–1961, less bad than sad, more a tired old loser. In the 1960s, Westerns adjusted to a different era. *The Dakotas* (1963) replaced *Cheyenne* on ABC Monday evenings, with Elam as "J. D. Smith," a rough-looking but decent deputy. He was promoted to full marshal the following year (1963–1964) on *Temple Houston* as "George Taggart." Audiences loved Elam best as over-the-top villains, most memorably as a mean gunslinger menaced by a pesky housefly in the opening sequence of Sergio Leone's *Once Upon a Time*

in the West (1968). He also played "Zack," family patriarch on *The Texas Wheelers* (1974); "Cully," trapper partner of James Arness, in *How the West Was Won* (1977); "Axel" on *Lucky Luke* (German-produced Western, 1993); and "Curtis" (*Lonesome Dove: The Series*, 1994–1995). An unsold pilot for *Cat Ballou* with Lesley Ann Warren, in which Elam played "Kid Shaleen," aired on 9/5/71. His made-for-TV Western movies include *The Over-the-Hill Gang* (10/7/69), *The Daughters of Joshua Cabe* (9/13/72), *The New Daughters of Joshua Cabe* (5/29/76), *Shootout in a One-Dog Town* (1/9/74), *Sidekicks* (3/21/74), *The Sacketts* (5/15/79), *Once Upon a Texas Train* (1/3/88), *Bonanza: The Return* (11/28/93), and *Bonanza: Under Attack* (1/15/95). SEE ALSO: James Coburn, Chad Everett, Jeff Hunter.

Ross Elliott

(1917–1999)

A veteran of Orson Welles's *Mercury Theater*, Elliott took part in the infamous Halloween 1938 radio broadcast of H. G. Wells's *War of the Worlds*. He had no trouble winning roles on TV and in movies, though they were always obscure and minor. He was not the first actor to play big brother Virgil on *The Life and Legend of Wyatt Earp* (Ray Montgomery), nor the last (John Anderson), though Elliott appeared in the part more than either of them, playing Virgil in most Dodge City episodes. He enacted Temple (son of Sam) Houston, a lawyer and shootist, in "The Reluctant Gun" (12/26/59) on *Death Valley Days*, and had the recurring role of the sturdy, steady "Sheriff Abbott" on *The Virginian*. SEE ALSO: John Anderson, Jeff Hunter, Hugh O'Brian.

Sam Elliott

(1944–)

••••••••••••••••••••••••••••••••

Like Tom Selleck, Elliott was born to be a Western star, in the right place (Hollywood) at the wrong time. His film debut came as a bit player in *Butch Cassidy and the Sundance Kid* (1969); he eventually married leading lady Katharine Ross after they met in 1978 on *The Legacy*. Elliott proved awkward at playing contemporary sex-symbol roles (*Lifeguard*, 1976), so he wisely opted instead for TV and upscale miniseries/movies. First was *The Sacketts* (5/15/79) from Louis L'Amour's third novel about Tennessee brothers on their way to New Mexico; Elliott played the oldest, "Tell," Selleck, "Orrin," and Jeff Osterhage, "Tyrel." This project set the pace for casting older TV/movie cowboys (Glenn Ford, Ben Johnson, L. Q. Jones) in supporting roles for nostalgia/authenticity. Next came *Wild Times* (1/24/80) as "Colonel Hugh Cardiff," a fictional hero who becomes a buffoonish Buffalo Bill Cody–style showman, based on a

REVIVING THE TRADITIONAL WEST-ERN: In the 1980s and 1990s, when Westerns all but disappeared from motion-picture screens, actor/producer Sam Elliott revived the genre in upscale TV miniseries and movies. Courtesy *Shadow Riders* Productions.

well-regarded Brian Garfield novel. *The Shadow Riders* (9/28/82) was derived from the L'Amour *Sackett* novels, though the names of the brothers were changed this time around owing to legal problems, with Elliott now "Dal Traven," Selleck and Osterhage his siblings, and wife Ross the female lead in a post–Civil War story. He also played "Chance McKenzie," a modern Westerner, in the short-lived soap *The Yellow Rose* (1983). Elliott enacted the title role and also assisted the producers with *Houston: The Legend of Texas* (1986, video title *Gone to Texas*), a superb TV epic and the best-ever film/TV treatment of Old Sam. Then it was back to L'Amour as the title character in the superb made-for-cable oater

The Quick and the Dead (2/28/87), *not* to be confused with the abominable 1995 film of that name. Elliott took some time out for non-Westerns: *Prancer* and *Road House*, both in 1989. He then produced *Conagher* (7/1/91) and *You Know My Name* (as Big Bill Tilghman, 8/22/99), and played General John Buford in *Gettysburg* and Virgil Earp in *Tombstone*, both in 1993, later portraying Bill Hickok in *Buffalo Girls* (4/30/95) opposite Anjelica Huston as Calamity Jane, from the Larry McMurtry novel. His best later TV role was as Captain Bucky O'Neil in John Milius's *Rough Riders* (7/20/97). Elliott's most memorable non-Western movie roles include "The Stranger" in the Coen brothers' *The Big Lebowski* (1998) and "Kermit Newman" in Rod Lurie's *The Contender* (2000). He delivered a powerful performance as "Lorne Lutch," a cancer-devastated former Marlboro Man, in *Thank You for Smoking* (2005), based on the real-life TV star David McLean. As to "new Westerns," attacked by most old-timers though defended by emergent twenty-first-century youth, Elliott alone reveals a wry, wise, balanced view. The traditionalist in him says, "I'm not [part of] the *Brokeback Mountain* crowd, I'm more of a purist." Then Elliott's progressive side adds: "but at the same time, it's a new day"—for a new audience, watching new Westerns. SEE ALSO: Tom Berenger, David McLean, Jeff Osterhage, Katharine Ross, Tom Selleck.

Leif Erickson
(1911–1986)

Born William Anderson, Erickson assumed the name of the Viking discoverer of America in order to stand out from the Hollywood pack. He experienced an unhappy love life, divorcing actress Frances Farmer late on the morning of 6/12/42 and marrying actress Margaret Hayes later the same day. They divorced three weeks later; he never remarried. Erickson had a nondescript career, with occasional roles in Westerns (*The Cimarron Kid*, 1952, Audie Murphy). He appeared in one sci-fi classic as the possessed father in *Invaders from Mars* (1953). TV Westerns included the lead in "The Eli Bancroft Story" (*Wagon Train*, 11/11/63) and the title character in "The Aaron Burr Story" (*Daniel Boone*, 10/28/65). Cast by producer William Claxton as "Big John Cannon," modeled after John Wayne, in *The High Chaparral* (1967–1971), Erickson played an ornery, narrow-minded Arizona rancher dealing with familial and business problems. The offbeat relationships and on-location shooting in Old Tucson allowed this series to stand out as the strongest of all family-oriented (in an adult sense of that term) Westerns of the late sixties. SEE ALSO: Linda Cristal, Cameron Mitchell, Frank Silvera.

Dale Evans

(1912–2001)

••••••••••••••••••••••••••••••••

Frances Octavia Smith (though some claim her actual name to be Lucille Wood Smith) from Uvalde, Texas, headed for Memphis and Chicago to break in as a radio singer. She experienced three failed marriages before her successful one to Roy Rogers, whom she met after a talent scout spotted the young beauty and brought her to LA for a Fox contract. Evans mostly played modern girls, typecast as (hard as this is to believe today) a naughty one at that. Her first Western was *In Old Oklahoma* (1943), as saloon floozy "Cuddles" opposite John Wayne. When Evans joined Rogers for *Cowboy and the Senorita* (1944), their chemistry clicked onscreen, and off as well. The two were married after his wife's passing and her latest divorce. Its title aside, *The Roy Rogers Show* (1951–1957) emerged as *their* series: Evans's job as a waitress in the town café allowed her access to info that helped Rogers to track down the baddies. Evans often rode alongside him (on her horse, Buttermilk) with her pistol drawn, firing at fleeing outlaws even as Rogers did, displaying a rough-hewn equality of the sexes in action. Evans penned the song "Happy Trails (to You)," which they sang together while the closing credits crawled over their image. In real life, things turned considerably less rosy: Three of their children died young. Evans turned to religion and shared her faith with fans in a series of popular inspirational books. She appeared with Rogers in another series, the ranch-style musical *The Roy Rogers & Dale Evans Show* (1962). Later still Evans hosted her own chat show, the short-lived *A Date with Dale* (1996). SEE ALSO: Pat Brady, Roy Rogers.

Gene Evans

(1922–1998)

••••••••••••••••••••••••••••••••

If the term "a face in the crowd" didn't already exist, it would have to be created to describe this low-key character actor, his stern countenance well known to movie/TV fans though his name remains elusive. The Arizona-born World War II vet (Purple Heart, Bronze Star winner) enjoyed amateur theatrics overseas and headed to Hollywood after the war. His first role came with a Republic Western, *Under Colorado Skies* (1947). He won the lead as the tough combat sergeant in low-budget, high-impact combat films for writer/director Sam Fuller: *The Steel Helmet* and *Fixed Bayonets!*, both in 1951. Evans played strong supporting roles in big projects (*The Bravados*, 1958, Gregory Peck) and was top-billed as "Rob McLaughlin," turn-of-the-century Montana rancher, in *My Friend Flicka* (1956–1958). With wife "Nell" (Anita Louise), he raised son "Ken" (Johnny Washbrook) and the title horse. Next came the role of the gunman "Loco Crispin" on *Texas John Slaughter* (1960). Evans found work as a subtle scene-stealer for Sam Peckinpah, notably as "Clete" in *The Ballad of Cable Hogue* (1970), and played dozens of world-weary lawmen, cattlemen, and soldiers on *Gunsmoke, Rawhide*, etc. His last significant TV Western role was as "McGregor," a Scottish frontiersman, in *The Alamo: Thirteen Days to Glory* (1/26/87). SEE ALSO: Johnny Washbrook.

(Peter Breck and Richard Long). She played Steve McQueen's love interest in his final Western, the dreary *Tom Horn* (1980). Evans was married to John Derek (1968–1974) after Ursula Andress but before Bo. Having learned from Babs how to be a matriarch, Evans later played one on *Dynasty* (1981–1989), where she was reunited with Stanwyck. SEE ALSO: Peter Breck, Charles Briles, Richard Long, Lee Majors, Steve McQueen, Barbara Stanwyck.

Linda Evans

(1942–)

••••••••••••••••••••••••••••••••••

Evans's first TV appearance was on *Bachelor Father* (10/13/69) as a fifteen-year-old girl harboring an "impossible" crush on star John Forsythe. A quarter of a century later, Evans played his wife on *Dynasty*. She was often associated with Westerns, beginning with a role as Brandon De Wilde's girlfriend in Disney's *Those Calloways* (1965). Evans was picked for *The Big Valley* (1965–1969) as TV's answer to movie star Yvette Mimieux: "Audra Barkley," daughter to "Victoria" (Barbara Stanwyck), Evans portrayed a naïve, willful, charming girl of the West who regularly suffered a new crush on some handsome older man passing by. Intriguingly, Audra had a more intense relationship with her illegitimate half-brother "Heath" (Lee Majors) than with her respectable sibs

Chad Everett

(1936–)

••••••••••••••••••••••••••••••••••

Everett's first TV cowpoke role was as "Deputy Del Stark" on *The Dakotas* (1963), the second-to-last Warner Bros. TV Western. Born Raymond Lee Cramton, he played a young punk out to make his reputation (a role patented by Richard Jaeckel and Skip Homeier in *The Gunfighter*, 1950) in B oaters *Return of the Gunfighter* and *The Last Challenge* (both 1967) up against old-timers Robert Taylor and Glenn Ford, respectively. Everett found long-term employment on the primetime soap *Medical Center* (1969–1976) as the idealistic "Dr. Joe Gannon," then returned to the Western genre as a fictional army major on NBC's *Centennial* (1978). He played "Wyatt Earp III," descendant of the legendary lawman, in *The Rousters*, a movie of the week (10/1/83), then in a short-lived series. In it, Everett ran a traveling carnival, keeping things peaceful with Granddad's Buntline. Everett announced during an early 1970s *Dick Cavett Show* that he considered his wife a piece of personal property, causing feminist Lily Tomlin to walk off the set. SEE ALSO: Jack Elam, Michael Greene.

Jason Evers

(1922–2005)

A journeyman TV actor, Evers played "Pitcairn" in *Wrangler*, the 1960 summer replacement for Tennessee Ernie Ford. This six-episode series boasted several unique elements, including a focus on the daily work of an expert with horses. This also represented TV's only attempt to videotape rather than film a Western. Most viewers missed the polished quality of celluloid. Seven years later, Evers played "Jim Sonnett," the missing gunfighter for whom Walter Brennan and Dack Rambo search in *The Guns of Will Sonnett*. SEE ALSO: Walter Brennan, Dack Rambo.

Roger Ewing

(1942–)

Ewing made his film debut as a rugged PFC in Frank Sinatra's sole directing effort, *None But the Brave* (1965), then played "Thad Greenwood" on *Gunsmoke* (1965–1967). SEE ALSO: James Arness, Burt Reynolds.

Richard Eyer

(1945–)

This redheaded, freckle-faced child actor had seemingly been born to play Huck Finn, though he never nabbed that role. He enacted plenty of others, though: a boy who stands up to gangster Humphrey Bogart in *The Desperate Hours* (1955), Gary Cooper's scrappy son in the Civil War–era *Friendly Persuasion* (1956), the title character in *The Invisible Boy* (1957) with Robby the Robot, a genie in Ray Harryhausen's *The 7th Voyage of Sinbad* (1958), and the son of Virginia Mayo, traveling through Indian country with Clint Walker and Brian Keith, in *Fort Dobbs* (1958). His TV work included a Western classic: In *G. E. Theater*'s "The Trail to Christmas" (12/15/17), Eyer was cast as a runaway boy who learns the meaning of the holiday from saddle tramp James Stewart. His only series role came as "David Kane," growing up on the frontier in *Stagecoach West* (1960). Eyer also played the "Montana Kid," a teenager hoping to become a gunslinger but talked out of that profession by Steve McQueen, on *Wanted: Dead or Alive* (9/5/59). Eyer left acting to pursue a career in education and at this writing teaches third grade in Bishop, California. SEE ALSO: Robert Bray, Steve McQueen, Wayne Rogers.

Richard Farnsworth

(1920–2000)

••••••••••••••••••••••••••••••••••

A native Angeleno, expert rider Farnsworth was hired to perform stunts in films and began playing bits, then major roles. His career took off with *Red River* (1948), in which he served as Monty Clift's stunt double and one of John Wayne's riders in the finale. Farnsworth played larger roles in *Monte Walsh* (1970, Lee Marvin) and *Blazing Saddles* (1974, Mel Brooks) and received an Oscar nomination for Best Supporting Actor in *Comes a Horseman* (1978), in which he delivered a strong performance in the melancholic role of a doomed old-timer. TV Western roles included "J. W. Stevens," a throwback to old-time lawmen, in *The Texas Rangers* (1981), and a similar part as "Cody McPherson" in *The Boys of Twilight* (1992) with Wilford Brimley and Ben Browder as their young sidekick "Tyler Clare." Farnsworth played lawman Bill Hickok in *The Legend of* *the Lone Ranger* (1981) and outlaw Bill Miner in *The Grey Fox* (1982). TV movies included *Wild Horses* (11/12/85), with Kenny Rogers as a rodeo veteran, and *Desperado: The Outlaw Wars* (1989). Farnsworth received an Oscar nomination for Best Actor as "Alvin Straight" in *The Straight Story* (1999), a fact-based yarn about an aging Westerner embarking on his final odyssey via a tractor. He took his own life after learning he suffered from terminal cancer. SEE ALSO: Wilford Brimley, Alex McArthur.

Tommy Farrell

(1921–2004)

••••••••••••••••••••••••••••••••••

A lackluster movie career, with bits in B actioners like *Atom Man vs. Superman* and *Jungle Jim in Pygmy Island*, both 1950, preceded one TV

Western role. During the third season of *The Adventures of Rin Tin Tin*, Rand Brooks ("Corporal Boone," a character *not* related to the frontier hero) left the cast. On 12/12/58, Farrell took up the slack as "Corporal Thad Carson," who *was* supposedly a descendant of *that* frontier hero. Carson arrived at Fort Apache wearing a buckskin jacket decorated with beads and had to be taken down a peg before fitting in with the boys of B Company. Shortly after, Brooks returned and Farrell left, but not before they costarred in several episodes. He played "Jay O'Hanlon" on *Bourbon Street Beat* in 1959–1960 and fleetingly appeared as a party guest in *Breakfast at Tiffany's* (1961). SEE ALSO: Lee Aaker, Rand Brooks, James (L.) Brown, Joe Sawyer.

 ## William Fawcett
(1894–1974)
••••••••••••••••••••••••••••••

While teaching theater at Michigan State University, this Ph.D. was challenged by students who couldn't grasp why he didn't head for Hollywood. After World War II, Fawcett did precisely that, playing old rivermen, prospectors, and ranchers in over 200 Western movies/TV shows. Continuing roles included "Old Higgins" on *Rin Tin Tin* and top hand "Pete" on *Fury*. SEE ALSO: Lee Aaker, Bobby Diamond, James (L.) Brown, Peter Graves.

Paul Fix
(1901–1983)
••••••••••••••••••••••••••••••

Son of an upstate New York brew master, Fix served in the U.S. Navy during World War I, then drifted to LA and committed to acting, which he had always enjoyed. He toured the country in a troupe that also included a pre-stardom Clark Gable. Three hundred movie roles (countless more on TV) followed, many of them in Westerns, including the best-remembered of all, Bill Boyd's *Hoppys*, *Bar 20 Rides Again* (1935). The following year, he worked for John Ford for the first time in *The Prisoner of Shark Island*. Earlier, Fix had met Ford's eventual star, John Wayne, when they were cast together in *Three Girls Lost* (1931). Fix mentored young Duke, teaching him not only to act (or more correctly *react*) but also how to perform that near-choreographed gunman's walk, Wayne's visual signature. A writer as well as multifaceted actor, his credits include coauthorship of the screenplay for Wayne's *Tall in the Saddle* (1944). The two were also effective together in *Red River* (1948) as a trail boss and a drover who wants to quit. He played the role of "Micah Torrance," the lawman in North Fork who calls on "Lucas McCain" (Chuck Connors) to help bring baddies to justice, on *The Rifleman* (1958–1963). Fix's best movie role was as a fair-minded judge in *To Kill a Mockingbird* (1962). Four

Wagon Trains followed, including one title role in "The Amos Billings Story" (3/14/62). He was a semi-regular as Cochise during *The High Chaparral*'s 1967–1968 season. Strong movie roles followed, as the doomed Pete Maxwell in Sam Peckinpah's *Pat Garrett & Billy the Kid* and the "Old Outlaw" in Wayne's *Cahill U.S. Marshal*, both in 1973. His daughter Marilyn is the wife of another TV/movie Western veteran, Harry Carey, Jr. SEE ALSO: Harry Carey, Jr.; Chuck Connors.

Eric Fleming
(1925–1966)

As rugged trail boss "Gil Favor" on *Rawhide* (1959–1966), Fleming shouted the memorable final line for most episodes: "Head 'em up; move 'em out!" In the final season, Clint Eastwood's "Rowdy Yates" took over the drive after Fleming, who had carefully saved his money, announced he would not return. He purchased a ranch in Hawaii and figured he'd retire early with his girlfriend. Unlike some TV stars (Fleming's earlier series was the low-budget actioner *Major Del Conway of the Flying Tigers*, 1951, replaced by Ed Peck), Fleming did not take acting too seriously. He had no desire for fame, only for a quiet life. Sadly, he didn't get to enjoy that. MGM sought Fleming out and talked him into starring in a Peru-lensed actioner, *High Jungle*. Filming

a scene on the Huallaga River rapids, Fleming was sucked into a whirlpool and drowned. Other than *Rawhide*, he is best remembered as the male lead in the cult classic *Queen of Outer Space* (1958), costarring with Zsa Zsa Gabor. During the 1966 season of *Bonanza*, Fleming appeared in several different roles. SEE ALSO: Paul Brinegar, Clint Eastwood, John Ireland.

Henry Fonda
(1905–1982)

Like close friend/sometime costar James Stewart, the Nebraska-born "Hank" early on struck producers as far too easygoing a rube to ever act in a Western. Then John Ford offered him the lead in an "Eastern," *Drums Along the Mohawk* (1939), and a frontier icon emerged. Fonda resembled Gary Cooper in that precious few of his films *were* Westerns, though most of his excursions into the genre proved so fine—*Jesse James* (as big brother Frank, 1939), *The Ox-Bow Incident* (1943), *My Darling Clementine* (Wyatt Earp, 1946), *Fort Apache* (a thinly disguised Custer, 1948), and *The Tin Star* (1957)—that in our collective imagination we recall him as appearing in more than he did. Between 1959 and 1961, Fonda became the only A-list movie star to appear in (and coproduce) a weekly show, *The Deputy*, though his name-above-the-title status enraged many viewers. As territorial marshal

"Simon Fry," Fonda would show up briefly at an episode's beginning only to head off on some mission after appointing the peace-loving but fast-with-a-gun local (Allen Case) to keep an eye on things. This approach allowed Fonda to shoot all his scenes for an entire season in a few weeks, then perform on Broadway while his footage was scattered over thirty-nine episodes. During the first year, he made substantial appearances in only six episodes; in the second, thirteen. Viewers noticed that, despite a lofty star's presence, most stories were contrived and clunky. Talk about a possible hour-long version for the 1961–1962 season never went far. Fonda had greater luck in 1967 when he played the lead in the first-ever made-for-TV Western movie, Don Siegel's *Stranger on the Run* (10/31/67), which garnered strong reviews and a large audience. SEE ALSO: Allen Case, Wallace Ford, Betty Lou Keim.

Scott Forbes

(1920–1997)

••••••••••••••••••••••••••••••••

This Englishman migrated to Hollywood and found work, including one major film Western, *Rocky Mountain* (1950), with Errol Flynn. He worked mostly on TV, in regular weekly shows (*Suspense*, 1953; *Danger*, 1954) and highbrow golden-age dramas by Shakespeare (*King Lear*, 1953) and Dickens (*Great Expectations*, 1954). Desilu picked Forbes to star in their

second (and, as it turned out, final) planned series of TV epics. *The Adventures of Jim Bowie* (1956–1958) seemed to be a sure thing, combining the best elements of two previous hits: the early frontier setting from Disney's *Davy Crockett* with the storytelling approach explored by Desilu on their hit *The Life and Legend of Wyatt Earp*. The show was based on *Tempered Blade* by Monte Barrett, that author on board to write/supervise scripts. Forbes, who resembled sketches of the real Bowie, proved to be well cast, delivering such cornball lines as "Well, dog my cats!"

The first episode, "The Birth of the Blade" (9/7/56), set the pace for what would follow: a combination of fact and fiction. The design of the Bowie knife was presented much as it occurred, though with Jim's role (his brother Rezin actually designed the weapon) played up. Several action scenes (Jim is inspired to make the knife after a wrestling match with a bear, then employs the blade against a passel of bad guys) were added for impact. The show went further than *Earp* as to historical accuracy: Not only was Rezin (Peter Hansen) a continuing character, but Mom (Minerva Urecal) showed up as well. During the second season, as Jim wandered into Texas, episodes introduced Don Veramendi (Sidney Blackmer) and his daughter Ursula (Eugenia Paul), with plans to depict Bowie's marriage into an aristocratic Spanish family. As with *Earp*, a wide

array of historical characters became recurring visitors: painter John James Audubon (Robert Cornthwait), Texas settlers Sam Houston (Denver Pyle) and Deaf Smith (Vic Perrin), and pirate Jean Lafitte (Peter Mamakos). The need for fresh material became clear when the hero began running into people his prototype had likely never met: Johnny Appleseed (Robert Ellenstein), president Andrew Jackson (Leslie Kimmell), Seminole Chief Osceola (Abel Fernandez) . . . even Davy Crockett (George Dunn), whom the real Bowie never ran into before the Alamo.

In a unique way, *Bowie* rated as five rotating series sharing the same central character. The hero altered his style of dress and his attitude for successive situations: the Tennessee backwoods, gaudy/bawdy New Orleans, Creole/Cajun swamplands, the wild Texas plains, and the elegance of elite Latino culture. Ken Darby and the King's Men supplied the same sort of catchy vocal chorus they had provided for *Earp*. Ratings were strong, but problems soon developed. Advertising execs realized that the deadly knife had become a symbol of the products being marketed to suburbanites, so the bloody fights were toned down. In some later episodes Jim did not use his famed weapon at all, disappointing viewers. Toward the end of the second season, ABC threw in the towel. Having been allowed to believe his series would carry the character through to death five seasons later,

Forbes stormed off the set. Producers scurried to complete the season without their star! In desperation, the writers fashioned the final script, "The Puma" (5/23/58), in which a new, fictional character is mistaken for Bowie. Forbes had cut off his nose to spite his face. He found occasional jobs on episodic TV (including one in *Trackdown*, ironically enough *Bowie*'s competition during its final season), though most producers were in no hurry to sign a troublesome star. Forbes returned to England and found some film/TV work there. SEE ALSO: Hugh O'Brian, Kenneth Tobey.

Glenn Ford

(1916–2006)

• •

Looking like a taller Audie Murphy with a naughty twinkle in his eye, Glenn Ford proved highly effective in oaters and was well-teamed with William Holden at Columbia Pictures, first in *Texas* (1941), a prewar fun Western, and later in *The Man from Colorado* (1948), an unrelentingly grim postwar item. Ford proved equally adept at other genres: film noir (*Gilda*, 1946), soap opera (*A Stolen Life*, 1946), police procedural (*The Big Heat*, 1953), social drama (*Blackboard Jungle*, 1955), service comedy (*Don't Go Near the Water*, 1957), and erotic thriller (*Experiment in Terror*, 1962). An impressive list of A Westerns established him as a genre star (*Jubal* [1956], *The Fast-*

est *Gun Alive* [1956], *3:10 to Yuma* [1957], *Cowboy* [1958], *The Sheepman* [1958], and *Cimarron* [1960]), often in the employ of Delmer Daves and Anthony Mann. Ford shifted to TV for *Cade's County* (1970–1971) as "Sheriff Sam Cade," policing the modern Southwest in a jeep with Edgar Buchanan along as chief deputy "J. J. Jackson," Victor Campos their young Hispanic assistant "Rudy," Jill Banner providing romantic interest as "Melanie," and Mike Road as Sam's boss "D. A. Forbes." Son Peter Ford played the newly appointed deputy "Pete." A Henry Mancini jazz score lent this show an original flavor. Good news: high ratings. Bad news: *Cade* proved to be so expensive to produce that CBS canceled it anyway. TV films and miniseries followed, including one superior Western, *The Sacketts* (4/15/79). SEE ALSO: Edgar Buchanan, Sam Elliott, Tom Selleck.

Wallace Ford
(1898–1966)
••••••••••••••••••••••••••••••••

British-born Samuel Jones found himself stranded in Toronto as a child and went on the road with his friend Wallace Ford. When that youth was killed trying to hop a passing freight train, Jones took his name to honor the dead boy's memory. Work in vaudeville and on Broadway led to a film career including roles in John Ford's Irish movies but none in his classic Westerns. The aspiring performer did find jobs in A and B Westerns for other filmmakers. In the early 1959 episodes of *The Deputy* he played store owner "Herb Lamson" who, like all of Wally's characters, revealed uncannily sad eyes. SEE ALSO: Allen Case, Henry Fonda, Betty Lou Keim.

Steve Forrest
(1924–)
••••••••••••••••••••••••••••••••

Younger brother of 1940s screen star Dana Andrews, Steve Forrest, like his brother, rated as classically handsome and impressively charismatic onscreen. His greatest TV success came in two contemporary action shows: *The Baron* (1966–1967) and *S.W.A.T.* (1975–1976). Forrest always proved effective in Westerns, usually in the second lead: with Anthony Quinn in *Heller in Pink Tights* (the title refers to Sophia Loren) and Elvis Presley in *Flaming Star*, both in 1960. He proved memorable as a Ringo-type gunman in the episode "The Guns of Johnny Rondo" on *The High Chaparral* (2/6/70). Next came the role of "Devlin" in *The Hanged Man* (3/14/74), a pilot for a show that did not happen, in which Forrest played a gunman who, surviving execution, belies his name and becomes angelic. He was slated to play the lead in a *Leatherstocking* series that failed to take, though two TV movies were aired, *The Last of the Mohicans* (11/23/77) and *The Deer-*

slayer (12/18/78), with Ned Romero playing his blood brother "Chingachgook." Forrest effectively incarnated the real-life lawman Charles Siringo, "the man in the straw hat," in *Wanted: The Sundance Woman* (10/1/76), and later played "Wes Parmalee" in *Dallas* (1986); Forrest's accent (he was a real Texan) came across wonderfully on that show. His final TV oater role to date was as shootist "Mannon" in *Gunsmoke: Return to Dodge* (9/26/87). SEE ALSO: Ned Romero, Katharine Ross.

Robert Forster

(1941–)

••••••••••••••••••••••••••••••••

Forster received a football scholarship to the University of Rochester, where he studied psychology and became interested in theater. His first film role was in a notorious flop—a showy supporting part in *Reflections in a Golden Eye* (1967) John Huston's Elizabeth Taylor–Marlon Brando teaming from a Carson McCullers novel. Forster fared better in *The Stalking Moon* (1968), a suspense Western, as Gregory Peck's mixed-race friend, the type of role ordinarily associated with Charles Bronson. He played an important lead in Haskell Wexler's *Medium Cool* (1969), about politics and media. Forster hoped TV might provide stardom and played in *Banyon* (3/15/71), a TV movie that preceded *Chinatown* in reviving noir/pulp private detectives. Though it

became a weekly show, the ratings were not there. The same held true for the contemporary Western *Nakia*, likewise a TV movie (4/17/74), then a brief-lived series, with Forster cast as a Native American deputy torn between a desire to help his people and his oath to uphold the law, the conflict often forcing him to make hard decisions. Gloria DeHaven played townswoman "Irene," Taylor Lacher deputy "Hubbel," and John Tenorio, Jr., the young Native American "Half Cub." The show attempted to be relevant to timely issues after Dee Brown's *Bury My Heart at Wounded Knee* introduced the vast public to Indian rights issues but lasted a mere thirteen weeks. Forster maintained a low profile afterward; Quentin Tarantino came to the rescue with *Jackie Brown* (1997), for which Forster received a Best Supporting Actor nomination. His most recent TV series role was as "Marshal Sisco" on *Karen Sisco* (2003–2004) with Carla Gugino. SEE ALSO: Arthur Kennedy.

Preston Foster

(1900–1970)

••••••••••••••••••••••••••••••••

An obscure performer, Foster was undeservedly so considering his fine work in *The Last Mile* (1932), *I Am a Fugitive from a Chain Gang* (1932), and Ford's *The Informer* (1935). His most significant Western role was as the gambler "Oakhurst" in the superb

1937 version of Bret Harte's *The Out-casts of Poker Flat*. Foster achieved TV stardom as "Captain John Herrick," owner of a tug in LA Harbor, in *Waterfront* (1954–1956). He played the second lead (to Tony Young) in *Gunslinger* (1961), cast as cavalry commander "Zach Wingate." Foster eventually returned to his first loves: writing, directing, and acting in live theater as the executive producer of El Camino Playhouse in California. SEE ALSO: Tony Young.

Douglas (V.) Fowley

(1911–1998)
••••••••••••••••••••••••••••••

One of Hollywood's most durable character players, Fowley appeared in well over 200 films/TV shows, ranging from supporting roles to bit parts. His most memorable role was as the harried director who tries to draw a convincing performance out of a talentless silent star in the greatest of all movie musicals, *Singin' in the Rain* (1952). Fowley's versatility can be seen in *The Life and Legend of Wyatt Earp*. During the first season, he played real-life Doc Fabrique, a crusty old sawbones in Wichita, not unlike the fictional "Doc Adams" on *Gunsmoke*. When Earp traveled to Dodge, Fowley took on the role of young alcoholic/consumptive Doc Holliday. Virtually no one watching realized these notably different parts were performed by the same person, so complete was his transformation. Col-

lette Lyons accompanied him early on as "Big Nose" Kate Fisher, called "Mrs. Holliday" here though the marriage likely had been common law. In 1966 he returned to TV as "Grandpa Hanks" on *Pistols 'n' Petticoats*. SEE ALSO: Myron Healey, Hugh O'Brian, Ann Sheridan, Milburn Stone.

Charles Frank

(1947–)
••••••••••••••••••••••••••••••

This handsome star of the daytime soap *All My Children* (1970–1975) left that show (taking costar/wife Susan Blanchard with him) to appear in the made-for-TV movie *The New Maverick* (9/3/78), followed by the series *Young Maverick* (1979), which lasted less than two months. He played "Ben," cousin to the beloved brothers from the hit 1950s show. Ben held an Ivy League degree but could not resist a good game of poker, with Blanchard cast as his romantic interest, "Nell." The tall, sad-eyed, sardonic-voiced John Dehner rambled around as "Marshal Edge Troy." SEE ALSO: James Garner, Jack Kelly, Roger Moore.

Don Franklin

(1960–)
••••••••••••••••••••••••••••••

When *The Young Riders* premiered (1989), the all (white) boys' club that the Pony Express had in fact been was politically corrected to include

a Native American, a "hearing challenged" (mute) boy, and even a girl.
The only thing missing for full diversity was an African American. At the
start of season two, that oversight
was corrected with the addition of
runaway slave "Noah Dixon," providing one more example of how writers and producers introduce historical
inaccuracies that render the West as a
mythic territory open to reinterpreta-
tion for the needs/desires of successive eras and their unique/specific
audiences. SEE ALSO: Stephen Baldwin, Josh Brolin, Ty Miller, Anthony
Zerbe.

Dean Fredericks
(1924–1999)
••••••••••••••••••••••••••••••••

Another World War II vet turned
actor, Fredericks briefly used his own
name, Fred Foote, then for a while
worked as Norman Frederic. His
first film was a Western, with Fredericks playing a lynch mob member
in *Jesse James vs. the Daltons* (1954).
Then came "Kaseem," the loyal native
sidekick to the title hero (Johnny
Weissmuller) on *Jungle Jim* (1955–
1956). Next up was "Komawi," the
peace-loving Comanche chief on *The
Adventures of Rin Tin Tin* (1954–
1957). Comic strip creator Milt Can-
iff was even then searching for the
right performer to play the lead on
Steve Canyon (1958–1960), an NBC
adventure show about a Cold War
Air Force ace. The star-in-embryo

changed his name to Dean Fredericks in hopes of taking his career in
a whole new direction. When the
series floundered, he returned to
Indians, this time as "Crowfeather,"
archenemy of the title hero (Dewey
Martin) on Disney's *Daniel Boone*
(1960–1961). Fredericks also played
the lead in *The Phantom Planet*
(1961), a low-budget but notably
clever sci-fi cult film. SEE ALSO: Lee
Aaker, James (L.) Brown, Joe Sawyer.

Robert Fuller
(1933–)
••••••••••••••••••••••••••••••••

Fuller enacted an alienated young
man with an attitude in several TV
Westerns before winning the second
lead as a 1950s-style teenager anachronistically transplanted to the frontier in *Laramie* (1959–1963). His "Jess
Harper" wandered onto the Sherman
Ranch, where this dark, brooding
misfit provided an effective contrast
to clean-cut "Slim" (John Smith). No
sooner had that show run its course
on NBC than Fuller was added to
Wagon Train as the new chief scout,
"Cooper Smith." When that series
moved to ABC to make room for
The Virginian (1962) on Wednesday
evenings, there was no designated
"second-billed star" to support John
McIntire; the ratings faltered owing
to competition from NBC's new
ninety-minute "super-Western." ABC
shifted *Wagon Train* to Mondays,
now also in a ninety-minute format.

Denny Miller had earlier joined the cast as "Duke Shannon," so *Train* briefly boasted characters sharing nicknames with bright lights of the theatrical oater, Gary Cooper and John Wayne. For the final season, the show cut back to the traditional hour approach on early Sunday evenings. Fuller later played controversial army officer William J. Fetterman in "Massacre at Fort Phil Kearney" (10/26/66; *Bob Hope Presents the Chrysler Theatre*) and replaced Steve McQueen as "Vince," Yul Brynner's second-in-command of the magnificent ones, in *Return of the Seven* (1966). He enjoyed a huge late-career success with *Emergency!*, produced by Jack Webb. Notable trivia: Fuller played dual roles on an installment of *Walker, Texas Ranger* (5/19/01), qualifying as the only actor to be killed *twice* (by Chuck Norris) in a single hour episode of any series. SEE ALSO: John McIntire, Denny (Scott) Miller, John Smith.

James Garner

(1928–)

••••••••••••••••••••••••••••••

Big and broad shouldered, with twinkling eyes and a sweetly sardonic line delivery, James Garner stood out from the Warner Bros. posse; he alone was destined for Hollywood superstardom. A Korean War vet and Purple Heart winner, the easygoing James Bumgarner first appeared on Broadway in *The Caine Mutiny Court Martial* (1954), where he observed Henry Fonda plying his craft. Warner Bros. signed Garner as a contract player and stuck him in studio program pictures to test his merit. In *The Girl He Left Behind* (1956), Garner stole every scene from nominal lead Tab Hunter. On TV, he was cast as a young army lieutenant, first on the non-WB *Zane Grey Theater's* "Stars over Texas" (12/28/56), then for WB on the first-ever episode of *Cheyenne*, "Mountain Fortress" (9/20/55). In a later episode of that show, "The Last Train West" (5/29/56), Jim played a laconic Westerner named "Bret." His own series a foregone conclusion, WB hired Alan Le May (*The Searchers*) to pen an unconventional scenario. The result was "Bret Maverick," a charming coward. *Maverick* premiered in the fall of 1957 on Sunday evenings and, for the first time, ABC could compete with the powerhouse that was Ed Sullivan thanks to this black-garbed gamblin' man.

Bret didn't cheat at cards, because he didn't need to; he was that good. Comfortable when forced to use his fists, Bret balked at the thought of a gunfight because he was slow on the draw and an inaccurate shot, providing a strong (and the first) contrast to those all-but-identical heroes played by virtually interchangeable actors.

Maverick emerged as an ever more comedic series that, to use today's terminology, deconstructed TV Western formulas. "Gun-Shy" (1/11/59) genially spoofed the original adult Western *Gunsmoke*. As audiences came to expect laughs as well as action, Garner's comic timing would be employed to great advantage. "Pappy" (9/13/59) had Bret, who loved to drawl, "Well, as my ol' Pappy used to say . . ." teamed up with the old codger, also played by Garner.

The only problem: This hour-long show took eight days to film. The solution was to cast Jack Kelly as "Bart," leading to one of TV's most appealing "brother" acts. Yet Garner would always remain *Maverick* in most people's eyes, even after Roger Moore (as "Beau"), then Robert Colbert ("Brent"), showed up. Like Clint Walker, Garner became sick of the WB routine: low wages, no residuals, and too often no stunt double for dangerous scenes. He bolted after the third season (after filming one episode), arguing that a Warner Bros. contract amounted to slavery, pretty much what Bette Davis had said twenty years earlier. Fortunately, this was a different era; while she had been forced back to work, Garner legally won the right to walk away and pursue movie work. Hollywood was glad to have him. William Holden could no longer play cynical young men, and Garner proved just right for such antiheroic figures. He replaced Rock Hudson as the leading man in Doris Day romantic comedies (*The Thrill of It All* and *Move Over, Darling*, both 1963). *The Great Escape* (1963) was supposed to transform him from star to superstar, but Steve McQueen demanded so much screen time that Garner's role had to be trimmed. Superstardom did come the next year when, in *The Americanization of Emily* (1964), opposite Julie Andrews, he played a World War II version of the amiably antiheroic Bret, delivering choice dialogue by Paddy Chayefsky. Garner had established himself as one of Hollywood's in-demand leading men.

He embodied a no-nonsense Wyatt Earp, first in *Hour of the Gun* (1967) for John Sturges, and later in *Sunset* (1988) for Blake Edwards. *Duel at Diablo* (1966) teamed Garner with Sidney Poitier, both in cowboy garb. After a return to the old Maverick mode in Burt Kennedy's delightful *Support Your Local Sheriff* (1969) and a so-so sequel, *Support Your Local Gunfighter* (1971), Disney cast Garner in the appealing quasi-Western *The Castaway Cowboy* (1974). But this new decade featured its own movie stars: Jack Nicholson, Dustin Hoffman, Al Pacino, etc. Able to find no place in the post-Woodstock cinema, Garner returned to TV, beginning with *Nichols* (1971–1972) as a dedicated lawman in the turn-of-the-century West. Audiences missed the old Bret bravura, so the writers tried to salvage things. In what was to have been the first-season finale, an

MOONLIGHT GAMBLER: James Garner changed the image of the TV Westerner beginning in 1957 as "Bret," the first and best-remembered of the lovable cowards who constituted TV's *Maverick* clan. Courtesy ABC/Warner Bros. Television.

outlaw shot the heroic Nichols in the opening scene. His *brother* (a Maverick homage), also played by Garner, showed up to solve the crime, the opposite of the strait-laced (expired) sibling, as such a throwback to what Garner always did best: offhand/casual humor. All this tinkering proved to be in vain; NBC canceled the show anyway.

Garner next played a Maverick-like modern-day private eye in *The Rockford Files* (1974–1980), with Western veteran Noah Beery, Jr., as dad "Rocky." He returned as Bret in the made-for-TV movie *The New Maverick* (9/3/78) with Charles Frank as "Ben," teaming again with the newcomer for the opening episode of a *Young Maverick* series. Big

Jim's presence proved disastrous for the show: Everyone wished *he* was the star. After Garner exited, the series quickly died. He returned for a season in *Bret Maverick* (1981–1982), answering the question "Whatever happened to that lovable lug?" Bret had finally settled down, owning a ranch as well as a saloon in a small Arizona town. Ed Bruce played his business partner "Tom Guthrie," Stuart Margolin Bret's sometime sidekick "Philo Sandeen," Jack Garner (Jim's brother) "Jack the Bartender," with Simone Griffeth the seductive "Jasmine DuBois." Garner played yet another fictional Western hero who had become mythic thanks to TV, "Woodrow Call" in *Streets of Laredo* (11/12/95), the part previously essayed by Tommy Lee Jones (*Lonesome Dove*, 1989), Jon Voight (*Return to Lonesome Dove*, 1993), Lee Majors (*Lonesome Dove: The Series*, 1995), and Jonny Lee Miller (*Dead Man's Walk*, 1996). A sequel to the classic miniseries from a Larry McMurtry novel, the new piece detailed Call's later exploits as a tracker. Playwright/actor Sam Shepard replaced Tim Scott (from *Return to Lonesome Dove*) as "Pea Eye Parker."

In 1994 Garner played "Marshal Zane Cooper" in *Maverick* (the movie), starring Mel Gibson as "Bret." Garner joined Clint Eastwood and Tommy Lee Jones for the sci-fi Western *Space Cowboys* (2000). Aging gracefully and always in demand, he stepped in as "Grandpa Jim" on *8 Simple Rules . . . for Dating My Teenage Daughter* (2002–2005) following John Ritter's passing. James Garner remains a true national treasure. SEE ALSO: Robert Colbert, Charles Frank, Jack Kelly, Roger Moore.

Sean Garrison

(1937–)
••••••••••••••••••••••••••••••

This young hopeful played the sporadic role of cowboy "Andy Gibson" on the 1958–1959 season of *Sugarfoot*, then was briefly touted as "the new John Gavin" (who had been the new Rock Hudson) by Universal in the mid-1960s. Garrison played the male lead opposite the magnificent Jean Seberg in a horrible combination

of soap opera/suspense, *Moment to Moment* (1965). He won the second lead (to no less than John Mills) in *Dundee and the Culhane* (1967) as an Irish cowboy assisting a British barrister on the frontier. Despised by critics and audiences, the show was canceled after a dozen episodes. SEE ALSO: Will Hutchins, John Mills.

John Gavin

(1931–)
••••••••••••••••••••••••••••••

A fifth-generation Angeleno, Gavin claimed descent from the distinguished Golenor family, which settled Southern California during the Spanish era. As brilliant as he was handsome, John Golenor graduated from Stanford with high honors, his field of expertise Latin American economic history. Universal Pictures signed the Rock Hudson lookalike to a studio contract, changing his last name. He appeared in a pair of classics (*Psycho* and *Spartacus*, both 1960) before slipping into light comedies with Sandra Dee. Gavin holds the distinction of starring in the last Warner Bros. TV Western, a short-lived version of Max Brand's beloved *Destry*, which ran for several months in 1964. This low-key, soft-spoken hero had previously been portrayed by Tom Mix (1932), James Stewart (1939), and Audie Murphy (1954), as well as by Joel McCrea in the 1950 feature *Frenchie*, the name there altered to Tom "Banning." For

Gavin's series, the lead's first name was changed to "Harrison." Following *Destry*'s demise, Gavin wisely drifted away from acting and became a successful businessman and diplomat, serving as (among other things) President Reagan's ambassador to Mexico, where Gavin's wife (former actress Constance Towers of *The Horse Soldiers*, 1959) always stood by his side. SEE ALSO: Audie Murphy, Ronald Reagan.

Jock Gaynor
(1929–1998)
••••••••••••••••••••••••••••••••

This actor played "Deputy Marshal Heck Martin" on the first season (1960–1961) of NBC's *Outlaws*. SEE ALSO: Don Collier, Barton MacLane, Slim Pickens, Bruce Yarnell.

Gina Gillespie
(1951–)
••••••••••••••••••••••••••••••••

The younger sister of Mouseketeer Darlene Gillespie, who played in *Corky and White Shadow* (1956), Gina costarred as "Tess Wilkins," an orphaned child found and cared for by Indian marshal "Sam Buckhart" (Michael Ansara), on *Law of the Plainsman* (1959–1960). As in *The Rifleman* with Chuck Connors and Johnny Crawford (a show created by the same team), Gillespie and Ansara would have a heart-to-heart talk at the end of each episode, Buckhart

explaining that he did not *want* to kill all those people, but . . . Gillespie left showbiz and became a lawyer, unlike her sister, who left show business, became a criminal, and went to jail. SEE ALSO: Michael Ansara.

Jack Ging
(1931–)
••••••••••••••••••••••••••••••••

Ging's career began with *Ghost of Dragstrip Hollow* (1959), leaving him nowhere to go but up. During the final (1961–1962) season of *Tales of Wells Fargo,* in an hour-long expansion of NBC's early evening Saturday slot, he joined the cast as "Beau McCloud," handling most six-gun chores now that "Jim Hardie" (Dale Robertson) had settled down to ranch. After that came episodic TV: "Johnny O'Rourke" (alias Johnny Behind the Deuce) on *The Life and Legend of Wyatt Earp* (10/11/60) and Southern Civil War Commander John Singleton Mosby on *Willie and the Yank* (1967), a miniseries within Disney's Sunday anthology. SEE ALSO: Tod Andrews, Dale Robertson, Kurt Russell.

Danny Glover
(1946–)
••••••••••••••••••••••••••••••••

This gifted actor made his first major impression as lovable "Moze" in *Places in the Heart* (1984) and detestable "Albert" in *The Color Purple*

(1985), both important in establishing his remarkable acting range. Glover played the too-often-overlooked African American folk hero "John Henry" on TV in *Tall Tales and Legends* (1986), as well as "Malachi Johnson," a black cowboy, in Lawrence Kasdan's well-intentioned if overblown *Silverado* (1985). "Joshua Deets" proved his equality every day on the trail in the classic *Lonesome Dove* (2/5/89). Glover proved equally notable as "Sergeant Washington Wyatt" in *Buffalo Soldiers*, a made-for-Turner-TV Western (12/7/97) saluting men of color in the post–Civil War frontier army; Glover also executive-produced. SEE ALSO: Robert Duvall, Louis Gossett, Jr.

Mark Goddard

(1936–)

Goddard joined the *Johnny Ringo* cast in its second episode, "Cully" (10/8/59), titled after the nickname of his character "William Charles, Jr.," a young punk transformed into a dedicated deputy by the lead (Don Durant). He also played the dashing "Major Dan West" in *Lost in Space* (1965–1968) when, in the decade of the New Frontier, sci-fi pushed Westerns off the air. Soap opera credits include *One Life to Live* (1981) and *Doctors* (1982). Goddard left acting to teach students with behavioral problems and earned a master's degree in education. He is a relative of the

famed rocket scientist Robert Goddard. SEE ALSO: Don Durant, Karen Sharpe (Kramer).

Jacques Godin

(1930–)

This popular Canadian actor, veteran of countless movies/TV shows in that country, starred in a CBC show during the late 1950s that was simultaneously broadcast in the United States. Godin played Pierre Esprit Radisson (Paul Muni in the 1941 film *Hudson's Bay*) during his early years as a humble trapper who in time would become the fur industry's empire-builder. The series, called *Radisson* in Canada, was redubbed *Tomahawk* (to create a false sense that this would be an action show) in the United States. Kids tuned in expecting a video adaptation of the then-popular DC comic of that name. Instead, they discovered a somber series, the only TV Western (Eastern) to deal with daily details of pioneer life: the manner in which traps were set, difficulties involved in building canoes, sudden snowstorms, etc., rendered strikingly realistic owing to on-location shooting. Julien Bessette showed up several times as a hostile Indian, and Percy Rodrigues a friendly one. This show is often confused with *Hudson's Bay* (1959), which dealt with fictional (if accurately rendered) employees of Radisson's eventual mega-company. SEE ALSO: Barry Nelson.

Pedro Gonzalez-Gonzalez

(1925–2006)

∙∙∙∙∙∙∙∙∙∙∙∙∙∙∙∙∙∙∙∙∙∙∙∙∙∙∙∙∙∙∙∙∙

Pedro Gonzalez-Gonzalez played the short, sweet-spirited, simple-minded, smiling, silly, and often singing Latino sidekick to Anglo heroes, notably John Wayne in *Rio Bravo* (1959). On TV, he enjoyed a similar relationship to Barry Nelson on *Hudson's Bay* (1959), and as "Pedro Vasquez" with Rory Calhoun on *The Texan* (1959–1960). His broad caricature of the Hispanic stereotype caused him to be written off as the Mexican Stepin Fetchit once America entered the age of political correctness. SEE ALSO: Rory Calhoun, Barry Nelson.

Leo V. Gordon

(1922–2000)

∙∙∙∙∙∙∙∙∙∙∙∙∙∙∙∙∙∙∙∙∙∙∙∙∙∙∙∙∙∙∙∙∙∙

When Don Siegel filmed his ultra-realistic prison picture *Riot in Cell Block 11* (1954) in San Quentin, only one member of his cast had formerly been an inmate there: Leo Vincent Gordon. Large and beefy, with snake eyes, a mean mouth, and a disquieting voice, Gordon had no trouble finding work as movie/TV villains. Early on he played "Ed Lowe," husband to Geraldine Page, whom John Wayne must kill before he can marry her in *Hondo* (1953). Duke's fatal shot would be reemployed in the opening of *The Shootist* twenty-three years later. Gordon also

starred with Wayne in *McLintock!* (1963), as the only man Big John ever referred to as "pilgrim" other than James Stewart (in *The Man Who Shot Liberty Valance*, one year earlier). Gordon played Bill Doolin on *Stories of the Century* (6/10/54) and William Clarke Quantrill in *Quantrill's Raiders* (1958). He was introduced as "Big Mike McComb" in the first-ever episode of *Maverick*, "War of the Silver Kings" (9/22/57), later appearing in four others, including the series' best-ever episode, "According to Hoyle" (10/6/57), with Diane Brewster debuting as the seductively sneaky "Samantha Crawford." A prolific writer, Gordon penned scripts for low-budget horror (*The Wasp Woman*, 1960) and big-scale World Ware II epics (*Tobruk*, 1967). His final Western role came as a cameo as a card player in *Maverick* (1994). SEE ALSO: James Garner, Jack Kelly.

Louis Gossett, Jr.

(1936–)

∙∙∙∙∙∙∙∙∙∙∙∙∙∙∙∙∙∙∙∙∙∙∙∙∙∙∙∙∙∙∙∙∙∙

Gossett, who received a Best Supporting Actor Oscar for *An Officer and a Gentleman* (1982), found roles in many TV/film Westerns/historical pieces: "Isak Poole" in *Young Rebels* (1970–1971), playing a black hero of the Revolutionary War; *Skin Game* with James Garner (1971); "Black Bart" in a TV remake of *Blazing Saddles* (*Black Bart*, 4/4/75); "Fiddler" in *Roots* (1977); gunfighter "Van Leek" in *El Diablo* (7/22/90); and cowboy "Isom Pickett" (a combination of two real-life people, Isom Dart and Bill Pickett) in *Return to Lonesome Dove* (11/4/93).

Stewart Granger

(1913–1993)
••••••••••••••••••••••••••••••••••

This deliciously droll light comedy–drama performer from London boasted a Cary Grant–style panache though he never achieved that actor's status. Granger established an image in MGM swashbucklers *The Prisoner of Zenda* and the exquisite *Scaramouche* (which features the longest sword fight in film history) as always doing all his own stunt work. His finest performance came as pirate "Jeremy Fox" in Fritz Lang's *Moonfleet* (1955). Granger played in some Westerns, beginning with the minor-league *The Wild North* (1952), then it was on to the big time in Richard Brooks's powerful, grim, sadistic *The Last Hunt* (1956, Robert Taylor) and Henry Hathaway's irresistible knockabout comedy *North to Alaska* (1960, John Wayne). As studios shut down during the 1960s, he headed for Europe where he played German author Karl May's American scout "Old Surehand" in *Frontier Hellcat* (1964), a project typical of that era's Teutonic Westerns, with Elke Sommer in the title role and Pierre Brice as his Indian pal "Winnetou." Granger headed back to LA for *Men from*

Shiloh (1970–1971), a revamping of *The Virginian*, as "Colonel Alan MacKenzie," final owner of the title ranch and typical of British aristocrats who journeyed to the American West for capitalistic ventures. Born James Stewart, Granger changed his name after arriving in Hollywood to avoid confusion with the Western movie icon of that name. SEE ALSO: Charles Bickford, Lee J. Cobb, John McIntire.

Kirby Grant

(1911–1985)
••••••••••••••••••••••••••••••••••

In 1939 producer Jesse Lasky had a grand idea: create a radio-motored talent search called "Gateway to Hollywood." The winner was young Kirby Hoon, though after all the accolades were done and he had been renamed Grant, the young man found no film work. He opted for B Westerns, including *Singin' Spurs* (1948), which led to a Poverty Row film series as Royal Canadian Mountie "Ron Webb," beginning with *Call of the Klondike* (1950). Grant reached TV stardom in *Sky King* (1952–1959) as a rich, successful modern rancher who kept a twin-engine Cessna airplane, *Song Bird*, ever ready on his Arizona spread, the Flying Crown. Whenever villains showed up, King and his pretty niece "Penny" (Gloria Winters) flew off to corral the varmints. Kids ate it up and, when the series ended, Grant (who never again appeared on TV or in a film) parlayed his one memorable role (the series continued in syndicated reruns until the late 1960s) into a cottage industry as a rodeo-circuit celebrity. Eventually he left show business to become public relations director for Orlando's Sea World. Astronauts at Cape Canaveral learned that their flying cowboy hero lived nearby and wished to honor him. Delighted, Grant left work to drive downstate and accept an award. On the way, he was killed in a traffic accident. SEE ALSO: Gloria Winters.

Rodney A. Grant
(1959–   )
••••••••••••••••••••••••••••••

A member of the Omaha tribe, Grant was one of numerous Native Americans employed by Kevin Costner in his overrated *Dances with Wolves* (1990). Grant's role as "Wind in His Hair" earned him accolades and helped prove there were indeed gifted Native American actors. His next project, ironically, turned out to be the one Costner had originally hoped to do: Custer and Little Big Horn. In *Son of the Morning Star* (2/3/91), Grant played Chief Crazy Horse, the first full-blooded Native American to do so. He received little screen time as "Mangas Coloradas" in Walter Hill's so-so *Geronimo: An American Legend* (1993), then returned to TV as "Chingachgook" in *Hawkeye* (1994). Grant's youthful good looks suggested the way "Sagamore" might

have appeared in the earlier *Deer-slayer* adventure. More recently, Grant dropped out of acting to pursue family interests, accepting a position on the Board of Directors for the Boys and Girls Club of Cheyenne County, South Dakota. SEE ALSO: Lee Horsley.

Peter Graves
(1926–   )
••••••••••••••••••••••••••••••

Brother of James Arness, Graves was likewise tall and handsome, yet a smirking quality made him appear as weak inside as he was rugged on the surface in *War Paint* (1953, Robert Stack), *Canyon River* (1956, George Montgomery), and Billy Wilder's *Stalag 17* (1953), a classic World War II POW serio-comedy. He played Morgan Earp in *Wichita* (1955), in a rare role as a hero. In fall 1955, even as big brother Jim debuted on *Gunsmoke*, Peter won a series lead, though he initially feared it might ruin his career. *Fury* (1955–1960), titled after a magnificent stallion (played by Highland Dale), concerned twentieth-century ranch life. As "Jim Newton," Graves received top billing, but scripts favored the scene-stealing Bobby Diamond as son "Joey" and that incredible horse. Worse, what was supposed to be a primetime series got bumped to a Saturday morning juvenile slot. Graves took time off to act in the Erskine Caldwell–esque *Bayou* (1957); the distributor added steamy sex scenes, changed the title

to *Poor White Trash*, and then cir-
culated the film as a sleazy drive-in
item. Somehow, Graves's career survived all of this. He returned to TV
as "Christopher Cobb," an Australian
cowboy with a black bullwhip, in
Whiplash (1960–1961, syndication);
directed brother Jim in a memorable
Gunsmoke, "Which Dr." (3/19/66);
and starred as Daniel Boone in a two-
parter on *The Great Adventure*. "Kentucky's Bloody Ground" (4/3/64)
accurately chronicled the crossing
into Kan-Tuc-Kee, including the
death of young James Boone (Teddy
Eccles). "The Siege of Boonesborough" (4/10/64) depicted a ten-day
battle with the Shawnees. Graves
then guest-starred on the "Run a
Crooked Mile" (10/20/66) episode
of *Daniel Boone*, uniting Graves with
Fess Parker, two of TV's Boones
together. Playing "Gabe" in this episode was Arthur Hunnicutt, who had
portrayed Crockett, Parker's other
legendary role, in Republic's *The
Last Command* (1955). Two Crock-
etts, two Boones, all together for the
first and only time! Graves finally
achieved superstardom as secret agent
"Jim Phelps" on *Mission: Impossible*
(1967–1973; 1988–1990). He revived
his career in the eighties hit *Airplane!*,
revealing a previously untapped
gift for self-satire. He more recently
played "John 'The Colonel' Camden"
in *7th Heaven* (1997–2007). SEE ALSO:
James Arness, Arthur Hunnicutt, Fess
Parker.

Charles D. Gray
(19??–????)

Gray is yet another actor who disappeared in the mists of time. No record
exists as to his life before or after a
brief career. Veteran producer/direc-
tor Charles Marquis Warren took a
liking to this young newcomer and
awarded him a part in *Cattle Empire*
(1958). The following year, Warren
turned the film into the TV series
Rawhide, bringing most of the actors
along, but not Gray. Between 1959
and 1964, Gray was added to the cast
as "Clay Forrester," a shady drover.
Small roles in two important Westerns, *Wild Rovers* (1971) and *Junior
Bonner* (1972), followed. SEE ALSO:
Clint Eastwood, Eric Fleming, Sheb
Wooley.

Graham Greene
(1952–)

This Canadian-born member of the
Oneida tribe, an Indian rights activist
as well as actor, first attracted attention as "Kicking Bird" in *Dances with
Wolves* (1990). A grim countenance
served Greene well, leading to roles
in superior TV movies including the
title role of "Ishi" in *The Last of His
Tribe* (3/28/92) and the Peace Maker
in *The Broken Chain* (12/12/93).
Greene had continuing parts as
"Leonard Quinhagak" (*Northern
Exposure*, 1992–1993), "Red Hawk"

(*Lonesome Dove: The Series*, 1994), "Sherman Blackstone" (*Wolf Lake*, 2001–2002), and "Conquering Bear" (*Into the West*, 2005), all of which played off his dignified image. He served as the host of *Exhibit A: Secrets of Forensic Science* (1997–2001) and was recently acclaimed for his stage work at Shakespeare festivals.

Lorne Greene

(1915–1987)

This Canadian-born, classically trained actor (courtesy of Queen's University) had the bombastic, stentorian, resonant voice to prove it. As CBC's "Voice of Doom" during World War II, Greene became associated with bad news, sternly delivered. He was well cast in *Studio One*'s live version of George Orwell's *1984* as "Big Brother" (9/21/53). This led to cold, calculated characters in Westerns *The Hard Man* (1957, Guy Madison) and *The Last of the Fast Guns* (1958, Jock Mahoney); on TV, Greene embodied a no-nonsense cavalry officer in "Gold, Glory, and Custer" (1/4/60–1/11/60), an ambitious *Cheyenne* two-parter. His first series part came as "Captain Mitchell" on *Sailor of Fortune* (1955–1956). In films, he excelled as the heartless prosecuting attorney in *Peyton Place* (1957). *Bonanza* creator Fred Hamilton meanwhile envisioned an epic adult Western about a distant, aloof father with three alienated

sons. Having seen Greene's previous work, Hamilton grasped that Greene was perfect. "Ben Cartwright" in the first two seasons (Saturday evenings) did appear as gruff. When the show switched to Sundays, becoming family-friendly, all the characters were re-imagined, with Ben now jovial and heartwarming in the number-one TV Western of the decade. Greene also cut a popular record, "Ringo," in the mid-sixties, a talking ballad about that legendary gunfighter. Following *Bonanza*, he was the narrator of the fine *Appointment with Destiny* (an updated *You Are There*) installment (1972–1973), "Showdown at O.K. Corral." *Griff* (1973) flopped, but Greene returned on *Battlestar Galactica* (1978–1979) as "Commander Adama." His final TV role came as a laconic, cynical, uninterested Sam Houston in *The Alamo: Thirteen Days to Glory* (1/26/87). Greene was in the process of planning a new *Bonanza* series (he would play Ben as an older man) at the time of his passing. SEE ALSO: Dan Blocker, Michael Landon, Pernell Roberts.

Michael Greene

(19??–????)

This nondescript leading man played "Deputy Vance Porter" on *The Dakotas* (1963), with Larry Ward, Jack Elam, and Chad Everett. SEE ALSO: Jack Elam, Chad Everett, Larry Ward.

Tom Greene

(19??–)

••••••••••••••••••••••••••••••••••

A child actor turned successful producer and writer, Greene created and starred (as "Heywood Floyd") in the short-lived (six episodes) *Wildside* (1985), about vigilantes ridding a town of outlaws. The cast included William Smith as "Brodie"; J. Eddie Peck as "Sutton Hollister"; Howard Rollins, Jr., as "Bannister Sparks"; and a young Meg Ryan as the prettiest girl around. SEE ALSO: William Smith.

Roosevelt Grier

(1932–)

••••••••••••••••••••••••••••••••••

Los Angeles Rams footballer Grier helped to disarm Sirhan Sirhan following the assassination of Robert F. Kennedy (6/6/68). He joined the *Daniel Boone* cast for the final season (1969–1970) as "Gabe Cooper," a big, burly, sweet-spirited runaway slave who finds solace—and equality!—in Boonesborough. SEE ALSO: Fess Parker.

James Griffith

(1916–1993)

••••••••••••••••••••••••••••••••••

This shamefully underrated character actor in Westerns, modern dramas, and comedies could play the harmless town drunk one week and a cold-blooded killer the next. His endless credits range from one-liners to strong supporting roles, including real-life good guys and badmen: William Quantrell (*Fighting Man of the Plains*, 1949), the Apache Kid (*Indian Territory*, 1950), Pat Garrett (*The Law vs. Billy the Kid*, 1954), Bob Dalton (*Jesse James vs. the Daltons*, 1954), Doc Holliday (*Masterson of Kansas*, 1954; and *Buffalo Bill, Jr.*, 4/18/55), Davy Crockett (*First Texan*, 1956), and John Wesley Hardin (*Maverick*, 2/1/59). Griffith played Abraham Lincoln numerous times: in *Stage to Tucson* (voice only, 1950), *Cavalcade of America* (2/4/53), *Apache Ambush* (1955), and as a Lincoln lookalike on *The Lone Ranger* (2/7/57). He assumed regular roles as the suavely shifty "Aaron Adams" on *Trackdown* (1957–1958) and "Deputy Tom Ferguson" on *U.S. Marshal* (1959–1960). His last significant part was as "Coll," the Stan Laurel half of a cryptic comedy team (his Oliver Hardy, Laurie Main as "Stinch") during *Daniel Boone*'s 1966–1967 season. SEE ALSO: John Bromfield, Robert Culp, Fess Parker.

Gary Grubbs

(1949–)

••••••••••••••••••••••••••••••••••

Grubbs played the guitar-strummin' Georgie Russell in several disastrous *Davy Crockett* made-for-TV films between 1988 and 1989. He later played "Harlin Polk" on *Will & Grace*

(1998–1999) and "Bullit" on *The O.C.* (2006–2007). SEE ALSO: Tim Dunigan, Buddy Ebsen.

Clu Gulager

(1928–)

••••••••••••••••••••••••••••••

This Oklahoma-born relative of Will Rogers picked up the nickname Clu as a kid after his pet clu-clu bird. He served in the U.S. Marines during the postwar era, then headed for Paris to join an experimental theater group before going to Hollywood. Gulager performed in live TV dramas (*U.S. Steel Hour*, *Studio One*, etc.) during the mid- to late 1950s and on episodic TV afterward. His star-making performance as Vincent "Mad Dog" Coll on *The Untouchables* (11/19/59) caused people to take notice of this eccentric/exciting actor who combined the qualities of Nick Adams and Vic Morrow with a menacing redneck undercurrent. Gulager seemed a natural for William H. Bonney in *The Tall Man* (1960–1961), with Barry Sullivan as Sheriff Pat Garrett. Next came the role of "Emmet Ryker" during *The Virginian*'s middle period (1964–1968) as a not-quite-evil badman who redeems himself by pinning on a deputy's badge. Nearly endless TV/film credits included one more series, *The Survivors* (1969), a flop despite Lana Turner and George Hamilton receiving top billing in this glossy soaper. His most intriguing movie roles were as

"Abilene," a modern-day tight-lipped cowboy in Peter Bogdanovich's *The Last Picture Show* (1971), from the Larry McMurtry novel, and as one of two title characters (the other Lee Marvin) in *The Killers* (1964), a Don Siegel actioner originally intended by Universal as the first-ever made-for-TV movie. When results proved too violent for NBC, the film (also known as *Johnny North*) instead received a theatrical release. SEE ALSO: James Drury, Doug McClure, Barry Sullivan.

Moses Gunn

(1929–1993)

••••••••••••••••••••••••••••••••

Cofounder (in the mid-sixties) of the Negro Ensemble Company, Gunn was also the sometime star of innovative director Joseph Papp's Shakespeare productions with African American casts. Film roles (*The Great White Hope*, 1970; *Shaft*, 1971) led to casting as the cook "Jebediah Nightlinger" in a short-lived 1974 series, *The Cowboys*, based on a theatrical film about a rancher (John Wayne) forced to employ boys ages twelve to fifteen for a hazardous cattle drive. Roscoe Lee Browne played Jeb in the film, assuming command when Wayne's character died. The show opened after the youths returned to New Mexico, with Diana Douglas as "Widow Andersen" (Allyn Ann McLerie in the film) protecting her ranch with the help of the local marshal (Jim Davis), the title characters, and Jeb. On TV, the cowboys were A. Martinez ("Cimarron"), Robert Carradine ("Slim"), Sean Kelly ("Jimmy"), Kerry MacLane ("Homer"), Clint Howard ("Steve"), Mitch Brown ("Hardy"), and Clay O'Brien ("Weedy"). Martinez and Carradine repeated their film roles; Kelly and O'Brien from the film were recast as different youths. Gunn later played "Kintango" in *Roots* and "Carl Dixon" on *Good Times*, both in 1977. As traditional oaters gave way to farm-oriented family drama, Gunn portrayed "Joe Kagen" (*Little House on the Prairie*, 1977–1981) and "Moses Gage" (*Father Murphy*, 1981–1983), both for producer Michael Landon. SEE ALSO: Keith Carradine, Jim Davis, Clint Howard, Michael Landon, A. Martinez.

Merle Haggard

(1937–)

This blue-collar redneck (and *damn proud of it*) country singer had grassroots politics that were hard to pin down: "Working Man Blues" sounded like Steinbeckian liberalism, though "The Fightin' Side of Me" attacked longhairs and defended Nixon. Haggard harbors a lifetime love for Westerns: He performed the title song for *Chisum* (1970) with John Wayne, hosted *Death Valley Days* (1975), and played the rough-hewn "Cisco Calendar" in *Centennial* (1978).

Dan Haggerty

(1941–)

Haggerty's lifestyle provided his inroad to the movie business. A bodybuilder by the sea, he was cast as precisely that in *Muscle Beach Party* (1964). A motorcycle enthusiast, he

built the choppers for *Easy Rider* (1969) and played a longhair. Likewise, Haggerty's love for and interest in animals caused him to be picked up for the indie film *When the North Wind Blows* (1974), a huge hit in rural areas where townsfolk despised the era's "new cinema" (*Midnight Cowboy, Taxi Driver*, etc.). Producer Charles E. Sellier, Jr., spotted Haggerty and cast him in *The Adventures of Frontier Fremont* (1976), the first of the Sunn Classic Pictures to alter history and transform mountain men from despoilers of the Rockies to protectors of nature. In an age when John Denver records sold big-time ("Rocky Mountain High"), the public, hungry for a Western hero but having OD'd on cowboys (for the time being, at least), bought it. The bigger and better follow-up was *The Life and Times of Grizzly Adams* (1974). In it James Capen Adams, accused of a crime he did not commit (at least not in the movie), runs off to the mountains and raises a beloved bear cub, Ben (a reference to *Gentle Ben*?). The movie spawned an intensely popular if short-lived TV series of the same name (1977–1978), with Don Shanks on board as Indian pal "Nakoma" and Denver Pyle as "Mad Jack." Haggerty revived Grizzly for *Once Upon a Starry Night* (1978), *Legend of the Wild* (1981), and a made-for-TV movie, *Capture of Grizzly Adams* (2/21/82), here turning himself in to authorities in hopes of keeping daughter "Peg" (Sydney Penny) out of an orphanage. Pop-culture claim to fame: Haggerty was the only actor to have his name slab *removed* from Hollywood Boulevard! It was to have been for actor *Don* Haggerty. Today both men are represented by their immortalized names. SEE ALSO: Don Haggerty, Denver Pyle.

Don Haggerty
(1914–1988)
••••••••••••••••••••••••••••••

A reliable TV/B Western character actor, Haggerty excelled at playing seemingly respectable lawmen or ranchers who turn out to be crooked. These included train robber Sam Bass in the 3/4/54 *Stories of the Century*, and "Marsh Murdock," the Wichita mayor who under false pretenses talks Wyatt into leaving Ellsworth and taking a job in Marsh's town during the second half of *The Life*

and *Legend of Wyatt Earp*'s first season (1955–1956) on the air. He later played cowhand "Wes" on *Texas John Slaughter* (1960–1961). SEE ALSO: Dan Haggerty, Hugh O'Brian, Tom Tryon.

Alan Hale (Jr.)
(1921–1990)
••••••••••••••••••••••••••••••

Alan Jr. (he dropped that distinction following his dad's death in 1950) enjoyed a character-actor career as varied as his father's. A big, genial, and easygoing guy (often the rugged but sentimental sidekick to the hero) in everything *but* Westerns, Gene Autry convinced Hale to give them a try; Autry cast him in two singin' cowboy flicks, *Rim of the Canyon* and *Riders in the Sky*, both in 1949. Hale played the older brother of Richard Jaeckel (killed in the opening scene) who tracks Ringo (Gregory Peck) in the seminal *The Gunfighter* (1950). Back in the Autry stable, he played in two dozen guest spots on Autry-produced shows—*The Range Rider, Annie Oakley*, etc.—between 1950 and 1954. He played the big buddy to Audie Murphy (*Destry*, 1954) and Kirk Douglas (*The Indian Fighter*, 1955). Real-life Westerners included Johnny (Behind the) Deuce on *Adventures of Wild Bill Hickok* (7/1/51), the Sundance Kid in *The Three Outlaws* (1956, with Neville Brand as Butch Cassidy), Cole Younger in *The True Story of Jesse James* (1957), Sam Bass on *Colt .45* (5/17/59), and the historical frontier engineer on *Casey Jones* (1957–1958), a kiddie Western featuring a young Bobby Clark as "Casey Jr." Hale wore a railroading costume with a holstered brace of Colt .45s. His other series included the lowbrow actioner *Biff Baker, U.S.A.* (1952–1954), and of course "The Skipper" on *Gilligan's Island* (1964–1967). Hale had a recurring role as the easygoing gunfighter "Sculley" on *The Texan* (1958–1960). His most popular film role was as Porthos, one of the Three Musketeers, in *At Sword's Point* and *Lady in the Iron Mask* (both 1952) and as an older man in *The Fifth Musketeer* (1979). Utterly unpretentious, Hale owned the LA restaurant Lobster Barrel. When not off on acting assignments, he greeted his delighted customers at the door dressed in his "Skipper" outfit! SEE ALSO: Gene Autry, Neville Brand, Rory Calhoun, Bob Denver, Richard Jaeckel, Audie Murphy, Dub Taylor.

Ty Hardin

(1930–)

••••••••••••••••••••••••••••••

Texas-raised Orrison Whipple Hungerford, Jr., won the nickname Ty as a kid since everyone considered him a typhoon of energy. He rates as the least talented of all TV Western stars and, after a brief run in that capacity, had the most embarrassing personal history afterward. He showed up

briefly as a lazy cowboy in *Last Train from Gun Hill* (1959, Kirk Douglas). Under contract to Warner Bros., Hardin became the nominal lead in *Cheyenne* during the 1958–1959 season when Clint Walker walked over a salary dispute. In a bizarre move, the show continued under its original name, with Hardin (his stage name derived from famed gunfighter John Wesley Hardin) as "Bronco Layne," with no explanation as to why a series titled for one cowboy now focused on another. When Walker returned in 1959, *Cheyenne* shifted to Mondays, with the cocky Hardin continuing in the Tuesday slot, the biweekly opus now more appropriately titled *Bronco*, alternating with *Sugarfoot*. Hardin also played Bronco on *Sugarfoot* ("Angel," 3/6/61) and *Maverick* ("Hadley's Hunters," 9/25/60) before *Bronco* and *Sugarfoot* were both absorbed into the early Monday evening slot, the title now changed to *The Cheyenne Show*. After cancellation in 1963, Hardin did some film work, notably (his most believable performance) as a cold-blooded Nazi in *Battle of the Bulge* (1965, Henry Fonda) and an equally mean character in the Argentinean B+ Western *Savage Pampas* (1966, Robert Taylor). Several ultra-cheap European-lensed Westerns followed, plus one historical character, Major Marcus Reno, in *Custer of the West* (1968). Hardin returned to the United States, gave up acting, and became an evangelical preacher in

Arizona. Even as most such religious leaders labored at creating ever better relations between all Christians and Jews, Hardin assumed a hard-line divisive approach, spreading vitriolic anti-Semitism and excluding Catholics as "impure" Christians. Actors who worked with him in the old days confided that the easygoing Bronco was less the true Hardin than the fascist he had played in *Bulge*. The great irony: Hardin idolized Elvis Presley, blissfully unaware that the King was part Jewish, part Catholic. Hardin then formed the Arizona Patriots, an extremist group that stockpiled weapons for what they believed to be a coming war with the American military. He engaged in vicious baiting of public officials, local and national, qualifying as an equal-opportunity hater: Conservatives and liberals, Republicans and Democrats, Bush and Clinton were all perceived as evil in Hardin's eyes. He defied the IRS and founded the anti-tax group Common Law Institute. He and his crew were perceived as so dangerous (with a potential to bomb federal buildings) that the government deemed it necessary to raid Hardin's patriot camp, confiscating an immense load of weapons from that Aryan Nation base. Hardin then fled to Washington State. He was the only living TV cowboy star *not* invited to appear in *The Gambler Returns: Luck of the Draw*. SEE ALSO: Will Hutchins, Kenny Rogers, Clint Walker.

Rosemary Harris

(1927–)

A superb stage and golden-age TV actress, Harris won occasional movie roles (*The Boys from Brazil*, 1978; *Tom & Viv*, 1994) and rare appearances in upscale TV films (*Holocaust*, 1978; *Death of a Salesman*, 1996). Her contribution to the Western genre came as "Minerva" on *The Chisholms* (miniseries, 1979–1980; weekly series, 1980–1981), less a formula Western than a large-scale family saga set on the 1840s frontier. Her give-and-take with Robert Preston, who did *not* play a "Ben Cartwright" ideal any more than she played a "Victoria Barkley" supermom, allowed this one a sharp realistic edge. SEE ALSO: Robert Preston.

John Hart

(1917–)

This athletic young man's ability to perform stunts helped him, like lookalike Jock Mahoney, win roles in low-budget projects, where he performed double-duty. Though he played mostly bits in Poverty Row items, Hart did get to play the lead in one serial, *Jack Armstrong* (1947). When Clayton Moore left ABC's most popular series, *The Lone Ranger* (1952–1954), Hart became John Reid's masked alter-ego, with

Jay Silverheels still playing "Tonto." Dumped when Moore came back, Hart forever after referred to himself as "the 'other' Lone Ranger." Low-budget filmmakers turned TV mavens Sam and Sig Newfield decided on an adaptation of the public-domain *Leatherstocking* saga. *Hawkeye and the Last of the Mohicans (1957)*, a syndicated "Eastern," earned high ratings on indie stations with Hart as the scout. The show was derived less from the Cooper book than from a B-movie adaptation, *The Iroquois Trail* (1950, George Montgomery), a loose interpretation in which "Natty Bumppo" became "Nat Culver," true for the series as well. To save money, the show was shot in Canada; however unintentionally, this added to the realism. During outdoor winter scenes, viewers could watch the characters breathing in the freezing air. Hart later played cowhand "Narbo" on *Rawhide* (1961–1962). He revived the "Lone Ranger," first on *The Greatest American Hero* ("My Heroes Have Always Been Cowboys," 4/29/81), then on *Happy Days* ("Hi Yo, Fonzie Away," 2/9/82). The always agreeable Hart played one of six Texas Rangers bushwhacked by the Cavendish gang in *The Legend of the Lone Ranger* (1981); Moore passed on the offer. SEE ALSO: Lon Chaney, Jr.; Clayton Moore; Jay Silverheels.

David Hartman

(1935–)

Hartman came across as a goofy-looking leading man, thanks to a toothsome grin. His first series role was on *The Virginian* (1967–1969) as "George Foster," a quiet, thoughtful newcomer to the Shiloh Ranch, which provided quite a contrast to the rowdy cowboys. Hartman seemed more at home in contemporary guises: doctor (*The Bold Ones: The New Doctors*, 1969–1970), teacher (*Lucas Tanner*, 1974–1975), and host of ABC's *Good Morning America* (1975–1987). SEE ALSO: James Drury, Stewart Granger, Doug McClure.

John Hawkes

(1959–)

Hawkes left rural Minnesota to hitchhike around the country, becoming part of a band (King Straggler) and winning plum roles in films: with George Clooney in *The Perfect Storm* (2000) and Keanu Reeves in *Hard Ball* (2001). David Milch, *Deadwood*'s (2005–2006) creator, considered Hawkes precisely right for Jewish pioneer Sol Star though the actor is not Jewish. Nonetheless, he was well cast as a man who wants only to succeed at merchandising but finds himself drawn into violent action due to his friendship/partnership with Sheriff Seth Bullock (Timothy Olyphant). Social significance: This qualifies as the first time a major character in *any* TV Western series had been identified as a member of that minority group. SEE ALSO: Ian McShane, Timothy Olyphant, Molly Parker.

Jimmy Hawkins

(1941–)

••••••••••••••••••••••••••••••

This talented child actor stepped in front of the cameras for the first time at age three and enjoyed success for a decade and a half. He played "Tommy Bailey," James Stewart's freckle-faced son in Frank Capra's Christmas classic *It's a Wonderful Life* (1946), and spoke for the first time onscreen in another (notably different) Stewart vehicle, Anthony Mann's *Winchester '73* (1950). Producer Gene Autry cast Hawkins as "Tagg," the fictional freckle-faced little brother to Gail Davis on *Annie Oakley* (1954–1957). The character proved a perfect ploy to engage little boys who might not otherwise have been interested in a show focusing on a woman, Tagg serving as an audience surrogate for this aspect of the home audience. Afterward he played "Scotty," frequent date of Shelley Fabares's teenage heroine on *The Donna Reed Show*. The mischievous-looking redhead starred in the pilot for an *Andy Hardy* TV series, well cast in Mickey Rooney's old role, but NBC did not pick it up. He later produced several specials

and made-for-TV movies. Hawkins is often confused with Jimmy Boyd, a lookalike child star who had a hit record with "I Saw Mommy Kissing Santa Claus." SEE ALSO: Gene Autry, Gail Davis, Brad Johnson.

Russell "Lucky" Hayden

(1912–1981)

••••••••••••••••••••••••••••••

Born Pate Lucid, Hayden won the role of "Lucky Jenkins," handsome young ladies' man sidekick to the mature "Hopalong Cassidy" in *Hills of Old Wyoming* (1937). He played the part in over thirty Bill Boyd films, concluding with *Wide Open Town* (1941). Sick of being a second fiddle, Hayden broke away and starred in his own low-budget "Lucky" series (Rand Brooks replaced him in the *Cassidy* saga). In each movie, Lucky had a different last name: "Haines," "Chandler," "Bannon," "Dawson," "Lawson," and "Lawrence" among them. He starred in one early TV show, *The Marshal of Gunsight Pass* (1950). Unhappy with its direction, Hayden dropped out, soon to be replaced by Eddie Dean. Hayden wanted to produce, and did so with three series, first starring as "Pat Gallagher" in *Cowboy G-Men* (1952), with Jackie Coogan his pal "Stoney Crockett." In partnership with fellow cowboy actor Dick Curtis, Hayden built one of the most authentic of all California-based Western sets, Pioneertown, and shot his next show,

Judge Roy Bean (1956), there, occasionally appearing as Texas Ranger "Steve Allison." Hayden saved money as a producer by not having to pay (or more accurately, paying himself) one actor's salary and for use of the location. This held true with *26 Men* (1957–1959), the most memorable among his series. He later filmed a half-hour pilot called *30 Minutes at Gunsight* (1963), with Marty Robbins as the town overseer, Hayden a genial drifter, and music by the Sons of the Pioneers. With the era of TV Westerns then fast fading, this one did not sell. Shortly thereafter, Hayden retired. SEE ALSO: Edgar Buchanan, Jack Buetel.

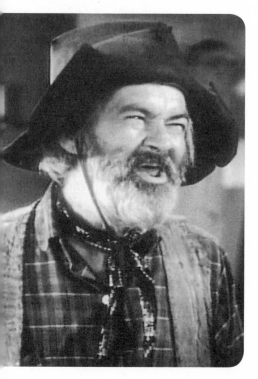

George "Gabby" Hayes

(1885–1969)

This native of upstate New York literally ran away from home to join a circus, then switched to a traveling troupe of actors before landing in vaudeville. Hayes believed he would prosper on the Broadway stage, but his entire life savings was lost in the 1929 stock-market crash. To reboot his career, Hayes headed for Los Angeles and the lucrative movie business. After winning small character roles in several *Hopalong Cassidy*s, he became Bill Boyd's regular sidekick, "Windy." When letters poured in indicating that Hayes rated as big (perhaps bigger) a draw as the top-billed star, he demanded a salary increase. When turned down, Hayes walked. Legally prohibited from using "Windy" (actually, he did so one final time, in *The Untamed Breed*, 1948), he instead went by the sobriquets "Pop," "Soupy," "Grizzly," "Flash," "Pesky," "Wildcat," "Dusty," "Judge," "Drag," "Shanghai," "Grandpaw," "Chuck," "Slack," and even "Dude" before settling on "Gabby," borrowed from an annoying animated character in the Fleischer

THE WORLD'S GREATEST SIDEKICK: Gabby Hayes played second fiddle to more movie cowboys than any other actor. TV allowed him top billing for the first time on two popular series. Courtesy George Hayes estate.

Bros.' animated *Gulliver's Travels* (1939). Hayes provided comic relief to more B-movie heroes than any other sidekick: Roy Rogers, Gene Autry, William Elliott, Bob Steele, Randolph Scott, and John Wayne. Between 1950 and 1954, he served as the live host of *The Gabby Hayes Show*—fifteen minutes, five days a week. Here he serialized B Westerns and told tall tales. The closing bit, still warmly recalled today by those who were young at the time, stands as an early TV example of deconstruction. Hayes loaded a cannon with oats or wheat, pointed it at the camera, warned kids to step back from their TV sets, and fired away (germs of grain hurled at the onlooker's screen) to prove that Quaker cereals really were "shot from guns." In 1956, he returned with a new format (the title remained the same) for thirteen weeks, hosting edited PRC films starring Lash La Rue, Eddie Dean, Tex Ritter, and Buster Crabbe. Hayes had not appeared in any of them, the sidekick role mostly portrayed by Al "Fuzzy" St. John. SEE ALSO: Gene Autry, Roy Rogers.

Ron Hayes

(1929–2004)

A veteran of 1950s Warner Bros. Westerns—*Cheyenne*, *Bronco*, *Maverick*, *Colt .45*, etc.—Hayes never did get one of his own, so he left ABC

to play Wyatt Earp on NBC's *Bat Masterson*. On *The Life and Legend of Wyatt Earp*, the title character had no mustache but second-lead Bat did; on *Masterson*, that situation would be reversed, Wyatt now sporting a mustache. The *Earp* show took place mostly in the mid-1870s; *Masterson* was set a decade later. On *Earp*, the title character appeared as a youthful man, the second lead a teenager; *Masterson*'s title character appeared early-middle-aged, the second lead an older man. Hayes later starred in *Everglades* (1961–1962) as "Lincoln Vail," a modern marshal patrolling the Florida swamps. He then appeared in the Disney miniseries *Gallegher Goes West* (1967); as "Dr. Phil Brewer" on *General Hospital* (late 1960s); as "Garth Holden" on *Lassie* (1971–1972); and as "Hank Johnson" on *Dallas* (1980–1981). SEE ALSO: Gene Barry, Alan Dinehart, Hugh O'Brian.

Myron Healey

(1923–2005)

This tall, rugged performer mostly played villains and took on multiple bad-guy roles in kiddie-oriented oaters (*Annie Oakley*, *The Gene Autry Show*, etc.) during the 1950s. He later showed up on virtually every adult Western (*Wagon Train*, *Bonanza*, etc.). His specialty in trade was a laconic, cynical fellow, often a sheriff who made a strongly positive first impression only to turn out crooked. Healey played outlaw Bob Dalton on "The Dalton Gang" episode of *Stories of the Century* (3/18/54); another historical figure, Dick Broadwell, involved in the Coffeyville raid in "The End of the Dalton Gang" (*You Are There*, 5/12/57); Doc Holliday on *The Life and Legend of Wyatt Earp* in 1958–1959 when Douglas V. Fowley, who ordinarily played the part, left to fulfill a movie commitment. Then Healey headed for Disney, where he enjoyed one of his few heroic roles as "Peter," second-in-command to Colonel Francis Marion (Leslie Nielsen) on *The Swamp Fox* (1959–1961). He also penned a pair of B theatrical films, *Texas Lawmen* and *Colorado Ambush* (both 1951). SEE ALSO: Jim Davis, Douglas V. Fowley, Leslie Nielsen.

Kelo Henderson

(1923–)

Born Paul Henderson, this lumbering giant had little experience when he was hired to play the fictional ranger "Clint Travis" on *26 Men* (1957–1958), a syndicated show about understaffed Arizona Rangers circa 1900. He looked a great deal like Clint Walker but possessed none of that performer's charisma. Henderson's only other credit was in the low-budget spaghetti Western *Mercenaries of the Rio Grande* (1965). SEE ALSO: Tristram Coffin.

Robert "Buzz" Henry

(1931–1971)

A Colorado-born rope rider, Henry's nickname derived from half a dozen juvenile Westerns he starred in as a child, including *Buzzy Rides the Range* (1940). As a young adult, the professional stuntman often won small roles in big Westerns: *Rocky Mountain* (1950, Errol Flynn), *Jubal* (1956, Glenn Ford), and *Waterhole #3* (1967, James Coburn), doubling for those stars during "gags." For Disney, he played the outlaw "Durango Dude" in *Corky and White Shadow* (1956) and Seventh Cavalryman Lieutenant Crittenden (*Tonka*, 1958). Henry died in a freak motorcycle accident shortly after his fortieth birthday. SEE ALSO: Chuck Courtney, Buddy Ebsen.

Barbara Hershey

(1948–)

Born Barbara Herzstein in a non-gentrified area of Hollywood, this withdrawn child escaped into the world of acting. Hershey played Sally Field's friend "Ellen" on *Gidget* (1965–1966) and the lead as "Kathy" on *The Monroes* (1966–1967), an important if short-lived nouveau oater with a female central character, an orphaned teen trying to hold her siblings together on the hostile frontier. Michael Anderson, Jr., appeared as her brother "Clayt," Keith and

Kevin Schultz the cute twins "Jefferson" and "Fennimore," Tammy Locke "Little Amy," and Ron Soble the scruffy half-breed "Dirty Jim." Filming took place in Jackson Hole, Wyoming, for authenticity; stories posited land barons as menacing to anachronistic flower-power young people. Hershey later played "Moonfire," the Native American woman in "The Peacemaker," a memorable episode of *The High Chaparral* (3/3/68) about race relations. She performed a semi-regular role on *Kung Fu* (1974) as the Asian "Nan Chi" while in a relationship with star David Carradine, calling herself "Seagull" at the time in memory of the dead bird in the teen film *Last Summer* (1969). Hershey's only other theatrical Western was *The Last Hard Men* (1976) with Charlton Heston and James Coburn. Her many other big movies include *The Stunt Man* (1980), *The Right Stuff* (1983), *The Natural* (1984), and *Beaches* (1988). She returned to the TV Western as "Clara Allen" in *Return to Lonesome Dove* (11/14/93). SEE ALSO: Michael Anderson, Jr.; David Carradine; Ben Johnson.

Charlton Heston

(1923–2008)

The granite-jawed movie legend proved particularly effective as larger-than-life figures, notably with biblical trappings: Moses in *The Ten Commandments* (1956) and the title character in *Ben-Hur* (1959), the latter his Oscar-winning Best Actor nod. He appeared equally at home in Westerns, some memorable: *The Big Country* (1958), with friend Gregory Peck, and *Will Penny* (1968), one of the finest portraits of an American cowboy ever captured on film. Heston also played Andrew Jackson in *The President's Lady* (1953) and *Buccaneer* (1958), Bill Cody in *Pony Express* (1953), plus a thinly disguised Al Seiber in *Arrowhead* (1953), William Clark in *The Far Horizons* (1955), and Henry Hooker in *Tombstone* (1993). One of the few big-time stars who felt comfortable doing quality TV, Heston made a TV-cowboy appearance in the *Schlitz Playhouse of Stars* Western "Switch Station" (5/17/57). He later narrated the TV epic *Texas* (4/16/95), based on a James Michener novel.

Darryl Hickman

(1931–   )

A child actor, Hickman appeared in such classics as *The Grapes of Wrath* (1940) and *Leave Her to Heaven* (1945). He played the older brother of his own younger brother Dwayne on the contemporary comedy *The Many Loves of Dobie Gillis* (1959–1960) and the troubled navy cadet "Dusty Rhodes" (*Men of Annapolis*, 1957–1958). For his first

Western role, on *Texas John Slaughter* (1959–1960), Hickman played "Ashley Carstairs" from Kentucky. Initially the youth idolizes Big John (Tom Tryon), then turns nasty, hoping to become a fast gun, and has to be put in his place by the former mentor. Hickman next starred in *The Americans* (1961), an ambitious Civil War drama about two brothers, "Jeff" (Richard Davalos) and "Ben" (Hickman) Canfield, who fight for the South and North, respectively. Scripts (mostly set in the West) focused on one or the other brother, sometimes both. Hickman's journeyman acting career in time gave way to behind-the-scenes work in production and as an acting coach. SEE ALSO: Richard Davalos, Tom Tryon.

Joel Higgins

(1943–)

Higgins starred in the easygoing, short-lived, low-key comedy oater *Best of the West* (1981–1982) as "Sam Best," a pilgrim who travels to Copper Creek with wife "Elvira" (Carlene Watkins) and son "Daniel" (Meeno Peluce), only to have the marshal's star forced upon him. He proved good at the job, *Destry*-like, to the chagrin of town boss "Tillman" (Leonard Frey) and hulking henchman "Frog" (Tracey Walter). He fared better as "Edward Stratton III" on the hit sitcom *Silver Spoons* (1982–1987).

Terence Hill

(1939–)

Born in Venice to an Italian father and a German mother, Hill abandoned university studies to pursue a film career. He often teamed with Bud Spencer in low-grade spaghetti Westerns as "Trinity" and "Cat Stevens." Hill appeared in one important film: the Sergio Leone-produced *My Name Is Nobody* (1973). Any hopes for Hollywood stardom dimmed when *Mr. Billion* (1977) flopped. He eventually played the lead in and directed *Lucky Luke* (1991), a live-action adaptation of the immensely popular European comic book/cartoon. Hill did a TV series two years later with Ron Carey playing his archenemy "Joe Dalton." He earned a large following on the continent, but the *Luke* concept, like Hill himself, failed to work in translation.

Darby Hinton

(1957–)

Several years before this child actor won the role of young Israel on *Daniel Boone*, his father, Ed, died in a plane crash. The tousle-haired boy bonded with TV father Fess Parker. When the series finished its six-year run, that relationship did not end, for Parker faithfully remained a mentor to Hinton as the boy grew to manhood. Some of that maturation took place on TV; in one episode, "The Ordeal of Israel Boone" (9/21/67), young Hinton played the leading role. In the last episode, "Israel and Love" (5/70/70), home viewers watched as the little boy they had come to love grew up. Hinton developed an interest in martial arts, his skills on display in later features *Firecracker* (1981) and *Malibu Express* (1985). SEE ALSO: Patricia Blair, Fess Parker.

Pat Hogan

(1920–1966)

Hogan specialized in playing brutal, nasty Native Americans, beginning with Yellow Hand in *Pony Express* (1953), in which he engaged in a memorable fight to the death with Charlton Heston as Cody. Hogan played Neche in "Geronimo" on *Stories of the Century* (with Chief Yowlachie in the title role; 2/14/54) and the lead in "Cherokee Bill" (2/1/55) on the same series. He also starred as Dull Knife in *Chief Crazy Horse* (1955) and the rare sympathetic Indian "Mungo" in Anthony Mann's underrated *The Last Frontier* that same year. As "Chief Red Stick" of the Creek/Choctaws on *Davy Crockett* (TV, 1954; film, 1955), he had another memorable fight (though not to the death), with Fess Parker. Hogan won semi-regular roles as "Black Cloud" (*Brave Eagle*, 1955–1956), Victorio (*Broken Arrow*, 1957), and Geronimo (*Texas John Slaughter*,

1960–1961). He was reunited with Parker for "The Returning" (1/14/65) on *Daniel Boone*. His final film role before his premature passing was in *Indian Paint* (1965). SEE ALSO: Keith Larsen, Fess Parker, Chief Yowlachie.

Earl Holliman

(1928–)

The consummate good ol' boy, this Louisiana native could play either nice kids like deputy Charlie Bassett in *Gunfight at the O.K. Corral* (1957) or bad ones (*Last Train from Gun Hill*, 1959), both John Sturges Westerns starring Kirk Douglas. On TV, Holliman performed one of each. In the inventive series *Hotel de Paree* (1959–1960), he played the Sundance Kid, just released from five years in jail for killing a man in Georgetown, Colorado. Sundance returns to the scene of the crime with plans of terrifying the victim's widow (Jeanette Nolan) and daughter (Judi Meredith). Instead, he takes a job at their establishment (there *is* a Hotel de Paree in Georgetown), by implication romancing each when not spending time with his pet lhasa apso, Useless, or using silver dollars, arranged in a band on his black hat, to blind opposing gunfighters before shooting them down. Ratings were so-so; CBS considered dropping the supporting cast so Holliman could return the following season as a more typical wanderer in *The Sundance Kid*, then scrapped the project. In 1962–1963, he returned as "Mitch Guthrie," a modern rodeo rider traveling the circuit with young brother Andy (Andrew Prine) in *The Wide Country*. The show's leisurely tone did not click; it was canceled after one season. In the 1970s, Holliman enjoyed steady employment on *Police Woman* with Angie Dickinson. SEE ALSO: Strother Martin, Judi Meredith, Jeanette Nolan, Andrew Prine.

Dennis Hopper
(1936–)

As a *Rebel Without a Cause* (1955) cast member, Hopper had been inspired (like friend/sometime roommate Nick Adams) by James Dean to view William H. Bonney as the nineteenth-century precursor to alienated modern teens. Hopper played Bonney-inspired roles in three early *Cheyenne*s: "The Travelers" (1/3/56), "Quicksand" (4/3/56), and "The Iron Trail" (1/1/57). In the first, Clint Walker says of Hopper's crazed outlaw: "I saw Billy Bonney once; this boy's *worse!*" Hopper then played Bonney himself in "Brannigan's Boots," the premiere episode of *Sugarfoot* (9/17/57). Hopper also played Billy Clanton in *Gunfight at the O.K. Corral* (1957), then yet another variation in *From Hell to Texas* (1958). On the "Find a Sonnett, Kill a Sonnett" episode of *The Guns of Will Sonnett* (12/8/67), he twirls a pair of pistols while giggling: "Just like Billy the Kid!" Hopper helped invent the New Cinema for the Youth Movement as both director and costar of *Easy Rider* (1969), now riding a cycle rather than a horse. His final Western TV role to date was as the de-romanticized/deglamorized Doc Holliday in *Wild Times* (1/24/80). SEE ALSO: Nick Adams, Will Hutchins, Clint Walker.

Lee Horsley
(1955–)

An authentic Texas rodeo rider with stage experience in big musicals, Horsley eased into TV Westerns beginning with "Captain Cain," as the only man who could stand up to the title characters in *The Wild Women of Chastity Gulch* (10/31/82). His first series role came in the quasi-Western *Matt Houston* (1982–1985), as a modern millionaire Texan living in LA, solving crimes as his hobby; Paul Brinegar (*Rawhide*) played top ranch hand "Lamar." Horsley won the lead in the cop show *Bodies of Evidence* (1992–1993), with George Clooney as his young partner. He then starred in the period Western *Paradise* (1988–1991) as gunman "Ethan Allen Cord," who reforms when his dying sister sends her four children from St. Louis to the frontier: "Claire" (age thirteen, Jenny Beck), "Joe" (eleven, Matthew Newmark), "Ben" (nine, Brian Lando), and "George" (five, Matthew Patrick Carter). Responsibility changes Cord;

H

OLD AND NEW: On *Paradise*, Lee Horsley (*center*) played fictional marshal "Ethan Allen Cord," who calls on historical heroes Bat Masterson (Gene Barry, *left*) and Wyatt Earp (Hugh O'Brian, *right*) to help him catch the bad guys; this marked the first time Barry and O'Brian had played those roles together, despite the long-held misconception that the two performers were regularly seen side-by-side during the 1950s. Courtesy CBS.

he buys a farm from banker "Amelia Lawson" (Sigrid Thornton) so as to make an honest living for family but, like "Lucas McCain" (Chuck Connors) on *The Rifleman*, finds himself drawn back into gunplay to protect the title town. Fortunately, a wise Native American, "John Taylor"

(Dehl Berti), hung around to offer sage advice. The most memorable episode ("A Gather of Guns," 9/10/89) had Cord calling on Bat Masterson (Gene Barry) and Wyatt Earp (Hugh O'Brian) for help. During the final season, the title was changed to *Guns of Paradise*, with Cord now the marshal while pursuing a more serious relationship with Amelia. He played the lead in *Hawkeye* (1994–1995), a single season spinoff of the popular *The Last of the Mohicans* movie, with Horsley as Cooper's "Natty Bumppo," Rodney A. Grant as "Chingachgook," and former *Wonder Woman* Lynda Carter as the take-your-breath-away pioneer woman "Elizabeth Shields" (*not* a Cooper creation). Horsley later played the prodigal father "Seamus O'Neil" on *Snowy River: The McGregor Saga* (1995), an Australian Western. SEE ALSO: Rodney A. Grant, Sigrid Thornton.

Robert Horton

(1924–   )

The good news for this exceptionally handsome actor was that his second TV series (his first, *Kings Row*, had been a ratings disaster in 1955) quickly climbed to the number-one spot. *Wagon Train* debuted in 1957 with Horton as the caravan's scout, "Flint McCullough." The bad news: From day one, Horton felt exploited as a beefcake star, never allowed to stretch as a "serious" actor. He also failed to fit in with the top-billed Ward Bond and other cronies from the John Ford stock company. Soon Horton appeared exclusively in stories that had Flint, and *Wagon Train* then became two alternating series. He left the moment his four-year contract was up. He returned to TV

Westerns with *A Man Called Shenandoah* (1965–1966) as an amnesiac Civil War vet, one of many such shows created in the aftermath of *The Fugitive*'s success. Horton played the lead in a routine movie of the week, *The Dangerous Days of Kiowa Jones* (12/25/66), a busted pilot. Afterward, the only film work Horton could find was in low-budget science-fiction fare like *The Green Slime* (1968). SEE ALSO: Ward Bond, John McIntire, Denny (Scott) Miller, Terry Wilson.

Clint Howard

(1959–   )

A talented child actor, Howard played "Leon" in *The Andy Griffith Show* (1962–1964), alongside brother Ron as "Opie." He also played "Mark Wedloe," son to Dennis Weaver's naturalist, in *Gentle Ben* (1967–1969), teamed with a pet bear; Henry Fonda's son "Jody" in the TV version of John Steinbeck's *The Red Pony* (3/18/73); and amiable "Steve" in *The Cowboys* (1974). His multitude of character-actor credits include parts in most of his director-sibling's films, beginning with *Grand Theft Auto* (1977). Pop-culture claims to fame: Howard played "Eaglebauer" in *Rock 'n' Roll High School* (1979) and provided the voice of "Roo" in Disney's *The Many Adventures of Winnie the Pooh* (1977). SEE ALSO: Robert Carradine, A. Martinez, Dennis Weaver.

CHARACTER PEOPLE: One great pleasure of the TV genre is provided by scene-stealing actors, including Arthur Hunnicutt. Courtesy ABC, NBC, and CBS.

Arthur Hunnicutt

(1910–1979)

••••••••••••••••••••••••••••••••

Arkansas born, Hunnicutt specialized in redneck roles both in comedy (*The Kettles in the Ozarks*, 1956) and drama (*The Big Sky*, 1952). He received an Oscar nomination for Best Supporting Actor as "Uncle Zeb" in the latter, offering a highly accurate depiction of a Rocky Mountain man. Earlier, Hunnicutt played "Jeeter Lester," the lead role in the stage production of Erskine Caldwell's *Tobacco Road*, embodying the backwoods rascal immortalized by Charlie Grapewin in the 1941 film. Hunnicutt played "Arkansas," sidekick to Charles Starrett, in six oaters during the early 1940s. He appeared in what may have been the first-ever live play on TV, *You Can't Take It with You* (11/18/45). His superb supporting roles in big films include a mail rider in *Broken Arrow* (1950, Delmer Daves, director, with James Stewart), a world-weary Yank in *The Red Badge of Courage* (1951, John Huston, director, with Audie Murphy), and an old rodeo rider in *The Lusty Men* (1952, Nicholas Ray, director, with Robert Mitchum). Several continuing roles on TV include the aged "mustanger" on *Elfego Baca* (1959), and a Revolutionary War volunteer in *The Swamp Fox* (1961), both for Disney. He played the real-life Westerners Davy Crockett in *The Last Command* (1955), Simon Kenton (whose full story has *never* been told on TV or in movies) in "Daniel Boone" (*The Great Adventure*, 1964), and an aged Butch Cassidy (*Cat Ballou*, 1965). Hunnicutt also incarnated "Old Obie" on *Bonanza* (1963–1964), then united with another Crockett, Fess Parker, as a guest star on *Daniel Boone* (10/20/66). His best-remembered role was as a sidekick to both Wayne and Mitchum in Howard Hawks's *El Dorado* (1966). SEE ALSO: Peter Graves, Dewey Martin, Fess Parker.

Jeff(rey) Hunter

(1926–1969)

••••••••••••••••••••••••••••••••

So handsome that it hurt, Henry Herman McKinnies, Jr., from Louisiana, also revealed a natural talent at acting. He ought to have become a huge star, but everything that could go wrong did. A speech and radio undergraduate at Northwestern, later a grad student at UCLA, Hunter appeared in an LA mounting of an Arthur Miller play; a Fox talent scout spotted Hunter and hurried to sign the obvious star-in-embryo before rival Paramount nabbed him. As a contract player, Hunter appeared in studio programmers, many of them Westerns: *Three Young Texans* (1954), Little Dog in *White Feather* (1955), Owen (son of John) Brown (*Seven Angry Men*, 1955), Matuwir (*Seven Cities of Gold*, 1955), *The Proud Ones* (1956), *Gun for a Coward* (1957), Frank James in *The True Story of Jesse James* (1957, with Bob Wagner in the title role), and *The Way to the Gold* (1957). He was married to Barbara Rush, a beautiful brunette, from 1950 to 1955. Hunter's banner year: 1956, when he played the second lead to John Wayne (*The Searchers*, on loan to Warner Bros.) and to Fess Parker (*The Great Locomotive Chase*, on loan to Disney). Hunter's Fox contract ran out in 1959; while that destroyed many players, Hunter appeared ready to come into his own with Ford's *Sergeant Rutledge* (1960), Nicholas Ray's *King of Kings* (1961), and Darryl F. Zanuck's *The Longest Day* (1962). His historical roles on TV include John Fremont (*Destiny, West!*, 1/24/60) and Walter Reed (*Death Valley Days*, 3/6/62). Ford wanted Hunter to repeat his role as the army lieutenant from *Rutledge* in the blockbuster *Cheyenne Autumn* (1964). Hunter turned down the part (which went to Pat Wayne) in favor of WB's most

ambitious TV Western: *Temple Houston* (1963–1964). Universal's *The Virginian* had proven that a ninety-minute color "epic" approach could work; NBC wanted no one but Hunter to play Sam Houston's lawyer son, to be supported by the up-and-coming James Coburn as his cynical sidekick. The pilot received theatrical release as *The Man from Galveston* (1963). Sadly, the show was then rushed into production and cut back to sixty minutes. Coburn bailed, replaced by Jack Elam as "Taggart." Other regulars included Frank Ferguson (the fair but stern "Judge Gurney"), Chubby Johnson (reckless "Concho"), Mary Wickes (motherly "Ida"), and James Best (countrified "Gotch"). All was to no avail: What was supposed to be a special series had been downgraded to one more routine oater; twenty-six episodes were filmed and aired.

NBC sensed Hunter's potential and starred him as "Captain Pike" in the pilot episode for *Star Trek* ("The Cage"). His then-wife laughed during the screening and told the network and producer Gene Roddenberry that her husband was "a movie star" and as such would not be reduced to playing Captain Video. William Shatner was then cast as "Kirk"; TV superstardom followed. Hunter found himself reduced to episodic TV and ever less prestigious European flicks. He was reunited with Fess Parker as a villain on *Daniel Boone* (12/1/66) exactly one decade after they starred together in *Chase*. Hunter suffered a stroke and a bad fall after shooting the not-bad B Western *Joaquin Murietta* (1965) as that legendary outlaw. He played Captain Frederick Benteen in the insipid "epic" *Custer of the West* (1968). Hunter would have been perfect for the lead in that one, though it went to a miscast Robert Shaw. Sensing failure was imminent, his second wife had long since walked out. Hunter begged for the part on *The Brady Bunch* (1969) that went to Robert Reed but was turned down as "too handsome." Whether he died from an accident or took his own life shortly thereafter remains an ongoing Hollywood mystery. SEE ALSO: James Coburn, Jack Elam, Fess Parker, William Shatner.

Will Hutchins

(1932–)

••••••••••••••••••••••••••••••••

This lean, lanky, likeably low-key performer was signed to a contract at Warner Bros. in hopes of developing him into a naïve, sincere Midwestern farm boy, à la the young Henry Fonda or James Stewart. In 1957, the studio needed a new Western to rotate with the biweekly *Cheyenne* (then two years on the air) on Tuesday nights. The manner in which *Sugarfoot* (1957–1961) was synthetically created reveals much about that studio's *modus operandi*. The title and theme song (Max Steiner) were lifted from a 1951 Randolph Scott Western (its name changed to *Swirl of Glory* for

TV release to avoid confusion). *Sugarfoot*'s plot was borrowed almost verbatim from the 1954 *Boy from Oklahoma* starring Will Rogers, Jr. Two of the show's supporting actors, Sheb Wooley and Slim Pickens, repeated their earlier film roles in the TV pilot so that scenes from the feature film could be incorporated, bringing down the budget of the TV adaptation, *always* the primary motivating factor at Warner Bros. TV. In the movie, Tom Brewster (aspiring lawyer/drifting cowpoke) refused to touch a gun, and instead employed his lariat (like the star's famous father). For TV, Tom reluctantly wore a pistol, bringing him more in line with formulaic Westerners. After three years of rotation with *Cheyenne* or *Bronco*, *Sugarfoot* was for its fourth and final season incorporated into a Monday night package. When Hutchins's episodes ran in Europe, they were retitled *Tenderfoot*, as international audiences were unlikely to grasp the original idiomatic Texas expression. Following cancellation and the end of Hutchins's studio contract, he starred in two sitcoms, Hey, Landlord (1966), and (as "Dagwood Bumstead") Blondie (1968–1969). Hutchins appeared in three Elvis musicals as well as one notable Western, Monte Hellman's *The Shooting* (1967, Jack Nicholson). In time, Hutchins grew disenchanted with acting, starting a second career in show business as a clown. SEE ALSO: Ty Hardin; Will Rogers, Jr.; Clint Walker.

Jill Ireland
(1936–1990)
••••••••••••••••••••••••••••••

While navigating a divorce from David McCallum (*The Man from U.N.C.L.E.*) to marry Charles Bronson, Ireland played Jean Arthur's role in the belated TV version of George Stevens's *Shane* opposite David Carradine in the Alan Ladd part. The hiring of a British actress attests to the impact of the British Invasion when this series premiered (1966). SEE ALSO: Charles Bronson, David Carradine, Christopher Shea.

John Ireland
(1914–1992)
••••••••••••••••••••••••••••••

This Canadian-born (that *was* his real name) actor exploded onto the screen in Lewis Milestone's *A Walk in the Sun* (1945), the first of the ultra-realistic post–World War II combat films, as "Windy," a philosophic loner. Other supporting roles in A movies followed: Ford's *My Darling Clementine* (1946) as Billy Clanton, and Robert Rossen's *All the King's Men* (1949, Best Supporting Actor nominee). On the set of Hawks's *Red River* (1948), Ireland dared to court leading lady (and producer/director's "friend") Joanne Dru; the filmmaker responded by reducing Ireland's part ("Cherry Valance"), a laconic gunfighter, in

MEANEST MEN IN THE WEST: Often, the villains were far more memorable than the heroes. John Ireland played both. Courtesy CBS/United Artists Films.

size, scope, and scenes. Ireland and Dru married shortly thereafter but were divorced in 1957. The Western genre became his B-movie staple: *The Doolins of Oklahoma* (1949) as Bitter Creek Newcomb; Samuel Fuller's *I Shot Jesse James* (1949) as Bob Ford; and *Little Big Horn* (1951). He also played many leads in unmemorable films, as well as supporting ones in biggies like *Gunfight at the O. K. Corral* (1957) as Johnny Ringo, *Spartacus* (1960), and *55 Days at Peking* (1963). Though Ireland seemed a natural for a Western series and shot several pilots, none sold. During *Rawhide*'s final season (1965–1966), he replaced Eric Fleming, playing "Jed Colby" and bringing his cowboy variation on Bogart—brooding presence, angular frame, menacing eyes, mellow voice—to that long-running hit.

Unfortunately, the show, by then on its last legs, was canceled at mid-season. Afterward, Ireland played in low-budget American oaters and spaghetti Westerns, in TV guest roles, and in soap operas. His last great shot at Western stardom came in *Bonanza: The Next Generation* (3/23/88), a TV movie/pilot about "Captain Aaron Cartwright," who assumes ownership of the Ponderosa following Ben's death. This was an interesting concept and appropriate for its era via the ethical issue of allowing miners to work the land, which would mean big profits for the Cartwrights but would spoil the environment. Once again rating as a bridesmaid rather than the bride, Ireland's show was not picked up by a network. SEE ALSO: Clint Eastwood, Eric Fleming, Michael Landon, Jr.

Richard Jaeckel
(1926–1997)
••••••••••••••••••••••••••••••

A mail courier on the 20th Century-Fox lot, Jaeckel was spotted by a casting director who had been assigned to round out the ensemble for *Guadalcanal Diary* (1943). Jaeckel played the role of a U.S. Marine well, then joined the military; following war's end, Jaeckel appeared in the least (*Battleground*) and most (*Sands of Iwo Jima*) jingoistic films on the subject, both in 1949. His long association with Westerns began in 1950 as the young punk "Eddie" shot by Gregory Peck's Ringo at the beginning of *The Gunfighter*. Jaeckel played the cocky sidekick to Glenn Ford in both *3:10 to Yuma* (1957) and *Cowboy* (1958). His best-known role was as Lee Marvin's assistant in *The Dirty Dozen* (1967). His finest performance was as Paul Newman's goofy/doomed brother in *Sometimes a Great Notion* (1971, which won Jaeckel an Oscar nomi-

nation). He covered many TV roles: Billy "The Kid" Bonney on *Stories of the Century* (1/30/54), "Tony Gentry" on *Frontier Circus* (1962) as the front man encountering problems in every town, and Grat Dalton in *The Last Day* (2/15/75). Supporting roles included *Spenser: For Hire* (1985–1987) and *Baywatch* (1989–1994). His last significant Westerns had him playing adversaries of his old character William Bonney, in *Chisum* (1970) and *Pat Garrett & Billy the Kid* (1973). SEE ALSO: John Derek, J. Pat O'Malley, Chill Wills.

Waylon Jennings
(1937–2002)
••••••••••••••••••••••••••••••

Jennings chose not to step aboard the plane that carried fellow Texan Buddy Holly, Ritchie Valens, and the Big Bopper to their deaths that night in 1959. Like Johnny Cash, he embodied a Man in Black outlaw singer with strong ties to Westerns. Beloved for his famed duet with Willie Nelson, "Mammas Don't Let Your Babies Grow Up to Be Cowboys," Jennings narrated *The Dukes of Hazzard* (1979–1985) and sang the popular theme song. He costarred with fellow "Highwaymen" Cash, Nelson, and Kris Kristofferson in *Stagecoach* (5/18/86); Jennings had originally been slated to play the "Ringo Kid," though in truth he was not up to the acting demands and so was recast as the gambler "Hatfield," Kristofferson assuming the central character. Jennings reteamed with Kristofferson, Nelson, and Travis Tritt for *Outlaw Justice* (1/24/99), as a bandit gang reforms to find the man who shot down a onetime member. Jennings appeared briefly in the film version of *Maverick* (1994) as "The Man with Concealed Guns." SEE ALSO: Johnny Cash, Kris Kristofferson, Willie Nelson.

CHARACTER PEOPLE: One great pleasure of the TV genre is provided by scene-stealing actors, including Ben Johnson. Courtesy ABC, NBC, and CBS.

Ben Johnson
(1918–1996)
••••••••••••••••••••••••••••••

An Oklahoma-born roper, Johnson was hired by Howard Hughes as a wrangler on location for *The Outlaw* (1943). After the shoot, Johnson escorted horses to LA and found work there as a stunt double for John Wayne. He played "Travis" in three Ford films: *She Wore a Yellow Ribbon* (1949), *Wagon Master* (1950), and *Rio Grande* (1950). Though on the verge of big-time stardom, Johnson became embroiled in an argument with "Pappy" (director John Ford) that got him bounced from the stock company until 1964 (*Cheyenne Autumn*). A disappointed Johnson quit movies and returned to the rodeo circuit but could not break even. Supporting roles in big pictures included a famed fistfight with Alan Ladd in *Shane* (1953), a shootout with Marlon Brando in *One-Eyed Jacks* (1961), and a confrontation with Charlton Heston in *Will Penny* (1968). He reached stardom in minor oaters (*War Drums*, 1957) and worked for Sam Peckinpah in *Major Dundee*

(1965), *The Wild Bunch* (1969), and *Junior Bonner* and *The Getaway* (both 1972). Johnson won a continuing role in *The Monroes* (1966–1967) as an unscrupulous one-armed cowboy, "Sleeve." He agreed to do *The Last Picture Show* (1971) only if his "cuss-words" were removed; they were, and Johnson won an Oscar for Best Supporting Actor. His historical characters include John Colter (*Grayeagle*, 1977) and Jim Bridger (*Dream West*, 4/13/86). Johnson played key roles in upscale TV Westerns: *The Sacketts* (5/15/79), *Wild Times* (1/24/80), and *The Shadow Riders* (9/28/82). He then enacted "Bronc Evans," an old-timer who assumes management of the Ponderosa ranch, in *Bonanza: The Return* (11/28/93) and *Bonanza: Under Attack* (1/15/95). SEE ALSO: Michael Anderson, Jr.; Sam Elliott; Barbara Hershey; Michael Landon, Jr.; Tom Selleck.

Brad Johnson

(1924–1981)
••••••••••••••••••••••••••••••

Tall, handsome, and broad shouldered, nonetheless Johnson projected an aura of easygoing, well-meaning incompetence. This served him well on *Annie Oakley* (1954–1957) as deputy "Lofty Craig," unable to complete the job without help from female lead Gail Davis. Johnson offered a similar characterization on *The Life and Legend of Wyatt Earp* as Ed Masterson (4/2/57), Bat's affable brother,

who unwisely moved into law enforcement. Other good/bad men include outlaw John Wesley Hardin (*Zane Grey Theater*, 3/26/59) and lawman Bill Tilghman (*Death Valley Days*, 2/13/60). SEE ALSO: Gail Davis, Alan Dinehart, Jimmy Hawkins.

Brad Johnson

(1959–)
••••••••••••••••••••••••••••••

A bland, uncharismatic performer, Johnson was picked by Steven Spielberg for the Van Johnson role in the remake of *A Guy Named Joe* (1943), *Always* (1989), one of that director's few flops. Johnson had been a pro rodeo rider, then appeared in beer commercials and as a Marlboro Man. Sporadic film/TV work includes the TV Western *Ned Blessing: The Story of My Life and Times* (1993), in which an old man about to hang recalls his life, each incident providing an episode. This strained attempt to create a noir sensibility proved to be devoid of solid characters or involving plots, while Johnson clearly lacked the right stuff to make it click. The show premiered to a large audience, revealing that Westerns *could* make a comeback. As viewers realized how tedious this would be, they turned away in droves; *Ned Blessing* was canceled after five broadcasts. Afterward, Johnson played small roles on TV: the historical Henry Nash in *Rough Riders* (7/20/97), from writer/director John Milius; *Crossfire Trail* (1/21/01,

Louis L'Amour); and *Comanche Moon* (2008, Larry McMurtry). He also starred in the brief-lived *Soldier of Fortune, Inc.* (1997–1999).

Russell Johnson
(1924–)

••••••••••••••••••••••••••••

This World War II flying ace studied acting under the G.I. Bill. After many supporting roles in sci-fi (*It Came from Outer Space*) and B+ Westerns (*Tumbleweed*, both 1953), Johnson turned vicious as the Sundance Kid (1958) to Neville Brand's Butch Cassidy, both taken to task (according to a notoriously unhistorical account) by Sheriff Pat Garrett (George Montgomery) in *Badman's Country* (1958). The following year, Johnson went over to the right side of the law as "Marshal Gib Scott" on *Black Saddle*. He hoped for but did not win the lead in *Ben Casey* (1961), instead settling for "The Professor" on *Gilligan's Island*. SEE ALSO: Anna-Lisa, Peter Breck.

Chris(topher) Jones
(1941–)

••••••••••••••••••••••••••••

Orphaned at an early age, Jones was raised partly in Boys Town, later going AWOL from the service after only a few days. He hungered to be an artist like his institutionalized mother, but owing to a slight resemblance to James Dean (in looks, not talent), Jones found himself pushed into acting with *The Legend of Jesse James* (1965–1966), a TV whitewashing of the gang leader during the post–Civil War years. Allen Case played older brother Frank, Ann Doran their mother, and Richard H. Cutting the young Woodrow James; John Milford, David Richards, and Tim McIntire were cousins Cole, Jim, and Bob Younger. The show followed the usual TV approach of eliminating the male hero's wife so as to make him appealing as a fantasy figure. The single-season show remains noteworthy as the precursor to *Bonnie and Clyde* (1967), romanticizing outlaws of the past as metaphors for the then-emerging Youth Movement. Jones appeared in one cult film, *Wild in the Streets* (1968), as a rock 'n' roller elected president by teens once they get the vote. Legendary filmmaker David Lean chose Jones for the male lead in *Ryan's Daughter* (1970), a famous flop; Jones's English accent proved so bad that another actor had to dub in the voice. Jones drifted into the LA drug culture and turned down his one chance for a big comeback when Quentin Tarantino offered him a plum role in *Pulp Fiction* (1994). SEE ALSO: Allen Case, Robert J. Wilke.

Dick ("Dickie") Jones
(1927–)

••••••••••••••••••••••••••••

This Texas-born son of a journalist displayed amazing gifts at horsemanship before age five. Hoot Gibson picked Jones up for a child star in a traveling Wild West show, Dickie dazzling audiences with wild stunts. Gibson set up interviews in LA, and "Dickie" moved into *Our Gang* shorts and features. He provided the voice of "Henry Aldrich" on the radio and played parts in B Westerns (*Hollywood Round-Up*, 1937, Buck Jones). He scored occasional big pictures, performing Samuel Clemens as a child in *The Adventures of Mark Twain* (1944, Fredric March). As a teenager, he played the young rebel in *Rocky Mountain* (1950, Errol Flynn) and a frightened U.S. Marine on Sirabachi (*Sands of Iwo Jima*, 1949, John Wayne). Gene Autry chose Jones to play his young pal in *The Strawberry Roan* (1948), followed by numerous teen roles on *The Gene Autry Show* and *Annie Oakley*. For *The Range Rider* (1951–1953), Jones embodied "Dick West," All-American-boy sidekick to Jock Mahoney. Horsemanship and Mahoney's stunt credentials saved Autry paying professional gagmen, as the two stars did their own work. Then it was on to his own show, *Buffalo Bill, Jr.* (1955–1956), the young hero no relation to William F. Cody. A foundling without a name discovered by "Judge Ben Wiley" (Harry Cheshire), Bill was raised in Wileyville with his annoying little sister, "Calamity" (Nancy Gilbert). A perennial juvenile, even after hitting thirty, Jones played one more young sidekick, this time to Bill Cord in the short-lived *Pony Express* (1959). He would have portrayed "Billy Joe" in the *Night Rider* series (1962) with Johnny Cash as "Johnny Laredo," but the pilot didn't sell. His final role was in Spencer Gordon Bennet's retro-fifties B Western *Requiem for a Gunfighter* (1965), with Rod Cameron, Johnny Mack Brown, and Colonel Tim McCoy. Jones left acting to pursue business/carpentry careers. Pop-culture claim to fame: Jones provided the voice of the puppet hero in Walt Disney's *Pinocchio* (1940). SEE ALSO: Gene Autry, Harry Cheshire, Bill Cord, Jock Mahoney.

L. Q. Jones

(1927–)

Texas native Justus McQueen fit so perfectly into his role as a goofy U.S. Marine in his first film, Raoul Walsh's *Battle Cry* (1955), that he took that character's name, "L. Q. Jones." Shortly he had built a career playing a more cunning, in some ways openly nihilistic, version of the good ol' boy for which James Best became known. Jones won a regular role on the first season of *Cheyenne* (1955–1956) as "Smitty," a sketch artist and mapmaker working for the U.S. Cavalry and accompanied by the title scout (Clint Walker). Warner Bros. dropped Smitty when they decided the show would work best with a loner hero. As the deadly but good-natured gunman "Pecos Hill," Jones stole *Buchanan Rides Alone*

(1958) from the top-billed Randolph Scott. He appeared in many war films and Westerns, including two with Elvis, *Love Me Tender* (1956) and *Flaming Star* (1960). He costarred as the cowboy "Pee Jay," a semi-regular on *Rawhide*'s 1965 season, and the lanky Westerner "Belden" on *The Virginian* (1963–1967), in addition to roles on *Gunsmoke, Wagon Train,* etc. Jones teamed with Strother Martin as a wickedly comic duo in Sam Peckinpah's *The Wild Bunch* (1969) and *The Ballad of Cable Hogue* (1970). He played "Sheriff Lew Wallace" on the Texas soap opera *The Yellow Rose* (1983–1984) and old-timer "Nathan 'Duke' Wayne" on *Renegade* (1994–1996, Lorenzo Lamas). Jones penned the script (from a Harlan Ellison sci-fi story) and directed the cult classic *A Boy and His Dog* (1975). SEE ALSO: Sam Elliott, Strother Martin, Clint Walker.

Stan Jones

(1914–1963)

●●●●●●●●●●●●●●●●●●●●●●●●●●●●●●

This U.S. Park Ranger/naturalist had a hobby: writing songs that reflected the heritage of the American West. When he performed one called "Ghost Riders in the Sky," friends insisted it was good enough to sell. Recorded by numerous artists, the ballad soon became a standard, launching Jones on a career as a composer for Westerns, notably by John Ford and Walt Disney. Filmmakers marveled at Jones's uncanny ability to write new tunes that sounded like authentic folk ballads. Ford, who in *Fort Apache* (1948) and *She Wore a Yellow Ribbon* (1949) had employed historical music, experimented in the third Cavalry Trilogy entry, *Rio Grande* (1950), with Jones's originals. Viewers adored them; "Yellow Stripes" proved so convincing as a frontier army theme that John Sturges incorporated it into *Escape from Fort Bravo* (1953). Jones's most famous song for a Ford film was the title number for *The Searchers* (1956). In addition to having Jones create music for *Wagon Master* (1950), Ford also allowed him to act. Shortly Jones would play "The Sheriff" in one of the last theatrical singin' cowboy films, *The Last Musketeer* (1952, Rex Allen). He wrote "Wringle Wrangle" for *Westward Ho the Wagons!* (1956), then showed up in most Disney Westerns for which he composed the music. He played one of Andrews' Raiders in *The Great Locomotive Chase* (1956). He was a regular in two Disney TV shows: *The Adventures of Spin and Marty* (1955), serialized on the late afternoon *Mickey Mouse Club,* as "Frank," one of the Triple R wranglers who teaches modern boys the Code of the West; and *Daniel Boone* (1960–1961) as "Doc Slocum," a pioneer traveling over the Cumberland Gap into Kentucky with the title character (Dewey Martin). Next he played "Deputy Olson" in *Sheriff of Cochise* (1956–1957). Jones also essayed one historical character, General Ulysses S. Grant, in the opening sequence of Ford's *The Horse Soldiers* (1959). His final (small) movie role was in *Invitation to a Gunfighter* (1964, Yul Brynner). SEE ALSO: Roy Barcroft, John Bromfield, James Griffith, Dewey Martin, Fess Parker.

Tommy Lee Jones
(1946–)

••••••••••••••••••••••••••••••

This Oscar winner for Best Actor in a Supporting Role (*The Fugitive*, 1993) is always well cast as glib, mean-spirited types, including baseball's Ty Cobb (*Cobb*, 1994). Jones was likewise just right for the hard-bitten Texas Ranger turned cattleman "Woodrow F. Call" in the classic miniseries *Lonesome Dove* (2/5/89). When Jon Voight played Call in the sequel *Return to Lonesome Dove* (1993), *not* written by Larry McMurtry, he revealed more sensitivity, delighting some fans while angering others. The role of *young* Call was played by Jonny Lee Miller in the prequel *Dead Man's Walk*. SEE ALSO: Robert Duvall, James Garner, Danny Glover.

TALL, WIDE, AND HANDSOME: If any TV actor came close to capturing the magic of Hollywood's greatest Western movie star John Wayne for the small screen, it was Brian Keith, who appeared in such theatrical films as *The Raiders* and on Sam Peckinpah's classic if short-lived series *The Westerner*. Courtesy Universal, NBC.

Betty Lou Keim

(1938–)

This pretty actress is best remembered for her role as Arthur Kennedy's wild daughter in *Some Came Running* (1958). In early (fall 1959) episodes of *The Deputy*, she played "Fran McCord," the sister of the title character (Allen Case) and a would-be love interest for "Marshal Simon Fry" (Henry Fonda). SEE ALSO: Allen Case, Henry Fonda, Wallace Ford.

Brian Keith

(1921–1997)

Son of actor Robert Keith, Brian appeared onstage with his dad at age two, then did his first film (*Pied Piper Malone*, 1924) at age three. Following U.S. Marine Corps service in World War II, Keith seriously pursued acting. His premiere Western role came as a cavalry captain in *Arrowhead* (1953, Charlton Heston); this was followed by a similar role in *Run of the Arrow* (1957, Rod Steiger). Keith's

first series role was as "Matt Anders," anti-Commie tough guy, in the contemporary actioner *Crusader* (1955–1956), solidifying Keith's John Wayne image. Sam Peckinpah was even then searching for a young Duke type to play "David Blassingame" in a series that would deglamorize the historical figure of the cowboy. The pilot "Trouble at Tres Cruces" aired on *Zane Grey Theater* (3/26/59), and the series *The Westerner*, a lost gem, commenced the following fall. Blassingame (accompanied by dog Brown, who had played Old Yeller for Disney two years earlier) drank heavily, cheated at cards, came on to married women, tried to avoid work, and generally made a nuisance of himself, along with friendly enemy "Burgundy Smith" (John Dehner). The show's purposefully slight narratives projected a wonderfully anecdotal appeal, but the shock to the American system proved too much: NBC canceled the low-rated show after thirteen episodes. Keith further nurtured his Wayne image in Peckinpah's first feature, *The Deadly Companions*, reinforcing this image in the Disney comedy *The Parent Trap*, both from 1961, each film featuring Duke's favorite leading lady, Maureen O'Hara. Keith replaced Fess Parker as the lead in the Disney Westerns *Ten Who Dared* (1960), *Savage Sam* (1963), and *The Tenderfoot* (1964). His extensive TV/movie work included the hit comedy *Family Affair* (1966–1971). Keith's Western roles included "Tank Logan" in *The Quest* (1976), "Sheriff Axel Dumire" in *Centennial* (1978), and "Andrew Blake" in *The Chisholms* (1979). In *Hooper* (1978), he played "Jocko," foster father to Sally Field's character, based on TV cowboy Jock Mahoney. Keith's historical figures include Senator Thomas Hart Benton on *Profiles in Courage* (11/8/64), Teddy Roosevelt in *The Wind and the Lion* (1975), and Buckshot Roberts in *Young Guns* (1988). Admired as a total professional, Keith was precisely that . . . and much more. SEE ALSO: John Dehner.

DeForest Kelley
(1920–1999)

The Atlanta-born actor will be forever remembered as "Dr. McCoy," the grim/foreboding medical officer aboard the spacecraft "Enterprise" on *Star Trek* (1966–1969) and the later theatrical films based on the franchise.

Before and after that show, Kelley appeared in numerous TV/movie Westerns. His key genre distinction: Kelley played more historical figures involved in Tombstone and the O.K. Corral incident than any other actor. On TV's original docudrama *You Are There*, he enacted the outlaw leader Ike Clanton in a 1955 version of the famed shootout. Two years later Kelley played Morgan Earp, deputy marshal, in *Gunfight at the O.K. Corral*. In 1959, he showed up as a variation on outlaw Curly Bill Brocious (renamed "Curley Burne") in *Warlock*. Finally, in season three, episode six, of *Star Trek* (broadcast 10/25/68), almost eighty-seven years to the day after the real-life showdown), he and other cast members were propelled back in time to that event. "Bones" found himself at the corral in the guise of outlaw Frank McLowery. SEE ALSO: William Shatner.

Daniel Hugh Kelly
(1952–)

A soap-opera star ("Frank Ryan" on *Ryan's Hope*, 1978–1981), Kelly went primetime as Mark "Skid" McCormick on *Hardcastle and McCormick* (1983–1986). He played an early-middle-aged "Ben," Lorne Greene's character in the original *Bonanza*, on *Ponderosa* (2001–2002), a prequel. SEE ALSO: Matt Carmody, Jared Daperis, Drew Powell, Gareth Yuen.

Jack Kelly

(1927–1992)

••••••••••••••••••••••••••••••••

The classically handsome younger brother of movie actress Nancy Kelly played the lead in WB's *Kings Row* (1955–1956). After supporting film roles (notably in MGM's *Forbidden Planet*, 1956), he returned to Warner Bros./ABC when it became clear that their new hit *Maverick* had run behind schedule. Writers hastily created brother "Bart" who, for the remainder of the 1957–1958 season, starred in every third episode. Then, for the next two years, Kelly alternated with James Garner's "Bret" on a weekly basis, the two occasionally costarring. Kelly expressed frustration that Garner received the best comedy scripts, while he was handed routine dramas and conventional romantic pieces. When Big Jim abruptly left following the third season, Kelly assumed top billing with Roger Moore added as English cousin "Beau." The dew had long since evaporated from the lily, as diminished ratings proved. For the fifth/final year (now in a less-prestigious late-afternoon Sunday slot), *Maverick* consisted of a baker's dozen new episodes starring Kelly, with reruns featuring Garner. He later revived the character for *The New Maverick* (1978), *Bret Maverick* (1982), and *The Gambler Returns: The Luck of the Draw* (11/3/91). Kelly also played several real-life Westerners: Clay Allison (*Stories of the Century*, 7/15/54), Doc Holliday (*The High Chaparral*, 10/29/67), and Sheriff John Behan (*Young Billy Young*, 1969). SEE ALSO: Robert Colbert, James Garner, Roger Moore.

Adam Kennedy

(1922–1997)

••••••••••••••••••••••••••••••••

Kennedy played the young reporter "Dion Patrick" in early episodes of *The Californians* (1957–1958) when that show rated less as a generic Western than as a social drama set in the West with a large ensemble cast. Dion sought out behind-the-scenes stories of diverse people who drifted into San Francisco following the discovery of gold: prospectors, con men, and honest townspeople. Many episodes took place in the Chinatown district, endowing this show with a unique flavor, though in truth most Western cities boasted large Asian populations. Ratings were low; *The Californians* settled in as a more typical Western, Kennedy's character phased out before the first season concluded. Afterward, Kennedy received some episodic TV work, eventually finding greater success as a novelist/screenwriter. He penned *The Domino Principle* (1975), later adapted for a film by Stanley Kramer. SEE ALSO: Richard Coogan, Sean McClory.

Arthur Kennedy

(1914–1990)

••••••••••••••••••••••••••••••••

One of the finest American actors of the twentieth century, Kennedy studied drama at the Carnegie Institute of Technology, then became a member of Maurice Evans's touring Shakespeare troupe, and finally hit Broadway as "Biff" in the original production of *Death of a Salesman*. He proved an excellent interpreter of Arthur Miller roles, also playing in *All My Sons, The Crucible*, and *The Price*. Kennedy always appeared at his best in cynical roles, particularly as the corrupt (and fictional) Indian agent in *They Died with Their Boots On* (1941, with Errol Flynn as Custer) and an H. L. Mencken–like newspaperman (*Elmer Gantry*, 1960, with Burt Lancaster). Kennedy received five Oscar nominations but never won the statuette. Westerns became a cottage industry in his diverse career; 1952 proved to be Kennedy's most memorable year, playing in Anthony Mann's *Bend of the River*, Nicholas Ray's *The Lusty Men*, and Fritz Lang's *Rancho Notorious*. He portrayed real-life Westerners Jim Younger (*Bad Men of Missouri*, 1941), the Sundance Kid (*Cheyenne*, 1947), and Doc Holliday (*Cheyenne Autumn*, 1964). In *Nakia*, first a TV movie (4/17/74), then a brief series, he starred as "Sheriff Sam Jericho," a contemporary lawman in the Southwest attempting to maintain a sense of fairness as Anglos and Indians came into conflict, dealing with each case on its own merits. Afterward, sad to say, Kennedy accepted desultory work in sexploitation flicks like *Emmanuelle on Taboo Island* (1976) with Laura Gemser. SEE ALSO: Robert Forster.

Douglas Kennedy

(1915–1973)

••••••••••••••••••••••••••••••••

The term *taciturn* best describes the stoic presence of this New York native/Amherst grad who appeared on virtually every TV Western, kiddie or adult, during the late 1950s. A veteran of character roles in theatrical films, he enacted historical figures by playing villainous versions of men who heretofore had been heroes: Wild Bill Hickok (*Jack McCall Desperado*, 1953) and Colonel George Custer (*Sitting Bull*, 1954). In the TV medium, Kennedy was cast mostly as legendary outlaws like Bill Longley (*Stories of the Century*, 5/20/54) and Mysterious Dave Mather (*The Life and Legend of Wyatt Earp*, 9/8/59). His only lead, and a hero at last, came as "Steve Donovan" in *Steve Donovan, Western Marshal* (1955–1956), an inexpensive syndicated Western for the kiddie market. In several episodes, vaudeville veteran (and onetime sidekick to Allan "Rocky" Lane) Eddy Waller showed up as his pal "Rusty." Thereafter, Kennedy returned to playing bad guys, including "Manuel" on

Disney's *Zorro* (1959). SEE ALSO: Guy Madison, Wayne Maunder.

Wright King

(1923–)

Talented and offbeat in appearance, King was not handsome enough for a leading man nor quirky enough to be typed as a character actor. His first TV role came as "Midshipman Bascomb" on *Captain Video and His Video Rangers* (1949); this was soon followed by a small part in *A Streetcar Named Desire* (1951). King enjoyed constant work in live TV drama during the golden age and episodic TV afterward, including B Westerns *The Young Guns* and *Stagecoach to Fury*, both in 1956. King played real-life Western gunmen Charley Ball in the *You Are There* presentation "The End of the Dalton Gang" (5/12/57) and Billy Thompson (the last name altered, to "Townsend") in *The Gunfight at Dodge City* (1959). He became a regular in two series, one forgotten, the other a classic. First up was *Boots and Saddles* (1957–1958), a syndicated story about the Fifth Cavalry, with King as "Private Bennett." Then, in 1959–1960, came *Wanted: Dead or Alive*, a hit although star Steve McQueen would soon bolt for the movies. The solution was to introduce King as "Jason Nichols," an aspiring bounty hunter mentored by "Josh Randall." At the third season's conclusion, Josh would marry and

settle down while Jody took over the lead, carrying that sawed-off Winchester. Audience response proved indifferent, so CBS axed the show. King worked regularly until retirement in 1987, including eight appearances on *Gunsmoke*. SEE ALSO: Steve McQueen, John Pickard.

John Forrest "Fuzzy" Knight

(1901–1976)

A slack-jawed vaudeville performer, Knight had been discovered by Mae West, who cast "Fuzzy" in her Western comedy *My Little Chickadee* (1940). He found work at Universal as a sidekick to Johnny Mack Brown, Bob Baker, and Tex Ritter and played "Sagebrush" on *The Gene Autry Show* (1950–1951) whenever Pat Buttram proved to be unavailable. Knight's nickname was revived for his role as "Private Fuzzy Knight" on Buster Crabbe's *Captain Gallant of the Foreign Legion* (1955–1957). His final oater was *Hostile Guns* (1967). SEE ALSO: Pat Buttram.

Kris Kristofferson

(1936–)

This Texas-born U.S. Air Force brat, Golden Gloves boxer, Rhodes scholar, and intellectual cowboy with liberal political leanings took odd jobs in Nashville to support his songwriting career. When Johnny Cash recorded "Sunday Morning Coming Down," and Janis Joplin "Me and Bobby McGee," both in 1970, Kristofferson gained status as a songwriter, then as a performance star. He played a bit part in Dennis Hopper's underwhelming *The Last Movie* (1971), the lead in the underappreciated *Cisco Pike* (1972), then took second billing to James Coburn in *Pat Garrett & Billy the Kid* (1973), though he in truth was all wrong as the runty New Yorker William Bonney; Bob Dylan, as sidekick "Alias," would have been a better choice. Kristofferson played in *Freedom Road* (10/29/79), a high-level TV Western costarring Muhammad Ali in a post–Civil War social commentary, and somehow survived *Heaven's Gate* (1980), a ponderous retelling of the Powder River War. Then it was back to TV, with the role of Jesse in *The Last Days of Frank and Jesse James* (2/17/86), costarring Johnny Cash as Frank; and Ringo Kid in *Stagecoach* (5/18/96), with the other Highwaymen (Cash, Willie Nelson, and Waylon Jennings) in support. He also starred in the superior genre piece *The Tracker* (3/26/88) as a dogged man pursuing deadly outcasts. For revered indie writer/director John Sayles, Kristofferson played in *Lone Star* (6/21/96) as a modern-day sheriff coming to terms with tragic incidents in the history of a Texas town. He narrated *Dead Man's Gun* (1997–1999), about the ill-fated S&W single-action Schofield .44 pistol, and proved effective as a Louisiana prison escapee who heads southwest with a pal (Scott Bairstow) in *Two for Texas* (1/18/98), eventually becoming a hero at the San Jacinto battle (1836). Kristofferson then appeared in *Outlaw Justice* (1/24/99), a notably brutal TV oater. He recreated the Billy Bonney role (voice only, in the English-language version) for *Requiem for Billy the Kid* (2006). SEE ALSO: Johnny Cash, Waylon Jennings, Willie Nelson.

Joe Lando

(1961–)

A Hollywood cook turned performer, Lando cut his TV teeth on the soap opera *One Life to Live* (1990–1992). He played handsome/heroic "Byron Sully," an utterly romanticized mountain man, on *Dr. Quinn, Medicine Woman* (1993–1997), as well as in two follow-up TV movies. He also played the contemporary Western rancher "Pete Ritter" on *Wildfire* (2005–2006). SEE ALSO: Genevieve Cortese, Jane Seymour.

Michael Landon

(1936–1991)

Born Eugene Maurice Orowitz in Queens, New York, to parents who were Jewish and Irish Catholic, Landon headed to the West Coast on an athletic scholarship (UCLA) that was terminated due to an arm injury. He worked odd jobs (gas-station attendant, etc.) and drifted into acting. Darkly handsome, with an arrogant demeanor and wounded eyes, Landon had little trouble finding James Dean–type alienated roles in junk movies such as *I Was a Teenage Were- wolf* (1957) and *High School Confiden- tial* (1958). One staple of TV adult Westerns in the late 1950s was the punk kid going up against an aging gunfighter. In 1957, Landon all but cornered the market with "Eddie," the part played by Richard Jaeckel in *The Gunfighter* (1951), in "End of a Gun" (*The 20th Century-Fox Hour*, 1/9/57), the TV remake with Richard Conte in Gregory Peck's role; "Claude" in "Too Good with a Gun" (3/24/57), menacing Robert Cummings on *G.E. Theater*; "Tad" in a modern juvenile delinquency tale reset in the Old West in two episodes of *Tales of Wells Fargo* (5/7/57, 11/18/57); and the kid who takes on

John Payne in "The Restless Gun" (*Schlitz Playhouse of Stars*, 3/29/57), a pilot for a later series. Landon won the lead in a fine B-budgeter, *The Legend of Tom Dooley* (1959), inspired by the Kingston Trio hit.

Meanwhile, NBC was casting the upcoming *Bonanza*. The hour-long show had been designed as a rough-and-tumble adult drama that would deal with the boys' volatile personal relationships and mixed emotions about their gruff father, "Ben" (Lorne Greene). Pernell Roberts was set to play the rational "Adam," and Dan Blocker the genial "Hoss." Producer David Dortort needed some suitably edgy kid for "Little Joe," the short, quick-tempered son. After viewing Landon's TV/screen credits, Dortort knew that Landon was the one. The series, shot in color, premiered as a Saturday evening show, NBC's attempt to find something to stand up against the powerhouse of Jackie Gleason on CBS. Though ratings hardly went through the roof, *Bonanza* did make a dent in the Great One's virtual monopoly of the 7:30 (EST) time slot. After two semi-successful years, NBC had to decide whether to continue with the show or cancel it. *Bonanza* was given a second chance in the 9 p.m. (EST) Sunday evening slot. Within weeks of the switch, it soared into the top ten, then hit number one.

Like most long-run series, *Bonanza* had to reinvent itself on the basis of audience reaction. Cards and letters made clear that an ador-

ing public perceived the show as fun family fare. Since adult Westerns had run their course, NBC entirely revamped *Bonanza*, with enmities between brothers and their father phased out. The show's new identity emerged as an all-male love fest, each episode featuring some new trial for the Cartwrights that they would withstand owing to not only individual courage but loyalty to one another. This impacted Little Joe (the adjective would in time be dropped, in part because the diminutive Landon began wearing lifts), who matured into a fine young man, a tad on the arrogant side though supremely good-natured. These were, after all, the 1960s, when the previous decade's rebels mostly grew as domestic as their parents had been.

And *they* were the audience for *Bonanza*.

Landon gradually emerged as the show's centerpiece. Fan mail, particularly from female viewers, revealed how deeply America had fallen in love with Landon. Shortly, the number of "Joe episodes" increased, featuring him in relationships with father Ben or brother Hoss. Any fear that Pernell Roberts' one-man exodus in 1965 might damage the workings of a hit proved short-lived; his absence had no impact on ratings. Landon found himself in a position to make greater demands. A gifted writer (twenty episodes) and director (fourteen), he now became *Bonanza*'s auteur, the unofficial architect of

OH, BROTHER! WHAT A SHOW!: Westerns of the 1950s focused on loners; the 1960s variation of the genre dealt with family: Dan Blocker (as "Hoss," *left*) and Michael Landon ("Little Joe") enjoy a quiet moment on *Bonanza*. Courtesy NBC.

where this series was headed. Most memorable among his writing/directing efforts was "The Younger Brothers' Younger Brother" (3/12/72), in which Hoss is mistaken for a member of the famed outlaw clan. The episode featured light yet edgy comedy (with Strother Martin brilliant as Cole Younger), setting the stage for Landon's successful post-*Bonanza* career. The utterly unexpected death of Blocker following the completion of the 1971–1972 season left the series in limbo. Landon came up with a "new" *Bonanza*: Whereas in the past, every woman whom one

of the brothers (or father) became interested in dropped dead so that the male foursome could continue, why not opt for a realistic approach and have Joe marry? He would move away from the ranch, into a place of his own; these episodes would alternate with ones focusing on Ben and the ranch hands. Essentially, Landon had invented *Little House on the Prairie*, though NBC execs failed to grasp his strong concept. Though Joe was allowed to marry a newcomer, "Alice Harper" (Bonnie Bedelia), in "Forever" (9/12/72), she turned up dead later in that episode. The public, which sensed this was the right moment for *Bonanza* to change with the times, flooded NBC with angry calls and letters. More important, they turned off the show, now in an early-evening weekday slot. No sooner had Joe tracked down his wife's killers and moved back home than the series was canceled.

Landon had been right: The large-scale family Western that dominated the late 1960s, be it a patriarchy (*Bonanza, The Virginian*) or matriarchy (*The Big Valley*), was over and done with. A different era called for a different type of show, not a Western per se (though perhaps set in the West), focusing on a full family engaged in farming rather than ranching. *The Waltons* became a hit on CBS, as did Landon's next show, *Little House on the Prairie*, which he produced, directed, and wrote as well as starred in as Charles Philip Ingalls, ostensibly based on books by Laura Ingalls Wilder. The much-loved series costarred Karen Grassle as wife Caroline (one wonders if Bonnie Bedelia was offered the part first), Melissa Gilbert as Laura (frequently a narrator), Lindsay and Sidney Greenbush alternating as Carrie, and Melissa Sue Anderson as Mary. In this emergent era, when the divorce rate soared and the idea of conventional marriage with children would be challenged, TV, as the most conservative of mass media, responded by offering images (more romanticized than realistic) of the traditional family unit, the Ingalls

(or Waltons) surviving through their common bond(s) any dire situations of the 1870s or 1930s. Yet such shows also displayed a progressive side. Feminism, the cause célèbre of the early 1970s, made itself felt through the presence of strong women who, though married, were anything but trophy wives.

Landon also successfully produced *Father Murphy* (1981–1983) and starred in (as an angel) as well as writing, producing, and directing *Highway to Heaven* (1984–1989), an answer to all those who in the 1980s expressed a lack of faith. But his four-pack-a-day smoking habit finally caught up with him. Diagnosed with cancer, Landon spoke sensitively about his plight on two installments of best friend Johnny Carson's *The Tonight Show* (1/19/90, 2/15/91). His funeral was attended by Ronald and Nancy Reagan, who had always appreciated Landon's support of the Republican Party and their own conservative values. SEE ALSO: Dan Blocker, David Canary, Lorne Greene, Pernell Roberts, Guy Williams.

Michael Landon, Jr.

(1964–)
••••••••••••••••••••••••••••••

Like his dad a producer, director, and writer as well as an actor, Michael Jr. played "Benjamin 'Benj' Cartwright," son of the missing-in-action (with the Rough Riders) Joe. Ben travels from the East to save the threatened

Ponderosa ranch from spoilers of the environment in a trio of made-for-TV *Bonanza* movies: *The Next Generation* (3/23/88); *The Return* (11/28/93), for which he was also credited with the story; and *Under Attack* (1/15/95). SEE ALSO: John Ireland, Ben Johnson, Michael Landon.

Allan "Rocky" Lane

(1909–1973)

••••••••••••••••••••••••••••••

Queen of the serials Linda Stirling (1921–1997) had a kind word to say about every B-movie actor she costarred opposite, with one exception: Allan "Rocky" Lane, her leading man in *The Tiger Woman* (1944). Stirling considered Lane something less than a gentleman, his grim, hard appearance suggesting a career as a villain rather than a hero. Lane dropped out of Notre Dame, despite football-field prowess, to pursue acting in stock, then on Broadway. Hollywood beckoned, and he appeared in a gaggle of nondescript studio films without attracting attention. Then Lane entered the world of B Westerns as "Dave King" in *King of the Royal Mounted* (1940), from a Zane Grey story, and Red Ryder in *Santa Fe Uprising* (1946). Lane's initial series entries were strong enough to ensure follow-ups. He also did more than two dozen quickies under his own name, at which point the "Rocky" moniker took hold. When B Westerns gave way to TV, he tried reviv-

ing *Red Ryder*, executive-producing the series, but something went awry. Lane was replaced almost immediately by Jim Bannon. He later played real-life gunfighter Johnny Ringo on Disney's *Texas John Slaughter* (1960). Lane is best remembered today as the off-screen voice to the title horse on *Mister Ed* (1958–1966). SEE ALSO: Jim Bannon, Don Durant, Tom Tryon.

Helmut Lange

(1923–)

••••••••••••••••••••••••••••••

When Karl May's novels about the American frontier proved popular as Teutonic Westerns in the early 1960s, it only stood to reason that someone in Germany would then adapt their inspiration, James Fenimore Cooper's *Leatherstocking* quintet. Euro-TV actor Helmut Lange played "Natty Bumppo" in *Die Lederstrumpferzählungen*, with Pierre Massimi as "Chingachgook." Patrick Peuvion was also onboard as "Harry March." SEE ALSO: Steve Forrest, Lee Horsley.

Joi Lansing

(1929–1972)

••••••••••••••••••••••••••••••

Born Joyce Wassmansdorff in Salt Lake City, Utah, this minor-league Monroe became a model, then acted in bit parts in minor movies (*Queen of Outer Space*, 1958). Her first TV Western role was as the blonde who

L

rocked the West on *The Adventures of Wild Bill Hickok* (1/30/55). Lansing swiftly became typecast as a photographic model (playing "Shirley Swanson" on *Love That Bob!*, 1956–1959, then herself on *I Love Lucy*, 11/26/56). Next came "Goldie," a wide-eyed, innocent-looking con woman on *Klondike* (1960). Lansing was best known as "Gladys (Mrs. Lester) Flatt" on *The Beverly Hillbillies* (1963–1968). Pop-culture claim to fame: She married George Reeves' man of steel (sort of) on *Superman* (3/31/58). SEE ALSO: Mari Blanchard, James Coburn, Ralph Taeger.

Keith Larsen

(1926–2006)

••••••••••••••••••••••••••••••

This World War II U.S. Navy vet turned actor specialized in Native American roles owing to his darkly handsome looks. His first Indian role was as "Pau" in *Hiawatha* (1952), a B-movie reduction of Longfellow's poem with Vince Edwards in the title part. He played a rare Anglo role as Bat Masterson in *Wichita* (1955), with Joel McCrea as Wyatt Earp. A more typical part was as the Apache Kid in *Apache Warrior* (1957) with Jim Davis. Larsen received top billing in *Brave Eagle* (1955–1956), a noble if juvenile attempt to make a fictional Native American of the Great Plains the lead in a Western

series, with Anthony Numkena as the adoring child "Keena," Kim Winona as the beautiful "Morning Star," Bert Wheeler (of the legendary Wheeler & Woolsey comedy team) as mountain man "Smokey Joe," and Pat Hogan as the sinister "Black Cloud." The show might have been a huge hit in some kiddie slot (Saturday morning or Sunday afternoon), but instead *Brave Eagle* went up against Disney on Wednesdays and thus rated as dead on arrival. Larsen's next series role was on *Northwest Passage* (1958–1959) as Major Robert Rogers, the French and Indian Wars commando leader played by Spencer Tracy in the classic 1940 film. Actually, Larsen would have been better cast as second lead "Langdon Towne" rather than the craggy, controversial leader. The show ran opposite *Maverick* on Sundays and so had little chance for survival. Larsen's third series, *The Aquanauts* (1960), featured an hour-long rip-off of *Sea Hunt* opposite *Wagon Train* on Wednesdays; this one lasted half a season. Larsen disappeared for years but reemerged in nature-oriented B Westerns that he produced, wrote, directed, and starred in (often featuring son Eric): *The Trap on Cougar Mountain* (1972), *Young and Free* (1979), and most notably *Whitewater Sam* (1977), as a real-life mountain man/survivalist. SEE ALSO: Don Burnett, Buddy Ebsen, Pat Hogan.

Al "Lash" La Rue
(1917–1996)

Like some other TV/movie performers (Bruce Willis included), La Rue took acting lessons to overcome a speech impediment. Working as a hairdresser, he was spotted by R. E. Tansey, a producer at low-budget PRC, then on the lookout for a tough type to play the antihero "Lash." Tansey noted La Rue's resemblance to Bogie and cast him as a dark-clad man with a whip, high atop his horse Black Diamond, accompanied by trusty sidekick Al "Fuzzy" St. John. Referred to as "Cheyenne Davis" or the "Cheyenne Kid" beginning with *Song of Old Wyoming* (1945), he switched to his own name in *Dead Man's Gold* (1948). La Rue's last film was *The Frontier Phantom* (1952). The following year, he hosted *Lash of the West*, in which he and prairie cook "Flapjack" (Cliff Taylor) presented shortened versions of his old films. La Rue appeared as outlaws John Wesley Hardin and Sam Bass on *Judge Roy Bean* (1956–1957, precise dates n.a.). When *The Life and Legend of Wyatt Earp* switched to Tombstone (fall 1959), La Rue was cast as Sheriff John Behan, archenemy of the hero. He delivered solid work, but La Rue blew it owing to personal demons (then on his tenth or twelfth marriage, depending on the source, and drinking heavily, slowing down production). For the 1960–1961 season, La Rue was replaced by the reliable Steve Brodie. La Rue eventually starred in an X-rated film spoofing his old image, *Hard on the Trail* (1971), a career low point. He enjoyed a career comeback thanks to Kris Kristofferson and Willie Nelson, who offered him small roles in *Stagecoach* (5/18/86) and *Pair of Aces* (1/14/90). SEE ALSO: Edgar Buchanan, Hugh O'Brian.

Harry Lauter
(1914–1990)

Lauter specialized in corrupt weaklings, particularly in B Westerns and episodic TV, making more than 250 appearances. He went over to the right side of the law once, memorably, in *Tales of the Texas Rangers* (1955–1958) as "Clay Morgan," intrepid partner of "Jace Pearson" (Willard Parker). SEE ALSO: Willard Parker.

Melissa Leo
(1960–)

Leo played "Emma Shannon," a mature woman who feeds and cares for Pony Express youths, in the first season of *The Young Riders* (1989–1990). Unsatisfied with the role, she bowed out and was replaced by Clare Wren in a similar part, "Rachel Dunne." SEE ALSO: Clare Wren.

Nan Leslie

(1926–2000)

Like Audrey Totter of _Cimarron City_, this B-Western movie veteran joined an ambitious series only to find herself phased out as the focus shifted to conventional male leads. Her first film had been an oater: _Under Western Skies_ (1945), followed by several opposite Tim Holt (_Wild Horse Mesa_, 1947; _Guns of Hate_, 1948); she also became his leading lady off-screen, if rumors are to be believed. Leslie was then romantically linked with the star/producer of _The Gene Autry Show_ (1950–1955) when she played various roles on his series. There were great hopes for her role as "Martha McGivern" when _The Californians_ debuted in 1957. Her townswoman was always prominent in this ensemble show about eclectic types in San Francisco during the gold rush days. Other cast members included Howard Caine as "Schaab," Herbert Rudley as "Brennan," Art Fleming as "Pitt," and Carole Mathews as "Wilma." Low ratings meant the intriguing approach was soon scrapped; Richard Coogan was brought in as one more tall-in-the-saddle marshal, and Leslie and the others were dropped. SEE ALSO: Richard Coogan, Adam Kennedy, Sean McClory.

Robert (Bob) Logan

(1941–)

A Robert Wagner lookalike, if more conventionally masculine, Logan was signed by Warner Bros. as a contract player in the late 1950s. His first claim to fame occurred when Edd Byrnes tired of his role as hipster/carhop "Kookie/Gerald Lloyd Kookson III" on _77 Sunset Strip_ (1958). Logan replaced him as bookworm "J. R. Hale." His career took off five years later, when Logan was picked to join the _Daniel Boone_ cast as "Jericho Jones" (4/29/65), producer Parker making good use of Logan's athletic gifts in "The Tortoise and the Hare" (9/23/65). Arrogance caused Jericho to briefly be seduced into a traitorous political scheme in "The Aaron Burr Story" (10/28/65). In time Logan would write, produce, direct, and star in popular nature-oriented indie films, _Adventures of the Wilderness Family_ (1975) the most memorable. SEE ALSO: Jimmy Dean, Leif Erickson, Fess Parker.

Robert Loggia

(1930–)

New York City–born Italian American Loggia graduated from the University of Missouri (Columbia) with a journalism degree, then switched to acting. After rave reviews on

THE SPANISH WEST: Robert Loggia as real-life lawman turned lawyer Elfego Baca brought a much-appreciated new dignity to the Latino image; that's Annette Funicello to his left. Courtesy Walt Disney Productions, Buena Vista Releasing.

Broadway for Lillian Hellman's *Toys in the Attic*, he won a bit part (along with Steve McQueen) in *Somebody Up There Likes Me* (1956) with Paul Newman as Rocky Graziano. Walt Disney picked Loggia to star in *Elfego Baca* (1958–1960), a ten-episode series on "Frontierland" inspired by the autobiography of a lawman turned lawyer. Baca's claim to fame derived from his survival in a New Mexico gunfight when, as a Hispanic deputy, he was surrounded by racist Texas cowboys in a small pueblo building, then fired on for days

before help arrived. This won Baca the nickname "El Gato," the cat with nine lives. Like all Disney Westerns, *Elfego Baca* was lavishly filmed on location with movie-quality scripts, production values, and cast. The show remains notable as the first instance in which a Latino character had been portrayed on TV without the patronization that marred *The Cisco Kid*. Baca emerged as a well-rounded, three-dimensional character, portraying not only a no-nonsense sheriff but also a serious student and eventual attorney, the pride of the New Mexico Spanish community. Loggia later starred in the modern-day mystery show _T.H.E. Cat_ (1966–1967) as yet _another_ man with feline qualities. He also appeared in _Emerald Point N.A.S._ ("Admiral Bukharin," 1983–1984), _Mancuso, F.B.I._ ("Nick," 1989–1990), _The Sopranos_ ("Feech La Manna," 2004), and _Queens Supreme_ ("Judge O'Neill," 2003–2007). Loggia had memorable movie roles as a detective (_Jagged Edge_) and a mobster (_Prizzi's Honor_), both in 1985. SEE ALSO: Henry Darrow, Duncan Renaldo.

Richard Long
(1927–1974)
••••••••••••••••••••••••••••

This elegant, sophisticated leading man looked like a cross between Cary Grant and Dick Powell, hardly qualifying him as a typical Western star. Then again, Long did play the son "Tom" in the _Ma and Pa Kettle_ series as well as Frank James in _Kansas Raiders_ (1950), so there must have been a touch of country in him. As a contract player at Warner's in the late 1950s, Long was perfect for "Gentleman Jack Darby," charming con man, on _Maverick_. He also portrayed the suave detective "Rex Randolph" on _Bourbon Street Beat_ (1959–1960) and _77 Sunset Strip_ (1959–1962). Then it was back to Westerns and the roles of "Paul Durand," dignified outlaw in _The Tenderfoot_ (1964), a Disney miniseries starring Brandon De Wilde; and "Jarrod Barkley," the educated

brother who mainly stayed in town and worked as a lawyer while his siblings ran the ranch on _The Big Valley_ (1965–1969). Long later returned to contemporary comedy as the second-billed team member on _Nanny and the Professor_ (1970–1971). SEE ALSO: Peter Breck, James Garner.

Jack Lord
(1920–1998)
••••••••••••••••••••••••••••

Born John Joseph Patrick Ryan in New York, this gifted artist saw his paintings hanging in the New York Metropolitan Museum of Art and the British Museum of Art while still in his teens. In the U.S. Navy during World War II, Lord was asked to perform in training films, and, bitten by the acting bug, joined the Actors Studio following his discharge. Often cast as Neville Brand types (if considerably more handsome), in _Man of the West_ (1958) and _The Hangman_ (1959), his best TV guest role was as the lead in "The Outcast" (_Bonanza_, 1/9/60). Writer/producer Leslie Stevens (_Left-Handed Gun_, 1958), cinematographer Conrad Hall (_Cool Hand Luke_, 1967), and director Tom Gries (_Will Penny_, 1968) picked Lord as the lead in a contemporary Western, _Stoney Burke_ (1962–1963), about a good-natured rodeo rider always dreaming of winning the golden buckle but never quite hitting that high note. A top-notch cast included Warren Oates ("Ves Painter"), Bruce

Dern ("E. J. Stocker"), and George Mitchell and Robert Dowdell ("Cal" and "Cody Bristol"). The low-key approach and on-location shooting created an authentic feel for "the circuit," but audiences didn't buy ABC's rodeo show any more than they did NBC's (*Wide Country*, 1962–1963). Lord was considered for the role of "Captain Kirk" on *Star Trek* and played the lead in the minor Universal Western *Ride to Hangman's Tree* (1967, a remake of *Black Bart*, 1948). He achieved iconic status as "Steve McGarrett," leader of the *Hawaii Five-O* detective team (1968–1980). Lord took up permanent residence in the islands. SEE ALSO: Bruce Dern, Earl Holliman, Warren Oates, Andrew Prine.

Jackie Loughery
(1930–)

••••••••••••••••••••••••••••••

A Brooklyn-born beauty, Loughery won the first-ever "Miss USA" pageant, which led to decorative roles in minor films, including a Venusian Amazon in *Abbot and Costello Go to Mars* and a royal handmaiden in *The Veils of Bagdad*, both in 1953. She added glamour to the syndicated *Judge Roy Bean* (1956) as "Lettie," blonde niece of Edgar Buchanan. Her only film lead came in 1957, opposite Jack Webb in *The D.I.* They married shortly afterward but divorced in 1964. SEE ALSO: Edgar Buchanan, Jack Buetel, Russell Hayden.

Robert Lowery
(1913–1971)

••••••••••••••••••••••••••••••

Robert Larkin Hanks from Kansas City, Missouri, headed west and became a B-movie actor. His roles included Pat Garrett in *I Shot Billy the Kid* (1950, with Don "Red" Barry as Bonney) and "Big Tim Champion" (*Circus Boy*, 1956–1957), owner of a frontier traveling show. He later played "Buss Courtney," a shifty/regal townsman, in *Pistols 'n' Petticoats* (1966–1967), and a similar upscale-sleaze role in *McLintock!* (1963), with John Wayne.
SEE ALSO: Noah Beery, Jr.; Andy Clyde; Micky Dolenz; Ann Sheridan.

John Lupton
(1928–1993)

••••••••••••••••••••••••••••••

Following roles as a soft-spoken, serious-minded man of courage/conviction in *Battle Cry* (1955) and *The Great Locomotive Chase* (1956, as William Pittenger, author of a book about a Union Civil War group known as Andrews' Raiders), Lupton won the role of Tom Jeffords, played by James Stewart in the movie version, *Broken Arrow* (1950), when the film was remade for TV as part of the *20th Century-Fox Hour* anthology (5/1/56). Jeffords had been a real-life honest Indian agent (a true rarity!) who dealt with Apache chief Cochise (Ricardo Montalban, replaced by

Michael Ansara for the 1956–1958 series). Feeling constrained by the format, Lupton left after two years (causing the cancellation of a successful show) to pursue "serious" acting interests. Most notable among them was *Jesse James Meets Frankenstein's Daughter* (1966), *not* to be confused with *Billy the Kid versus Dracula* (1966), both from quickie director William Beaudine. SEE ALSO: Michael Ansara.

"HEY, WILD BILL—WAIT FOR ME!" Adult Westerns at least made an attempt at historical accuracy, but juvenile oaters presented a fanciful version of frontier life even when the hero was reality-based: Guy Madison (*left*) as James Butler Hickok and Andy Devine as the fictional sidekick "Jingles Jones." Courtesy Guy Madison Estate.

Barton MacLane

(1902–1969)

••••••••••••••••••••••••••••••••

A star college athlete (Wesleyan), author/producer of plays, and musical virtuoso, MacLane rated as a true Renaissance man in every guise but one: movie actor. Early on, his barrel-like physique and rough-looking face caused MacLane to be cast as hard, mean-spirited types, mostly in modern roles (*"G" Men*, 1935; *Gangs of Chicago*, 1940) and occasional Westerns (Jack Slade in *Western Union*, 1941). In *The Maltese Falcon* (1941), MacLane played the less sympathetic of two police detectives (the nicer one, Ward Bond) on the tail of Sam Spade (Humphrey Bogart). In the late 1950s, his image began to mellow, first with the ongoing role as kindly "John Scanlon" on *Tales of Texas John Slaughter* (1959), then as "Marshal Caine" (a purposeful rekindling of Gary Cooper's "Will Kane" in *High Noon*, 1952) on the first season of *The Outlaws* (1960–1961). The intriguing premise had Caine and his deputies perceived from the point of view of whichever particular outlaw they happened to be trailing that week, causing the "good guys" to appear menacing. The ratings were not there, so NBC restructured the series with a more typical approach, focusing on the heroes, MacLane dumped in favor of younger leads. SEE ALSO: Don Collier, Bruce Yarnell.

Guy Madison

(1922–1996)

••••••••••••••••••••••••••••••••

Born Robert Ozell Moseley, Madison was serving in the U.S. Coast Guard during World War II when he was spotted by super-producer David

O. Selznick, even then searching for a fresh face to play a handsome young sailor in *Since You Went Away* (1944). Next up came a role in *Till the End of Time* (1946) as a returning vet, his best buddy played by Bill Williams; a few years later, they would star in *The Adventures of Wild Bill Hickok* and *The Adventures of Kit Carson*, respectively, a pair of entertaining juvenile TV oaters with little if any relationship to those historical figures. Madison's hero would be accompanied by plump sidekick "Jingles" (Andy Devine) between 1951 and 1958. Rugged but soft-spoken, Madison proved perfect for Western films as well as TV, including *The Charge at Feather River* (1953), later re-imagined as a first-season *Cheyenne* episode. Madison later drifted to Europe to star in Teutonic/spaghetti Westerns, *Son of Django* (1967) the best of a bad lot that dimmed his once-flourishing career. SEE ALSO: Clint Walker, Bill Williams.

Jock (Jack) Mahoney

(1919–1989)

• •

The remarkable athletic abilities of this U.S. Marine Corps vet opened doors to stunt work in B Westerns. His tall frame, handsome face, and mellifluous voice qualified Mahoney as a natural for onscreen work. Following bit parts, then strong supporting roles, Mahoney finally picked up his first lead in the oddly titled *Roar of the Iron Horse, Rail-Blazer of the Apache Trail* (1951). Gene Autry liked what he saw and cast Jocko in *The Range Rider* (1951–1953), billed as "Jack." This show qualified as one more fantasy version of the Old West: the man-with-no-name hero who rode around with his young sidekick "Dick West" (Dick Jones). The fringe on Range Rider's buckskin jacket rates as the longest ever seen on TV. This highly appealing, extremely successful show with much marketing of hats, guns, costumes, etc., led to star billing in B+ theatrical Westerns, *Joe Dakota* (1957) the best among them with its strong Indian rights theme. In the late 1950s, with the shift toward more adult TV Westerns, Mahoney would be billed as "Jock" (real name Jacques O'Mahoney) in *Yancy Derringer* (1958–1959) as a onetime wealthy plantation owner reduced to working as a professional gambler during the post–Civil War era. Elegant clothing, a thin mustache, plus a New Orleans setting all added to the moody impact with gaslight/shadowy nighttime settings and appropriate period music. The title character lived up to his name, his small pistols hidden everywhere, including one up his sleeve. When Yancy flexed his muscles, this gun would pop out on a spring and into his hand. Always lurking down the next alley was Pahoo-Ka-Ta-Wah (X. Brands), a silent, stoic Indian sidekick carrying an eight-gauge shotgun. Mahoney followed this single-season cult hit with a role as the enemy of Gordon Scott in *Tarzan the Magnificent* (1960), then two stints as the hero in *Tarzan Goes to India* (1962) and *Tarzan's Three Challenges* (1963). A stroke in 1973 slowed down his career, though Mahoney still worked occasionally. He was Sally Field's stepfather in *Hooper* (1978), with then-couple Field and Burt Reynolds more or less playing themselves. Brian Keith played the character of "Jocko." SEE ALSO: X. Brands, Dick Jones, Brian Keith.

Lee Majors

(1939–)

••••••••••••••••••••••••••••••••

The Kentucky-raised Harvey Lee Yeary yearned to be a star athlete, until a serious injury while playing university football for Eastern Kentucky ended that dream. Handsome looks helped him succeed in Hollywood; in time he achieved TV superstardom via a performance as "Captain Steve Austin" (*not* a descendent of the founder of Texas) on two hit shows in the mid- 1970s, *The Six Million Dollar Man* and *The Bionic Woman*. Majors continued to play rugged men of action into the 1990s on the Vietnam-based series *Tour of Duty* as "Pop Scarlet." Westerns were always essential to Majors's career; his second film, *Will Penny* (1968), from writer/director Tom Gries, ranks as a classic. This remarkably honest piece about the daily life

of typical cowboys featured Majors as the young drover "Blue." Earlier, Majors had caught the attention of Lou Morheim, associate producer at Gardner/Laven/Levy. Morheim was even then putting together *The Big Valley* and cast Majors as "Heath Barkley," black sheep of the family. The matriarchy (headed by Barbara Stanwyck) featured a daughter (Linda Evans), three grown sons (Peter Breck, Richard Long and, briefly, Charles Briles), plus Majors as an illegitimate son of her late husband by an Indian woman. A daring concept for the time, Heath served as a catalyst who created sparks within the family unit, bringing the ABC show to dramatic levels (particularly during the first two seasons) never reached on NBC's higher-rated *Bonanza*. In truth, though, such situations sometimes made *The Big Valley* feel less like a Western than a soap opera set on the frontier—and, as such, a forerunner to *Dallas* and *Dynasty*.

Looking like a combination of Paul Newman and Elvis Presley, Majors served as the focus for more episodes than any of his male costars. In 1968, when it appeared that *The Big Valley* would be canceled after three solid years, the actor signed with John Schlesinger, one of the era's great writer/directors, for the role of "Joe Buck," a contemporary Texan who travels to Manhattan, in *Midnight Cowboy* (1969), the eventual Best Picture of the Year Oscar winner. Then ABC picked up Majors's series for one more season; Majors had to drop out, and the part went to Jon Voight. Majors had to content himself with the 1970–1971 season of *The Virginian* (as it morphed into *Men from Shiloh*) as "Roy Tate," a gunman intent on going straight. Majors later starred in several made-for-TV Westerns, including *High Noon, Part II: The Return of Will Kane* (11/15/80), reprising the role that won Gary Cooper his second Oscar. Sadly, this proved to be a sequel in name (title and character) only. Majors is also recalled today as the husband of Farrah Fawcett during the late 1970s. SEE ALSO: Peter Breck, Charles Briles, Linda Evans, Richard Long, Barbara Stanwyck.

Dewey Martin

(1923–)

•••••••••••••••••••••••••••••••

Sometimes referred to as "TV's other Daniel Boone," Martin is a Texas native like the more famous Fess Parker. His first oater had been the Civil War–era Western *Kansas Raiders* (1950), playing Jim Younger to Audie Murphy's Jesse James. Discovered by Howard Hawks, Martin then won a supporting role in *The Thing from Another World* (1951) and, when Montgomery Clift did not sign on, as "Boone Caudill" in *The Big Sky* (1952), second lead to Kirk Douglas in a striking adaptation of A. B. Guthrie, Jr.'s epic novel about early mountain men. A lack of

TV'S "OTHER" DANIEL BOONE: Difficult as it may be to believe, Fess Parker wasn't the only actor to play the legendary frontiersman; Dewey Martin had earlier essayed the role in Disney's four-part miniseries (1960–1961). Courtesy Walt Disney Productions, Buena Vista Releasing.

chemistry with the egregious Douglas (Hawks had been hoping for the kind of sparks that flew between Clift and John Wayne in *Red River*, 1948) caused Martin to be ruled out as a movie star. Next came two busted TV pilots, *Cavalry Patrol* (1956) for Charles Marquis Warren (Martin cast as a brash lieutenant) and *Man of Fear* (1958) for James Sheldon (all wrong for the intellectual Doc Holliday). Walt Disney hired Martin for his upcoming *Daniel Boone* miniseries, along with a fine supporting cast: Mala Powers as wife Rebecca; Richard Banke as brother Squire; three Corcoran kids (Kevin, Brian, and Kerry) playing James, Israel, and Jemima Boone; Anthony Caruso a sympathetic Chief Blackfish; and Dean Fredericks the evil "Crow-feather." The first episode ("The Warrior's Path," 12/4/60) nicely chronicled Boone's discovery of a passage through Cumberland Gap, thanks to the inspiration of explorer John Finley (Eddy Waller). Initially, the series stuck so close to the facts that Martin wore a felt hat instead of a coonskin cap (the real Boone complained the latter made his head itch). "And Chase the Buffalo" (12/11/60) also rated as strong (though no bison appeared onscreen), covering the financial, political, and legal matters impeding Boone's move to Kentucky, which began at the finale. After that, everything went wrong: Silly melodramatics involving a fictional Romeo and Juliet–type couple on the run bogged down "The Wilderness Road" (3/12/61), the fascinating construction of the title frontier highway never once shown! Worst of all was "The Promised Land" (3/19/61). No one involved knew what to do with the fact that James Boone died in an Indian attack at this moment in history. Instead he was "almost killed," which left the series with nowhere to go. How could they explain James still being around while sticking to the facts, as the series had promised to

do? If the *Crockett* shows had begun the cycle of Disney TV Westerns on the highest note possible, then this, the last such undertaking, provided a disappointing fizzle. The following year, *Tales of Wells Fargo* went from a half-hour to a sixty-minute format. Martin hoped to win the role of Dale Robertson's new partner, but it went instead to newcomer Jack Ging. Martin appeared in one more theatrical Western, *Seven Alone* (1974), as a sad-faced father whose death leaves the title children to fend for themselves on the menacing frontier. SEE ALSO: Dean Fredericks, Peter Graves, Rick Moses, Fess Parker.

Ross Martin
(1920–1981)

Born Martin Rosenblatt on New York's lower East Side, this trouper went on the vaudeville circuit with Bernard West ("Martin and West"), toured in *Guys and Dolls* as "Nathan Detroit," then was discovered by Blake Edwards. That writer/director showcased Martin in both dramatic (*Experiment in Terror*, 1962) and comedic (*The Great Race*, 1965) films. Martin reached Western series fame as "Artemus Gordon," a government agent, in *The Wild Wild West*, with Robert Conrad as the stolid hero. Martin, on the other hand, got to act big-time, assuming myriad identities via accents and disguises. The strain of this tour-de-force exasperated an already existing heart condition. He joined Conrad for two TV-movie follow-ups, *The Wild Wild West Revisited* (5/9/79) and *More Wild Wild West* (10/7/80). His final appearance was also in a TV Western, *I Married Wyatt Earp* (1/10/83). SEE ALSO: Bruce Boxleitner, Robert Conrad.

Strother Martin
(1919–1980)
••••••••••••••••••••••••••••••••

Indiana born and bred, Martin excelled at swimming/diving during World War II, leading to a promotion to full instructor; he later taught these skills to the stars' children in Hollywood. Martin soon found work as a "swimming extra" in water-themed films and became a popular character actor, beginning with "Lem Boots," a lovable hick in the original *Lassie* (1956–1957). His first major Western role was as a mournful failed outlaw in "A Stone for Benny French" (*Trackdown*, 10/3/58). A latecomer to the John Ford stock company, Martin played scurvy cowards in *The Horse Soldiers* (1959) and *The Man Who Shot Liberty Valance* (1962). When Sam Peckinpah assumed Ford's old role as the top Western director, he cast Martin in his first film, *The Deadly Companions* (1961). Previously Martin had costarred in *Hotel de Paree* (1959–1960), an offbeat forgotten gem, as storeowner/cracker-barrel philosopher "Aaron Donager," whose dry wit helped that series sparkle.

Martin's greatest film role was as the wicked "Captain" in *Cool Hand Luke* (1967) who informs Paul Newman, "What we got here is a failure t' c'mmunicate!" His real-life Western roles included Ed Schieffelin, the man who discovered Arizona's greatest mine, in "Silver Tombstone" (*Death Valley Days*, 2/26/67), and Cole Younger in "The Younger Brothers' Younger Brother" (*Bonanza*, 3/12/72). Martin appeared in all three of 1969's big Westerns: *True Grit, Butch Cassidy and the Sundance Kid*, and *The Wild Bunch*. His final Western role before expiring after a heart attack was as "Parody Jones" in *The Villain* (1979) with Kirk Douglas. SEE ALSO: Earl Holliman, Michael Landon, Judi Meredith, Jeanette Nolan.

A. Martinez
(1948–)
••••••••••••••••••••••••••••••••

This half-Indian (Apache, Blackfoot), one-quarter-Mexican, one-quarter-European played semi-pro baseball and performed in a rock 'n' roll band before he turned to acting full-time. Martinez is best known for simmering, brooding, quick-to-anger Native American/Latino roles and early in his career won a stand-out part as "Cimarron" in *The Cowboys* (1972) with John Wayne, playing an angry young Hispanic teen on a fateful cattle drive. When that movie was reconfigured for a TV series two years later *sans* the Duke (killed in the film), Martinez returned in his role, though now a more mature character. This marked a significant advancement for the depiction of Latinos on TV in general and in Westerns in particular. Later Martinez played "Marquez" in *Centennial* (1978) and "Low Wolf" in *Born to the Wind* (8/19/82). He provided a powerful presence as young Juan in *Seguin* (1982), an under-budgeted but worthwhile if little seen *American Playhouse* PBS film chronicling the roles of Tejanos in defense of the Alamo. Henry Darrow played his father, Don Erasmo

Seguin; Edward James Olmos provided a brilliant cameo as Santa Anna. Martinez later played "Daniel Morales" on *L.A. Law* (1992–1994) and Agent "Nick Cooper" on *Profiler* (1996–1997). He won a daytime Emmy for the role of "Cruz" on *Santa Barbara*. SEE ALSO: Henry Darrow, Robert Loggia.

Lee Marvin

(1924–1987)

• •

Everyone knows there were only two wagon masters on *Wagon Train*: Ward Bond as "Major Seth Adams" (1957–1961) and John McIntire as "Captain Chris Hale" (1961–1965). Wrong! The third appeared between them, if for only one episode (3/15/61). After Bond's passing, producers/writers knew that to replace the lovably gruff star would be impossible. They decided to try something totally different and hope audiences would accept it. The choices were narrowed down to two candidates: McIntire as Hale, embodying Adams's gentler side without the rough exterior, or Lee Marvin as "Jud Benedict," a character as mean as Seth seemed to be on the outside, who was meaner still inwardly. A transitional episode featured them in conflict for the caravan, with two endings written (some claim filmed!) in which each wins out in the end. The behind-the-camera team could then wait until the last minute to decide who

THE IN-BETWEEN WAGON MASTER: Many recall Lee Marvin's Oscar-winning performance in *Cat Ballou*, but few remember the single episode of *Wagon Train* when he played the caravan's leader. Courtesy CBS/United Artists Films.

would emerge as the show's next star. They decided on McIntire and killed off Marvin. At the time, Marvin—who had hoped to land a TV Western ever since his earlier police show, *M Squad* (1957–1960), concluded—initially expressed his disappointment. But everything happens for a reason. John Ford was so taken with Marvin's giggling criminality in that episode that he cast him as the title villain who takes on John Wayne *and* James Stewart in *The Man Who Shot Liberty Valance* (1962), a role Marvin would have had to pass up if saddled with weekly TV. *That* film was seen by Elliot Silverstein, then searching for an actor to play "Kid Shelleen" in *Cat Ballou* (1965) after Kirk Douglas turned him down. Marvin won an Oscar, and the longtime character actor at last became an A-list star. Later Westerns included the well-remembered *The Professionals* (1966) and, greater still, the tragically neglected *Monte Walsh* (1970). SEE ALSO: Ward Bond, John McIntire.

Tim Matheson

(1947–)

• •

An urbane appeal rendered Matheson perfect for "smart" contemporary roles ranging from Eric "Otter" Stratton in *Animal House* (1978) to Vice President "John Hoynes" on *The West Wing* (1999–2006). He was a less-than-likely candidate for Westerns but did play regular roles

in four: *Bonanza* (1972–1973) as "Griff King," a recent arrival to the Ponderosa; *Quest* (1976) as "Quentin Beaudine," the more soft-spoken of two brothers searching for their sister, held captive by Indians; *How the West Was Won* (1978) as young frontiersman "Curt Grayson"; and (voice only) *The Legend of Calamity Jane* (1997), an animated show, in the role of cavalry officer "John O'Rourke." Matheson also appeared as outlaw Emmet Dalton in *The Last Day* (2/15/75). SEE ALSO: Lorne Greene, Kurt Russell, Richard Widmark.

Wayne Maunder

(1935–)

• •

A Canadian-born baseball hopeful, Maunder failed to make the major leagues and instead studied psychiatry at a California junior college. He took a role in a school play and found himself hooked on acting. Discovered by a 20th Century-Fox talent scout, Maunder was signed to star in *Custer* (1967) with no previous film/TV experience. This approach to a controversial historical figure presaged the later film *Patton* (1970) by portraying a rebel working within the system, brashly disregarding rules and superior officers and somehow making his wild decisions work—at least until the last stand, never featured on this show, which lasted only seventeen episodes due to low ratings. The irony was that *Custer* had become a

Woods appeared in several episodes as Captain Myles Keogh, owner of the famed horse Comanche, the sole military survivor of the Little Big Horn debacle. Romantic interest was provided by Mary Ann Mobley as "Ann Landry," headstrong resident of Fort Hays. Maunder next showed up as "Scott" in another Fox Western, *Lancer* (1968–1970), as the Boston-raised estranged son of a frontier patriarch (Andrew Duggan) who heads west to resolve relationships with his stern father and half-brother (James Stacey). Afterward, Maunder tried soft-core porn (Russ Meyer's *The Seven Minutes*, 1971). His final film role was as "Cavanaugh" in *Porky's* (1980). Maunder currently produces indie films. SEE ALSO: Andrew Duggan, Peter Palmer, Slim Pickens, James Stacy.

THE FALLEN HERO: George Armstrong Custer degenerated in popular-culture depictions from a great American patriot in films like *They Died with Their Boots On* (1941) to a racist lunatic, notably in *Little Big Man* (1970). TV attempted to reboot his earlier image in a brief-lived Custer series during the late 1960s starring Wayne Maunder. Courtesy ABC.

huge hit in Europe, where dedicated viewers didn't grasp why new episodes failed to appear. Perhaps one reason the series didn't click stateside was that, in keeping with the earlier (but now dated) 1950s approach (*The Life and Legend of Wyatt Earp*, etc.), the writers eliminated wife Elizabeth Bacon Custer. TV viewers in the late sixties were veering toward shows that depicted mature adult relationships (*The High Chaparral*). Grant

Donald May

(1927–   )
••••••••••••••••••••••••••••••••

Classically chiseled facial features and a matching physique made this male mannequin a natural for TV. He landed the role of "Cadet Charles C. Thompson," host/occasional star of the primetime *West Point* (1956). Warner Bros. signed him to a contract, then cast May as "Samuel Colt, Jr.," when Wayde Preston walked out on *Colt .45* early in 1959. By this point, WB no longer searched for interesting types, favoring hunks who appeared cloned from one standard model. The following year, May turned up as a reporter on *The Roaring 20's* (1960–1962), WB's disastrous attempt to adjust *The Untouchables'* gangster era to early Saturday evening family fare. Then he took work in daytime soaps including *One Life to Live* (1968), plus some nighttime glitz (*Falcon Crest*, 1985). SEE ALSO: Wayde Preston.

Kermit Maynard

(1897–1971)

• •

Less popular with audiences though better liked in the Hollywood community than his older brother, Ken, Kermit first worked as a stunt double for Ken, then headed off to play "Tex," who with his horse Rocky rode the range in several low-budget oaters plus several Northers as a Royal Canadian Mountie (most notably *Trails of the Wild*, 1935). When his C-movie stardom abruptly ended, easygoing Kermit (unlike his now out-of-work brother) found no trouble picking up "extra" jobs. He holds the distinction of being billed as the "Outlaw's Henchman" in more Westerns than any other performer. In the 1950s, Maynard was hired by Gene Autry for just such parts in Autry's own weekly show as well as the Autry-produced *The Range Rider*. Maynard also hosted *Saturday Roundup* (1951), a live TV Western hoedown with songs, bits and pieces of folklore, and some movie clips.

Alex McArthur

(1957–   )

• •

A role on *Knots Landing* ("Ken Forest," 1985–1986) established McArthur's TV profile. He starred in a quintet of TV movies beginning with *Desperado* (4/27/87), inspired by the Glenn Frey/Don Henley ballad. Elmore Leonard concocted the role of "Duell McCall," a wrongly accused man on the run searching for a witness who can prove his innocence. The show ripped off *The Fugitive*, though McCall's missing man had two arms. The hero's personality was modeled on the Man with No Name from the Clint Eastwood/Sergio Leone spaghetti Westerns. Lise Cutter played "Nora Malloy," the woman who stands by her man. The film rates as acceptable if unexceptional. McArthur's second entry, *The Return of Desperado* (2/15/88), offered less than that, recycling the old B-movie device of a crooked sheriff committing crimes and blaming others, Cutter sorely missed. *Desperado: Avalanche at Devil's Ridge* (5/24/88) proved better, thanks to a savvy script by cult author Larry Cohen and the presence of Rod Steiger as a desperate man who forces McCall to rescue his "kidnapped" daughter; plus there was the return of Nora. The fourth, *Desperado: The Outlaw Wars* (1989; specific date of broadcast n.a.), in which McCall learns he has fathered a son with Nora, qualifies as the best by far, bolstered by strong performances: Richard Farnsworth as a serious-minded lawman, James Remar as a cold-blooded killer, plus stalwarts Buck Taylor and Geoffrey Lewis. The fifth and final film, *Badlands Justice* (12/17/89), was uplifted somewhat by the charismatic Patricia Charbonneau as the new female lead, though the original concept had by now been watered down. McArthur's only other contact with the genre was a role as "Johnny Coburn" on the *Dead Man's Gun* "Sleepwalker" episode (2/5/99). Fans consider his best non-Western role to be "Gabriel" on *Charmed* (1999).

Sean McClory

(1924–2003)

••••••••••••••••••••••••••••••

A well-regarded member of Dublin's Abbey Players, McClory was discovered by John Ford while shooting the non-Western *The Quiet Man* (1952) in that Irish city. McClory then tried for a Hollywood career, but he put on pounds, diminishing his initial leading-man appeal though his acting ability led to strong character roles. Ambitious producers Felix E. Feist and Robert Sisk were assembling *The Californians* and cast McClory as "Jack McGivern," an honest townsman in San Francisco circa 1850, who was sickened when his city became overrun by gold-crazed lowlifes. At night, Jack secretly heads up the vigilantes in hopes of ending the wave of street violence by fighting fire with fire. This proved to be the only Western during the genre's golden age to focus on vigilantism as "upstanding" citizens donned masks under the moonlight to take the law into their own hands. The public did not buy it, so two-thirds of the way into the first season, San Francisco hired its first marshal, and McClory was soon phased out. He later played the over-the-hill pioneer "Ben Dodge" on *How the West Was Won* (1978). SEE ALSO: Richard Coogan, Adam Kennedy, Nan Leslie.

Doug McClure

(1935–1995)

••••••••••••••••••••••••••••••

Boyishly charming in an ingratiating way, McClure seemed a natural for teen-heartthrob status (appearing in the rock 'n' roll youth movie *Because They're Young*, 1960, with Dick Clark) on the order of Tab Hunter, Troy Donahue, and Gardner McKay. Alone among them, McClure enjoyed a long run as a TV star, plus some nominal movie work. Early on, he earned a role in an important A film as the younger brother of Texicans Audie Murphy and Burt Lancaster in *The Unforgiven* (1960), from an Alan Le May novel. His first series was *Overland Trail* (1960), one more *Wagon Train* wannabe, with McClure in the Robert Horton role, named "Frank 'Flip' Flippen." William Bendix played

"Fred Kelly," his older, wiser mentor. NBC put the series up against *Maverick* on Sunday nights and canceled the show after six months. McClure immediately moved into high-class international intrigue with *Checkmate* (1960–1962), a series about cerebral detectives that also featured Sebastian Cabot and Anthony George. His most famous part was as "Trampas" on *The Virginian* (1962–1970), though in truth he could hardly embody the nasty sort of Westerner that this role, as created by Owen Wister, called for. McClure might have been far better cast as "Steve," the silly and easygoing sidekick to James Drury. Sensing this, the behind-the-scenes team eliminated Steve (Gary Clarke), reconceiving Trampas as a goodhearted cowhand. As a Universal contract player, McClure appeared in minor movies like *The King's Pirate* (1967). His next two series were flops, in part owing to McClure's miscasting, first as a sophisticated government agent in the Bond-like *Search*, aka *Probe* (1972–1973), then as "Cash Conover," a dude-like dandy and owner of a San Francisco gambling palace in *Barbary Coast* (1975–1976; McClure's role had been originated in the TV movie by Dennis Cole). After his contract expired, McClure alternated between drive-in action flicks (*At the Earth's Core*, 1976) and occasional TV appearances ("Jimmy Brent," *Roots*, 1977). Before his death from lung cancer, McClure did cameos in *Maverick* (1994) as a riverboat gambler

and in *The Gambler Returns: The Luck of the Draw* (11/3/91) and *Kung Fu: The Legend Continues* (10/16/95). SEE ALSO: William Bendix, Gary Clarke, James Drury.

Colonel Tim McCoy

(1891–1978)

••••••••••••••••••••••••••••••

While a student at Chicago's St. Ignatius College, young McCoy decided to relax by catching a live Wild West traveling show. Hours later, he left the theater a changed man. McCoy headed west and talked the foreman of a Wyoming ranch into giving him a job. When not busy studying horses or the use of a lariat, McCoy ingratiated himself with local Native Americans, learning their spoken and sign languages. He took time out to serve in World War I, earning the rank he would proudly bear his entire life. When the newly formed Paramount Pictures set out to film the first epic Western, *The Covered Wagon* (1925), director James Cruze hired McCoy to talk his Indian friends into participating. Afterward, as hooked on Western movies as on the West itself, McCoy moved to Hollywood with the crew. Between his first B movie, *The Thundering Herd* (1925, Jack Holt), and his last, *West of the Law* (1942, Buck Jones), the colonel starred in over ninety oaters, including roles as the hero "Lightning Bill Carson" in the 1930s and "U.S. Marshal Tim McCall" in the 1940s. Aficionados consider *Phantom Ranger* (1938) his best. McCoy's career ended when he reenlisted in his beloved U.S. Army to serve in World War II. Upon his return, he fulfilled his long-held desire by creating his own Wild West extravaganza, the last of the touring cowboy shows modeled on those created by Buffalo Bill Cody and Ned Buntline half a century earlier. In the early days of TV, McCoy appeared on a local Los Angeles station on Saturday afternoons as the host of *The Tim McCoy Show* (1952). Unlike other hosts, McCoy did not rely on clips from old movies. Softly, succinctly, and with great certainty, he explained the ways of the real West, particularly the beauty of Native American lifestyles. Even without big shootouts or stampedes, McCoy held audiences spellbound thanks to his vast knowledge and obvious passion for the material. He made a final appearance in Mike Todd's spectacular *Around the World in Eighty Days* (1956) as the cavalry officer who rides up with troops and saves a train threatened by marauding Indians.

Jody McCrea

(1934–)

In 1959, three actors simultaneously played Bat Masterson on TV: Alan Dinehart on ABC's *The Life and Legend of Wyatt Earp*, Gene Barry on NBC's *Bat Masterson*, and Jody McCrea on *Wichita Town*. On the last, the name was altered to "Ben Matheson" to avoid confusion. McCrea had been hired by father Joel, who played an Earp-like role. Most of Jody's early parts were in his dad's films: *The First Texan* (1956) and *Trooper Hook* and *Gunsight Ridge*, both 1957. He appeared in the intriguingly awful exploitation flick *Young Guns of Texas* (1962) alongside Jim Mitchum and Alana Ladd. McCrea's biggest if most dubious success was as surfer "Deadhead" in the popular mid-1960s *Beach Party* films. He convinced his father to come out of retirement (Joel had not done a major film since Sam Peckinpah's elegiac *Ride the High Country*, 1962) to play Jody's character as an older man in the opening sequence of *Cry Blood, Apache* (1970), a brutal and embarrassing exploitation flick. SEE ALSO: Gene Barry, Alan Dinehart, Joel McCrea.

Joel McCrea

(1905–1990)

In B+ Westerns, he played characters not unlike the ones Henry Fonda essayed in A oaters: Wyatt Earp, played by Fonda in Ford's *My Darling Clementine* (1946), would be played by McCrea in *Wichita* (1955). McCrea did not possess Fonda's level of talent (nor did he ever pretend to), yet he did work for two of Hollywood's finest: Alfred Hitchcock (*Foreign Correspondent*, 1940) and Preston

LIKE FATHER, LIKE SON: Young Jody McCrea (*left*) joins legendary dad Joel for *Wichita Town;* though they assumed fictional names, their characters were based on Bat Masterson and Wyatt Earp. Courtesy NBC.

Sturges (*Sullivan's Travels*, 1941). He had always hoped to do Westerns, though he'd been cast in pretty much everything but during the 1930s, when the adult variety dried up after the failure of Raoul Walsh's *Big Trail* (1930). The Western's big comeback occurred late in the decade and, even before Ford's trend-setting *Stagecoach* (1939), McCrea starred in two biggies: *Wells Fargo* (1937) and *Union Pacific* (1939), and in time as William Frederic Cody in *Buffalo Bill* (1944). He later settled in with studio programmers, including a solid remake of *The Virginian* (1946), a role which more than fifteen years earlier had turned Gary Cooper into a star. Best of all was *Four Faces West* (1948), the *only* Hollywood oater in which no one fires a gun. Other historical characters included Sam Houston in *The First Texan* (1956) and Bat Masterson in *The Gunfight at Dodge City* (1959). His favorite was Earp; McCrea had hoped to do a TV series on Wyatt's life, but Desilu beat him to the punch. Not easily discouraged, he headed up *Wichita Town* (1959–1960), Earp's name altered to "Mike Dunbar," with Carlos Romero around as a noble Latino, "Rico Rodriguez," and George N. Neise as "Dr. Nat Wyndham." Stuck in a weak late-night time slot by NBC, this fine series never found an audience. Shortly afterward, McCrea starred (along with Randolph Scott who, like him, had also played both Earp and Masterson) in Sam Peckinpah's second film, *Ride*

the High Country (1962). Both stars insisted they would retire thereafter. Scott, who had never appeared on TV, stuck to his guns. McCrea came back to the screen on four occasions, the worst *Cry Blood, Apache* (1970) and the best *Mustang Country* (1976). SEE ALSO: Jody McCrea.

John McIntire

(1907–1991)

••••••••••••••••••••••••••••••

His raspy voice was well known by moviegoers long before they ever saw McIntire's face; they knew him as the most famous narrator of the *March of Time* newsreel series. On film, he looked old even while still young. McIntire could play good and bad with equal effectiveness, notably as the evil father of Richard Widmark in John Sturges's *Backlash* (1956) and the devoted dad to Elvis Presley in Don Siegel's *Flaming Star* (1960). Best of all were men with mixtures of both, notably scout Al Seiber in *Apache* (1954) for Robert Aldrich. In his first TV series, *Naked City* (1958), McIntire revived the role of the New York cop created by Barry Fitzgerald in the film (1948). This did not work out: McIntire insisted his character be killed off because he so despised working with abrasive costar James Franciscus. Next he was cast as a father (a nice one) to Darryl Hickman and Dick Davalos in the opening episode (1/23/61) of *The Americans*, a brother vs. brother

M

Civil War series. When Ward Bond passed away and a new wagon master was needed, McIntire stepped in as "Captain Chris Hale" on 3/15/61 and stayed with *Wagon Train* for nearly four years. He had a recurring role as Timothy Patrick Bryan, father of Rebecca, wife of the title character on *Daniel Boone* (1965). When Lee Cobb left *The Virginian* (1966), Charles Bickford came on board (as "John Grainger") but soon passed away. Once more Big John stepped in, as brother "Clay," and McIntire again occupied *Wagon Train's* one-time Wednesday evening slot. "Hale" and "Grainger" were both strong yet gentle men; not so "hanging" Judge Isaac Parker, the boss to John Wayne in *Rooster Cogburn* (1975). The following year McIntire replaced *another* star, Buddy Ebsen, in *The New Daughters of Joshua McCabe* (5/29/76). He was married to gifted actress Jeanette Nolan and father to actor Tim McIntire. SEE ALSO: Charles Bickford, Ward Bond, Lee Marvin, Jeanette Nolan.

Dallas McKennon

(1919–)

Beginning in the early fifties, McKennon provided voices for animated characters including "Buzz Buzzard" in *Woody Woodpecker*, "Pedro" in Disney's *Lady and the Tramp*, and the title character *and* companion "Pokey" on *The Gumby Show* (1957), TV's earliest

attempt at interactive entertainment. His first onscreen performance had been in a Western: a miner in *Bend of the River* (1952, James Stewart). TV's equivalent to that movie star, Fess Parker, cast McKennon as "Cincinnatus," owner of a lodging house/bar, in *Daniel Boone* (1964–1969). When Albert Salmi (as sidekick "Yadkin") left two-thirds of the way through the first season, McKennon's role expanded to fill that void. Visitors to Disney theme parks hear his voice as Benjamin Franklin in the "American Adventure" presentation. SEE ALSO: Fess Parker, Albert Salmi.

David McLean

(1922–1995)

Big, rugged David McLean looked so "right" for Westerns that he was hired to star in a series though he had never before acted. In the summer of 1960 he played the title character in *Tate*, a thirteen-episode show about a maimed bounty hunter. He captured villains to face justice, not motivated by greed but to pay for surgery to repair his damaged hand, covered by a thick black glove and hanging in a sling. Patricia Breslin, veteran of the sitcom *The People's Choice*, played "Jessica," a sensitive woman who kept Tate's spirits up. A man of few words (Tate did after all have only one name), critics noticed something vaguely philosophical about him too. Though NBC did not continue

and 1965) to the tune of Elmer Bernstein's stirring theme from *The Magnificent Seven* (1960), raking in terrific paychecks plus all the cigarettes he could smoke. McLean continued acting as well, guest-starring on TV Westerns (usually as marshal or sheriff) and playing two legendary figures on *Death Valley Days*: scout Kit Carson (1/25/63) and Stephen Austin, founder of Texas (4/21/64). Then McLean learned he had developed cancer. This transformed him from a pitchman into the cigarette industry's harshest critic. He campaigned for an end to the TV ads he had helped initiate; his efforts were partly responsible for an eventual ban, which went into effect before he died. McLean provided the inspiration for the novel (and later film) *Thank You for Smoking*; in the movie, Sam Elliott's character is based on David McLean. SEE ALSO: Sam Elliott.

THE ORIGINAL MARLBORO MAN: David McLean's short-lived series *Tate* brought him to the attention of an advertising firm that turned his image into a visual metaphor for the cowboy lifestyle. A bitter irony: McLean died of cancer after consuming the cigarettes he was given free by employer Marlboro. Courtesy NBC.

Steve McQueen

(1930–1980)

Early on, McQueen won a bit part in *Somebody Up There Likes Me* (1956) starring Paul Newman. The two hit it off, remaining friendly over the years, even when the sobriquet "Superstar of the Sixties" referred to one or the other, a competition for top gun always present. McQueen's great dream was to one day receive star billing over his friendly competitor. When Newman let McQueen know

the series, Philip Morris advertising execs were impressed by McLean's presence. They had come up with a new campaign called the Marlboro Man and were busily searching for precisely the right person. And here he was. Shortly thereafter, the performer (now with two good arms) rode the range nightly (between 1960 he had found the perfect script to do together, McQueen replied that he would be glad to, as long as his name came first. As Newman had become a star earlier and was older, *his* name *had* to rank number one. McQueen would not budge, so the role in *Butch Cassidy and the Sundance Kid* (1969) went to Robert Redford. McQueen finally did get his way when he and Newman appeared together in *The Towering Inferno* (1974), with McQueen billed first.

Raised in a home for boys without families, McQueen never finished the ninth grade; while still a teenager, he joined the U.S. Marines. Only he and Martin Landau were admitted to Lee Strasberg's Actors Studio during a year in which thousands auditioned. His TV Western premiere was as outlaw Bill Longley on *Tales of Wells Fargo* (2/10/58). McQueen's career began to kick in when *The Blob*, a low-budget teen exploitation horror flick, killed at the box office. Simultaneously, the TV Western *Wanted: Dead or Alive* premiered on 9/6/58. The series aired on CBS where, along with the sturdy *Gunsmoke* and the offbeat *Have Gun—Will Travel*, McQueen's show became part of a Western block that "owned" Saturday night. The concept of a likeable bounty hunter was considered controversial at a time when most TV Westerns focused on stalwart lawmen. Writer John Robinson, who came up with the idea, gave "Josh Randall" a tryout on a more conventional oater.

BOUNTY HUNTER: Like James Garner and Clint Eastwood, Steve McQueen transcended his TV role ("Josh Randall" on *Wanted: Dead or Alive*) to become one of the screen's reigning stars during the 1960s. Courtesy CBS.

On 3/7/58, McQueen guest-starred on *Trackdown* with Robert Culp. When audiences warmed to the new character, CBS gave McQueen and Robinson the go-ahead for a series.

In the late 1950s, it was de rigueur that a Western hero should own a unique weapon. Josh carried "Mare's Leg," a Winchester rifle sawed off at each end and worn holstered by his side. Shortly there would be some confusion with another show, as Nick Adams (who resembled McQueen) carried a sawed-off shotgun on *The Rebel*. Far more significant is that McQueen offered something more than most TV Western actors. That he might be a film star became crystal-clear after *The Magnificent Seven* (1960), in which he stole every scene he had with the stoic Yul Brynner by developing bits of business that "Vin" would perform, causing audience's eyes to drift toward McQueen. This provided a perfect prototype for the future King of Cool's roles, though McQueen was miffed he did not get to play young "Chico," a role that went to Horst Buchholz. In *The Great Escape* (1963), he got to ride one of his beloved Triumph motorcycles on the screen, a scene not in the original script, rather added at McQueen's suggestion. The contemporary action thriller *Bullitt* (1968) featured a wild chase in a sports car. McQueen returned to the Western, period and modern, in *Nevada Smith* (1966), *The Reivers* (1969, a "Southern"), *Junior Bonner* and *The Getaway* (both for Sam Peckinpah, 1972), and *Tom Horn* (1980), his final Western/penultimate film. McQueen died of lung cancer shortly after completing *The Hunter* (1980), which took him full cycle, as that film's fact-based hero was a modern version of his bounty hunter role. SEE ALSO: Nick Adams, Robert Culp, Wright King.

THE TV WESTERN IN THE TWENTY-FIRST CENTURY: Forsaking any sentimentality, the genre took on a leaner, meaner form in *Deadwood;* Ian McShane is seen here as Al Swearengen, a charismatic villain worthy of Shakespeare's Machiavellians Richard III, Iago, and Macbeth. Courtesy HBO Films.

Ian McShane

(1942–)

••••••••••••••••••••••••••••••••

After studying at the Royal Academy of Dramatic Arts in London,

McShane enjoyed an impressive stage career, including Joe Orton's *Loot* and *The Promise* with Sir Ian McKellan and Dame Judi Dench. He produced, directed, and starred in *Lovejoy* (1986) for the BBC, then appeared as "Don Lockwood" on *Dallas* (1989). Often cast as a villain, most notably in *Sexy Beast* (2000), McShane would become a TV legend as evil Al Swearengen, the self-possessed, manipulative town boss in *Deadwood* (2004–2006). That show's scripts, far from traditional Western fare, were filled with expletives-not-deleted, most hailing from McShane's mouth. Al abused prostitutes and manipulated the redistricting of the Gulch to his own benefit, hoping to keep the famed camp from becoming part of any state so it would remain wide open, as such more profitable for him. McShane won a Golden Globe in 2005 for this impressive villain of Shakespearean (e.g., *Richard III*) magnitude. Swearengen also served as the archenemy of Sheriff Seth Bullock (Timothy Olyphant), in truth far from perfect himself though a good guy by comparison. SEE ALSO: Keith Carradine, Timothy Olyphant.

Christian Meier
(1970–)
••••••••••••••••••••••••••••••

This Peruvian-born musician (keyboardist with Arena Hash) and graphic designer found work as an actor in a dozen *telenovelas*, those Latino soap operas that achieved huge popularity in third-world countries. He was picked to play "Diego de la Vega" in *Zorro: La Espada y la Rosa* (2007), an expensive, ambitious filmed series loosely based on the revisionist novel *Zorro* (2005) by Isabel Allende. Broadcast in the United States over Telemundo, the second-largest producer of Spanish-language content in the world, the series reached syndication in nearly one hundred countries worldwide. *Zorro: La Espada y la Rosa* retained characters created by pulp writer Johnston McCulley, as well as others added by the Walt Disney company during the late 1950s, while integrating Allende's reimagining of the source material. TV writer Carolina Diaz fashioned this sexually charged version of the period piece set in early nineteenth-century Los Angeles, and the focus was once again on a righteous avenger. Now, though, Diego was *not* some pureblood Spanish Don who patronizes poor people unable to stand up for themselves, but a mestizo, half Spanish/half Indian, a man not only *for* the people but truly *of* the people. An interesting plot device had Diego impregnating two women, one of whom, "Esmeralda" (Marlene Favela), Zorro's true love, is the gorgeous daughter of the very villain (Arturo Peniche) Zorro must vanquish; this caballero proved himself a swordsman in *every* sense of the term. Incredibly popular with Anglo as well as Latin Americans (broadcast in Spanish with English subtitles), the series premiered on 2/12/07, running nightly in hour (occasionally ninety-minute) installments. Considering the mushrooming Spanish population in the United States, this may well suggest the shape of things to come for American TV in general and Westerns in particular. SEE ALSO: Duncan Regehr, Guy Williams.

Judi Meredith
(1936–)
••••••••••••••••••••••••••••••

Child skating star Judy Boutin drifted into acting after multiple accidents ended her career on ice. Picked up for the role of "Judi" on *The George Burns Show* (1959), she then had recurring roles in two oaters, as "Esmee Labaillaire," a gorgeous green-eyed mystery girl on *The Adventures of Jim Bowie* (1956), and "Monique Deveraux," the sweetly sexy teen daughter of Jeanette Nolan's owner of the title enterprise in *Hotel de Paree* (1959–1960). SEE ALSO: Scott Forbes, Earl Holliman, Jeanette Nolan.

Jan Merlin
(1925–)

Merlin's first TV job was as "Roger Manning," pal to the hero on *Tom Corbett, Space Cadet* (1950–1954). He then played the elegant, aristocratic "Lieutenant Colin Kirby," a former Johnny Reb traveling west after the Civil War in the company of Yanks Kent Taylor and Peter Whitney, on *The Rough Riders* (1958–1959). Merlin was more often a villain: In *Hell Bent for Leather* (1960), he steals the horse and identity of Audie Murphy. SEE ALSO: Kent Taylor, Peter Whitney.

Denny (Scott) Miller
(1934–)

This big, genial UCLA basketball star turned actor has the distinction of starring in the worst Tarzan movie ever made: *Tarzan, the Ape Man* (1959). He joined *Wagon Train* on 4/27/64 as "Duke Shannon," gradually easing out Robert Horton as the scout only to be forced out himself

two and a half years later by Robert Fuller. Irregular roles in other Westerns included "Sheriff Owen Kearney" in *Lonesome Dove: The Series* (1994–1995) and "Noah McBride" on *Dr. Quinn, Medicine Woman* (1996). He also enacted the "Gorton Fisherman" in a yellow slicker on popular TV ads. SEE ALSO: Robert Fuller, Robert Horton.

Kristine Miller
(1929–)

This Argentinean-born beauty found work in minor Hollywood fare as both good girls (Rebecca Bryan in *Young Daniel Boone*, 1950, opposite David Bruce) and bad women ("Lady DeWinter" in *The Three Musketeers*, 11/24/50, forerunner of the made-for-TV movies). She replaced Mary Castle on *Stories of the Century* as Jim Davis's female partner for the final thirteen (of thirty-nine) episodes, playing "Margaret Jones," or "Jonesy" for short. Though lovely to look at, Miller did not pack the punch Castle had in the first twenty-six. Her final role before retirement was on *Tales of Wells Fargo* (3/27/61).

Ty Miller
(1964–)

Miller played "The Kid" on *The Young Riders* (1989–1992), a Billy Bonney–type bad boy. That the character hailed from the South added an interesting edge, as the others were all Northern sympathizers in the days preceding the Civil War. He later had a recurring role as the "Tech Agent" on *Without a Trace* (2002–2008). SEE ALSO: Stephen Baldwin, Josh Brolin.

(Sir) John Mills
(1908–2005)

A world-class Shakespearean actor/producer/director, Mills became known early on to movie audiences for patriotic World War II films (Noel Coward's *In Which We Serve*, 1942), and later as "Pip" in David Lean's adaptation of Dickens's *Great Expectations* (1946). He displayed diversity in 1960 with a tour-de-force opposite Alec Guinness in *Tunes of Glory* and as the engaging patriarch in Disney's splendid *Swiss Family Robinson*. Mills won an Oscar (Best Supporting Actor) for the role of the village idiot in Lean's overblown *Ryan's Daughter* (1970). Three years earlier, he had starred in the disastrous TV series *Dundee and the Culhane* as the former, a British barrister traveling across the frontier, helping those in need and accompanied by a young gun (Sean Garrison). CBS quickly canceled the horrid show, and Mills moved on to bigger and better things. SEE ALSO: Sean Garrison.

Cameron Mitchell
(1918–1994)

The young Mitchell won acclaim as "Hap," younger son of "Willy Loman," in the Broadway/film (1951) versions of Arthur Miller's *Death of a Salesman*. He played hundreds of movie and TV roles but was typecast as a ne'er-do-well with a penchant for hard liquor and easy women thanks to second leads in *Garden of Evil* (1954, Gary Cooper), *The Tall Men* (1955, Clark Gable), and TV's *The Beachcomber* series (1962), in which he played a New York City advertising executive who chucks it all to enjoy the good life of sun and surf. He was perfectly cast as "Buck Cannon" on *The High Chaparral* (1967–1971), as the irresponsible brother of "Big John" (Leif Erickson), the owner of the Arizona ranch. Buck would get drunk, hang out with brother-in-law "Manolito" (Henry Darrow), and try to corrupt John's innocent son "Blue" (Mark Slade), even casting an occasional eye in the direction of John's younger wife, "Victoria" (Linda Cristal), helping to create a frank, ambitious, adult, realistic Western in every sense. Mitchell played three historical Westerners: Pete Kitchen on *Death Valley Days* (6/7/60), George Rogers Clark on *Daniel Boone* (2/17/66), and General Lew Wallace in the TV movie *The Andersonville Trial* (5/17/70). Mitchell appeared in many B-budget films, including schlock horror flicks (*Nightmare in Wax*, 1969) and European mini-epics (*The Last of the Vikings*, 1961), both of which tarnished his later career and image. SEE ALSO: Linda Cristal, Leif Erickson.

Guy Mitchell
(1925–1999)
••••••••••••••••••••••••••••••

This influential pop singer is sadly forgotten today, though his records far outweigh his Western films/TV appearances in importance. First a big-band singer with Carmen Cavallero, he then broke out on his own. Under Mitch Miller's guidance, Mitchell opted for a country-style sound just MOR enough to keep him on the mainstream as well as C&W charts. "My Truly Truly Fair" and "The Roving Kind," both 1951, stretched the limits of pop, preceding the rockabilly sound that was still five years off. He won roles in Western musicals, including the blandly conventional *Those Redheads from Seattle* (1953, Rhonda Fleming) and the decidedly *un*conventional *Red Garters* (1954, Rosemary Clooney). Both starred Gene Barry, soon to be one of TV's Bat Mastersons. The next logical step was a series. Initially, Mitchell seemed to have hit the jackpot when he was hired by producer/star Audie Murphy for the second lead in NBC's *Whispering Smith* as "Detective George Romack," a Colorado lawman who grabbed a guitar and sang a song in each episode, qualifying Mitchell

as one of the only singin' cowboys introduced to the public via TV. Then everything fell to pieces: Mitchell broke his arm and couldn't strum *or* shoot, so the show shut down. His only other appearance was in *The Wild Westerners* (1962), a throwback to cheap indies Sam Katzman had done for Columbia (*Masterson of Kansas*, 1954; *The Gun That Won the West*, 1955; etc.) in the 1950s. Mitchell then quietly slipped into obscurity. SEE ALSO: Gene Barry, Audie Murphy.

George Montgomery
(1916–2000)
•••••••••••••••••••••••••••••••

Born George Letz, this actor played many of the Old West's famous lawmen except the one he was born for: Wyatt Earp. Montgomery had been Desilu's first choice for that character as they developed the weekly series that eventually made a star out of Hugh O'Brian; Montgomery was so in demand for B+ theatrical Westerns then that he turned them down. He often danced around the Earp legend, appearing in films featuring other people in that role. Montgomery was cast as "Billy" Ringo in *Gun Belt* (1953, with James Millican as Earp), Bat in *Masterson of Kansas* (1954, Bruce Cowling), and Pat Garrett in *Badman's Country* (1958, with Buster Crabbe). In truth, Montgomery had been too old for Ringo and not dandyish enough for Bat, while an essential niceness made him an unlikely candidate for the grim Garrett. How much better if he had played the soft-spoken, fair-minded Wyatt instead.

Much like his lookalike Jock Mahoney, Montgomery first found work as a stunt man, his good looks causing him to be cast in bits, small roles, and eventually as heroes in B+ Westerns. He did play romantic leads (*Roxie Hart*, 1942), period-piece adventurers (*The Sword of Monte Cristo*, 1951), and even Raymond Chandler's hard-boiled detective "Philip Marlowe" in *The Brasher Doubloon* (1947). After incarnating "Lassiter," Zane Grey's seminal hero in *The Riders of the Purple Sage* (1941), Montgomery became a Western star: James Fenimore Cooper's hero Natty Bumppo in both *The Iroquois Trail* (1950), a loose adaptation of *The Last of the Mohicans*, and *The Pathfinder* (1952). In *Davy Crockett, Indian Scout* (1950), he enacted not the historical Davy Crockett but a fictional nephew. His most bizarre casting was in *Jack McCall Desperado* (1953), in which Montgomery played the title character, the man who shot James "Wild Bill" Hickok (Douglas Kennedy) in the back, McCall here portrayed as a jolly good fellow for doing so! Two years after turning down Desilu's offer, Montgomery filmed a pilot called *Thousand Dollar Gun* as "Buchanan Smith." It aired on 10/20/57 but was not picked up. He guest-starred on *Wagon Train* (1/8/58) in "The Jesse Cowan Story," then was approached by Richard Bartlett and Norman Jolley, a writing/producing/directing team, to headline *Cimarron City* (1958–1959), an "ambitious" Western: sixty minutes with an immense cast of characters. The "lead" would be the town itself, an ever-growing Oklahoma city. As in film versions of Edna Ferber's *Cimarron*, we would watch the place change a little each week as the story continued: Gold, cattle, and oil were the resources that made this the most important spot in the state. Perhaps the public was not yet ready for something so complex. Fans tuned in expecting Montgomery to play a lawman, whereas he portrayed "Matthew Rockford," a gentleman rancher recently elected mayor. Other cast members included Audrey Totter as townswoman "Beth Purcell"; John Smith as the young deputy "Lane Temple"; Stuart Randall as the aging sheriff "Art Sampson"; Dan Blocker and Don Megowan as the "Budinger" brothers, "Tiny" and "Grant"; Fred Sherman and Claire Carleton as "Burt" and "Alice Purdy," a serious-minded couple; and Addison Richards as the quick-to-anger neighbor "Martin Kingsley." When ratings (opposite *Have Gun—Will Travel* and *Gunsmoke* on CBS) were not what NBC had hoped for, *Cimarron* was pared down to a conventional oater with Matt, actual status aside, acting as a lawman, with handsome young Lane riding alongside him.

Afterward Montgomery returned to movies, producing, directing, and co-writing as well as starring in action films shot in the Philippines (*Guerillas in Pink Lace*, 1964). He starred in *Hostile Guns* (1967), one of ubiquitous filmmaker R. G. Springsteen's attempts to keep the B Western alive. Montgomery also spent time on his favorite hobbies: carpentry, sculpting, and architecture. SEE ALSO: Dan Blocker, John Smith, Audrey Totter.

Clayton Moore
(1914–1999)
••••••••••••••••••••••••••••••••

Moore worked as everything from a child circus performer to a male model before heading west to break into B movies. Initially Moore found work as bad guys, including one real-life outlaw, the lead in *Jesse James Rides Again* (1947) and *Adventures of Frank and Jesse James* (1948), both Saturday morning serials. He went over to the right side of the law as William Frederic Cody in *Buffalo Bill in Tomahawk Territory* (1952) and as a masked hero (*Ghost of Zorro*, 1949). Producers Jack Chertok and Paul Landers, then planning to bring the Lone Ranger to the small screen, spotted Moore in the latter. He possessed the right look but the wrong voice; they insisted he study and imitate Brace Beemer's stentorian approach from the radio show. Moore mastered the booming, commanding vocals, winning the role he played (with Jay Silverheels as "Tonto") from 1949 to

1951, when he dropped out due to a salary dispute. John Hart subbed between 1952 and 1954; Moore returned with the guarantee of a larger paycheck in the fall of 1954 and more scripts featuring him in whiskers as the "Old Prospector," another alter-ego for "John Reid," these new episodes filmed in color. After B+-movie spinoffs *The Lone Ranger* (1956) and *The Lone Ranger and the Lost City of Gold* (1958), Moore played the character once more, in the "Peace Patrol" episode of *Lassie* (5/10/59). He had a long, lucrative career appearing at various events, particularly those oriented to children. Moore was challenged in 1975 when the Wrather company decided to mount a new film starring unknown Klinton Spilsbury. They took Moore to court over the issue of whether he could continue to wear the black mask. Though Moore lost the suit, he slipped on dark sunglasses instead. After the film flopped, no one cared anymore when he went back to wearing a mask and billing himself as the *real* Lone Ranger—which, for millions of Americans, he always was. And always will be. SEE ALSO: John Hart, Jay Silverheels.

Roger Moore
(1927–)
••••••••••••••••••••••••••••••••

This dapper, elegant, and impossibly handsome Englishman hardly seemed right for TV Westerns, yet he did turn up in two for Warner Bros. Earlier, Moore had received a pair of simultaneous offers: The Royal Shakespeare Company wanted to make him "the next Olivier," a handsome and brilliant performer, while MGM offered to turn him into a romantic matinee star. Confused and conflicted, Moore approached the great Noel Coward, asking advice. That living legend replied: "Go for the money!" Moore did precisely that. His first series was *Ivanhoe* (1958–1959), an American-funded/British-produced swashbuckler. Then it was off to Hollywood and WB, Moore now top-billed on *The Alaskans* (1959–1960), one of several attempts to cash in on an interest over statehood (including TV's *Klondike* and the film *North to Alaska*, 1960, with John Wayne). Moore's show was set in Skagway; he played the shady gambler "Silky Harris," making a fortune fleecing miners. It might have worked except for a writers' strike. Fresh scripts stopped coming in at midseason. Desperate to keep going, WB offered "Kangaroo Court" on (5/8/60), which viewers recognized as a scene-for-scene redux of a *Maverick* episode aired the previous year.

Meanwhile, James Garner had walked. Desperate to keep *Maverick* on the air, Moore slipped in as a cousin in "Bundle from Britain" (9/18/60), playing "Beau," named after "Pappy," and was the white sheep of a clan that prided itself on living on the edge, always a shining

knight, thus embarrassing the family "tradition." But Moore balked at WB's formulaic approach, demanding movie roles. He was cast alongside Clint Walker in the B+ *Gold of the Seven Saints* (1961), though Moore expressed disappointment when it was hyped as "Cheyenne meets Maverick!" Like James Garner, he quit, apparently much happier as Simon Templar on *The Saint* (1962–1969, *not* for WB), and in due time as James Bond on the big screen. Moore was knighted not for acting (he had abandoned the Bard early on) but for his wondrous, all-consuming charity work for UNICEF and other worthy organizations. SEE ALSO: Robert Colbert, James Garner, Jack Kelly, Jeff York.

Terry Moore

(1929–)

Born Helen Koford, Moore became a perennial starlet and mistress (possible wife?) to Howard Hughes. She eventually posed for *Playboy* at age fifty-five, looking more luscious than ever. Her emotional range as an actress allowed Moore to bounce from innocent tomboy (*Mighty Joe Young*, 1949) to prowling sex kitten (*Peyton Place*, 1957). She won an Oscar nomination for Best Supporting Actress for *Come Back, Little Sheba* (1952). Moore transformed into a ripe Western woman of dubious morality if undeniable charms on

TV, beginning with "Dallas," a bad girl in bondage in the first *Rawhide* (1/9/59). Moore starred in *Empire* (1962–1963) as "Constance Garrett," a flirtatious, spirited, provocative ranch girl. In real life, Moore survived five husbands, six if you count Hughes. Her defining quote was "I hate silicone, because now *everyone* can have what I have." In Moore's case, it all came to her naturally. SEE ALSO: Clint Eastwood, Richard Egan.

Read Morgan
(1931–)
••••••••••••••••••••••••••••••••

A longtime Hollywood fixture, Morgan played "Sergeant Hapgood Tasker," a gruff cavalryman and occasional assistant to "Marshal Fry" (Henry Fonda) during the second season (1960–1961) of *The Deputy*. SEE ALSO: Allen Case, Henry Fonda, Wallace Ford.

Jeff Morrow
(1907–1993)
••••••••••••••••••••••••••••••••

His given first name was Irving; Morrow is best remembered today as "Exeter of Metaluna," a visitor from the stars with a notably high forehead in the sci-fi classic *This Island Earth* (1955). Also in the cast were two other stars of upcoming Westerns: Russell Johnson (*Black Saddle*) and Rex Reason (*Man Without a Gun*). Morrow's show, *Union Pacific* (1958–

1959), cast him as advance man "Bart McClelland," who traveled ahead of oncoming railroad work teams, troubleshooting with outlaws, Indians, and anyone else who might slow the march of what some called progress. SEE ALSO: Susan Cummings, Russell Johnson, Rex Reason.

Rick Moses
(1952–)
••••••••••••••••••••••••••••••••

This actor starred in the brief-lived (four episodes broadcast) *Young Dan'l Boone* (1977), produced by Jimmy Sangster, who had precious few previous connections with TV Westerns though he had written and/or directed numerous Hammer horror films. The idea here was to tell the story of Boone's adventures *before* he journeyed to Kentucky, allowing for an unofficial prequel to Fess Parker's hugely successful show of the sixties. Devon Ericson appeared as Rebecca Bryan (later Boone), Ji-Tu Cumbaka the African American "Hawk," and Eloy Casados the Native American "Tsiskwa." For historical accuracy, this show eliminated the famed coonskin cap, which the real Boone never wore. For audiences, Daniel Boone without that fur headpiece seemed like a day without sunshine. Moses later found regular work on the daytime soap *General Hospital*. SEE ALSO: Ji-Tu Cumbaka, Peter Graves, Dewey Martin, Fess Parker.

James Murdock

(1931–1981)

••••••••••••••••••••••••••••••

Before *Rawhide*, Murdock had one role on TV as a young outlaw on the "Deliver the Body" episode of *Have Gun—Will Travel* (6/7/58). Cast as "Mushy," the youngest member of the cattle-drive crew (1959–1965), he was assigned the thankless job of assistant to the cook (Paul Brinegar). In real life, such a person would be fifteen or sixteen, so Murdock was directed to play the part as a teenager, Johnny Reb cap perched high on his head of 1950s Elvis-style hair. As the actor was twenty-eight when the show began, he looked/sounded a tad ridiculous trying to express naïveté, ever a more serious problem as the series wore on. SEE ALSO: Paul Brinegar, Clint Eastwood.

Audie Murphy

(1924–1971)

••••••••••••••••••••••••••••••

A poor Texas farm boy, Murphy joined the U.S. Army in World War II, emerging as the most decorated veteran of what author James Jones called "the last good war." James Cagney suggested that Murphy try Hollywood; the likelihood of an A-movie career tanked when *The Red Badge of Courage* (1951), adapted from the Stephen Crane classic and directed by John Huston, died at the box office despite strong reviews.

Murphy became a Universal contract player throughout the 1950s, including several historical figures: Billy Bonney (*The Kid from Texas*, 1950), Jesse James (*Kansas Raiders*, 1950), Bill Doolin (*The Cimarron Kid*, 1952), and John Clum (*Walk the Proud Land*, 1956). He played the lead in the remake of *Destry* (1954) and himself in *To Hell and Back* (1955), with immense success. Murphy then won supporting roles in two A oaters: *Night Passage* (1957, James Stewart) and *The Unforgiven* (1960, Audrey Hepburn and Burt Lancaster). His best Western performance came as the cold-blooded killer in *No Name on the Bullet* (1959). One critic dismissed him as "a pint-sized Gary Cooper"; fans saw him that way, though from a positive perspective, as the baby-faced tough guy whose war record proved him to be the real deal.

Wisely sensing that TV was where he needed to go, Murphy worked behind the scenes as a producer on *Whispering Smith* (1961), taken from a fine 1948 Alan Ladd movie as well as from the actual files of a Denver, Colorado, policeman who sensed the times were changing in the 1870s and began employing scientific developments to help track down bad guys. The show began shooting in 1958 for a fall 1959 debut; everything that could go wrong did. Costar Guy Mitchell as sidekick "George Romack" broke an arm, making it impossible for him to play his guitar. Production shut down. No sooner was he back than Sam Buffington, cast as older captain "John Richards," committed suicide. Somehow, twenty-six episodes finally made it into the can; ready for the premiere, the show was then canceled due to a news special on national security. The series finally limped onto the air, but it was too little, too late. Murphy admitted that by the time *Smith* arrived, "The whole thing looked as if it belonged to an earlier era." As the 1960s emerged, Hollywood's system fell under siege; long-term contracts were dropped and onetime studio stars had to scrounge for low-budget Western roles. Murphy's life was complicated by lingering nightmares over war, leading to an addiction to prescription drugs and obsessive gambling. He was traveling to a business meeting when a plane crash took his life. SEE ALSO: Guy Mitchell.

Ben Murphy

(1942–)

Playing a young journalist on *The Name of the Game* (1969), Murphy acquired a reputation as a Paul Newman lookalike. When *Butch Cassidy and the Sundance Kid* (1969) scored huge at the box office and ABC designed a TV-movie knockoff, *Alias Smith and Jones* (1/5/71), what better actor for Butch's equivalent, "Kid Curry" aka "Thaddeus Jones"? Pete Duel played the other half of the duo. Western stalwarts Forrest

Tucker, James Drury, and John Russell were around to add nostalgia to the TV series that ran from 1971 to 1973. The lighthearted approach clicked with viewers; the easygoing quality of the show hit home in the laidback 1970s. Murphy returned to the genre as "Will" on *The Chisholms* (1979–1980), a big-budget, high-quality show about a family moving west, with Murphy as the oldest son of Robert Preston and Rosemary Harris, taking command when the father faltered along the way. Other (non-Western) TV series include *Griff* (1973), *Gemini Man* (1976), and *Dirty Dozen: The Series* (1988). SEE ALSO: Brett Cullen, Roger Davis, Pete Duel, Rosemary Harris, Robert Preston.

Don Murray

(1929–)

After stage work and golden-age live TV from New York, Murray made his film premiere as contemporary cowboy "Bo," obsessed with Marilyn Monroe as "Cherie" in *Bus Stop* (1956). He alternated between modern drama (*A Hatful of Rain,* 1957; *Sweet Love, Bitter,* 1967) and big Westerns (*From Hell to Texas,* 1958; *These Thousand Hills,* 1959). As TV finally caught up with movies regarding the civil rights movement, teamings of black-white heroes (à la *I Spy*) came into vogue, with *The Outcasts* (1968–1969) the most significant Western example. Mur-

INTEGRATING THE WESTERN: During the late 1960s, as the Civil Rights Movement assumed a central position in American society, popular culture reflected our country's changing sensibility: Otis Young (*left*) and Don Murray played a former slave and his one-time master who roam the frontier together on *The Outcasts*. Courtesy ABC.

ray played "Earl Corey," a former plantation owner who, following the Civil War, travels west in the company of the former slave "Jemal David" (Otis Young). Timely then, the series remains a time capsule of how the genre adjusted to changing times. Murray later enjoyed success on the glitzy TV soap *Knots Landing* (1979–1981) as "Sid Fairgate." SEE ALSO: Otis Young.

Charles Napier
(1936–)

••••••••••••••••••••••••••••••

This big, beefy actor with a granite jaw twice the size of Charlton Heston's comes across as a caricature of Brian Dennehy, with whom he is often confused, perhaps because Napier played a role in *Rambo: First Blood Part II* (1985) comparable to Dennehy's in the first film. Napier was discovered by Russ Meyer and appeared in many of his trash masterpieces (*Beyond the Valley of the Dolls*, 1970); he also became a great favorite of Jonathan Demme (*Something Wild*, 1986). Napier played "Major Red Buell" in the World War II series *Baa Baa Black Sheep* (1976), looking like a wild riff on John Wayne in *Flying Tigers* (1942). He costarred with Rod Taylor in two brief-lived TV Westerns: *The Oregon Trail* (1977) as "Luther Sprague," grizzly mountain man turned trail guide; and *Outlaws*

(1986) as "Wolf Lucas," a bandit who passes through time to the present day. SEE ALSO: Rod Taylor.

Barry Nelson
(1917–2007)

••••••••••••••••••••••••••••••

Nelson rates as a shamefully underrated actor, perhaps because his quietly handsome Nordic appearance caused him to resemble the blandest of all stars, Van Johnson. MGM signed Nelson to a contract in part to make Johnson aware that this more talented lookalike could always be substituted in a film should Johnson cause problems. This crippled Nelson's film potential, his best roles not coming until decades later as "Captain Harris" in *Airport* (1970) and "Stuart Ullman" in *The Shining*

(1980). He made a great impression as a Broadway performer (Tony-nominated for *The Act*), playing the male lead in *Mary, Mary* onstage (opposite the gifted Barbara Bel Geddes) and in the 1963 movie (with Debbie Reynolds). Nelson owns a bit of pop-culture/TV history as the first person ever to enact James Bond, in a 1954 version of Ian Fleming's *Casino Royale*. In his TV Western role as "Jonathan Banner" in *Hudson's Bay* (1959), he worked for the title company, coming into contact with varied people who wandered through the northern frontier—Europeans, from Russians to French to English, and numerous Native American tribes—some who wanted to work hard and get rich slowly, and others out to make a fast buck. The show was often confused with another series, CBC's *Tomahawk*, about the earlier founding of that fur company. SEE ALSO: James Coburn, Jacques Godin, Pedro Gonzalez-Gonzalez, Roger Moore, George Tobias.

Willie Nelson

(1933–)

••••••••••••••••••••••••••••••

Roadhouse, blues, folk, pop, mountain music, gospel, and outlaw country all come together in the unique songs Nelson writes and performs. Hailing from Depression-era Texas, he headed for Nashville, composed for Patsy Cline ("Crazy"), and belatedly became a headliner in the 1970s.

His first Western role came in *The Electric Horseman* (1979), a contemporary social comedy with Robert Redford and Jane Fonda. He incarnated the title legendary figure in *Barbarosa* (1982) and teamed with Kris Kristofferson for the first time in *Songwriter* (1984), an inside peek at the country music scene. The two hit it off; when Kristofferson (as Jesse) joined with Johnny Cash (Frank) for *The Last Days of Frank and Jesse James* (2/17/86), Nelson came along for the ride as General Shelby. He drafted Waylon Jennings and all four formed the supergroup the Highwaymen. In TV's *Stagecoach* remake (5/18/86), Nelson appeared in Thomas Mitchell's Oscar-winning role as Doc, the last name changed from "Boone" to Holliday. His most deeply personal indie (some would say vanity) project was *Red Headed Stranger* (1986), based on his balladic album, with Morgan Fairchild as the bad girl and Katharine Ross the good one. Then it was back to TV as "John Henry Lee," another larger-than-life bandit, pursued by Richard Widmark in *Once Upon a Texas Train* (1/3/88). The most interesting aspect of that film came in the nostalgic casting of TV Western stars in cameos: Chuck Connors; Ken Curtis; Jack Elam; Gene Evans; Dub Taylor; Harry Carey, Jr.; Don Collier; Hank Worden; and Stuart Whitman; with Jeb Adams subbing for his late father Nick. Nelson played "Marshal Elias Burch" on *Dr. Quinn, Medicine*

Woman (1996–1998), then reunited
with Kristofferson, Jennings, and
Travis Tritt (who took over the ailing
Johnny Cash's role) for *Outlaw Justice*,
aka *The Long Kill* (1/24/99). More
recently Nelson played "Uncle Jesse"
in the film *The Dukes of Hazzard: The
Beginning* (2005). SEE ALSO: Johnny
Cash, Waylon Jennings, Kris Kristofferson, Denver Pyle.

Leslie Nielsen
(1926–)
••••••••••••••••••••••••••••••

Son of a Canadian Mountie, this
Toronto arts/acting student can claim
blood relations to the legendary actor/
humanitarian Jean Hersholt. Much
work in golden-age TV drama gave
way to minor-league movie stardom in *Forbidden Planet* (1956) and
Tammy and the Bachelor (1957). His
first Western role came as a cattle
baron in *The Sheepman* (1958, Glenn
Ford). Nielsen was cast by Disney as
Colonel Francis Marion, Robin Hood
of the American Revolution, who
fights Colonel Tarleton (John Sutton)
and redcoats via guerilla tactics in the
Carolinas in *The Swamp Fox* (1959–
1961). This excellent quasi-Western's
superb cast included J. Pat O'Malley,
Louise Beavers, Clarence Muse,
Tim Considine (killed in the third
episode), Hal Stalmaster (as another
youth assuming Considine's place),
Myron Healey, and Arthur Hunnicutt as various early frontier raiders.
Nielsen played Colonel Custer in *The*

Plainsman (1966) and a bad guy in
Gunfight in Abilene (1967) opposite
Bobby Darin. After a recurring role
as "Vincent Corbino" on *Kung Fu*
(1975), he achieved full stardom by
spoofing himself as "Frank Drebin"
in *Police Squad!* (1982) and the *Naked
Gun/Airplane!* movies.

Jeanette Nolan
(1911–1998)
••••••••••••••••••••••••••••••

This popular radio actress from the
1930s met and married John McIntire; after that event, the two worked
together often. Nolan's film debut
had been as Orson Welles's wife in
Macbeth (1948). Her first Western
role was as "Ma Higgins" in *Saddle
Tramp* (1950). She played nearly a
dozen Western women nicknamed
"Ma" on TV and in films before
turning fifty. Her first series role
was on *Hotel de Paree* (1959–1960)
as "Annette Deveraux," the glamor-
ous older woman who with pretty
daughter "Monique" (Judi Meredith)
runs the title hotel. Nolan excelled
at playing women on the edge of
hysteria, including two for John
Ford: "Mrs. McCandless" in *Two
Rode Together* (1961) and "Nora Ericson" in *The Man Who Shot Liberty
Valance* (1962). She provided the
voice for the deceased "Norma Bates"
in Hitchcock's *Psycho* (1960), while
husband John appeared as the county
sheriff. Nolan became one of "The
Ensemble" for *The Richard Boone*

Show, an ambitious attempt at repertory company for TV (1963–1964). She played on several *Wagon Trains*, including the title role in "The Janet Hale Story" (5/31/61), about the lost love of wagon master "Chris" (McIntire). When McIntire assumed the part of ranch owner "Clay Grainger" on *The Virginian* (1967–1970), Nolan came onboard as wife "Holly," the tip of the iceberg in a tendency to shift Westerns away from single-parent situations to couples. Their extended family included Sara Lane as "Elizabeth" and Don Quine as "Stacey." Nolan appeared for the first time on *Gunsmoke* as "'Dirty' Sally Fergus" (3/1/71); she returned several times as the foul-mouthed, ornery, yet genuinely caring pioneer woman. The character was spun off as *Dirty Sally* (1974), leaving Dodge to head for the California goldfields in the company of young gunfighter "Cyrus Pike" (Dack Rambo), altering the lives of all she came into contact with for the better, thanks to her "Aw, shucks!" folk wisdom. Nolan played one of the ensemble of female stars in the feminist Western *The Wild Women of Chastity Gulch* (10/31/82), the ladies running that town while the men headed off to the Civil War. Her final film role came, fittingly, in a Western: "Ma Booker," mother of Robert Redford's cowboy in *The Horse Whisperer* (1998). SEE ALSO: John McIntire, Dack Rambo.

Tommy Nolan

(1948–)

Taking a cue from the movie classic *Shane* (1953), *Buckskin* told the story of a Western community as seen through the eyes of a ten-year-old, played by the gifted young Tom Nolan. He resembled *Shane*'s Brandon De Wilde and Tommy Rettig ("Jeff" on the original *Lassie*) in both appearance and talent. Scripts (even camera angles) were crafted so that we grasped "Jody" not only as the central character but also as our point of view. The hero figure for the boy was the stalwart "Marshal Tom Sellers" (Mike Road). Joey's mother, widow "Annie O'Connell" (Sally Brophy), ran a boardinghouse, so we (looking over Jody's shoulder) had an opportunity to study an assortment of characters, notably "The Newcombs" (Michael Lipton and Shirley Knight), longtime guests.

Chuck Norris

(1940–)

Oklahoma-born, California-raised, this U.S. Air Force veteran (Korea) grew intrigued with martial arts in the service and pursued studying/teaching after his return. His students included Steve McQueen and James Coburn. Norris trained alongside

MODERN MAN OF THE WEST: When the period Western fell into decline, other venues had to be created to continue the values inherent in the genre. Among the most successful was *Walker, Texas Ranger*, in which martial arts expert Chuck Norris provided an old-fashioned Lone Star hero in contemporary Texas. Courtesy CBS.

Bruce Lee and went up against him in his first major film, *Return of the Dragon* (1972). He retired (undefeated) as the Pro World Middleweight karate champ to pursue movies. The timing proved perfect as the karate craze even then picked up steam. Low-budget, high-impact action films followed, including the *Missing in Action* series during the 1980s (revealing the star's deep, ongoing concern for Vietnam vets). Norris's best film was *Lone Wolf McQuade* (1983), as a contemporary Texas Ranger who takes on and defeats David Carradine in the classic finale. The aura of the spaghetti Western proved highly effective and likely led to the decision to play "Cordell Walker" on *Walker, Texas Ranger* (1993–2001), as well as the brief-lived spinoff *Sons of Thunder* (1999). Though not a Western

per se (more a modern crime series), *Walker* allowed Norris to project his values as the last of the old-time lawmen, tolerant of an educated partner, "James Trivette" (Clarence Gilyard, Jr.), who brings scientific methodology into play. Executive-producer status allowed this conservative Republican to present his political views through the action drama. Norris's civil rights agenda (always emphasizing positive Latino, Native American, and black characters) also surfaced. He wrote five *Walker* scripts, including "Sons of Thunder" (5/4/97), with his son Aaron (who also directed) starring in this pilot for a spinoff. Norris most recently played Walker in *Walker, Texas Ranger: Trial by Fire* (10/16/05). SEE ALSO: David Carradine, James Coburn, Steve McQueen.

Warren Oates

(1928–1982)

• •

As hillbilly-ish in appearance as his name suggests, Oates graduated from the University of Louisville and served in the U.S. Marines. He played numerous menacing redneck maniacs on *Gunsmoke*, *Rawhide*, etc. Cast by Sam Peckinpah in *Ride the High Country* (1962) as one more Western wack job, Oates soon received larger roles in *Major Dundee* (1965) and *The Wild Bunch* (1969), and at long last a sympathetic lead in *Bring Me the Head of Alfredo Garcia* (1974), as well as the title character in John Milius's Westernized version of *Dillinger* (1973). His best movie role ever: the hard driver in Monte Hellman's bizarre road movie *Two-Lane Blacktop* (1971). Oates's first TV series role had been as "Ves Painter," a surly rodeo rider, in *Stoney Burke* (1962–1963). Oates always hoped to land his own series, recreating Bogart's part ("Charlie Allnut") in a pilot for *The African Queen* (1977, with Mariette Hart-

ley—his old *High Country* costar—as "Rose Sayer") and Wayne's "Rooster Cogburn" in *True Grit* (5/19/78, with Lisa Pelikan as "Mattie Ross"). Neither sold as a series. Oates may be best remembered today as the leering deputy who menaces Sidney Poitier in the Oscar-winning Best Picture *In the Heat of the Night* (1967). SEE ALSO: Jack Lord.

Hugh O'Brian

(1925–)

• •

Who was: a) the youngest drill instructor (age seventeen) in the history of the U.S. Marines; b) the performer who played Bud Abbott's role (opposite Buddy Hackett in a part intended for Lou Costello) in *Fireman Save My Child* (1954) when that famed comic duo turned the project down; c) the first choice to star in both *The Virginian* (1962) and *Cowboy in Africa* (1967–1968) on TV; d) the actor who played the final badman killed onscreen in a gunfight with John Wayne (*The Shootist*, 1976)? Answer to all of the above: Hugh O'Brian. Actor/director Ida Lupino discovered the handsome Irishman when, following his service discharge, O'Brian found steady work in a Santa Barbara stock company. Universal signed him to a contract, and many Western roles followed: "Lem" Younger (*The Return of Jesse James*, 1950); Lieutenant Lamar (*The Man from the Alamo*, 1953); American Horse (*White Feather*, 1955); and General Nelson Miles (*Gunsmoke: The Last Apache*, 3/18/90). His signature role as the renowned lawman in *The Life and Legend of Wyatt Earp* (1955–1961) was offered to O'Brian when George Montgomery turned the part down.

The series premiered on 9/6/55. The first episode, titled "Mr. Earp Becomes a Marshal," set the tone for what was to come with this unique series, following the actual line of the man's life, at least if one accepts the Stuart N. Lake biography at face value. By doing so over half a dozen years, the series—produced by Desilu and personally overseen by executive producer Louis F. Edelman and head writer Frederick Hazlitt Brennan— assumed a rare leisurely approach to the material that would be surpassed only by Disney's *Texas John Slaughter*. This resulted in an impressive if imperfect ongoing TV epic, chroni-

cling how law and order actually worked on the frontier.

A contrast to *Gunsmoke* (which throughout its long run was, like *Earp* during its second through fourth seasons, set in Dodge City, Kansas) begs consideration. However "adult" *Gunsmoke* appeared as to its psychological approach toward the characters, its writers revealed no historical sense of what a lawman's role (U.S. Marshal, town deputy marshal, county sheriff, city constable, etc.) in any Western community had actually been like. *Earp* provided the perfect contrast, along with an alternative definition of what an "adult" Western could be by offering accurate details of the day- to-day workings of a lawman with a highly political mayor, a self-serving town council, an often corrupt local judge, and other peace officers who may or may not have proved coopera- tive. In that first episode, Wyatt rode into small, lawless Ellsworth, Kansas, summoned by an old friend, Mar- shal Crawford (Dabbs Greer). Earp also discovered there a more recent acquaintance, young Bat Masterson (Alan Dinehart), jailed after running up against the powers-that-be. (The story of the Earp-Masterson initial meeting as buffalo hunters would not be told on the screen, large or small, until Lawrence Kasdan's 1994 *Wyatt Earp*, with Kevin Costner and Tom Sizemore.) The manner in which Wyatt put on a badge after Craw- ford's death at the hands of crazed Billy Thompson (Hal Baylor), then

FIRST OF THE FAST GUNS: Hugh O'Brian (Wyatt Earp, *left*) and Mason Alan Dinehart III (Bat Masterson) initiated the tradition of the adult TV Western in 1955. Courtesy Hugh O'Brian, Mason Dinehart, and Desilu.

faced down Billy's older brother Ben (Denver Pyle), had been duly recorded in Lake's *Frontier Marshal* (1931), drawn from that author's interviews with Earp during his final days in 1920s California. Earp then oversaw the making of a movie based on his life starring Tom Mix (subject of the fictionalized 1988 film *Sunset*). Some historians do question the historicity of the events as chronicled in Lake's tome. The denouement proved shocking to anyone weaned on earlier TV Westerns where "the bad guy" always received his just deserts. A judge in

the services of the Thompsons (the major money influence in the area) turned Ben loose after a slap on the wrist and a small fine. The judge then threw Earp and Masterson in jail for questioning his veracity. The episode ended ambiguously as Earp tried to decide if it was worth the effort to wear a badge. This issue would dog him throughout the series' run.

The "ballad" (de rigueur following *Davy Crockett*) was here sung not in period style but by the Ken Darby Singers in the manner of a barbershop quartet, planned as a signature of Desilu's historical Westerns though only one other such show, *Jim Bowie,* premiered the following year. Each episode of *Earp* played less as a story than an anecdote, not ending in any conventional sense, rather stopping when time ran out. The following week's installment picked up where the previous one had left off, an approach that would continue for half a dozen years, conveying a sense that this was one long "loop" covering what the title promised: a balance between the man's reality and his myth. Since "what really happened" now seemed long lost in the mists of time, Wyatt Earp had emerged as "partly fact and partly fiction," as Kris Kristofferson might put it.

Another distinction between *Earp* and other adult oaters was the dynamic quality of the relationships. The more formulaic shows would introduce a hero, supporting characters, and "the situation" in the first episode. If there was to be a "special gun," it too showed up at once, as in *Johnny Ringo.* After that, nothing would change, at least not until change could no longer be avoided when actors quit and their characters had to be replaced. *Earp* offered an entirely different approach. The first third of season one dealt with the character's brief Ellsworth stay. Anyone who thought Bat, seemingly established as a young sidekick like "Dick West" (Dick Jones) on *The Range Rider* (Jock Mahoney), would continue in that guise soon grasped

that here, as in life, *nothing* remains constant. Bat headed off on his own after four episodes, returning toward season's end following Wyatt's move to Wichita. The famed Buntline Special with an extended barrel, allegedly presented to Wyatt by dime novelist Ned Buntline (Lloyd Corrigan), would be gradually phased into the ongoing narrative toward the end of season one. Other figures, ranging from Doc Holliday (played by Douglas Fowley and occasionally Myron Healey) to Ben Thompson (Denver Pyle, later Walter Coy) and countless others (judges, mayors, sheriffs, etc.), were woven in and out as Wyatt moved again, at the beginning of season two, to Dodge. Finally, at the end of the fourth/start of the fifth season, the hero moved to Tombstone, Arizona, and his date with destiny at the O.K. Corral.

However admirable, the show's ambitions raised the bar so high that *Earp* could not always meet the standards it had set for itself. The biggest disappointment involved a number of fictional deputies, including "Hal" (William Tannen) and "Shotgun Gibbs" (Morgan Woodward). This precluded the full development of Wyatt's friendships with such remarkable figures as Big Bill Tilghman, Charles Bassett, and Luke Short, all of whom appeared only once or twice. The uniqueness of those friendships, each as fascinating as those with Masterson and Holliday, was never developed in full complexity. Even family issues between Wyatt and brothers Virgil and Morgan in Tombstone were played down so he could be accompanied instead by Gibbs, a "Festus Haggen" figure. Other weakness included a decision to eliminate the important women in Wyatt's life, leading to the timeworn male-fantasy approach. Pretty (fictional) women (beginning with Gloria Talbott as "Martha Connell") came and went. During the fifth season, episodes chronicled flirtations with "Emma Clanton" (Carol Thurston), beautiful kid sister to the bad-boy brothers, and Nellie Cashman (Randy Stuart), a real-life townswoman who, history tells us, disliked Earp. His constant companion in Dodge, Mattie Blaylock, never once appeared, while Josephine Marcus (Earp), who stood at the absolute epicenter of Wyatt's enmity with Sheriff John Behan (Lash La Rue, later Steve Brodie) in Tombstone, was merely suggested by a renamed version (Jean Allison as "Mina Marlin") who appeared once (2/14/61). The dramatization of the romantic triangle would, years later, drive the admirable *Tombstone* (1993). Depicting sequential marriages of real-life people would be done only once on TV, by Disney, on *Texas John Slaughter*.

All of that said, *Earp* nonetheless rates as an exceptional show. The final episodes presented events leading up to the O.K. Corral gunfight more accurately than any other TV or film presentation. Only here do

we learn the full truth: Following the death of Newman Haynes "Old Man" Clanton (Trevor Bardette), the gang split into factions, one run by Curly Bill Brocious (William Phipps) and Johnny Ringo (Peter M. Thompson in 1959–1960, then Norman Alden in 1961; John Pickard in 1957 as Johnny Ringgold, replaced by Britt Lomond in 1960–1961), the other by Ike Clanton (Rayford Barnes) and Tom McLowery (aka McLaury, Gregg Palmer). When the paranoid Ike began to fear that Curly Bill and Ringo considered him soft, Ike encouraged his younger brother Billy (Ralph Reed, Gary Gray), along with Tom and Frank (George Wallace) McLowery, to ride into Tombstone and strut around wearing guns. They were to back down the Earp faction (who had posted a "no guns in town" edict), then head home to the ranch, Ike's courage proven. The cowboys were stunned when the Earps confronted and attempted to disarm them, and an approximately thirty-second shootout no one wanted spontaneously occurred. This vivid delineation of the events would be followed by one more episode in which the Earps were tried but cleared of manslaughter. Sadly, the series then failed to follow up with the bushwhacking of Virgil (John Anderson, earlier played by Ross Elliott) and Morgan (Ray Boyle, aka Dirk London) that caused Wyatt, Doc, and several others to go on the vengeance trail. Earp buffs would have to wait for *Hour of the Gun* (1967) for disclosure of what happened next.

After Earp, O'Brian turned down *The Virginian* (the role went to James Drury) to concentrate on movies. He would make a cameo appearance as Earp in *Alias Jesse James* (1959) with Bob Hope and on "A Gather of Guns" (9/10/89) and "Body to Die For" (9/10/89) on *Paradise*, as well as *The Gambler Returns: The Luck of the Draw* (1991). Today, O'Brian oversees HOBY, the Hugh O'Brian Youth Leadership program, which recognizes gifted teens, particularly from poor families, encouraging them to pursue college, act, etc. SEE ALSO: John Anderson, Trevor Bardette, Gene Barry, Lloyd Corrigan, Alan Dinehart, Douglas (V.) Fowley, Myron Healey, Lee Horsley, Morgan Woodward.

Dan(iel) O'Herlihy
(1919–2005)

••••••••••••••••••••••••••••••

This Irish-born Shakespearean actor turned in a marvelous performance as "Macduff" in Orson Welles's *Macbeth* (1948). His first Western (actually Eastern) role was as a redcoat officer in *The Iroquois Trail* (1950). O'Herlihy's TV Western career began with a superior *Zane Grey Theater* episode, "The Bitter Land" (12/6/57, Peggy Wood). He was Oscar-nominated for his bravura performance in Luis Buñuel's excellent existential 1954 version of Daniel Defoe's *The*

Adventures of Robinson Crusoe. In the 1960s, as Westerns were reinvented, O'Herlihy would be top-billed as "Doc McPheeters" in ABC's big-scale adaptation of *The Travels of Jaimie McPheeters* (1963–1964), about a father and son (young Kurt Russell as the title character) on their way west with a caravan, the initial focus on their complex relationship. When the ratings proved weak, this initially intriguing series would be reduced to conventional fare, essentially a *Wagon Train* redux, with Charles Bronson signing on as a hard-bitten wagon master, O'Herlihy's role sadly diminished. He later played the "Old Man" in *Robocop* (1987) and its sequel, then returned to TV Westerns, intriguingly costarring with Russell (now fully grown), in an occasional role as "Matthew Hatcher" in *The Quest* (1976). SEE ALSO: Charles Bronson, Tim Matheson, Kurt Russell.

Merlin Olsen
(1940–)

••••••••••••••••••••••••••••••

This Rams football great (defensive tackle, 1962–1976) and component of the Fearsome Foursome made his film debut in *The Undefeated* (1969) with John Wayne, also featuring Roman Gabriel. He played "Perlee" on a memorable *Kung Fu* episode, "Nine Lives" (2/15/73). When Victor French left *Little House on the Prairie*, producer/star Michael Landon brought Olsen aboard in a similar role as "Jonathan Garvey," a pioneer with a notably strict wife, "Alice" (Hersha Parady, 1977–1981). Landon spun Olsen off to *Father Murphy* (1981–1983), in which "John Michael Murphy" poses as a priest to help the poor, particularly orphans, assisted by "Mae" (Katherine Cannon) and "Gage" (Moses Gunn) in this spiritual show with strong family flavor. Olsen later played the lead in a contemporary drama, *Aaron's Way* (1988). SEE ALSO: Michael Landon.

Timothy Olyphant

(1968–)

••••••••••••••••••••••••••••

Honolulu-born, this actor majored in theater and won fame as a competitive swimmer at the University of Southern California. Supporting film roles included *A Life Less Ordinary* (1997), *Rock Star* (2001), *The Girl Next Door* (2004), and the recurring part of "Bret Farraday" in *High Incident* (1997), a contemporary police drama. Olyphant played Seth Bullock, the central historical character in *Deadwood* (2004–2006), an intense, edgy HBO series credited with reviving interest in the genre if in a notably different form, stressing the ugly, unpleasant aspects of frontier life. Bullock arrives in the Gulch (a camp, not a town) at about the time of the Custer Massacre (6/25/1876), planning to kick-start his life as a store owner only to be befriended by down-and-out Marshal James Butler

Hickok (Keith Carradine). Wild Bill places Bullock in immediate conflict with the raunchy saloon owner/town boss Al Swearengen (Ian McShane). Following Hickok's assassination, Bullock finds himself forced into the position of unwitting hero when, out of loyalty to the deceased living legend, he becomes a local lawman in the West's meanest territory. SEE ALSO: Keith Carradine, Ian McShane, Molly Parker.

J. Pat O'Malley

(1904–1985)

••••••••••••••••••••••••••••

Had Alfred Hitchcock been born an actor rather than a director, he would likely have been J. Pat O'Malley. Short and plump, fussy and fidgety, with pursed lips and wide open eyes, the British-born character actor immigrated to America, where he never had trouble finding work on TV or in movies, on radio or onstage. Today he is perhaps best remembered for the voices he supplied in several Disney classics, including *The Wind in the Willows* ("Cyril," 1949), *Alice in Wonderland* ("The Walrus" and "The Carpenter," "Tweedledee" and "Tweedledum," 1951), and *The Jungle Book* ("Colonel Hathi of the Elephants," 1967). Disney also hired O'Malley for two live-action Westerns. He played "Perkins," befuddled butler to "Marty Markham," a spoiled rich kid (David Stollery), in *The Adventures of Spin and Marty* (1955) as well as two follow-up serials on *The Mickey Mouse Club* (ABC). He played a rare tough guy as Sergeant O'Reilly, member of the Revolutionary War outfit known as Marion's Men, in *The Swamp Fox* (1959–1961), with Leslie Nielsen as General Francis Marion; earlier on that series O'Malley had played a drunken redcoat. He also enacted "Judge Caleb," to whom Russell Johnson's lawman had to report, on *Black Saddle* (1959–1961); "Duffy," front man for a traveling show, on *Frontier Circus* (1961–1962); and an "Indian medicine man" on the 1965 season of *F Troop*. His non-Western roles included the tipsy "Walker" on *Captain David Grief* (1960), a South Sea island adventure, and the ever-bemused "Harry Burns" on *My Favorite Martian*'s 1963–1964 season. SEE ALSO: John Derek, Richard Jaeckel, Russell Johnson, Leslie Nielsen, Chill Wills.

Ryan O'Neal

(1941–)

••••••••••••••••••••••••••••••

This macho pretty boy attempted to forge a Redford-esque career, but an arrogant attitude, in life and onscreen, plus a limited acting range cut away his appeal. O'Neal first appeared as a regular on *Empire* (1962–1963), a contemporary Western, playing "Tal Garret," spoiled son of ranch matriarch "Lucia" (Anne Seymour), mentored toward manhood by rugged foreman "Jim Redigo" (Richard Egan). He found greater success in a similar role on the New England–set *Peyton Place*, premiering in 1964. *Love Story* (1970) made him a movie star (temporarily) after O'Neal somehow managed *not* to crack a smile while Ali MacGraw delivered the worst line in film history, courtesy of Erich Segal: "Love means never having to say you're sorry." Then came numerous films, mostly negligible. One big-screen Western featured O'Neal's best performance, as a young cowboy partnered with William Holden in *Wild Rovers* (1971). He is also known as Farrah Fawcett's on-again/off-again mate. SEE ALSO: Richard Egan, Terry Moore.

Jeff Osterhage

(1953–)

••••••••••••••••••••••••••••••

Like the better-known Bruce Boxleitner, this young actor hoped to revive the traditionalist TV Western. His first lead was as "John Golden" in *The Legend of the Golden Gun* (4/10/79), a Lone Ranger–like hero helping General Custer (Keir Dullea) track William Quantrill (Robert Davi). He played younger brother to Tom Selleck and Sam Elliott in *The Sacketts* (5/15/79) and *The Shadow Riders* (9/28/82) and was the voice of "Marshal Anderson" for the first-person shooter (FPS) video game *Outlaws* (1997). SEE ALSO: Sam Elliott, Tom Selleck.

(Walter) Jack Palance

(1919–2006)

Palance rates as the villain's villain, incarnating unadulterated evil in its various guises: Jack the Ripper (*Man in the Attic*, 1953), Attila the Hun (*Sign of the Pagan*, 1954), "Mr. Hyde" (*The Strange Case of Dr. Jekyll and Mr. Hyde*, 1968), and the Count (*Dracula*, 1973). All these were preceded by a memorable role in *the* classic Western: "Jack Wilson," the devil atop a horse in *Shane* (1953), up against the angelic Alan Ladd. Other Western roles included Apache Chief Toriano (*Arrowhead*, 1953) and cattle baron L. G. Murphy (*Young Guns*, 1988). Palance never starred on a TV Western, though he served as spokesman for Time-Life books when they offered handsomely bound copies of their Old West series to viewers (1975–1985). Wearing an outfit reminiscent of his dark garb from *Shane*, Palance grinned wickedly, then menacingly whispered about the

volumes: "They make me *feel* like I was really *there!*" For the better part of a decade, that qualified Palance as the most prominent Western figure on TV. When Billy Crystal began work on *City Slickers* (1991) and Clint Eastwood turned down the role of "Curly Washburn," Crystal recalled Palance's impact in those commercials and offered him the part, which won Palance a Best Supporting Actor Oscar that, as fans will recall, he accepted enthusiastically if hardly humbly.

Gregg Palmer

(1927–   )

Palmer broke into show business as a radio announcer via his commanding voice. A Universal Studios contract player in the early 1950s, he had small roles in movies starring Audie Murphy (*Column South*, 1953; *To Hell and Back*, 1955), early on billed by his birth name, Palmer Lee. He played Grat Dalton in *The Cimarron Kid* (1952), Jack Slade on *Stories of the Century* (3/4/55), Tom McLowery during *Wyatt Earp*'s final season (1960–1961), and Jim Bridger in Disney's *Kit Carson and the Mountain Men* miniseries (1977). His friendship with John Wayne during Duke's final years led to small parts in big films: *The Undefeated* (1969), *Chisum* (1970), *Big Jake* (1971), and the Duke's last hurrah, *The Shootist* (1976). SEE ALSO: Jim Davis, Audie Murphy, Hugh O'Brian.

Peter Palmer

(1931–)

Wisconsin born and Missouri raised, Palmer entered the University of Illinois via a football scholarship, afterward joining the military. He tried out for an "All Army Entertainment" contest, which he won. Palmer's spot on Ed Sullivan's *Toast of the Town* (8/11/57) was noticed by Hollywood producer Norman Panama and director Melvin Frank, who were then looking for an unknown to play the lead in the big musical *Li'l Abner* (1959). Palmer later played "Sergeant Bustard," a fictional Irish hard-drinkin' non-com at Fort Hays, Kansas, in *Custer* (1967). SEE ALSO: Michael Dante, Wayne Maunder, Slim Pickens.

Fess Parker

(1924–)

With the success of the three-part *Davy Crockett* series within Walt Disney's first weekly TV anthology during the 1954–1955 season, a virtual unknown named Fess Parker found himself propelled to international fame. Parker rates as the first Western superstar created *by* TV; Gene Autry, Roy Rogers, and William Boyd were *already* idols of youth when their shows began. Parker, Disney, and *Crockett* must also be credited with bridging the gap between the preceding kiddie Westerns (*Range Rider, Gene Autry*) and the adult oaters (*Cheyenne, Gunsmoke*) to follow. Ten years following the Crockett craze, Parker produced *Daniel Boone*, in which he again displayed those special qualities which Americans love best about Gregory Peck, James Stewart, and Will Rogers.

A graduate of the University of Texas, where he studied history and became involved in drama, Parker began picking up small film/TV roles before his big break came. These included outlaw Grat Dalton on *Stories of the Century* (3/18/54). Previously he had appeared alongside James Arness, another upcoming TV Western heavyweight, in *Island in the Sky* (1953, John Wayne). Parker and Arness then costarred in *Them!* (1954), the best of the 1950s Big Bug sci-fi films (in this case, ants). Disney meanwhile hoped to find a new face to portray Crockett in his first "Frontierland" shows for ABC's *Disneyland.* Someone mentioned Arness as a likely candidate, so Walt himself headed off to catch *Them!* He pondered Arness, uncertain. At the halfway point, Parker appeared (in a bathrobe) as a confused Texan in a mental hospital who had spotted the monsters. If the legend is to be believed, Walt leaped up, shouting *"That's* Davy Crockett!" and cast Parker alongside Buddy Ebsen playing Davy's sidekick, George Russel.

"The Ballad of Davy Crockett," by Tom Blackburn and George Bruns, not only provided transitions between various stages of Crockett's life but became the year's number-one hit song. Parker's country-ish recording, though popular, took second fiddle to a mainstream version by Bill Hayes. Parker reaped the greatest reward, though, becoming an immediate "name" in Westerns. This included drawbacks as well as pluses; he signed a long-term Disney contract as that studio's "own" Western-star hero. Shortly thereafter John Ford contacted Parker, hoping to costar him with Wayne in *The Searchers* (1956). Walt Disney flatly refused, arguing that this would take the edge off those films *he* planned to do with Parker; the star countered that *The Searchers* could only further promote him to the benefit of Disney as well as himself. Whether this incident diminished their initial warm feelings, the Disney-Parker relationship didn't work out as planned.

Initially, Disney considered doing a monthly *Crockett* episode during the second season, expanding on the first three historical shows (the Creek Indian War, the politics of Andrew Jackson, and the Alamo, all inspired by Crockett's own journals) with legends drawn from "The Crockett Almanacs" published during Crockett's later years and for more than a decade following his death. Only two made it to the small (and later big) screen, involving the hero with famed riverman Mike Fink (Jeff York). These were edited (as the original trilogy had been) into a second film that proved almost as successful as the first, though the "Crockett craze" had by then dimmed. Disney would take the franchise no further, instead starring Parker in movies: *The Great Locomotive Chase* (1956), *Westward Ho the Wagons!* (1956), *Old Yeller* (1957), and *The Light in the Forest* (1958). Though successful, none had the impact both men hoped for. When the contract ended, neither chose to renew, the lead in Disney Westerns passing to others, most often Brian Keith.

Parker appeared in several B+ Westerns, with Robert Taylor in *The Hangman* and Jeff Chandler in *The Jayhawkers!*, both in 1959. He filmed a pilot for the TV oater *The Code of Jonathan West*, which aired on *G.E. Theater* (as "Aftermath," 4/17/60), though none of the networks picked it up as a series. When Frank Capra's *Mr. Smith Goes to Washington* became a weekly sitcom with Parker in the James Stewart role and swiftly flopped, some wondered if he had a future in show business. Fate then stepped in. Disney (which had moved from ABC to NBC, where it became a Sunday night staple) opened the 1963 season with reruns of the first three *Crockett*s. Though they had been aired three times already on ABC *and* shown theatrically, the beloved shows tore through the ratings ceiling. Not wanting to waste a good thing, NBC's head honcho Bill Self wondered if Disney might rehire Parker and shoot new *Crockett*s. For whatever reason, Walt refused. Undaunted, Self considered asking Parker to produce a *Crockett* series, though Self admitted to being nervous about angering Disney. The compromise: *Daniel Boone*, which proved Self's thinking right: So long as Parker played a frontiersman in a coonskin cap, the audience would not care much *what* they called the character.

Who said there are no second acts in American life? In fall 1964, even as Disney reran the second two *Crockett*s on Sunday, Parker's new series (the actor now enjoying more TV exposure than ever) showed up on Thursdays. Though the tendency at the time was toward color, *Boone* initially appeared in black-and-white to keep down expenses, as the Fox studio tried to survive the financial disaster of *Cleopatra* (1963). As a result, *Boone*'s first season proved to be a mixed blessing. Shot largely on soundstages, it lacked the expansive look of not only *Crockett* but *all* of Disney's TV historical shows. Albert Salmi, a well-regarded actor, awkwardly played mountain-man sidekick "Yadkin," a role that screamed out for Jeff York. Even the fur cap Parker wore appeared too small for his head. But the supporting cast had a nice family-show feel, with Patricia Blair as wife Rebecca Bryan Boone, Veronica Cartwright and Darby Hinton their offspring Jemima and Israel. Ed Ames proved best of all as "Mingo," a Cherokee (though his name implied another tribe). Here was a significant landmark on the road toward a more enlightened portrayal of Native Americans on the theatrical/TV screen. The character of Mingo (actually half Anglo and half Indian, leading to fine scripts in which Mingo found himself conflicted as to loyalties) turned out to be Oxford educated (there *was* such a person on the frontier, if not necessarily a friend of Boone's). For the first time, impressionable viewers were treated to a Native American who spoke better English (the King's English, in fact) than his frontiersman friend.

The role of Mingo expanded even as Yadkin diminished. With this change in focus came an ever greater emphasis on Native Americans as something other than handy targets. This explains why an image in the

THE CIVIL RIGHTS WESTERN: More than any other actor, Fess Parker associated himself with genre pieces that conveyed respect for ethnicity. In Disney's *Davy Crockett*, with Buddy Ebsen (*rear left*) as "George Russel," he took up the cause of mistreated Cherokees. Courtesy Walt Disney Productions/Buena Vista Releasing. On his own *Daniel Boone* series, Parker emphasized the need for an integrated America, here seen with guest star Rafer Johnson as "Rawls." Courtesy NBC/Fesspar Productions.

first season's opening titles (Boone fires a long rifle and an Indian falls dead) had to be eliminated from the credits for the second through sixth seasons. In its place, Mingo joins Daniel as equals in the daily work of trapping. Indian fighting gradually gave way to stories emphasizing peaceful relationships between the races.

This must be credited to Parker who, following five producers during the first season, assumed the mantle of producer and, along with Aaron Rosenberg (executive producer), took control. Ever humble, Parker credits Rosenberg with most of the improvements, though in fact they partnered in transforming what could have been a routine Eastern/Western into a TV vehicle broadcast in the present that employed tales from the past to better things for America's future. *Boone* then rose in the ratings, coming into its own as a show rather than just a *Crockett* redux. Episodes were now shot in color, many on location. Whereas the addition of color diminished *Gunsmoke*, this proved the necessary element for *Boone* to click, as, instead of dusty streets in some cowtown, this show required the beauty of the first frontier's great outdoors.

Though ostensibly line producer, Barney Rosenzweig proved essential in realizing the vision. Only twenty-nine at the time and relatively inexperienced, he revealed his talent at once in the changes that soon appeared. Parker's costume changed from the traditional buckskin jacket to a vest that looked to have been designed by Indian friends. The new coonskin cap was larger and more appealing even than those worn in *Crockett*. These changes were far from cosmetic. Early on, an episode called "My Name Is Rawls" (10/7/65) introduced an emphasis on civil rights. The title character, played by sports great turned actor Rafer Johnson, appeared as the first of many runaway slaves to be welcomed in Boonesborough. As the years passed, TV's incarnation of that place became the original stop on the Underground Railroad. Woody Strode guest-starred in "Goliath" (9/29/66) during the third season; later continuing characters "Gabe" (Roosevelt Grier) and "Gideon" (Don Pedro Colley) took fine advantage of Parker's unprecedented TV showcase for African American talent.

Also essential to success was Jack Swain, first hired as cameraman, soon stretching above and beyond that by solidifying diverse elements. Soon *Boone* related less to the era in which it was supposedly set than to the mid-to-late 1960s, a vivid reflection (period trappings aside) of that time. As such, *Boone* exerted a greater positive influence on the American psyche than has been noted. Other TV shows (*I Spy, East Side/West Side*) also included black characters. But these series played to an urbane audience, as such preaching to the converted. *Boone*'s largest following was in the South, where the civil rights statement most needed to be heard. Week after week, Southerners drawn to the series (a country-western feel became more tangible after Jimmy Dean joined up as the guitar-strumming "Josh Clements") witnessed images of Anglo characters with whom they could readily associate overcoming old prejudices and learning to live with people of color—and, if to their own surprise, enjoying the experience.

How much any example of modern media can cause social change will be endlessly debated. No question, though, that when *Boone* premiered in 1964, racism remained a pressing problem in that part of the country. A few months before its debut, three civil rights workers were murdered in the "Mississippi Burning" incident. The degree to which Parker can be credited with creating a better America may be debatable; what can't be questioned is that he and *Boone* were on the right side of history, sharing an enlightened vision with their target audience.

No wonder, then, that one of the great African American actresses, Ethel Waters, made a rare guest-starring appearance in "Mamma Cooper" (2/5/70), playing the mother of Grier's Gabe. To this day, Parker remains rightly proud of that episode, one of four he directed. Tolerance as a way of life, and appreciation for what we now call diversity, reached beyond race: Another first lady of the legitimate stage, Julie Harris, appeared in "Faith's Way" (4/4/68), about an Anglo woman treated suspiciously by others owing to her "different" ways. In time she proves herself valuable to the community at large owing to her uniqueness as an individual, that statement summing up *Boone*'s main message. Clearly, we were tuning in to a Boonesborough of Parker's moral as well as artistic imagination; the wooden walls and other details appeared accurate enough for early pioneer days. Yet Parker also posited a paradigm for how we ought to conduct ourselves today.

Happily, this never turned didactic, the ongoing appeal always full-throttle entertainment. Israel even had a goose named "Hannibal" (modeled after "Samantha" in the 1956 film *Friendly Persuasion*) in the first season, and many wild-animal pets afterward. The notion of living at one with nature became so essential that in "The Thanksgiving Story" (11/25/65), a turkey Israel captures for the feast instead becomes their guest of honor, sitting beside the pioneers, nibbling on cornbread as neighboring Indians join settlers for what apparently is a vegetarian meal. If this is not precisely the way things were, it inarguably appeared exactly the way they ought to have been. Another key decision was to eliminate any attempt at historical chronology. The first season had taken place entirely during the days leading up to the Revolutionary War. Year two did *not* pick up there, the show from that moment on skipping back and forth over time in an almost surreal manner. Each week's story might be set in prewar, Revolutionary War, or postwar periods, though the characters remained always the same age. However much a violation of realistic time, this clearly functioned in the service of creating a broad overview of that era. Such an approach allowed for numerous historical figures to temporarily step onto the symbolic stage that this dramatic incarnation of Boonesborough had become: Benjamin Franklin, Patrick Henry, Aaron Burr, even the Marquise de Lafayette. Some historians complained, among other things, that Parker had further blurred an already-existing confusion between Crockett and Boone. To argue so is to miss the point. What Parker accomplished, in the most popular of our mass media, had been the creation of a mythic American hero, embodying the best in our own national character: firm traditional values tempered by a progressive acceptance of the need for gradual and positive change. At a time when the cowboy was disappearing from TV screens, Parker provided an alternative Western (or, if you prefer, Eastern) icon. *Boone* served as a transitional series between the Westerns that preceded it and those to follow. Here was a hero as straight in stature and values as those played by Autry, Rogers, and others. Yet *Boone* focused on *family*, shortly to become the new way of things as country/Midwestern settings replaced the far West for such 1970s shows as *The Waltons* and *Little*

House on the Prairie. Between the two forms, *Boone* combined the best of the past shows with a forward glance. The series premiered in one era of American morals and manners and concluded in an entirely other one.

Parker later starred in the TV film *Climb an Angry Mountain* (12/23/72), the pilot for a series that would have cast him as "Sheriff Elisha Cooper," solving crimes in the modern West, but the show was not picked up by NBC. Retired from show business, Parker today owns and runs an oceanfront resort in Santa Barbara, an intimate inn in Los Olivos, and a well-regarded/multi-award-winning winery. At the time of this writing, he is building another resort. SEE ALSO: Patricia Blair, Veronica Cartwright, Peter Graves, Darby Hinton, Dewey Martin, Rick Moses, Albert Salmi.

Molly Parker
(1972–)

••••••••••••••••••••••••••••••••

The British Columbian–born Parker, a hippie ballerina in her youth, matured into an offbeat beauty and subtle actress specializing in edgy parts: a necrophiliac in *Kissed* (1996) and a lap dancer in *The Center of the World* (2001). Her first Western role was as "Frances Phillips" in *Lonesome Dove: The Outlaw Years* (1996). Parker then hit her stride as "Alma Garret," a respectable widow stuck in the Gulch (*Deadwood*, 2004–2006) with her

THE WESTERN WOMAN REVISED: On *Deadwood* Molly Parker offered a vision of a frontier female who had little in common with earlier depictions of women. Courtesy HBO.

young ward "Sofia Metz" (Bree Seanna Wall). She became involved with the sheriff (Timothy Olyphant) until the sudden arrival of his wife Martha (Anna Gunn) and her son "William" (Josh Eriksson) by the lawman's deceased brother "Robert." This soap-opera-ish situation was rendered truly tragic through strong writing, a gifted cast, and vivid production values. SEE ALSO: Timothy Olyphant.

Willard Parker
(1912–1996)
••••••••••••••••••••••••••••••••

How highly unlikely it was that anyone would have bought a Manhattan-born man named Worster Van Eps as a cowboy! So he changed his moniker and became Willard Parker beginning with his first film, *The Devil's Saddle*

Legion (1937), a Dick Foran Western. Parker won the lead in *The Great Jesse James Raid* (1953) and eventually appeared as Jesse's cousin Cole Younger in *Young Jesse James* (1960). In between, he starred in one of the best-loved TV Westerns, *Tales of the Texas Rangers* (1955–1958), as "Jace Pearson," previously played by Joel McCrea on the radio. With partner "Clay Morgan" (Harry Lauter), Jace sets out to solve crimes in the Lone Star state. The show's uniqueness was that though the tales were all based on fact, the heroes were fictional and the incidents drawn from the entire history of the Rangers. The stars played the same characters each week, but viewers never knew whether they would show up in the Old West riding horses or in modern Texas in a car. No one out there in Television-land minded; the show proved highly popular in late Saturday morning/early Sunday afternoon slots. "The Eyes of Texas" was employed as the theme song, but with new words: "The tallest man in Texas stands before you, Jace Pearson is his name; beside him is his friend Clay Morgan, together they made fame!" SEE ALSO: Harry Lauter.

Michael Pate
(1920–2008)
••••••••••••••••••••••••••••••••

An Australian writer, director, producer, and actor, onstage as well as on screen/TV, Pate once played Jason to Dame Judith Anderson's title role in *Medea*. He adapted Colleen McCullough's acclaimed novel *Tim* into a film (1979) starring Mel Gibson. In Hollywood, Pate was quickly typecast as swarthy villains—Indians, Arabs, and Sicilians—in countless movies and TV shows. His first Indian role was as Apache chief Vittorio in *Hondo* (1953, John Wayne). Pate actually hesitated accepting the part, unsure whether anyone would "buy" him as a Native American! The role would be followed by Geronimo (aka Gokliya) on *Broken Arrow* (1956), Pate reviving that character in *Zane Grey Theater*'s "The Last Bugle" (11/24/60) and the recurring villain "Quintana" on *Zorro* (1958) opposite Guy Williams, as well as Toriano on *Laramie* (1960–1962), Crazy Horse in *The Great Sioux Massacre* (1965) and on *Branded* (1966). He played more Indians, sometimes sympathetic, on *Gunsmoke*, *Wagon Train*, *Rawhide*, *Daniel Boone*, etc. Talk about coming full circle! Pate's final role in Hollywood before returning to Sydney was Vittorio on TV's *Hondo* (1967), now opposite Ralph Taeger in John Wayne's part. SEE ALSO: Michael Ansara, Chuck Connors, John Lupton, Dick Powell.

John Payne

(1912–1989)

••••••••••••••••••••••••••••••

In his twilight years, John Howard Payne fondly related an old anecdote.

Having traveled on business to a third-world country, he checked in at his hotel and caught the man behind the counter staring. Then in broken English the fellow asked, "You an American cowboy star?" Surprised that anyone would recognize him after so many years, Payne smiled and nodded yes. No sooner had he stepped into his room than the phone rang. The head politico in the land expressed shocked delight that Payne was there, inviting him to attend a state dinner. Incredulous, Payne agreed, amazed that even in such a hidden corner of the world a one-time TV cowboy would receive royal treatment. During dinner, guests considered him skeptically, insisting he looked different in person. Gradually, the truth dawned on Payne: They thought they were wining and dining John *Wayne*!

Always self-effacing, Payne proved himself a versatile movie performer, particularly while under contract at Fox, playing the male lead in everything from Betty Grable musicals to noirs, romantic melodramas, action yarns, and Westerns. After his studio contract ended, Payne won the lead in one of Republic's best oaters, *Santa Fe Passage* (1955). On NBC's *The Restless Gun* (1957–1959) he played "Vint Bonner," a role James Stewart had performed on radio. Payne offered a quietly convincing portrayal as an aging gunfighter who wants to avoid violence. This was the only Western other than the fact-based *The Life and Legend of Wyatt Earp* (as well as Wyatt on *Bat Masterson*) in which the hero carried a Buntline Special. Bonner's featured not only a long barrel that could be added or removed but an adaptable rifle stock, allowing the fictional Bonner (like the real-life Earp) to transform his weapon from pistol to rifle for greater accuracy. During the first season, ratings ran high, though they dipped when the following fall *Gun* ran up against CBS's *The Texan*, which became the flavor of the season. An interesting bit of Americana: John Howard Payne was a direct descendant of the musician of that name who wrote "Home, Sweet Home." SEE ALSO: Rory Calhoun, Hugh O'Brian.

Guy Pearce

(1967–)
••••••••••••••••••••••••••••••

English born and Australian raised, Pearce has acted from age eleven. Following roles on several Australian soap operas (*Neighbours*, 1985–1989; *Home and Away*, 1991–1992), he hit the big time with *Snowy River: The McGregor Saga* (1993–1996), a down-under Western inspired by the Banjo Paterson poem about the pursuit and capture of a "brumby" (wild stallion). The series was set twenty-five years following the popular film (1982), with Pearce cast as "Rob McGregor," handling his American relative "Luke" (Josh Lucas); star-to-be Hugh

Jackman was also around as neighbor "Jones." Pearce's later film roles include two Westerners: "John Boyd," a clone of explorer Captain Fremont, in *Ravenous* (1999); and "Charlie Burns" in *The Proposition* (2005). SEE ALSO: Sigrid Thornton.

Christopher Pettiet

(1976–2000)
••••••••••••••••••••••••••••••

Pettiet added an intriguing element to *The Young Riders* (1991–1992) as Jesse James, that legendary bad boy providing contrast to the stalwart heroes. (Jamie Walters played older brother Frank.) He also starred as "Dean" on *MTV's Undressed* (1999) before dying of an accidental drug overdose. SEE ALSO: Stephen Baldwin, Josh Brolin, Ty Miller.

John Pickard

(1913–1993)
••••••••••••••••••••••••••••••

A U.S. Navy vet, Pickard's pop-culture claim to fame came as the model for that branch of the service's recruiting posters from the 1940s to 1960s. In his first Western role, Pickard played one of three brothers tracking Gregory Peck's Ringo in *The Gunfighter* (1950). Born to play a cavalryman, Pickard appeared in *Bugles in the Afternoon* (1952), *The Charge at Feather River* (1953), *Fort Yuma* (1955), and the unsold TV pilot *Cavalry Patrol* (1956). Pickard might have played "Matt Dillon" on *Gunsmoke*, but producer Charles Marquis Warren complained that he appeared too stiff in scenes with Amanda Blake as "Miss Kitty" and cast James Arness instead. Pickard played Johnny Ringo/Ringgold on the 1957 season of *The Life and Legend of Wyatt Earp* and the lead in *Boots and Saddles*, aka *The Story of the Fifth Cavalry* (1957–1958), a dimly remembered show about daily life on a frontier fort, filmed on location at Kanab, Utah, for authenticity. He played "Captain Shank Adams" with Patrick McVey ("Lieutenant Colonel Wesley Heyes"), Gardner McKay (later to star in *Adventures in Paradise*) as "Lieutenant Dan Kelly," Dave Willock ("Lieutenant Banning"), John Alderson ("Sergeant Bullock"), and Michael Hinn ("Chief of Civilian Scouts Luke Cummings"). Three years later Pickard received third billing (and a reduction in rank to sergeant) as "Murdock" on *Gunslinger*. He appeared on ten *Rawhide*s, often as the marshal of towns the drive passed by. Then it was back to bluecoats: Colonel Philip Sheridan on *Branded* (1966, Chuck Connors) and "Colonel Caine" on *How the West Was Won* (1977, James Arness). Pickard died in an accident on the family farm when attacked by a crazed bull. SEE ALSO: James Arness, Dewey Martin, Johnny Western, Tony Young.

Slim Pickens

(1919–1983)

••••••••••••••••••••••••••••••••

With a thick, raspy voice, combining the hint of a Southern accent with a Montana twang (though born Louis Burton Lindley, Jr., in California), this large, angular character actor worked as a cowboy from youth, joining the rodeo circuit, where he took on that most dangerous of jobs, the clown. He quit, insisting he would never make anything but slim pickings. Pickens's Hollywood career began with *Rocky Mountain* (1950), a big-budget Errol Flynn Western for Warner Bros. He played Rex Allen's sidekick, "Slim" (though that never described his physique), in *Colorado Sundown* (1952), and a dozen more B oaters. He left when roles in bigger films came his way, his B roles filled by Buddy Ebsen. Pickens was matched with an ornery mule in *Santa Fe Passage* (1955); the beast tried to bounce him off every ten seconds. He stuck with that varmint for as long as the mule lived, their high-flying animosity a signature bit in films and on TV. Pickens's memorable theatrical Western roles include a Texican in *The Last Command* (1955), a Civil War soldier in *The Great Locomotive Chase* (1956), an ornery hombre in *One-Eyed Jacks* (1961, for director/star Marlon Brando), a cantankerous cook in *Will Penny* (1968), and a spoof of his own tougher-than-leather image in Mel Brooks's *Blazing Saddles* (1974). He became part of Sam Peckinpah's stock company, playing in *Major Dundee* (1965), *The Ballad of Cable Hogue* (1970), *The Getaway* (1972), and *Pat Garrett & Billy the Kid* (1973).

Pickens played in lots of TV Westerns: as the mountain man Old Bill Williams in *The Saga of Andy Burnett* (1957–1958), comic-relief lawman "Slim" on *Outlaws* (1961–1962), humorous rodeo veteran (again, "Slim") on *The Wide Country* (1962–1963), and California Joe Milner in *The Legend of Custer* (1968). He later made occasional appearances as "Sheriff Gant" on *Bonanza* (1968–1970) and as various lawmen on *Alias Smith and Jones* (1971–1972). Pickens made appearances on two of TV's *Daniel Boone* shows: with Dewey Martin in "The Wilderness Road" (3/12/61) and with Fess Parker in "Dan'l Boone Shot a B'ar" (9/15/66). He is perhaps best remembered as "Major King Kong," pilot of the doomed bomber jet in Stanley Kubrick's masterfully mad dark comedy *Dr. Strangelove or: How I Learned to Stop Worrying and Love the Bomb* (1964). That role had originally been scheduled as Peter Sellers's fourth in the film, until the British actor had to ease off following medical problems. SEE ALSO: Rex Allen, Jerome Courtland, Fess Parker, Dewey Martin.

Dick Powell
(1904–1963)
••••••••••••••••••••••••••••••

A band singer turned lightweight leading man in WB Depression-era musicals, notably *42nd Street* (1933), Powell later emerged as a diminutive tough guy for noirs ("Philip Marlowe" in *Murder, My Sweet*, 1944) and one memorable oater, *Station West* (1948). He directed (*The Conqueror*, 1956), and produced TV shows under the Four Star banner, the company named for Powell's first series, *Four Star Playhouse* (1952–1956), with Powell, Charles Boyer, Ida Lupino, and David Niven the rotating stars in comedies and dramas. *Zane Grey Theater* (1956–1961) followed, for which Powell served as host, in addition to occasionally starring in stories derived from the famed Western author's work. The anthology ran for five and a half years, usually thirty-nine episodes per season. Powell wisely picked the best scripts for himself, appearing in more than a dozen. Best among them: *Ambush* (1/5/61), the searing story of complex relations within a cavalry unit, directed by movie veteran Budd Boetticher. As Grey material wore thin, the series switched to other Western works, including the pilots for eventual series from Four Star: *Wanted: Dead or Alive, The Westerner, Trackdown,* and *Johnny Ringo. Zane Grey* reruns were repackaged as summer replacement shows under the title *Frontier Justice* with hosts Lew Ayres (1958), Melvyn Douglas (1959), and Ralph Bellamy (1961). A year and a half into his new hour-long *The Dick Powell Show* (1961–1963), the actor succumbed to cancer, the result of filming *The Conqueror* on Nevada nuclear test sites. *Zane Grey* was rereleased shortly thereafter with Chuck Connors featured in newly filmed hosting spots. SEE ALSO: Chuck Connors, Robert Culp, Brian Keith.

Drew Powell
(1976–)
••••••••••••••••••••••••••••••

A role as "Cadet Drew" on *Malcolm in the Middle* (2000–2001) led to "Hoss Cartwright" on *Ponderosa* (2001–2002), about the ranch's early days in 1849. Hoss's actual first name turned out to be "Eric." SEE ALSO: Jared Daperis, Daniel Hugh Kelly, Gareth Yuen.

Robert Preston
(1918–1987)
••••••••••••••••••••••••••••••

This gifted actor achieved full stardom only later in life, ironically after abandoning Hollywood for Broadway. Signed at an early age to a long-term Paramount contract, he played mostly second leads in big films, while being top-billed in small ones, not unlike Robert Taylor (MGM) and Ronald Reagan (WB), though far more gifted than either. He left La-La

Land for wartime service in the U.S. Army Air Corps, returning to the studio afterward, often as the "best pal" in oaters: *Union Pacific* (1939, Joel McCrea), *Whispering Smith* (1948, Alan Ladd), and *Best of the Badmen* (1951, Robert Ryan). His best Western role was as the embittered Custer-like Civil War vet in *The Last Frontier* (1955) for Anthony Mann. Preston abandoned movies to pursue a stage career, winning two Tonys, including Best Actor for *The Music Man* (1957). Hollywood hesitated turning that hit into a lavish film, fearing that Preston did not rate as a box-office star, though no other actor dared do "Professor Harold Hill." He finally won the role, and the film proved a gigantic success. Preston now rated as a big-enough name to be billed alongside John Wayne, James Stewart, Henry Fonda, and Gregory Peck in *How the West Was Won* (1962) as the wagon master. He agreed to headline *The Chisholms* (1979–1980), an ambitious miniseries set in the West that avoided the usual clichés thanks to Evan Hunter's adaptation of his realistic book. Preston was cast as "Hadley Chisholm," a pre–Civil War Virginian who loses his land, picks up stakes, and leads his family to Oregon. Rosemary Harris appeared as wife "Minerva." Sons and daughters, as well as in-laws, were also in tow: Ben Murphy ("Will"), Brian Kerwin ("Gideon"), James Van Patten ("Bo"), Stacey Nelkin ("Bonnie Sue"), Susan Swift ("Annabel"), and Glynnis O'Connor ("Elizabeth"). A focus on family relations, good and bad, rather than Indian fighting transformed what might have been yet another go-round for *Wagon Train* into a memorable, intimate epic, far more suited to the era in which it was made, with *Little House on the Prairie* and *The Waltons* high in the ratings. Preston and most other cast members returned when *The Chisholms* became a weekly series (1980), Brett Cullen now playing "Gideon" and Swift recast as "Mercy." Next up was the role of Steve McQueen's father in Sam Peckinpah's uneven but winning contemporary rodeo film *Junior Bonner* (1972); and "Ben Sunday" in *September Gun* (10/8/83), Preston cast as an aging gunfighter helping a nun (Patty Duke) keep the peace. SEE ALSO: Ben Murphy.

Wayde Preston

(1929–1992)

· ·

Glenn was not the only man named Strange working in Westerns during the 1950s. William Erskine Strange, a TV star redubbed Wayde Preston, was Colorado born and Wyoming raised. After the Korean War he found work as a park ranger and musical performer on the rodeo circuit. Rugged good looks caused Warner Bros. to sign him for a contract with no previous acting experience. He played the lead on *Colt .45* (1957–1960), the least successful of the Westerns pro-

duced by that studio for ABC during the heyday of the TV oater. The fictional "Christopher Colt," seemingly a gun salesman for the company that bore his name, actually served as a government undercover agent/army captain, qualifying this show as the first to add an espionage element to the traditional Western format. In its late Friday spot, *Colt .45* failed to find an audience and was canceled after twenty-six episodes. The studio and network, however, refused to give up, transferring the actor and his character to the popular *Sugarfoot*, where Colt and "Tom Brewster" joined forces on three occasions to track down the "Canary Kid," a deadly outlaw and lookalike for the easygoing drifter hero. The following fall, *Colt .45* returned, first with reruns of the half-season already broadcast (the feeling was that few had seen them anyway), then with thirteen new episodes. Preston, hoping to make the show more authentic, now sported a handlebar mustache, the first TV cowboy to appear anything but cleanshaven since *Davy Crockett* on Disney.

Though ratings improved slightly in varied Tuesday and Sunday slots, the show's problems were far from over. Like Clint Walker and James Garner, Preston grew disgruntled about an actor's status at WB: though heroes to millions, as part of the studio's cowboy corral they received the lowest wages of any TV performers. When WB refused to provide a stuntman for a tricky sequence, Preston stalked off the set, shortly replaced by Donald May as cousin "Sam Colt, Jr." In an odd move, the episode in which Chris briefly introduces Sam, then rides off into the sunset, was shown *not* as the new star assumed the lead, rather as one of the *last* broadcasts during the third/final season. The following fall (9/25/60), *Maverick* (*sans* Garner) began its new season with "Hadley's Hunters," an episode that had Jack Kelly as "Bart" bumping into other Warner Bros. Western stars; a melancholy bit showed him entering Chris Colt's empty office, filled with cobwebs, holstered guns hanging on a wall peg and covered with dust. That moment served as a fond farewell not only to *Colt .45* but, shortly, to the entire first wave of TV Westerns which, one by one, were almost all soon canceled.

Like many others who had become minor names thanks to TV, Preston headed for Rome. Throughout the 1960s, he achieved stardom in spaghetti Westerns like *A Long Ride from Hell* (1968). Preston wrote about *la dolce vita* in a magazine article after that genre ended and he returned home. He eventually costarred with another WB maverick (pun intended), James Garner, in the medium-budget Western *A Man Called Sledge* (1970), directed by Vic Morrow, star of *Combat!* (1962–1967). SEE ALSO: James Garner, Will Hutchins, Jack Kelly, Donald May, Clint Walker.

Andrew Prine

(1936–)

••••••••••••••••••••••••••••••

Looking like a cross between Wright King and the young John Carradine, Prine made a strong impression in live TV drama before 1955 and in filmed series afterward. He delivered a powerful performance as James Keller, brother to Helen, in *The Miracle Worker* (1962). Prine's first series role was in *The Wide Country* (1962–1963) as "Andy Guthrie," younger brother of rodeo cowboy "Mitch" (Earl Holliman). The show presented a unique conflict as the older sibling attempted to warn Andy away from the circuit while pursuing it himself. Originally to have been titled *Rope Riders*, the show was canceled after only one season. Prine next showed up as William H. Bonney in "The Outlaw and the Nun" (Joan Hackett played the latter) on *The Great Adventure* (12/6/63). Seven years later he played Alex McSween, storeowner/acquaintance of the Kid, in *Chisum*, with John Wayne in the title role and Geoffrey Deuel, younger brother of Pete Duel (*Alias Smith and Jones*), as Billy. Prine played roles in multiple episodes of *Wagon Train, Gunsmoke*, etc., before and after his second series, *The Road West* (1966–1967). Here he played "Timothy Pride," part of a tight-knit pioneer family hoping to homestead. Costar Brenda Scott appeared as "Midge Pride"; the actors married that year, quickly divorced, and remarried the next year only to divorce again; they were remarried again from 1973 to 1978. Prine had constant TV work and small roles in big Westerns (*Bandelero!* with James Stewart, 1968; *Rooster Cogburn* with John Wayne, 1975), big parts in small ones (*Grizzly*, 1976, which he also co-wrote). On TV, he played "Major Duncan Heyward" in *Last of the Mohicans* (11/23/77) and one of the snowbound pioneers in *Donner Pass: The Road to Survival* (10/24/78). On the contemporary quasi-Western *Dallas*, he enacted "Harrison Van Buren III" (1989). For Ted Turner, Prine performed as Brigadier General Richard B. Garnett in both *Gettysburg* (1993) and *Gods and Generals* (2003). In 2006 he hosted interview segments, chatting with fellow TV/movie Western veterans, for the Encore Westerns Channel. SEE ALSO: Glenn Corbett, Steve Forrest, Earl Holliman, Jack Lord, Barry Sullivan.

Dorothy Provine

(1937–)

Bouncy and buoyant, often over-ecstatic, Provine won the title role in her first film, *The Bonnie Parker Story* (1958), playing a part that ten years later made a superstar of Faye Dunaway. Provine combined aspects of Doris Day, Carol Channing, and Betty Hutton. She always seemed best suited to period-piece roles: "Rocky Shaw," a giddy dance-hall girl in *The Alaskans* (1959–1960), and "Pinky Pinkham," an equally egregious speakeasy performer in *The Roaring Twenties* (1960–1962). Her best movie role was as Hayley Mills's older sister in Disney's *That Darn Cat!* (1965). SEE ALSO: Ray Danton, Donald May, Roger Moore, Jeff York.

Linda Purl

(1955–)

This Greenwich, Connecticut-born, Japanese-raised actress and jazz singer never found the right role to showcase her considerable talents. She played "Molly Beaton" in *Young Pioneers* (3/1/76), a TV movie focusing on a young woman, her husband "David" (Roger Kern), her friend "Dan" (Robert Hays), and the stalwart "Nettie Peters" (Mare Winningham), all trying to make a go of farming in the Dakota territory despite the constant menace of ruthless railroad interests. Huge ratings prompted a sequel, *Young Pioneers' Christmas* (12/17/76). The series began in 1978 with the cast intact; ratings were surprisingly low, causing the show to be canceled after three weeks. Purl later played "Charlene" on *Matlock* (1986–1987), "Claire" on *Port Charles* (1997), and "Sarah" on *First Monday* (2002).

Denver Pyle
(1920–1997)

••••••••••••••••••••••••••••••••

While recuperating from a wound
suffered at Guadalcanal, Pyle took
time off from his California job as
a riveter to try live theater. He was
signed to a Universal contract, where
Pyle appeared in countless films,
notably Audie Murphy Westerns
(*Column South*, 1953; *Ride Clear of
Diablo*, 1954). Scads of TV work,
mostly as laconic sheriffs, slow-minded sidekicks, and beady-eyed badmen,
followed. Desilu picked him to play
historical characters Ben Thompson,
a charmingly crooked cattleman who
looks out for his mentally challenged
younger brother Billy (Hal Baylor),
in *The Life and Legend of Wyatt Earp*;
and the heroic Sam Houston, always
trying to talk the title character into
giving Texas a try, on *The Adventures
of Jim Bowie*. Pyle scored a rare lead
in the "Deadwood Dick" episode
of *Death Valley Days* (10/1/66). His
two best movie roles were as Thim-
blerig in *The Alamo* (1960) with John
Wayne, and as Frank Harner, the old-
time Western lawman after the title
crooks in *Bonnie and Clyde* (1967).
More TV work followed as "Briscoe"
on *The Andy Griffith Show* (1963–

THE ECOLOGICAL WESTERN: In the mid-
1970s, the TV Western shifted from cowboys
to mountain men posited as environmentalist
heroes. In *The Life and Times of Grizzly Adams*,
"Mad Jack" (Denver Pyle, *left*) and the title
character (Dan Haggerty, *right*) welcome a
hot-air balloonist (Gene Conforti) to their
animal reserve. Courtesy NBC.

1966). In the 1970s the cowboy was
nowhere to be seen on TV, but not so
the mountain man. Pyle played "Mad
Jack" on *Grizzly Adams* (1977–1978),
then went country again for "Uncle
Jess" on *The Dukes of Hazzard* (1979–
1985) in an age when horses seemed
less attractive to young viewers than
red-hot cars. SEE ALSO: Scott Forbes,
Dan Haggerty, Hugh O'Brian, John
Schneider.

Randy Quaid

(1950–)

Houston born and raised, Quaid hopped on a bus and headed for Hollywood. Shortly, he had a hit in the contemporary Western *The Last Picture Show* (1971), playing a spoiled rich kid. Effective in the part despite not being conventionally attractive, the role revealed an enormous range that allowed Quaid to play roles as diverse as President Lyndon Johnson and Frankenstein's monster. He received an Oscar nomination for the part of the queasy sailor in *The Last Detail* (1973), a minor masterpiece. Numerous roles as real-life Westerners included brother Grat in *The Last Ride of the Dalton Gang* (11/20/79); Clell Miller in *The Long Riders* (1980)

with real-life brother Dennis as Clell's brother Ed; John Wesley Hardin in *Streets of Laredo* (11/12/95); and Doc Holliday in *Purgatory* (1/10/99). Quaid played the dimwitted "Lenny" in a superb TV version of John Steinbeck's *Of Mice and Men* (11/29/81), with Robert Blake as "George," then costarred with James Brolin in the TV film *Cowboy* (4/30/83). He returned to his breakthrough role in Peter Bogdanovich's *Texasville* (1990), a notably disappointing follow-up to *The Last Picture Show*. Quaid remains effective as Westerners, including the homophobic ranch owner in *Brokeback Mountain* (2005).

Steve Raines

(1916–1996)

••••••••••••••••••••••••••

A bit actor in B movies beginning with *Along the Oregon Trail* (1947), in which Raines had been billed simply as "Henchman Steve," Raines appeared in a dozen films starring Monte Hale, Allan "Rocky" Lane, Lash La Rue, and Audie Murphy. TV beckoned; Raines was briefly seen on endless episodes of *The Gene Autry Show*, *The Roy Rogers Show*, etc. Then came the role that changed everything, as a sardonic but dedicated drover in *Cattle Empire* (1958) for. Charles Marquis Warren. When the movie metamorphosed into the TV series *Rawhide*, Raines revived the role, his character now called "Jim Quince." Frustrated as to how few lines he had, Raines wrote the script "Incident at Rojo Canyon" (9/30/60) featuring a larger-than-usual part for himself. After *Rawhide*, he had

recurring roles as a "Stage Driver" on *Laredo* (1966) and *Gunsmoke* (1969–1970). SEE ALSO: Paul Brinegar, Clint Eastwood, Eric Fleming.

Ford Rainey

1908–2005)

••••••••••••••••••••••••••••••

This notably diverse character actor with a weathered face and Lincoln-esque appearance (he played the president several times), appeared in nearly two hundred film/TV roles. He played small parts in big oaters: *3:10 to Yuma* (1957), *The Badlanders* (1958), *Flaming Star* (1960), and *Two Rode Together* (1961). Rainey played Sheriff Brady on two early episodes of *The Tall Man*, "Forty-Dollar Boots" (9/17/60) and "The Lonely Star" (10/8/60). In one episode of *Cimarron*

Strip (9/14/67) he played "Marshal Tillman," a fictionalized version of real-life lawman Bill Tilghman. His final series role was as "Old Mickey" on *The King of Queens* (CBS, 1999–2003). SEE ALSO: Clu Gulager, Barry Sullivan, Stuart Whitman.

Gregg Rainwater
(1966–)
••••••••••••••••••••••••••••••

Rainwater played "Running Buck Cross," the half-Kiowa/half-Anglo/all-fictional member of the Pony Express in *The Young Riders* (1989–1992). His mixed heritage allowed for interesting plots as Indians menaced the mail service and Rainwater's character found himself caught in a culture clash. SEE ALSO: Stephen Baldwin, Josh Brolin.

Dack Rambo
(1941–1994)
••••••••••••••••••••••••••••••

Born Norman Rambo, Dack and his equally handsome brother Dirk seemed likely to become TV's first twin superstars. (A mole on Dack's left cheek was the only way anyone could tell them apart.) Fate had other plans. Dirk was killed by a drunk driver in 1967. Following study with Lee Strasberg, Dack won the role of Walter Brennan's grandson on *The Guns of Will Sonnett* (1967–1969). He played a similar part, if with a notably different lead, as the traveling

companion to aged pioneer woman Jeanette Nolan in *Dirty Sally* (1974). Afterward, he regularly worked on afternoon soap operas and the quasi-Western *Dallas* (as "Jack Ewing," 1985–1987). Dack died in 1994 owing to complications from the AIDS virus. SEE ALSO: Walter Brennan, Jason Evers, Jeanette Nolan.

Rudy Ramos
(1950–)
••••••••••••••••••••••••••••••

So impressive was Ramos' TV debut as the title character in "The Indian," a memorable antiracist episode of *The Virginian/Men from Shiloh* (1/20/71), the producers brought him in to fill the gap left by Mark Slade's departure from *The High Chaparral*. Ramos played "Wind," a half-breed youth searching for his identity in the racially polarized West, adding a strong civil rights/pro–Native American element to a show already renowned for its enlightened portrayal of Latino characters. His later work included the role of "Captain Ruiz" in *Dr. Quinn, Medicine Woman: The Movie* (5/22/99). SEE ALSO: Linda Cristal, Stewart Granger, Mark Slade.

Ronald Reagan
(1911–2004)
••••••••••••••••••••••••••••••

The status that Robert Taylor enjoyed at MGM in the 1930s, Ronald Reagan paralleled over at Warner Bros., playing the lead in small films, including two Saturday morning serials as "Brass Bancroft" of the Secret Service; and taking the second lead in movies starring the Big Boys (George Custer in *Santa Fe Trail*, 1940, with Errol Flynn as Jeb Stuart). His best-remembered parts were as George "The Gipper" Gipp for whom the team must win one in *Knute Rockne All American* (1940) with Pat O'Brien; the deeply disturbed "Drake" in *Kings Row* (1942); and a wounded serviceman in *The Hasty Heart* (1949). In the 1950s, his studio contract ended; Reagan's freelancing included the camp classic *Bedtime for Bonzo* (1951), in which he teamed with a chimp. A long string of B+ Westerns followed: *The Last Outpost* (1951); the 1953 remake of the 1932 classic *Law and Order* (as a thinly disguised Wyatt Earp); *Cattle Queen of Montana* (1954) with Barbara Stanwyck; and *Tennessee's Partner* (1955). He campaigned for but did not receive the Davy Crockett role on Disney's TV show. Reagan costarred with future wife Nancy in *Hellcats of the Navy* (1957). He filmed a pilot for a show that did not sell: the Western "The Long Shadow" (*Zane Grey Theater*, 1/19/61). He hosted (and owned a piece of) *G.E. Theater* (1954–1962), a filmed anthology including many oaters. Reagan replaced the beloved Stanley "Old Ranger" Andrews as host of *Death Valley Days* and starred in three installments: "The Lawless Have Laws" (10/1/65), "No Place for a Lady" (10/21/65), and "A City Is Born" (10/22/65). When approached by the Republican Party to run for governor of California, Reagan suggested pal Robert Taylor as his TV replacement, won the election, and, in 1980, attained the presidency. SEE ALSO: Fess Parker, Robert Taylor.

Rex Reason

(1928–)

••••••••••••••••••••••••••••••

This older brother of Rhodes Reason (*White Hunter*, 1957–1958) worked as a contract player (sometimes billed as Bart Roberts) at Universal. He played one historical character, the Apache warrior Naiche in *Taza, Son of Cochise* (1954), with Rock Hudson in the title role. Reason then won the lead as "Adam MacLean" in *Man Without a Gun* (1959), one of several journalistic Westerns. This syndicated series is often referred to as "the pacifist oater," featuring none of the usual violence, perhaps explaining why it (like *Jefferson Drum*) failed to grab a large audience. Harry Harvey played the town mayor, Forrest Taylor the doctor. SEE ALSO: Jeff Richards.

Rodd Redwing

(1904–1971)

••••••••••••••••••••••••••••••

A New York–born Chickasaw, Redwing holds the record as the fastest gun alive in TV/movie Westerns. In two-tenths of a second, he could reach for his pistol, draw, and fire. More amazing still, Redwing could then draw his sheathed knife and throw it at the target, the blade hitting precisely the spot where his bullet had just landed. Redwing taught every movie star how to handle a gun; in *Shane* (1953), close-ups of Alan Ladd's fast draw are actually Redwing. He received the same honors for TV, also playing Native American roles (*Gunsmoke, Rawhide, Wagon Train*, etc.) Redwing and Rico Alaniz won the continuing roles of Mr. Cousin and Mr. Brother, scouts for the marshal (Hugh O'Brian) on *The Life and Legend of Wyatt Earp* (1957–1959). Earlier, Redwing had played the title role in the popular movie serial *Son of Geronimo: Apache Avenger* (1952), with Chief Yowlachie cast as his father. SEE ALSO: Hugh O'Brian, Chief Yowlachie.

Jerry Reed

(1937–2008)

This Georgia-born country star (Jerry Reed Hubbard), known for his signature weathered cowboy hat and his egregious redneck comedy, was instrumental in crystallizing the Tennessee-to-Texas connection during the late 1970s/early 1980s. As a musical genre, country-western had officially existed since 1946, though many artists initially resented the "collapsing" of one form into another. All that changed with the beginning

of the polarization of politics (and pop culture) in America. Reed co-starred with Burt Reynolds in *Smokey and the Bandit* (1977) as modern-day outlaws in hot cars, pursued by old-time lawman (Jackie Gleason) in an era when truck-drivin' came to be seen as the contemporary equivalent of cowboyin'. His TV credits include "Detective Trace Mayne" (*Nashville 99*, 1977), "Traveler" (*Good Ol' Boys*, 6/7/79), and "J. D. Reed" (*The Concrete Cowboys*, 1979) as one more wanderer in today's West. SEE ALSO: Claude Akins, Burt Reynolds, Tom Selleck.

Duncan Regehr

(1952–)

A Canadian-born skating champ, expert boxer, stage veteran (Stratford Shakespeare Festival), and gifted artist (Smithsonian Institute collection), Regehr played the lead "Don Diego" in *Zorro*, aka *The New Zorro* (1990–1993), an hour-long syndicated hit during the era when Latino talents first began to dominate pop culture (although, in truth, Regehr's heritage is Russian). The show also starred James Victor ("Sergeant Mendoza"), Patrice Martinez ("Victoria"), and Henry Darrow (who played the aged Diego in *Zorro and Son* and here father "Alejandro"). Regehr enacted Pat Garrett in *Billy the Kid* (5/10/89) with Val Kilmer as Bonney, and later played "Shakaar" on *Star Trek: Deep*

Space Nine (1995–1997). SEE ALSO: Henry Darrow, Guy Williams.

Duncan Renaldo

(1904–1980)

••••••••••••••••••••••••••••••

Presumably born in Spain (though that locale has been much debated), orphaned at an early age, Renaldo arrived in America as a coal stoker on a third-world ship. A gifted painter, he broke into movies playing Latin lovers at MGM but found himself reduced to B-movie roles including the first Latino member of *Three Mesquiteers*, "Rico Rinaldo," most impressively in *Covered Wagon Days* (1940). Meanwhile, *The Cisco Kid* was about to be revived. Warner Baxter had originated the role on film in an A movie, *In Old Arizona* (1928), that diverged from O. Henry's conception of the Kid as an Anglo outlaw modeled on Billy Bonney, Henry's onetime jail-mate. Filmmakers transformed the character into a Mexican; the concept became a B-movie series, with Cesar Romero and Gilbert Roland each taking turns in the part. Renaldo won the lead in *The Cisco Kid Returns* (1945), with Martin Garralaga his sidekick "Pancho." He continued in that role for several more movies. In 1950, B Westerns gave way to TV. The Cisco Kid, "O. Henry's Robin Hood of the Old West," a bandit no longer, now emerged as an honest citizen *mistaken* for an outlaw by lawmen, with Leo Carrillo the latest Pancho. One of the first TV shows filmed in color (1950–1955), the series presents a tricky problem in the age of political correctness. On the one hand, it is admired for presenting impressionable children with a heroic Spanish role model. On the other, some carp that Cisco is a stereotype, a handsome 1920s cliché toned down in sexuality for the small screen and small fry. SEE ALSO: Leo Carrillo, Robert Loggia, Guy Williams.

Burt Reynolds

(1936–)

••••••••••••••••••••••••••••••

If you don't make it in this business while you're young, an old Hollywood adage insists, you're never going to make it. If any career defies this bit of Sunset Boulevard wisdom, it's that of Burt Reynolds. This former Florida State footballer labored long and hard to achieve stardom but didn't hit the big time until he was nearly forty. After three appearances on half-hour anthology shows, he was picked for the role of "Ben Frazer," assistant to "Grey Holden" (Darren McGavin) on *Riverboat* (1959). The two actors did not get along; when the series returned for a second season, Reynolds's role had been scuttled. Several years of episodic TV and B movies led to casting in the now hour-long *Gunsmoke*. In season eight, episode three (9/29/62), Reynolds rode into Dodge as "Quint

Asper," part Indian and bitter about harsh treatment at the hands of insensitive whites. This was the first of many times Reynolds (whose father was half Irish, half Native American; his mother, Anglo) would play such a role. As town blacksmith and part-time deputy to "Matt Dillon" (James Arness), Quint could be portrayed in a supporting role or as the lead any week. Close friends advised him not to walk away from a regular paycheck on a popular show. Still, convinced he ought to be a top-billed star, Reynolds did just that. He kicked around doing journeyman TV work and landed on *Hawk* (1966), as a Native American detective in New York (the show lasted one season). Reynolds cinched his reputation as a Western star in minor theatrical oaters: *Sam Whiskey* (1969), *100 Rifles* (1969), and *Navajo Joe* (1966). He appeared to be on a road to nowhere when all circumstances suddenly conspired in his favor. Reynolds dated the classy older woman Dinah Shore, was the first male to pose (semi)-nude in *Cosmopolitan*, and showed up on *The Tonight Show with Johnny Carson* in black leather, spoofing his sex-symbol image so well that Carson then offered Reynolds a guest-hosting job. When Charlton Heston and Henry Fonda each turned down the role in *Deliverance* (1972), Reynolds snatched it, kick-starting his movie career. Among the diverse pictures (comedies, both sophisticated and rube, action epics, and serious drama),

good, mediocre, and awful, he starred in one underappreciated Western: *The Man Who Loved Cat Dancing* (1973). SEE ALSO: James Arness.

Jeff Richards
(1922–1989)

••••••••••••••••••••••••••••••••

This pro-baseball player (real last name Taylor) for Oregon teams turned to acting, mostly in negligible films, with one exception: *Seven Brides for Seven Brothers* (1954), the classic dance-musical Western. Richards starred in the newspaper Western *Jefferson Drum* (1958–1959) as a widower in a small town with son "Joey" (Eugene Martin); the show played as *The Rifleman* with a press mightier than the Winchester. *Jefferson Drum* also featured Cyril Delavanti as "Lucius Coin," an old printer, and Robert Stevenson as "Big Ed," a bartender. Lacking enough action for genre buffs, the show lasted twenty-six weeks. SEE ALSO: Rex Reason.

Tex Ritter
(1905–1974)

••••••••••••••••••••••••••••••••

An honest-to-goodness Texan with the accent to prove it, Ritter boasted an authentically raspy voice for performing songs that achieved a delicate balance between cornball country and far Western, including "Deck of Cards" (1948), "I Dreamed of a Hillbilly Heaven" (1961), and most famous of all "High Noon (Do Not Forsake Me Oh My Darlin'" (1952), which he had performed in the film. Ritter's version was played mainly on Southern stations; Frankie Laine's cover became the mainstream pop hit. Earlier, he starred in low-budget oaters, mostly as "Tex" with a different last name in each film, "Ranger Tex Haines" the best remembered. Ritter married his constant leading lady Dorothy Fay. On TV, he appeared with Dick Powell and Nick Adams in "Sundown at Bitter Creek" on *Zane Grey Theater* (2/14/58). When two years later Adams received his own show, *The Rebel*, Ritter joined him for "The Ballad of Danny Brown" (4/9/61). Ritter hosted *Ranch Party* (1958), singing cowboy songs and passing the torch to young newcomer Johnny Cash. Afterward, he campaigned as a Republican for a U.S. Senate seat in Tennessee but did not win. Tex was the father of actor John Ritter. SEE ALSO: Nick Adams, Johnny Cash, Dick Powell.

Pernell Roberts

(1928–)

••••••••••••••••••••••••••••

A swarthy Georgia-born U.S. Marine Corps vet and college dropout, Roberts debuted in TV Westerns (*Trackdown*, 1958; and *Sugarfoot*, 1957–1958), then earned a major role as the shifty but likeable gunman in Budd Boetticher's superb *Ride Lonesome* (1959) with Randolph Scott. How lucky was he to be cast in *Bonanza*,

one of the most successful of all cowboy shows? Not very, according to Roberts, who considered the scripts corny. He had, after all, cut his teeth on the legitimate Broadway stage. He played "Adam Cartwright," the most serious of the three sons, from 1959 to 1965, then walked at the height of the show's popularity, leaving a lucrative paycheck behind to do artistically rewarding stage work. He occasionally showed up in Westerns including *Centennial* (1978), *Desperado* (1987), and *The Young Riders* (1990). Overall, Roberts appeared happier playing a doctor on *Trapper John, M.D.* (1979–1986), as much a Sunday night staple for many Americans during the 1980s as *Bonanza* had once been. SEE ALSO: Dan Blocker, Lorne Greene, Michael Landon, Guy Williams.

Roy Roberts

(1900–1975)

••••••••••••••••••••••••••••••

A Broadway vet, Roberts headed for Hollywood and character-actor status as a symbol of the Establishment, sometimes heroic (as a captain in *Guadalcanal Diary*, 1943), more often evil, huffy, occasionally pompous (as the hotel owner who refuses Gregory Peck a room because he may be Jewish in *Gentleman's Agreement*, 1947). Roberts played Doc "Summerfield" (based on the real-life Doc Sutherland, an Alamo medic) in *The Last Command* (1955). He enjoyed huge success in TV sitcoms as "Captain

Huxley" opposite Gale Storm in *The Gale Storm Show*, aka *Oh! Susanna* (1956–1960), "Admiral Rogers" in *McHale's Navy* (1963–1965), "John Cushing" in *The Beverly Hillbillies* (1963–1967), "Mr. Cheever" in *The Lucy Show* (1966–1968), "Norman Curtis" in *Petticoat Junction* (1963–1970), and "Frank Stephens" in *Bewitched* (1967–1970). All the while, Roberts enjoyed a twelve-year run as "Harry Bodkin," the feisty, self-important Dodge City banker on *Gunsmoke* (1963–1975). SEE ALSO: James Arness, Amanda Blake, Milburn Stone.

Dale Robertson

(1923–)

• •

Smug, surly, and supremely self-satisfied, Robertson never strayed far from that simple persona which served him well as a B-movie/TV Western star. Columbia's Harry Cohn, having spotted the teenager in a boxing match in Wichita, Kansas, offered the rugged seventeen-year-old the lead in his upcoming film, *Golden Boy* (1939), from an acclaimed Clifford Odets play. When Robertson refused due to family commitments, the part went to William Holden. Robertson eventually drifted to LA, where in his fourth film (and first Western), the B movie *Fighting Man of the Plains* (1949), he appeared as Jesse James. He went to work for 20th Century-Fox where, in an intriguing casting

coup, Robertson first played a small supporting role in the Civil War tale *Two Flags West* (1950); when Fox remade that film for TV in 1957, he played the lead, Joseph Cotten's part from the original. In between, Robertson played a fictional cavalry officer in *Sitting Bull* (1954), with J. Carrol Naish as the title character, the first of Hollywood's vehemently anti-Custer (Douglas Kennedy) films.

Tales of Wells Fargo (1957–1962), in which Robertson starred, was the first (though far from last!) oater introduced on TV via a filmed anthology show. The pilot aired on *Schlitz Playhouse of Stars* on 12/14/56; positive audience reaction propelled a series into production. Arriving on NBC's Monday evening schedule on 3/18/57, *Wells Fargo* immediately scored as a ratings hit with Robertson as "Jim Hardie," a fictionalized/whitewashed variation on real-life gunfighter John Wesley Hardin. Title aside, the show had little to do with the famed stagecoach line's daily operations. Hardie served as their chief troubleshooter, only occasionally riding in one of their vehicles. This proved a wise move, for those series that did deal with that mode of transportation (*Overland Trail*, *Stagecoach West*) quickly failed. *Tales of Wells Fargo* set the pace for the later *Pony Express* and Robertson's own *The Iron Horse* (1966–1968). When in the third season writers had trouble coming up with scripts, they recycled *Stories of the Century*'s earlier approach,

Jim now involved, if peripherally, with famed outlaws.

During the final season, *Tales of Wells Fargo* went the route of most TV Westerns, expanding to an hour with a big supporting cast, now featuring even *less* connection to the stage line. Hardie became a rancher outside San Francisco and, on rare occasions, helped out his old employer. Virginia Christine portrayed the mature woman "Ovie," who brought a feminine touch to the ranch; William Demarest played "Old Jeb," helping out with chores; Lory Patrick the delightful child "Tina"; and Mary Jane Saunders the precociously pretty teenager "Mary Gee." After the series ended, Robertson starred in several B theatrical Westerns, one particularly interesting: In *Law of the Lawless* (1964), he enacted a variation on the historical hanging judge Isaac Parker, redubbed "Clem Rogers" and transformed into a rugged Westerner, though that highly educated (if merciless) figure had been anything but. Fifteen years later, Robertson would enact Parker (under his real name) in a TV movie, *The Last Ride of the Dalton Gang* (11/20/79), again playing the role as a two-gun man rather than the taciturn, bookish fellow Parker had actually been. In between, he never once found himself out of work, playing the fictional gambler "Ben Calhoun," who wins the near-bankrupt title railroad in a poker game and gets serious about making a go of it, in the TV movie *Scalplock*

(4/10/66). This led to a year-and-a-half series, *The Iron Horse* (1966–1968). Appearing more than once were Roger Torrey as "Nils Torvald," a Goliath-like railroad construction worker; Gary Collins as "Dave Tarrant," executive in charge of laying new track; Woodrow Parfey as "Holmes," an older employee; and Robert Random as "Barnabas," the orphan who idolizes Ben.

Following cancellation, Robertson took over as the latest (of many) hosts for *Death Valley Days* (1969–1970), acting in three installments. He then played a real-life twentieth-century lawman in two made-for-TV movies, *Melvin Purvis G Man* (4/9/74) and *The Kansas City Massacre* (9/19/75), the former written by John Milius. With TV Westerns no longer prevalent, Robertson found roles in glitzy primetime soaps set in the modern West, in Colorado as "Walter Lankershim" on *Dynasty* (1981) and down Texas way as "Frank Crutcher" on *Dallas* (1982). SEE ALSO: Ellen Burstyn, Jack Ging, Ben Johnson, Douglas Kennedy, Warren Oates.

Robert Rockwell
(1920–2003)
•••••••••••••••••••••••••••••••••

A tall, handsome, soft-spoken star of light comedy, Rockwell replaced Jeff Chandler as "Mr. Boynton" on the *Our Miss Brooks* radio show opposite Eve Arden, then continued as her platonic love interest on TV (1952–

1956). He later played "Tom Bishop" on *Diff'rent Strokes* (1979–1984) and "Wally Overmier" on *Growing Pains* (1988–1990). Rockwell performed in one unconventional oater: *The Man from Blackhawk* (1959), as "Sam Logan," insurance investigator for the famed firm. A rarity among TV's frontier heroes, Logan wore a jacket and tie, preferring to ride into town in a surrey rather than on horseback. Each week, he arrived in some new place to decide if the family of the latest victim of a gunfight ought to receive financial compensation.

Kenny Rogers

(1938–)

••••••••••••••••••••••••••••

Dubbed "the overweight lightweight" by *Rolling Stone*, this purveyor of syrupy, sentimental pop standards delivered in a gravelly voice won acceptance as an outlaw-country artist by those who knew nothing about outlaw country. His most popular recording, "The Gambler" (1979), featured a balladic rendering of the title character's adventures including the phrase "you got to know when to hold 'em, know when to fold 'em." That song provided the premise for a TV movie, *Kenny Rogers as The Gambler* (4/8/80), with Rogers playing "Brady Hawkes," out to rescue his son with the help of young "Billy Montana" (Bruce Boxleitner). *The Adventure Continues* (11/28/83) had Brady, Billy, and tyke "Jeremiah

Hawkes" (Charles Fields) traveling on a train taken over by badmen. The sequel's routine plot was bolstered by the intriguing appearance of 1950s/1960s Western stars: Linda Evans, Cameron Mitchell, Johnny Crawford, and Roy Rogers as a drunk! In *The Gambler Returns: The Luck of the Draw* (11/3/91), Brady enters a marathon poker game. Far more intriguing than the plot: a "last roundup" approach, hinted at in the previous film, with numerous one-time genre stars showing up in their original roles or reasonable facsimiles: Gene Barry, Paul Brinegar, David Carradine, Chuck Connors, Johnny Crawford, James Drury, Linda Evans, Brian Keith, Jack Kelly, Doug McClure, Hugh O'Brian, Dub Taylor, and Clint Walker, with Claude Akins as Teddy Roosevelt and country performer Reba McEntire as "Burgundy Jones," a throwback to the charming con woman "Samantha Crawford" on *Maverick*. *The Gambler V: Playing for Keeps* (10/2/94) featured Brady and Billy *again* rescuing Jeremiah (now Kris Kamm) from outlaws Butch Cassidy (Scott Paulin) and the Sundance Kid (Brett Cullen).

Rogers's other appearances included *Rio Diablo* (2/28/93), one more *Searchers* redux, with Rogers and Travis Tritt looking for the latter's lost wife (beauty pageant winner Laura Harring). He guest-starred on *Dr. Quinn, Medicine Woman* (5/22/93), as pioneer "Daniel Watkins" and served as the host/narrator for *The Real West*

(1992), a pop documentary show criticized for numerous historical errors. SEE ALSO: Bruce Boxleitner.

Roy Rogers
(1911–1998)
••••••••••••••••••••••••••••••

Born Leonard Slye in Cincinnati, Ohio, the future Roy Rogers drifted to California at an early age, joined hillbilly musical groups, and helped form (with Bob Nolan) the Sons of the Pioneers, their hits including "Tumbling Tumbleweeds." They performed as backup singers in several B Westerns (Charles Starrett, Dick Foran), plus the big Bing Crosby musical *Rhythm on the Range* (1936). Rogers stepped out of the background for a solo bit in Gene Autry's *The Old Corral* (1936). Rogers borrowed his screen name from his childhood dentist, and starred as a lookalike for Billy Bonney in *Billy the Kid Returns* (1938) and the title character in *Jesse James at Bay* (1941). He went over to the right side of the law in *Young Buffalo Bill* (1940) and *Young Bill Hickok* (1940). Rogers proved effective as a punk with a bad attitude in *Dark Command* (1940), a big (and strange!) Civil War/John Wayne Western. Trigger had been around from the beginning; sidekicks were varied (Smiley Burnett, Gabby Hayes), as were leading ladies until Dale Evans arrived in *Cowboy and the Senorita* (1944). In a switch from a romanticized historical approach to an anachronistic vision of the frontier collapsed into a contemporary West as pioneered by Autry, Rogers headlined the best singing cowboy film ever made, *Don't Fence Me In* (1945), title song composed by Cole Porter. As B Westerns slipped into decline, Rogers played himself as a singing storyteller for Disney's animated *Pecos Bill* (1948), in which he and the Pioneers introduced their classic "Blue Shadows on the Trail." Rogers kept Bob Hope out of trouble in the big-budget *Son of Paleface* (1952), again lending Hope a comic hand (albeit briefly) in *Alias Jesse James* (1959).

TV beckoned; *The Roy Rogers Show* (1951–1957) became his mainstay (there were no further theatrical releases). The premise: Rogers ran the Double-R Ranch, with modern cowboys wearing .45s even as cars breezed by. Dale Evans worked as the waitress at a nearby café, sidekick Pat Brady hung around for goofy country comedy, and Trigger and super-dog Bullet (also a movie veteran) were also on hand. Their eventual ranch-style musical series, *The Roy Rogers & Dale Evans Show* (1962), appeared charmingly dated in the swingin' sixties. Later TV shows included *Saga of Sonora* (5/3/73), a bizarre, campy special featuring Rogers and Evans alongside Frankie Avalon, Zero Mostel, and "Mama" Cass Elliott. *Mackintosh and T.J.* (1975) presented Rogers as an aged drifter who mentors troubled youth. He guest-starred on *Wonder Woman* (1/29/77) as "J. P. Hadley," an old-timer helping Lynda Carter beat the bad guys, though only after she agreed to cover herself up. Today he is known by a new generation as the name (not unlike Colonel Sanders) for a chain of fast-food restaurants. SEE ALSO: Pat Brady, Dale Evans, George "Gabby" Hayes.

Wayne Rogers

(1933–)

••••••••••••••••••••••••••••••

An Alabama-born Princeton grad, Rogers dabbled in theatrics while in the service, then seriously pursued acting after his discharge. His first series role was in Stagecoach West (1960–1961) as "Luke Perry," a cowboy who throws in with "Simon Kane" (Robert Bray) to try to make a go of a stagecoach line. After that, his career remained low-key until the success of M*A*S*H as "Trapper John McIntyre" (1972–1975). Rogers eventually left show business for a career in investments. SEE ALSO: Robert Bray, Richard Eyer.

Will Rogers, Jr.

(1911–1993)

••••••••••••••••••••••••••••••

This son of America's famous part-cowboy/part-Indian political humorist and Western performer found himself typecast as his dad, playing Will Sr. as a cameo in Look for the Silver Lining (1949), the lead in The Story of Will Rogers (1952), and a

supporting role in The Eddie Cantor Story (1953, with Keefe Brasselle). Rogers landed the title part in a big Warner Bros. Western as "Tom Brewster," The Boy from Oklahoma (1954). When it became the Sugarfoot series two years later, the unknown Will Hutchins assumed the role. Rogers hosted The Pioneers, syndicated in the late 1950s, featuring recycled early Death Valley Days episodes with new introductions. SEE ALSO: Stanley Andrews, Will Hutchins, Guinn "Big Boy" Williams.

Ned Romero

(1925–)

••••••••••••••••••••••••••••••

Part Native American (Chitimacha), as well as part Spanish and French, Romero became the key transitional figure on TV from Anglo Indians to the real deal. Originally an operatic baritone, he switched to playing Native Americans and Latinos. Romero's regular roles on TV series include "Chips" (Shane, 1966), "Running Feet" (Custer, 1967), "Mendoza" (The High Chaparral, 1967–1968), "Sergeant Joe Rivera" (Dan August, 1970–1971), "Broken Foot" (Born to the Wind, 1982), "Judge Fivekills" (Walker, Texas Ranger, 1998–2000), and "River Dog" (Roswell, 1999–2000). His historical portraits in TV movies include Chief Joseph of the Nez Perce (I Will Fight No More Forever, 4/14/75); Chief Red Cloud, Lakota (Peter Lundy and the Medicine

Hat Stallion, 11/6/77); and Chief John Jolley, Cherokee (*Houston: The Legend of Texas*, 11/22/86). He also played the fictional characters "Chingachgook" in *The Last of the Mohicans* (11/23/77) and *The Deerslayer* (12/18/78), and "Wisa" in *The Mystic Warrior* (5/20/84). SEE ALSO: David Carradine, Sam Elliott, Leif Erickson, Steve Forrest, Wayne Maunder, Don Shanks.

Katharine Ross

(1940–)
••••••••••••••••••••••••••••••

With her classy looks and sophisticated demeanor, Ross hardly seemed a likely candidate to become one of the first ladies of TV Westerns, particularly after she shot to fame in Mike Nichols's *The Graduate* (1967) opposite Dustin Hoffman. Yet her next major role cast Ross opposite Paul Newman and Robert Redford in *Butch Cassidy and the Sundance Kid* (1969), the Old West outlaws (and their girl Etta Place) now made "hip" for modern viewers. That same year, Ross enacted a Native American woman in *Tell Them Willie Boy Is Here*. She was persuaded to revive Etta Place for a TV movie, *Wanted: The Sundance Woman* (10/1/76), in which she learns that the Kid may still be alive and sets out to find him. Ross played the female lead in *The Shadow Riders* (9/28/82), one of the earliest serious attempts to create a TV-movie Western on an epic scale, starring opposite husband Sam

WESTWARD THE WOMEN: The variety of American females who helped settle the frontier were well represented. Katharine Ross brought a fierce brand of feminism to *The Shadow Riders*. Courtesy Turner Television.

Elliott. She then became involved in her husband's attempts to provide high-quality oaters for the small screen, also appearing with him in *Conagher* (7/1/91). Earlier she guest-starred (as real-life Alamo survivor Sue Dickinson) in *Houston: The Legend of Texas* (11/22/86). That same year Ross played opposite Willie Nelson in *Red Headed Stranger*, based on the popular ballad. SEE ALSO: Sam Elliott, Willie Nelson.

Bing Russell

(1926–2003)
••••••••••••••••••••••••••••••

Never out of work, never a name star, the father of Kurt Russell (who often visited his dad on the set) made hundreds of movie/TV Westerns, notably as a Jayhawker in *The True Story of Jesse James* and a Texas bartender in *Gunfight at the O.K. Corral*, both in 1957. He appeared in virtually every TV Western, with one continuing character, "Deputy Clem Foster," trying to bring law and order to Nevada City in episodes of *Bonanza* (1963–1972). SEE ALSO: Lorne Greene, Kurt Russell, Ray Teal.

John Russell
(1921–1991)
••••••••••••••••••••••••••••••

Tall, dark, and handsome, this hero of Guadalcanal was a natural for movies, particularly Westerns, beginning with *Yellow Sky* (1948) as part of a gang led by Gregory Peck and Richard Widmark. He worked for Ford in *The Sun Shines Bright* (1953), exquisite Americana, afterward relegated to Republic B pictures, then the TV series *Soldiers of Fortune* (1955–1957), as a mercenary (with sidekick Chick Chandler). His other parts included Lieutenant Dickinson, Alamo officer, in *The Last Command* (1955), and Chief Gall in *Yellowstone Kelly* (1959). Russell reached full TV stardom as "Dan Troop" on *Lawman* (1958–1962), the marshal of Laramie, Wyoming, with young deputy "Johnny McKay" (Peter Brown). In concept, the show sounded like *The Deputy*, *The Tall Man*, and many other formulaic Westerns, though this one proved special. WB's top TV producers (Wil-

liam T. Orr, Jules Schermer), writers (Clair Huffaker, Burt Kennedy), and directors (George Waggner, Stuart Heisler) breathed fresh life into stock situations. Minimalist in approach, the star's imposing demeanor would often be silhouetted by lanterns on the late-evening frontier boardwalk. Russell then stepped into the hazy light, revealing a face as perfectly chiseled as Charlton Heston's, with drooping mustache for accuracy. Some work afterward included the recurring role of "William Dover," international man of mystery, on *It Takes a Thief* (1969, Robert Wagner). Then it was back to Westerns with *Alias Smith and Jones* (1/5/71), as one of several lawmen tracking the lighthearted outlaws, Russell also a regular on the weekly series version (1971–1972). He played notable villains in two Clint Eastwood Westerns: Bloody Bill Anderson in *The Outlaw Josey Wales* (1976) and the ruthless range boss in *Pale Rider* (1985). SEE ALSO: Peter Brown, Peggie Castle, Pete Duel, Clint Eastwood, Ben Murphy.

Kurt Russell
(1951–)
••••••••••••••••••••••••••••••

The son of actor Bing Russell played a scene with Elvis in *It Happened at the World's Fair* (1963) and later enacted the King in the TV movie *Elvis* (1979). At age twelve, Russell won the title role (though Dan

THE SEARCHERS REDUX: Themes from 1950s films were revived for TV in the 1970s and 1980s; here, two brothers (Tim Matheson, *left*, and Kurt Russell) attempt to find their sister, abducted by Indians, on *The Quest*. Courtesy NBC.

O'Herlihy as his father was top-billed) in the ambitious ABC failure *The Travels of Jaimie McPheeters* (1963–1964), based on the well-regarded Robert Lewis Taylor novel about a boy heading west with his widower dad. Regulars included Michael Witney as the wagon boss, "Buck Coulter"; James Westerfield and Sandy Kenyon, pioneers "John Murrel" and "Shep Baggott"; and Alan, Jay, and Merrill Osmond, "Micah," "Lamentations," and "Deu-

teronomy Kissel." Grim and realistic, the show offered high-quality drama but seemed all wrong for the Sunday evening family slot. Russell became a Disney youth star (*Computer Wore Tennis Shoes*, 1969), then headed back to the TV Western in *The New Land* (1974), a short-lived pioneer saga. He then played in *The Quest* (1976), a *Searchers* clone about the rugged young "Morgan Bodeen" on the lookout for his younger sister, abducted by Indians. Several episodes were re-cut and turned into the TV movie *The Longest Drive* (1976). Russell finally found his proper persona, an updated version of John Wayne, in the action flicks *Escape from New York* (1981) and *The Thing* (1982), both for John Carpenter. He eventually returned to Westerns as a complex Wyatt Earp in *Tombstone* (1993). SEE ALSO: Bonnie Bedelia, Charles Bronson, Tim Matheson, Dan O'Herlihy.

SHOOTING STARS OF THE SMALL SCREEN

Albert Salmi

(1928–1990)

••••••••••••••••••••••••••••••

Another of Hollywood's tragic figures, this brilliant actor suffered from
severe depression, which hurt his
career and in time took his life. After
World War II service, Salmi studied
at both the Actors Studio and the
American Theatre Wing; he won
roles on Broadway, including the
naïve cowboy "Bo Decker" in *Bus
Stop* (1955), then unwisely turned
down the lead in the movie opposite
Marilyn Monroe (1956), which made
an instantaneous star of Don Murray. Salmi preferred the stage and
live TV drama, though he did in time
move west, where the Brooklyn-
born actor became associated with
Western roles beginning with a
lovable Bo-like cowboy who courts
Audrey Hepburn in *The Unforgiven*,
then a brutal Southern redneck who
viciously beats Monty Clift in *Wild*

River (both 1960). Salmi won the role
of "Yadkin," sidekick to Fess Parker
on *Daniel Boone* (1964); an intense
Method actor, Salmi strained to fit in
but dropped out before the end of the
first season. He won the prestigious
Western Heritage "Wrangler" award
for "Holly" on *Gunsmoke*'s "Death
Watch" episode (1/8/66) and stole
the show from Dean Martin as a man
who will give up his beloved Gatling
gun only if somebody provides him
with a woman in *Something Big*
(1971). Salmi later played a small part
in Gore Vidal's *Billy the Kid* (5/10/89)
with Val Kilmer. Semi-retired in Spo-
kane, Washington, he and his wife
perished in a murder-suicide linked
to their joint addiction to legal drugs.
SEE ALSO: James Arness, Fess Parker,
Jeff York.

Joe Sawyer
(1906–1982)
....

Cop or crook, heroic U.S. Marine or cold-blooded murderer, all provided equal fodder for the man born Joe Sauer, a stalwart member of the WB stock company during the 1930s. Known for mistrusting eyes, a barrel-like body, and that melodious yet vaguely threatening voice, Sawyer played Curly Bill Brocious in *Frontier Marshal* (1939) and Butch Cassidy twice on TV, in *Stories of the Century* (6/3/54) and *Frontier Doctor* (11/15/58). His best movie roles were in *The Informer* (1935), *The Petrified Forest* (1936), and *The Grapes of Wrath* (1940). Sawyer mellowed with age, allowing him to be perfectly cast as "Sergeant 'Biff' O'Hara" (given name "Aloysius") on *The Adventures of Rin Tin Tin* (1954–1959), caring for orphan Rusty (Lee Aaker) while dealing with sidekicks Corporals Boone (Rand Brooks) and Carson (Tommy Farrell). His final role was as the hardy river boatman in the big Cinerama oater *How the West Was Won* (1962). SEE ALSO: Lee Aaker, Rand Brooks, James L. Brown, Tommy Farrell.

John Schneider
(1960–)
....

When contemporary country replaced the Old West as a TV staple in the 1970s, Schneider starred as "Bo" on *The Dukes of Hazzard* (1979–1985), a good ol' boy driving a hot car rather than riding a worn pony. He appeared in ABC's *Stagecoach* remake (5/18/86) as "Buck," the driver played by Andy Devine in John Ford's 1939 classic and by Slim Pickens in the 1966 theatrical flop. Schneider also played badman Jack McCall in *Wild Jack* (1/15/89) and two Western heroes, Davy Crockett in *Texas* (4/16/95) and Sam Houston in *True Women* (5/18/97). He enjoyed a regular role as frontiersman "Daniel Simon" on *Dr. Quinn, Medicine Woman* (1997–1998), then as "Jonathan Kent" (*Smallville*, 2001–2006). SEE ALSO: Johnny Cash, Waylon Jennings, Willie Nelson, Jane Seymour.

Rick Schroder
(1970–)
....

After winning the role as Jon Voight's son in *The Champ* (1979), Schroder then effectively moved from movie drama to TV sitcom with *Silver Spoons* (1982–1987). When that ended, he refused to (like most kid actors) disappear (or worse!), moving on to a diverse career beginning with the miniseries *Lonesome Dove* (2/5/89) in the role of "Newt Dobbs," youngest of the heroes and possible son of "Woodrow Call" (Tommy Lee Jones). Schroder's fine performance suggested strong possibilities as a retro Western star. He followed *Dove* up with the TV movie *Blood River* (3/17/91) as "Jimmy Pearls," fugitive from the law, pursued by cattle baron "Henry Logan" (John P. Ryan) and mentored by mountain man turned marshal "Patrick Culler" (Wilford Brimley). He revived the role of Newt for *Return to Lonesome Dove* (11/14/93), the more controversial of two sequels as the one *not* based on writings by Larry McMurtry. With Gus now deceased, Call (Jon Voight) deals with Newt's incarceration in jail along with his pal "Jasper" (Barry Tub); the story also follows Newt's marriage to "Ferris" (Reese Witherspoon) and employment by the mean-spirited cattleman "Dunnigan" (Oliver Reed). McMurtry it's not, but a sturdy and engaging TV oater? Yes. Schroder passed on the chance to continue as Newt in a weekly series (1994–1995) in order to concentrate on modern roles, including a standout performance in the Denzel Washington–Gene Hackman hit *Crimson Tide* (1995). He played cowboy "Otto MacNab" in *Texas* (4/16/95), though this would-be epic (based on a James Michener novel) didn't come close to *Lonesome Dove* in quality. Other roles include Detective Danny Sorenson on *NYPD Blue* (1998–2001) and recurring parts in *Scrubs* (2003), *Strong Medicine* (2005–2006), and *24* (2007). Schroder lived for many years with his wife and kids on a sprawling Colorado ranch but later sold it and moved to a ranch in California. An outspoken National Rifle Association member, he is also a fervent supporter of the Republican Party. SEE ALSO: Scott Bairstow, Robert Duvall, Danny Glover, Tommy Lee Jones.

Eric Schweig

(1967–)
••••••••••••••••••••••••••••••••

Of mixed Inuit and German descent, Schweig made a strong impression as "Uncas" in *The Last of the Mohicans* (1992), though that role was so trimmed in the editing room that viewers didn't grasp that in James Fenimore Cooper's novel, *he* was the title character! Schweig would be better served by Epenow in *Squanto: A Warrior's Tale* (1994, with Adam Beach in the lead). High-profile TV movie roles include Joe Brandt/Theyendangea in *The Broken Chain* (12/12/93), about the Iroquois Confederacy during the American Revolution; Wildcat (*Follow The River*, 4/22/95), chronicling the abduction of Mary Ingles (Sheryl Lee) by Shawnees; Sitting Bull (*Into the West*, 6/10/05); Sam George (*One Dead Indian*, 1/4/06), about a real-life peaceful protest turned deadly; and Chief Gall (*Bury My Heart at Wounded Knee*, 5/27/07), concerning the brutal U.S. Army–Indian dispute over the incendiary Ghost Dance that inspired Dee Brown's book (1970), in its time the first to raise America's consciousness about Indian rights. SEE ALSO: Adam Beach.

Pippa Scott

(1935–)

This ravishing, Broadway-trained redhead made her film debut as "Lucy Edwards," doomed fiancée of Harry Carey, Jr., in Ford's *The Searchers* (1956). She was an original cast member of *The Virginian* as "Molly" (1962), a woman from the East who tries to understand the Code of the West; the role had previously been played by Mary Brian (1929) and Barbara Britton (1946) on film. The episode that best showcased her talent was "It Tolls for Thee" (11/21/62), with Lee Marvin guest-starring. As the show gradually found its identity, writers found no room for her character, so Molly was eased out. Scott did considerable film and TV work afterward and was also a producer at Lorimar and Linden. SEE ALSO: Lee J. Cobb, James Drury, Roberta Shore.

Tom Selleck

(1945–)

At college, young Selleck hoped to sign up for an architecture class but found it full. He noticed an acting class listed just above and took that instead. Early roles included "The Stud" (to Mae West, Raquel Welch, and Farrah Fawcett) in the notorious flop *Myra Breckinridge* (1970) and a small part in the World War

A RETURN TO TRADITION: Tom Selleck, who likely would've been a superstar during the golden age of theatrical Westerns, maintained the sensibility of that classical genre in a series of memorable made-for-TV movies and miniseries. Courtesy *Shadow Riders* Productions.

II epic *Midway* (1976), headlined by Charlton Heston, soon a friend, mentor, and Selleck's lifelong idol. He played a recurring TV role as "Will Eubanks," contemporary wanderer of the West, in *The Concrete Cowboys* (1979). Known for unswerving integrity, Selleck had just signed on to do *Magnum, P.I.*, for Universal TV when Steven Spielberg offered him the role of "Indiana Jones." Selleck could have broken the contract but knew it was not the right thing to do. In a terrible irony, owing to a change in timing of the projects, he could have starred in both! Selleck's Hawaii-set show rated as a huge hit between 1980 and 1988. He performed in many marginal movies but enjoyed his greatest success on the small screen, particularly in Westerns. In *The Sacketts* (5/15/79) he played "Orrin," with Sam Elliott and Jeff Osterhage as his brothers; the trio reunited for *The Shadow Riders* (9/28/82) with different names. Selleck's finest film role came as the lead in *Quigley Down Under* (1990), an Aussie adventure that sparked a working relationship with director Simon Wincer. Selleck then starred in a series of high-class TV movies: *Last Stand at Saber River* (1/19/97, from the Elmore Leonard novel), *Crossfire Trail* (1/21/01), and best of all *Monte Walsh* (1/17/03), a superb remake of the classic 1970 Lee Marvin film. Selleck proved equally adept at contemporary comedy and drama, playing "Jack McLaren" on *The Closer* (1998) and Dr. Richard Burke, "Monica's older man," on *Friends* (1996–2000). More recently, he starred in an upscale series of TV movies as "Jesse Stone," police chief (2005–). Selleck is a National Rifle Association member and was a Reagan supporter in the 1980s, yet he considers himself an independent who supports candidates based on their values rather than by blind party allegiance. SEE ALSO: Sam Elliott, Jeff Osterhage, Jerry Reed.

Victor Sen Yung

(1915–1980)

Small in stature, this Asian American actor is best remembered for nearly twenty *Charlie Chan* movies as "Number Two Son Jimmy" to Sidney Toler and then Roland Winters, and as "Hop Sing," the short-tempered cook on *Bonanza* (1959–1973). A gifted Cantonese chef in real life, he authored *The Great Wok Cookbook* (1974). Yung was found dead under mysterious circumstances in his home. SEE ALSO: Dan Blocker, Lorne Greene, Michael Landon.

Jane Seymour

(1951–)

A real-life female counterpart to F. Scott Fitzgerald's "Jay Gatsby," Jane Seymour sprang from a platonic conception of herself. Born Joyce Penelope Wilhelmina Frankenberg to an Eastern European doctor father and his Dutch wife after they settled in England, she assumed the name of historical aristocracy and an upperclass English accent, effectively projecting herself as a combination of old-fashioned class and contemporary feminist enlightenment. Seymour's elegant aura and subtle sensuality, abetted by an imperfect/irresistible beauty (one brown eye and one green, a self-described "crooked

S

ROMANCE ON THE RANGE: Feminist values of the 1970s found their way into the TV Western via Jane Seymour as an Eastern woman who tames the heart of a handsome mountain man (Joe Lando) in *Dr. Quinn, Medicine Woman*, first on the weekly series, then in the subsequent made-for-TV movies. Courtesy CBS.

smile"), opened doors to showy roles including "Solitaire," the Bond girl in *Live and Let Die* (1973) and Bathsheba on the TV miniseries *Story of David* (1976). The latter form proved Seymour's métier; she starred in *Captains and the Kings* (1976), *Battlestar Galactica* (1978), and *War and Remembrance* (1988). Even today her lifestyle radiates class: She and fourth husband James Keach (Jesse James in *The Long Riders*, 1980) inhabit

an ancient mansion, St. Catherine's Court, near Bath in England.

Series creator Beth Sullivan chose Seymour for the lead in *Dr. Quinn, Medicine Woman* (1993–1998), a successful revisionist Western series that projected contemporary values in the same manner that earlier shows expressed the ideology of *their* times. Featuring a feminist woman as the focus of a Western series had been rejected after the failure of *Sara*

(1976), but by the 1990s—when mainstream women had absorbed many once radical values—the time seemed right. In all truth, though, *Dr. Quinn* likely would not have succeeded were it not for the charisma of the leading lady and strong chemistry with her leading man.

The premise had Dr. Quinn (her given name "Michaela" suggesting a class act though her nickname "Mike" made clear she was unpretentious), a "one of the guys" woman, leaving sophisticated Boston following the death of her father to practice in small Colorado Springs. Dr. Quinn initially received a less than enthusiastic welcome from the frontier populace unable to imagine its new doctor might be a *woman*. Diligently, firmly, but non-threateningly, she proved her worth. Even the most rugged male characters came to accept and even adore a lady who clearly had a great gift for medicine and an agenda to morally educate them that thankfully never turned shrill or didactic. Dr. Quinn gradually changed their point of view through actions that left no doubt a woman can do anything a man can, without her ever once making the mistake of preaching such values openly. In her personal life, Mike proved as traditional as she was progressive career-wise. "Byron Sully" (Joe Lando), a handsome mountain man, arrived on the scene; gradually they developed a deep love. The PR photographs of Seymour and Lando in each other's arms resembled the pluperfect couples on covers of paperback romance novels, which is how their relationship played out on the show. This resulted in an idealized fantasy for a largely female audience, implying as it did that a woman "could have it all."

A large cast included three orphan children of "Charlotte Cooper" (Diane Ladd) whom Mike took in: "Matthew" (Chad Allen), "Colleen" (Erika Flores, replaced by Jessica Bowman), and "Brian" (Shawn Toovey); John Schneider as Sully's best friend "Daniel Simon"; and Orson Bean as the curmudgeon "Loren Bray"; Geoffrey Lower as "Rev. Timothy Johnson" added a nice verisimilitude. The series also addressed the growing interest in/ revised thinking about Native Americans. Like Kevin Costner's *Dances With Wolves* (1990) and a product of the same era, Indians were here played as innocent/nonviolent, an image embodied by Nick Ramus as Chief Black Kettle; the U.S. Cavalry came across as a killing machine on horseback, led by the hissing and spitting General Custer (James Leland Adams). As with Costner's film, the result rated as politically correct but historically inaccurate; the serious plight of the American Indian was presented as a backdrop to a tear-jerker romance between two good-looking whites.

As the series continued, such situations grew ever more melodramatic, sometimes ludicrously so. Mike and

Sully married and had a child. But when actor Lando decided he might leave over a salary dispute, the writers ended the fifth season by having him fall over a cliff. This allowed execs more time to try to work out a deal. If they could, Sully would survive the fall; if not, a mourning Mike could find solace in the arms of Sully's equally handsome best friend. Lando did return, so Schneider was out. Despite such silliness, *Dr. Quinn* did occasionally tackle tough topics with integrity. "The Body Electric" (4/5/97) featured a visit from Walt Whitman (Donald Moffat). The townsfolk, who had by now learned to accept both women and Indians, revealed their homophobia, though that too would be corrected by the Mary Poppins–like heroine.

A seventh season was slated as the last, with all plot elements to be resolved over the course of the year. Instead, CBS suddenly canceled *Dr. Quinn*, though ratings remained high. During more than half a decade on the air, society had altered *again*. The public at large had become attracted to Quentin Tarantino–style edgy violence, and TV began to flirt with a *Pulp Fiction* (1994) style of storytelling. The target audience of *Dr. Quinn* had been the all-important under-forty female viewers whom advertisers hunger to reach. During the show's run, its audience remained loyal but aged, rendering the fans irrelevant. Outrage over cancellation

led to a pair of movie specials: *Dr. Quinn, Medicine Woman: The Movie* (5/22/99), about the family's later (1877) adventures in Colorado, and *The Heart Within* (5/12/01), in which they traveled to Boston and discovered the big city. Finding people there cynical, Mike longed for the rugged simplicity of the plains. Seymour later played the recurring role of "Genevieve" in *Smallville* (2004–2005), reuniting her with *Dr. Quinn* costar John Schneider. SEE ALSO: Joe Lando, John Schneider.

Rocky Shahan
(1918–1981)

One more stuntman who parlayed his authentic Western manner into acting roles, Shahan performed tricky "gags" on *The Range Rider* (1951), then served double-duty as a member of the "outlaw gang of the week." The same situation proved true in movies: *The Lusty Men* (1952, Robert Mitchum) and *Johnny Guitar* (1954, Sterling Hayden). Then came the little movie that made big changes in the lives of many actors: *Cattle Empire* (1958). Shahan was cast as "Quince," but when the film morphed into the *Rawhide* series, that role went to Steve Raines, with Shahan on board as "Joe Scarlett," a dour drover. SEE ALSO: Paul Brinegar, Clint Eastwood, Steve Raines.

Don Shanks
(1950–)
••••••••••••••••••••••••••••••••

An Illinois-born Native American, Shanks assumed roles in films and on TV when Anglos in makeup were finally phased out. He appeared in *The Life and Times of Grizzly Adams* (1974) and *The Adventures of Frontier Fremont* (1976), impressing viewers as "Uncas" in the TV movie *The Last of the Mohicans* (11/23/77), then as "Red Kettle" in *How the West Was Won* and *The Chisholms* (both 1979). His best TV-movie role ever: "Asha-wakie" in Louis L'Amour's *Down the Long Hills* (11/15/86). SEE ALSO: Dan Haggerty, Ned Romero.

Karen Sharpe (Kramer)
(1934–)
••••••••••••••••••••••••••••••••

This Texas-born actress made her film debut in *The Sniper* (1952), a fine film noir; though she never met that film's producer, Stanley Kramer, on site, she would marry him fourteen years later. On *Johnny Ringo* (1959), Sharpe enacted a townswoman, "Laura Thomas." Her role and that of her father, "Case Thomas" (Terence De Marney), were quickly written out, allowing a concentration on the relationship between the marshal (Don Durant) and a young deputy (Mark Goddard), thereby rendering *Ringo* all but indistinguishable from a dozen other TV oaters. In 2000,

shortly before the death of her husband, Sharpe Kramer produced a TV remake of *High Noon*, one of his most famous films, with Tom Skerritt in the Gary Cooper role of "Will Kane." SEE ALSO: Terence De Marney, Don Durant, Mark Goddard.

William Shatner
(1931–)
••••••••••••••••••••••••••••••••

Adored by *Star Trek* fans as "Captain Kirk," many critics dismissed Shatner as a pretentious/pompous performer. The Canadian-born Shat's first TV role came as "Ranger Bob" on the legendary *Howdy Doody* puppet show (1954). Shatner played small parts in big films (*Judgment at Nuremberg*, 1961), big ones in small flicks (*I Hate Your Guts!*, 1962), two *Twilight Zones*, an unsold *Alexander the Great* pilot (1964), and the brief-lived contemporary series *For the People* (1965), before at last winning the lead in TV's best-loved sci-fi series. His later *Barbary Coast* began as a TV movie (5/4/75), with Shat cast as "Jeff Cable," a government agent in San Francisco who hides out in a lavish gambling den owned by an old friend (Dennis Cole). Cable employed a series of disguises (old man, Asian immigrant, rowdy cowpoke, drunk, etc.) to bring baddies to justice. In the series, Doug McClure took over Cole's role as the friend. This lavishly produced attempt to recapture the glory days of Clark Gable/Spencer

Tracy matchings failed to catch on and was canceled by NBC after several months. Shatner later enjoyed considerable success with *T.J. Hooker* and *Boston Legal* on TV, as well as a highly popular series of *Star Trek* movies. SEE ALSO: Doug McClure.

Christopher Shea

(1958–)

••••••••••••••••••••••••••••••••

Shea played little "Joey Starrett" (Brandon De Wilde in the 1953 movie) in the brief-lived TV version of *Shane* (1966). His greatest success came as the voice of "Linus" in six animated *Charlie Brown* TV specials. SEE ALSO: David Carradine, Brandon De Wilde, Jill Ireland.

Ann Sheridan

(1915–1967)

••••••••••••••••••••••••••••••••

Texas-born Clara Lou Sheridan won a beauty contest that ensured a Paramount screen test. As the "Oomph Girl," Sheridan came across as a tart-tongued modern girl, winning dramatic roles while under contract to Warner Bros., notably in *They Drive by Night* (1940) opposite Bogart. She later pursued an independent career in comedies, including Howard Hawks's *I Was a Male War Bride* (1949, Cary Grant).

Sheridan appeared with Errol Flynn in two big-scale Warner's Westerns, *Dodge City* (1939) and *Silver River* (1948). A guest spot on *Wagon Train* (1962) brought her to the attention of TV producers, who offered Sheridan the lead in *Pistols 'n' Petticoats* (1966–1967), an interesting attempt to revive the TV oater at a time when the genre had given way to cornball country comedies like *Petticoat Junction*. Creator George Tibbles included a large dose of rowdy hillbilly humor but set his series in the Old West, also incorporating the budding feminist movement by having Sheridan play "Henrietta Hanks," a strong female who brings law and order to Wretched, Colorado. "Grandma" (Ruth McDevitt), who had taught Henrietta how to shoot, provided strong support. The cast spanned three generations, with Carole Wells as Henrietta's daughter "Lucy" ready to take up the torch. Overwhelmed by the female trio were young sheriff "Harold Sikes" (Gary Vinson), old range boss "Buss Courtney" (Robert Lowery), and local tribal leader "Eagle Shadow" (Lon Chaney, Jr.). "Grandpa Andrew" (Doug Fowley) helped out too. Though ratings were acceptable, the show was canceled after Sheridan abruptly became ill, then passed away midway through an abbreviated single season. SEE ALSO: Lon Chaney, Jr.; Douglas (V.) Fowley; Robert Lowery.

Roberta Shore

(1943–)

A child/teen actress, Shore is best remembered for stints on *Father Knows Best* (1958) and various Walt Disney TV (*Annette*, 1958) and film (*The Shaggy Dog*, 1959) projects. A member of the original cast of *The Virginian* (1962–1965) as "Betsy Garth," the pretty/perky adopted daughter of "Judge Henry" (Lee J. Cobb), Shore decided to leave acting for marriage. She was written out of the series with a wedding (to Glenn Corbett) on "The Awakening" episode (10/13/65). Following her Mormon faith, she moved to Salt Lake City to raise a family, later working as a disc jockey there. SEE ALSO: Randy Boone, Lee J. Cobb, Glenn Corbett.

Frank Silvera

(1914–1970)

This Jamaican-born African American studied at Northwestern for a career in law. Acting beckoned, beginning with the American Negro Theatre in Harlem and the Actors Studio. Silvera won a nomination for a Tony award for his role in the 1963 stage play *The Lady of the Camellias*. His light skin allowed Silvera to play virtually any ethnic person, so he was often cast as Latinos. His best film roles were as

"Huerta" in *Viva Zapata!* (1952, Elia Kazan) and "Rapallo" in *Killer's Kiss* (1955, Stanley Kubrick). TV stardom arrived as "Don Sebastian Montoya" in *The High Chaparral* (1967–1970). Silvera provided an accurate portrait of a Spanish patriarch, which revealed the new maturity of TV Westerns in setting the record right historically via dignified Hispanic characters. Silvera died in an accident; his final film, *Valdez Is Coming* (1971), was released posthumously. SEE ALSO: Linda Cristal, Henry Darrow.

Jay Silverheels

(1912–1980)

The precise date of his birth is uncertain, but Harold J. Smith (his original name) was a pureblooded Canadian Mohawk. Silverheels's first notable role came as "Osceola," contemporary descendant of the great chief, in *Key Largo* (1948, Humphrey Bogart). Silverheels costarred in the B movie *The Cowboy and the Indians* (1949) with Clayton Moore. Their chemistry clicked, so when Moore was picked for the lead in *The Lone Ranger*, Silverheels came along for the ten-year ride on TV and in feature films. The role was notable in that "Tonto" rated as *not* a sidekick but a full partner with "John Reid," conveying the civil rights message to kids via an exciting melodrama. The actor could also

THE REAL DEAL: "Tonto" rates as TV's first Native American hero, seen here with saddle pal "John Reid" (Clayton Moore) in *The Lone Ranger*, "Silver" in the background but "Scout" nowhere to be seen. Authenticity was provided by the casting of an actual Indian, Jay Silverheels, in the role. Courtesy *Lone Ranger* Enterprises, ABC.

be menacing, playing Geronimo in three films: *Broken Arrow* (1950), *The Battle at Apache Pass* (1952), and *Walk the Proud Land* (1956). Other historical figures include Tecumseh (*Brave Warrior*, 1952), Red Cloud (*Jack McCall, Desperado*, 1953), and Natchez *(Texas John Slaughter*, 1960). Silverheels also played James Fenimore Cooper's "Chingachgook" in *The Pathfinder* (1952). He delivered his best performance ever in the lost gem *Indian Paint* (1965), with Johnny Crawford as a sensitive young brave. SEE ALSO: Johnny Crawford, John Hart, Clayton Moore, Tom Tryon.

Richard Simmons

(1913–2003)
••••••••••••••••••••••••••••••

"On, King! On, you huskies!" So shouted the hero of *Sergeant Preston of the Yukon* (1955–1958), a Thursday evening staple on CBS, as he and his dog team tore across a snowy terrain in the lawless (at least until Preston arrived) Yukon of the 1890s. After the badmen had been subdued, the mountie would hug his lead dog and say, "Well, King, another case *closed!*" That's how it worked in half the shows, though dogsleds were absent from those episodes that took place in summer. Then, in bright red uniform, Preston rode into action. The only star of juvenile Westerns to sport a mustache, Simmons had become interested in acting while a University of Minnesota student; he took

several years off to vagabond around the world on tramp steamers, settling in LA to work with horses until the handsome fellow was spotted and signed by MGM. Simmons appears to have been fated for the role, as his first speaking part in a film had been as a redcoat in *King of the Royal Mounted* (1940).

Robert F. Simon

(1908–1992)
••••••••••••••••••••••••••••••

A solid TV/movie character actor with over 200 credits, Simon played the decent-minded sheriff in *Gunman's Walk* (1958), starring Van Heflin, and the anti-racist New Mexico deputy "Ed Morgan" in the *Elfego Baca* series (1958). He also played Brigadier General Alfred Terry, the stern but understanding commanding officer of the title character in *The Legend of Custer* (1968), but was better known as "Frank Stephens" (*Bewitched*, 1964–1971) and J. Jonah Jameson (*The Amazing Spider-Man*, 1978–1979). SEE ALSO: Robert Loggia, Wayne Maunder.

Mark Slade

(1939–)
••••••••••••••••••••••••••••••

Originally a gifted cartoonist, Slade accidentally discovered acting while at Worchester Academy in Massachusetts, then headed for Hollywood. He played "Patrick Hollis," the perennially sick sailor in *The Wackiest Ship in the Army* (1965–1966) with Jack Warden, which led to his casting in one of TV's best "big" Westerns, *The High Chaparral*. For the first three seasons (1967–1970), Slade played "Billy Blue Cannon," son of "Big John" (Leif Erickson); this father-son relationship between a John Wayne–type reactionary dad and a James Dean–type confused/sensitive son resulted in a realistic portrayal of a dysfunctional family, in sharp comparison to the gooey love fest viewed earlier each Sunday evening on *Bonanza*. Slade's Billy Blue came off as marginally mentally challenged, a concept developed further after Slade left the show to write/star in "Cliffy," a notable episode of *The Rookies* (3/3/75). Slade enjoyed one historical role as the young Captain U. S. Grant on *The Life and Times of Grizzly Adams* (4/5/78). He eventually returned to his first love, art. SEE ALSO: Linda Cristal, Leif Erickson, Cameron Mitchell.

John Smith

(1931–1995)

••••••••••••••••••••••••••••••

Smith played several real-life Westerners shortly after breaking into Hollywood: the outlaw John Sontag on *Stories of the Century* (2/8/55), Frederick (son of John) Brown in *Seven Angry Men*, and James Earp in *Wichita* (both 1955). His best screen role was as historical character William Wesley Van Orsdel, a man of the cloth attempting to end violence on the frontier and known to the congregation as Brother Van, in *The Lawless Eighties* (1957). Smith alternated between big roles in small films (*Hot Rod Girl*) and small ones in big movies (*Friendly Persuasion* as "The Wrestling Quaker," both 1956). His first TV Western role came courtesy of *Cimarron City* (1958–1959), an ambitious big-scale (if single-season) series, as "Deputy Sheriff Lane Temple," a green but dedicated lawman. In the fourth/best episode, "Twelve Guns," Luana Patten played his love interest. The two actors married soon thereafter but eventually divorced. *Laramie* (1959–1963) originally focused on two brothers, "Slim Sherman" (Smith) and young "Andy" (Robert Crawford, Jr.), trying to survive in Wyoming after their father's death by punching cattle on a small ranch that also served as a stagecoach stop, allowing for guest stars/diverse plots. Following a healthy four-season run, Smith won one big movie role, in Henry Hathaway's *Circus World* (1964). His final recurring role was as "Ed Dow," the no-good husband of a ranch lady (Katherine Browne) also loved by the title hero (Ralph Taeger), in *Hondo* (1967); these roles had been played by Leo V. Gordon, John Wayne, and Geraldine Page, respectively, in the film. Real name: Robert Van Orden; he changed it because he wanted to be the only man named John Smith in show business! SEE

ALSO: Dan Blocker; Robert Crawford, Jr.; Robert Fuller; Leo V. Gordon; George Montgomery; Ralph Taeger.

William "Bill" Smith
(1934–   )

••••••••••••••••••••••••••••••

Smith's Missouri-born, Depression-era family left the Dust Bowl and headed for the West Coast in hopes of a fresh start. Young Bill, an angelically beautiful child, found work as the "little boy" in the notable movie *The Ghost of Frankenstein* (1942). Decades later, he would be third-billed on *Laredo* (1965–1967) as "Joe Riley," a muscular Texas Ranger. Smith relished rather than resented his status as King of the Bs when full-fledged stardom proved elusive, appearing in biker flicks (*Angels Die Hard*, 1970), as the assassin of sexy space vampires (*Invasion of the Bee Girls*, 1973), and as leader of the title group in *Seven* (1979), Andy Sidaris's initial trash-action master-piece. He played the pioneer "Amos Martin" on *Daniel Boone*'s final season (1969–1970) as well as the real-life frontiersman Henry Brown, an occasional figure on *Death Valley Days*. Smith engaged in highly memorable big-screen fights with Rod Taylor in *Darker Than Amber* (1970) and Clint Eastwood in *Any Which Way You Can* (1980). He did a cameo as the dad of Arnold Schwarzeneg-ger in *Conan the Barbarian* (1982), appeared as Wyatt Earp on *Fantasy*

Island (3/18/78), and played recurring roles as the evil "Falconetti" (*Rich Man, Poor Man*, 1976) and the heroic "Kimo Carew" (*Hawaii Five-O*, 1979–1980). Smith still works regularly, mainly for the sheer fun of it since business investments have made him a wealthy man. SEE ALSO: Neville Brand, Peter Brown, Philip Carey.

Suzanne Somers
(1946–   )

••••••••••••••••••••••••••••••

A former Playboy model, Somers played ditzy "Chrissy" on the sit-com *Three's Company* (1977–1981) with John (son of Tex) Ritter. A Vegas entertainer and survivor of a dysfunctional/alcoholic family in childhood, Somers battled breast cancer in maturity. Her one Western role, as "Hildy Granger" on *She's the Sheriff* (1987–1989), represented a weak attempt to cash in on feminism while maintaining an old-fashioned sex symbol of the dumb blonde type. When her husband dies, Hildy is appointed law officer in a cowtown; Guich Koock, George Wyner, and Leonard Lightfoot were her deputies; Nicky Rose and Taliesin Jaffe the children; and Pat Carroll her friend "Gussie." The show paled in compari-son to the similar/earlier short-lived *Pistols 'n' Petticoats*. Somers later costarred in *Step by Step* (1991–1998) with Patrick Duffy (*Dallas, Texas*). SEE ALSO: Ann Sheridan.

David Soul

(1943–)

••••••••••••••••••••••••••••

A pop singer turned actor, Soul
became famous as the latter half of
the *Starsky and Hutch* team (1975–
1979) with several quasi-Westerns to
his credit. He played "Joshua Bolt"
in *Here Come the Brides* (1968–1969),
TV's non-musical version of *Seven
Brides for Seven Brothers* (1954); in
it, a Seattle logger (Robert Brown
and Bobby Sherman played Soul's
brothers) brings one hundred young
women from the East to marry his
frustrated mill crew workers. Soul
later starred in the notable flop *The
Yellow Rose* (1983–1984), a modern
Texas soaper, as "Roy Champion."

James Stacy

(1936–)

••••••••••••••••••••••••••••

An LA acting hopeful, Stacy made his
debut in a small part as a reporter in
Sayonara (1957, Marlon Brando); he
played a singing sailor the next year
for the same director (Josh Logan) in
South Pacific. His first TV Western
appearance was as the cocky young
gunslick "Johnny Tully" on *Have
Gun—Will Travel* (12/1/62). Stacy
became sidetracked in the Beach
Party flicks *A Swingin' Summer* and
Winter A-Go-Go (both 1965). Then
it was back to oaters; the role of "Joe
Bravo" on *Cimarron Strip* (1/4/68)
led to the top-billed part of "Johnny

Madrid," castoff son of a California rancher (Andrew Duggan), on
Lancer (1968–1970); Stacy played a
moody, violent half-Indian shootist
trying to accept his Boston-raised
half-brother (Wayne Maunder).
Motorcycling with a girlfriend, Stacy
was sideswiped by a drunk driver;
she died, and he lost his left arm and
leg. He made a comeback in 1975 as
a paraplegic reporter in Kirk Douglas's Watergate-era Western *Posse*.
SEE ALSO: Andrew Duggan, Wayne
Maunder.

Barbara Stanwyck

(1907–1990)

••••••••••••••••••••••••••••••••

Born in Brooklyn as Ruby Stevens,
this semi-beautiful woman/near-great
actress held her own against a studio-
era stable of queen bees (Bette Davis,
Joan Crawford) through sheer belief
in herself as a superstar, leading to
four Oscar nominations. Stanwyck
played diverse roles as a light comedi-
enne (*The Lady Eve*, 1941), film noir
temptress (*Double Indemnity*, 1944),
tear-jerking diva (*Stella Dallas*, 1937),
flippant career woman (*Meet John
Doe*, 1941), and cocky stripper (*Ball
of Fire*, 1941). Occasionally, she also
starred in feminist Westerns: *So Big!*
(1932), from Edna Ferber's novel, in
which she played "Selina," a pam-
pered society girl coming into her
own on the rugged frontier, by director William Wellman; *Annie Oakley*
(1935, George Stevens); and *Union*

ALL IN THE FAMILY: Queen of the West Barbara Stanwyck, as "Victoria Barkley," introduces her matriarchal dynasty: "Audra" (Linda Evans), "Jarrod" (Richard Long, in buggy), "Heath" (Lee Majors), and "Nick" (Peter Breck, *right*). Courtesy ABC.

Pacific (1939, Cecil B. DeMille). In the 1950s Stanwyck became ever more associated with this genre, both as wily bad women (*Blowing Wild*, 1953; *The Violent Men*, 1955) and as worn but decent ones (*Cattle Queen of Montana*, 1954; *The Maverick Queen*, 1956). Her best such role: the complex female lead, part good/part bad, in iconoclast Sam Fuller's *Forty Guns*

(1957). The opening sequence of Babs, looking butch in black and riding a huge white horse, with the title gunmen following behind, remains a classic image of the strong-willed woman having her own way in a man's world.

Stanwyck made four appearances on *Zane Grey Theater*, including a pilot that did not sell: *The Lone*

Woman (10/8/59), as a Selina-like frontierswoman. She then played a similar role, "Kate Crawley," on two *Wagon Trains* (9/16/63–1/27/64). Meanwhile, the times they were a-changin', *The Feminine Mystique* (Betty Friedan) appeared in print. The timing couldn't have been better for an alternative to *Bonanza*: *The Big Valley* (1965–1969), positing matriarchy for the first time in a TV Western. Stanwyck played "Victoria Barkley," running a ranch in San Joaquin Valley near Stockton and keeping several sons and one daughter in line while proving a woman in charge could succeed. She later took on a similar role in the 1970s-style glitzy primetime soaps *Dynasty* (1985) and *The Colbys* (1985–1986). SEE ALSO: Peter Breck, Charles Briles, Linda Evans, Richard Long, Lee Majors.

Bob Steele

(1907–1988)

••••••••••••••••••••••••••••••

This short, wiry actor with mean eyes and a gravelly voice appeared in more TV/movie Westerns than any other person, estimated at over 300 parts ranging from extra work to bit parts, major and minor as well as some leads. The son of a director, Steele began working for dad Bob Bradbury (Steele's real name was also Bob Bradbury) alongside his brother Bill in a series of inexpensive Pathe shorts, *The Adventures of Bob and Bill*. He employed his real name as

a Hollywood juvenile but switched to the tougher-sounding moniker after being picked for *The Mojave Kid* (1927). Steele won top billing in a string of *Billy the Kid*s (competing with Buster Crabbe's series) and as "Tucson Smith" in *Three Mesquiteers*. Steele won great supporting roles in major movies: Curley, the insecure husband of a flirtatious wife, in *Of Mice and Men* (1939), from the Steinbeck novel; and a menacing hitman (appearing twice his actual size) in *The Big Sleep* (1946), from Raymond Chandler's book. Then he headed back to Monogram, PRC, and the upscale (at least in comparison) Republic for more Westerns, Westerns, Westerns. On TV, Steele guest-starred on virtually every show, plus had regular gigs as Hugh O'Brian's "deputy" in Wichita (1955) on *The Life and Legend of Wyatt Earp* episodes; cowboy "Ben" on Disney's *Texas John Slaughter* (1960); and "Trooper Duffy" on *F Troop* (1965–1967). SEE ALSO: Hugh O'Brian, Tom Tryon, Forrest Tucker.

Charles Stevens

(1893–1964)

••••••••••••••••••••••••••••••

Born in Solomonsville, Arizona, this half-Mexican, half-Apache youth left his hometown when hired for Miller Bros.' 101 Ranch Wild West show, one of several dozen minor-league imitations of Buffalo Bill's traveling spectacular. Such live acts all but disappeared with the advent of motion pictures, so many veteran performers headed to Hollywood. Stevens had the good fortune to begin at the top, hired by D. W. Griffith to appear in the first major American film, *The Birth of a Nation* (1915). He was soon befriended by Douglas Fairbanks (Sr.) and performed in most of that legendary swashbuckler's costume films. Stevens's future typecasting was sealed when, in 1930, he played "Injun Joe" in the John Cromwell–directed version of Mark Twain's *Tom Sawyer* and, later that year, a treacherous half-breed in Raoul Walsh's *The Big Trail*. From then on, Stevens played Mexicans, Indians, and half-breeds; shifty, treacherous figures with sad, confused eyes and an uncertain, whiney voice, in 150 feature films. In a bizarre casting coup, Stevens played Indian Charlie, a real-life henchman of the Clanton gang, in three films about the O.K. Corral: *Frontier Marshal* (1939), *Tombstone: The Town Too Tough to Die* (1942), and John Ford's classic *My Darling Clementine* (1946), the character's name altered to "Indian Joe" in the latter. His great hope was to win the title role in *Geronimo* (1939), though the part went to a more noble-looking Native American actor, Chief Thundercloud. Stevens's greatest satisfaction came when he was finally cast as Geronimo in *The Adventures of Rin Tin Tin* (1954–1958), since Charles Stevens was in fact the grandson of that Apache

chief! SEE ALSO: Lee Aaker, James (L.) Brown, Joe Sawyer.

James Stewart
(1908–1997)

Most 1950s movie stars would have nothing to do with TV, though there was one notable exception: this "Aw, shucks!" actor. Television, to Stewart, appeared not a lesser medium than movies, but rather (like radio, which he had also done) another venue to tell a type of story that could not work on the big screen. He starred in three memorable *G.E. Theater* half-hour episodes. In "The Windmill" (4/24/55), adapted by Borden Chase from a story by Ernest Haycox, Stewart played the appropriately named "Joe Newman," a simple farmer who enters a shooting match in hopes of winning enough money to buy the title object for his struggling farm. "The Town with a Past" (2/10/57) cast Stewart as a drifter who finds himself in the middle of a standoff between a gruff old townswoman (Beulah Bondi) and the incoming railroad. "The Trail to Christmas" (12/15/57) retold Dickens's *A Christmas Carol* in a frontier setting; Stewart served as both on-camera story-teller and director. For *Lux Playhouse*, he directed and narrated "Cowboy Five Seven" (7/17/59), relating the daily events of a typical modern cowboy. On *Startime*, Stewart appeared as a westernized fairy godfather to

S

Lois Smith as the title character in "Cindy's Fella" (12/15/59), Gower Champion's Western musical version of the Cinderella story.

SEE ALSO: Gary Cooper, Henry Fonda, Glenn Ford.

Raymond St. Jacques
(1930–1990)
••••••••••••••••••••••••••••••

Born James Arthur Johnson in Connecticut, this prolific writer, director, and actor is often cited as the first African American to play a continuing role on a weekly TV Western. He was added to the *Rawhide* cast in 1965 as "Simon Blake." The show's omission up to this point was indefensible, as it is estimated that one out of every five cowboys was a person of color. This former Actors Studio student, a veteran of the American Shakespeare Festival, is notable for his fine work in such significant films as *Black Like Me* and *The Pawnbroker*, both 1964. His last significant historical role was as Frederick Douglass in *Glory* (1989).

SEE ALSO: Clint Eastwood, James Edwards, Otis Young.

Milburn Stone
(1904–1980)
••••••••••••••••••••••••••••••

If the expression "crusty, cranky curmudgeon" didn't already exist, it would have had to be created to describe "Doc Adams," Milburn Stone's character on *Gunsmoke* (1955–1975). Never had he known such success in a long career that ran the gamut from the vaudeville circuit to the legitimate stage before landing in Hollywood and laboring in mostly lousy movies for Monogram. He performed in thrillers, melodramas, as well as pretty much everything except Westerns, with one exception: *The Great Train Robbery* (1941, Bob Steele). Stone's best roles were in John Ford films: Stephen A. Douglass (opposite Henry Fonda) in *Young Mr. Lincoln* (1939) and John "Black Jack" Pershing in *The Long Gray Line* (1955). Then came *Gunsmoke* and a two-decade job to turn any character actor green with jealousy. Stone rarely missed an episode, though a heart attack in 1971 knocked him out for a while; Pat Hingle subbed as "Dr. Chapman." Seven years after he passed away, Stone appeared in *Gunsmoke: Return to Dodge* via a stock-footage flashback. By the way, Adams's first name was "Galen."

SEE ALSO: James Arness, Amanda Blake.

Glenn Strange
(1899–1973)
••••••••••••••••••••••••••••••

Hulking George Glenn Strange worked as a cattle rancher, rodeo rider, and deputy sheriff in New

Mexico before drifting into entertainment. His frightening looks led to casting as bad guys in Westerns (over 200), including Cole Younger in *Days of Jesse James* (1939). Multitalented, Strange not only wrote the title song for the movie *Westward Ho* (1935) but provided the vocal performance for John Wayne when young Duke admitted he could not carry a tune. During the 1940s, Strange became the final actor (after Boris Karloff, Bela Lugosi, and Lon Chaney, Jr.) to play Frankenstein's monster in Universal's horror series and appeared alongside Chaney (as the Wolf Man) and Lugosi (as Dracula) in the grand finale, *Abbott and Costello Meet Frankenstein* (1948). He played "Butch Cavendish" (based on the outlaw Butch Cassidy) in the first-ever episode of TV's *The Lone Ranger* (9/15/49) and continued in that part on an irregular basis throughout the show's run. Strange played the lovable "San Noonan," bartender at the Longbranch saloon, on *Gunsmoke* between 1961 and 1973. He was preceded as bartender by Clem Fuller as "Clem" (1958–1961); Strange shared duties with Rud Sooter as "Rudy" (1965–1967) and was followed by Robert Brubaker (who had earlier played stage driver "Jim Buck," 1957–1962) as "Floyd" (1974–1975). SEE ALSO: James Arness, Amanda Blake, Ken Curtis, Rodd Redwing, Burt Reynolds, Milburn Stone, Dennis Weaver.

Randy Stuart

(1924–1996)

••••••••••••••••••••••••••••••••

Best remembered today for her role as "Louise Carey," wife of Grant Williams in *The Incredible Shrinking Man* (1957), Stuart had played a "Louise" before that, on TV, as the wife of Alan Hale on *Biff Baker, U.S.A.* (1952–1954). During the 1959–1960 season of *The Life and Legend of Wyatt Earp*, she enacted Nellie Cashman, owner of a Tombstone eatery still in existence today. The writers took a liberty here: On the show, the highly respectable Nellie was portrayed as an admirer of the hero. In reality, Nellie did not care for the Earps, once describing them as dark-suited men strutting self-importantly about town. SEE ALSO: Hugh O'Brian.

Yvonne Suhor

(1965–)

••••••••••••••••••••••••••••••••

Suhor played "Louise McCloud" on *The Young Riders* (1989–1992), a teenage girl who passed herself off as a boy (shades of Shakespeare's romantic comedies) to ride with the Pony Express. Fanciful, perhaps, but politically correct, which was required of a TV Western by the time this one appeared. SEE ALSO: Stephen Baldwin, Josh Brolin, Ty Miller.

Barry Sullivan
(1912–1994)

••••••••••••••••••••••••••••••

The New York City–born Broadway actor and golden-age-of-live-radio performer won his first major movie role in the Western *The Woman of the Town* (1943) as "King Kennedy," a combination of two actual Western gunmen done in by Bat Masterson (Albert Dekker in the film). He returned to Westerns infrequently but effectively, thanks to his low-key, laconic delivery, playing Tom Horn in *Bad Men of Tombstone* (1949), then appearing in *Texas Lady* (1955), and as a thinly disguised Wyatt Earp ("Griff Bonnell") in *Forty Guns* (1957). Sullivan delivered a top performance as a charismatic killer in *Seven Ways from Sundown* (1960) and a no-nonsense twentieth-century plainsman in *Tell Them Willie Boy Is Here* (1969); he also played in the spaghetti Western *Take a Hard Ride* (1975) and as rancher John Simpson Chisum in Sam Peckinpah's *Pat Garrett & Billy the Kid* (1973). Earlier, Sullivan had played Garrett in *The Tall Man* (1960–1962), the third of his TV series (others include non-Westerns *The Man Called X* (1956) and *Harbourmaster*, aka *Adventure at Scott Island* (1957–1958).

Sadly, *The Tall Man* rated as a disappointment. The New Mexico range war involving Garrett and William Bonney (Clu Gulager) rates as one of the most complex events in frontier history, helping explain why no film version has ever done full justice to the sprawling saga. A two-season TV series would have been perfect to cover every angle, even as final two seasons of *The Life and Legend of Wyatt Earp* (1959–1961) did with the unfolding events in Tombstone. Instead, producers decided to fictionalize everything. Other than the names of the two leading characters, most others (Lew Wallace, John Chisum, John Tunstall, etc.) were ignored (though Ford Rainey did show up twice as Sheriff Brady). Billy the Kid here became a reluctant deputy to Sheriff Garrett; in each episode they rode off to capture fictional outlaws, reducing this to a clone of *The Deputy*.

Sullivan starred in another oater, *The Road West* (1966–1967), an ambitious failure that attempted to revive the glory days of *Wagon Train* (finally canceled a year earlier) while adjusting its once-successful format to the emergent style and emphasizing the element that 1950s oaters had ignored: family. "Ben Pride" and his clan trekked cross-country to the promised land; they included "Kip" (Kelly Corcoran), "Midge" (Brenda Scott), "Grandpa" (Charles Seel), and the lovely traveling companion "Elizabeth Reynolds" (Kathryn Hays). SEE ALSO: Glenn Corbett, Clu Gulager, Audie Murphy, Andrew Prine, Ford Rainey, Kenny Rogers.

Ralph Taeger
(1936–)

This towering 6'3" Clint Walker lookalike seemed a natural for Westerns though he was born in Queens, New York. Taeger played "Big Mike Halliday" in the Northern *Klondike* (1960) for half a season on NBC. He returned seven years later as the gunfighter/cavalry scout "Lane" in *Hondo* (1967), based on John Wayne's popular 1953 movie. He later found employment as a car salesman and tennis pro. Dubious claim to fame: On the 9/8/67 *Hondo* telecast, Taeger became the last TV cowboy ever to be staked out on plains and tortured by Indians. SEE ALSO: Noah Beery, Jr.; James Coburn.

Gloria Talbott(t)
(1931–2000)

A native Angeleno, Talbott claimed descent from one of the city of angels' founding families. She made her TV debut on *Adventures of Wild Bill Hickok* (12/9/51) as the Latina "Consuelo," leading to typecasting as exotic, often mysterious dream girls, including a gypsy on *The Gene Autry Show* (8/25/53). She was cast as a Native American in *The Oregon Trail* (Fred MacMurray) and *Alias Jesse James* (Bob Hope), both from 1959. Talbott's pop-culture claim to fame: she was the first actress to play Pocahontas on TV, in "America's First Great Lady" (*TV Reader's Digest*, 3/21/55). This eerie, offbeat, hypnotic beauty enjoyed a simultaneous B-movie career as a scream queen, in *Daughter of Dr. Jekyll* (1957) and *I*

AN AMERICAN PRINCESS: Among her other TV western credits, Gloria Talbott was the first actress to play Pocahontas on television. Courtesy ABC.

in Westerns, including Emmett Dalton in *Jesse James vs. the Daltons* and Arkansas Dave Rudabaugh in *The Law vs. Billy the Kid*, both in 1954. Tannen moved over to the right side of the law as the fictional "Deputy Hal Norton" during *The Life and Legend of Wyatt Earp*'s second season (1956–1957). Ironically, Tannen later played Earp's enemy Ike Clanton in "After the O.K. Corral" on *Death Valley Days* (4/28/64). Two other "occasional" roles were as pioneer "Calvin Moss" on *Daniel Boone* (1967) and "The Bartender" on *The High Chaparral* (1967–1968). SEE ALSO: Cameron Mitchell, Hugh O'Brian.

Married a Monster from Outer Space (1958, Tom Tryon). She played "Martha Connell," Hugh O'Brian's love interest, during the first season of *The Life and Legend of Wyatt Earp* (1960–1961) and later "Moneta" on *Zorro* (1959). Talbott enacted a historical frontierswoman in *Death Valley Days*' "Kate Melville and the Law" (5/4/65). Her final Western role was as another Indian girl in *Arizona Raiders* (1965, Audie Murphy). SEE ALSO: Gene Autry, Hugh O'Brian, Tom Tryon, Guy Williams.

William Tannen
(1911–1976)
••••••••••••••••••••••••••••••••
This veteran of three hundred movies and TV shows played mostly small roles, often as the menacing figure

Buck Taylor
(1938–)
••••••••••••••••••••••••••••••••
Born Walter Clarence Taylor III, Taylor studied art at college and became fond of sketching Western scenes during breaks on *Gunsmoke*. He was first introduced as "Newly O'Brien" (1967–1975), a gunsmith, in "The Pillagers" (11/6/67), using the skills of his profession and quick wits to save himself and "Miss Kitty" (Amanda Blake) when captured by outlaws. Taylor later costarred in the TV movie *The Busters* (5/28/78), with Bo Hopkins and Slim Pickens as rodeo veterans. His scores of credits include two real gunmen, Dynamite Dick in *Cattle Annie and Little Britches* (1981) and Turkey Creek Jack Johnson in *Tombstone* (1993).

Taylor played "Detective Bussey" on *Dallas* (1990–1991) and Ben Lily in *Comanche Moon* (2008), from the Larry McMurtry novel. Today he is a Western artist living in Texas, known for his preference for watercolors. SEE ALSO: Amanda Blake, Dub Taylor.

Dub Taylor
(1907–1994)
••••••••••••••••••••••••••••••

In his 250 movie and TV roles, mostly Westerns, Taylor is best remembered as the father of "C. W. Moss" (Michael J. Pollard), who convinces his son to betray the title characters in *Bonnie and Clyde* (1967). Between 1940 and 1949, he served as the sidekick ("Cannonball," with varied last names) to "Wild" Bill Elliott, Don "Red" Barry, Tex Ritter, Russell "Lucky" Hayden, and Charles Starrett; to the least well-remembered of all cowboy stars, Tex Harding; and finally to Jimmy Wakely. Over time Taylor developed his unique costume, never wearing a shirt, instead allowing his dirty long-john underwear top to suffice, his ragged getup incongruously topped off with a worn bowler hat. Taylor made the transition to more ambitious B+ Westerns, including *Riding Shotgun* (1954, Randolph Scott), and an A Western, *The Fastest Gun Alive* (1956, Glenn Ford). He played a classic early TV role as the dishonest "Rattlesnake Jones" on the "Lucy Goes to the Rodeo" episode of *I Love Lucy* (11/28/55). Taylor showed up as "Wallie Sims," sidekick to Alan Hale, Jr., on the *Casey Jones* kiddie Western (1957–1958), taking care of the depot while the hero was off railroadin'. He was supposed to become the sidekick to Brian Keith on *The Westerner*, beginning 10/7/60, but that series was abruptly canceled. Taylor played the real-life cowboy-coot known only as "Chicken Bill" on *Death Valley Days* (10/14/67) and won a continuing role as the eccentric "Bryan Pfeiffer Farnum" on *Gunsmoke* (1967), the same year his son Buck joined the cast as "Newly O'Brien."

In time, Taylor became part of Sam Peckinpah's stock company, appearing in *The Wild Bunch* (1969), *Junior Bonner* and *The Getaway* (both 1972), and *Pat Garrett & Billy the Kid* (1973). His final series role was as the irascible "Houston Lamb" on *Little House on the Prairie* (1980–1981). By now it seemed all but immoral to mount an homage to old Westerns without him, so Dub was cast as "Old-Timer" in the saloon sequence of *Back to the Future Part III* (1990). In *The Gambler Returns: The Luck of the Draw* (1991), he once again played the sidekick to "Dave Blassingame" (Brian Keith) of *The Westerner*. His final role was as the hotel clerk in *Maverick* (1994). SEE ALSO: James Arness; Don Barry; Bill Elliott; Alan Hale, Jr.; Brian Keith; Michael Landon; Steve McQueen; Denver Pyle; Kenny Rogers; Buck Taylor.

Kent Taylor

(1907–1987)

Born Louis William Weiss, Taylor early on worked mostly in 1930s/1940s B urban mysteries. A slick, seedy look made him precisely right to play *Boston Blackie* (1951–1953) on TV, taking over the role of a shady sometime-thief portrayed by Chester Morris on film. Westerns seemed less likely, though Taylor had played Doc Holiday (*sic*) in *Tombstone: The Town Too Tough to Die* (1942), then the title character in *Frontier Gambler* (1956), a low-budget Western redux of the classic noir *Laura* (1944). On *The Rough Riders* (1958–1959), he starred as "Captain Jim Flagg," the Union veteran headed west in the company of his former sergeant and a young Johnny Reb. Everything about the show was, to say the least, different, with no introductory story to explain how the characters met or why they were traveling together. Most episodes proved stronger on mood than narrative, the trio seemingly stuck in a swamp from which, as in a *Twilight Zone* episode, they could not escape. During the title sequence, an unseen narrator attempted to convince us that this had *something* to do with the charge up San Juan Hill half a century later. SEE ALSO: Jan Merlin, Peter Whitney.

Robert Taylor

(1911–1969)

Born Spangler Arlington Brugh, MGM's all-purpose lightweight lead (Ronald Reagan's job over at Warner's), Taylor found himself all but eaten alive by the overpowering Garbo in *Camille* (1936). He came into his own during the following decade as a tough guy in Westerns (*Billy the Kid*, 1941), World War II actioners (*Bataan*, 1943), and big spectacles (*Quo Vadis*, 1951). He played Gable-like cowboys in *Westward the Women* (1951), *Ride, Vaquero!* (1953), *The Last Hunt* (1956), *The Law and Jake Wade* (1958), and *The Hangman* (1959). On TV, Taylor starred as "Captain Matt Holbrook" on *The Detectives* (1959–1962), appearing in mostly bad B movies after that, with one exception: the admirable *Return of the Gunfighter* (1967). When close friend Reagan left his job hosting *Death Valley Days* for politics, he suggested Taylor as a replacement. Taylor proved an effective host between 1966 and 1969 (until his death from cancer), also occasionally starring, most notably in "Lady with a Past" (11/19/68, Mariette Hartley) and in "The Pieces of the Puzzle" (5/11/68) as James Reavis, self-styled baron of Arizona, a role earlier played by Vincent Price in the theatrical film of that name (*The Baron of Arizona*, 1950). SEE ALSO: Stanley Andrews, Merle Haggard, John Payne, Ronald Reagan.

Rod Taylor

(1930–)

••••••••••••••••••••••••••••••

Alfred Hitchcock claimed this strapping Australian might be the next Cary Grant and cast him in *The Birds* (1963). John Ford rather saw Taylor as the next John Wayne, awarding him the lead in *Young Cassidy* (1965). Combining the best qualities of both, Taylor ought to have become a superstar but never quite touched the highest rung on Hollywood's ladder. He often played in Westerns, beginning with *Top Gun* (1955), then in the Tim Holt role in the Warner Bros. TV remake of *The Treasure of the Sierra Madre* (1948) called "The Argonauts" (*Cheyenne*, 11/1/55). His early film roles included the quasi-Westerns *Giant* (1956) and *Raintree County* (1957). His first TV series, *Hong Kong* (1960), was done in by a time slot opposite *Wagon Train* on Wednesday evenings. Taylor played the romantic lead opposite a young Jane Fonda (*Sunday in New York*, 1963) and an aging Doris Day (*The Glass Bottom Boat*, 1966). In 1967, he attempted to bring back the classic one-man/one-name Western (*Shane, Hondo, Jubal,* etc.) with *Chuka* (1967); audiences were more in the mood for *The Wild Bunch* and *Butch Cassidy*. After losing the lead in *Planet of the Apes* (1968) to Charlton Heston, Taylor headed back to TV. The turn-of-the-century quasi-Western TV movie *Powderkeg* (4/16/71) became the series *Bearcats!* (costarring Dennis Cole), with Taylor as "Hank Brackett," a soldier of fortune riding around in a Stutz. The show had a big budget but few viewers and lasted for only thirteen episodes. Then came *The Oregon Trail* (1/10/76) as "Evan Thorpe," a family man heading for Oregon in 1842. This TV movie featured Blair Brown as the beautiful "Jessica Thorpe," Andrew Stevens and Tony Becker as sons "Andrew" and "William," Gina Mari as "Little Rachel," and Douglas Fowley as "Old Eli." Eventually, thirteen episodes of a series were filmed, but only eleven were broadcast. Taylor's most popular genres were Westerns and sci-fi; these were combined in *Outlaws*, Taylor playing "John Grail," in which a bandit and his cohorts are sucked through a time tunnel to today and become detectives. Taylor costarred with William Lucking ("Pike"), Charles Napier ("Wolf"), Patrick Houser ("Billy"), and Richard Roundtree ("Ice"). The show lasted only thirteen episodes. Taylor then worked with John Wayne on *The Train Robbers* (1973), playing a Forrest Tucker type from Republic's 1950s B films. He later became a regular as the larger-than-life Lone Star resident "Gordon Cahill" on *Walker, Texas Ranger* (1996–2000). SEE ALSO: Douglas Fowley, Charles Napier, Chuck Norris.

Ray Teal
(1902–1976)
••••••••••••••••••••••••••••••

This versatile character actor accrued over three hundred movie/TV credits during a forty-year career, only occasionally playing a good guy (courageous World War II captain in *Back to Bataan*, 1945). More often he was to A Westerns what Roy Barcroft was to the Bs: smarmy, self-serving, mean-spirited, slyly grinning villains in *Streets of Laredo* (1949), *Along the Great Divide* (1951), and *Montana Belle* (1952) as Emmett Dalton. TV allowed Teal to play stern but upstanding good guys: the neighbor "Jim" in the original *Lassie* (1956–1957), and the glum but dedicated "Sheriff Coffee" of Virginia City in nearly one hundred *Bonanzas* between 1960 and 1972.
SEE ALSO: Lorne Greene, Michael Landon.

Sigrid Thornton
(1959–)
••••••••••••••••••••••••••••••

This Australian star of movies and TV made her first impact as "Jessica Harrison" (opposite Tom Burlinson's "Jim Craig") in the down-under Western *The Man from Snowy River* (1982) and its sequel, *Return to Snowy River* (1988). She later played the spirited, proto-feminist female banker "Amelia Lawson" on *Paradise* (1988–

1991) who falls for the reformed gunfighter "Cord" (Lee Horsley). SEE ALSO: Lee Horsley.

Chief Thundercloud
(1899–1955)
••••••••••••••••••••••••••••••

Born Victor Daniels to part-Cherokee parents, Thundercloud created the role of "Tonto" in the serial *The Lone Ranger* (1938). He appeared in many Native American roles in movies and on TV, most famously playing Geronimo three times: in *Geronimo* (1939), *I Killed Geronimo* (1950), and *Buffalo Bill, Jr.* (3/1/55). SEE ALSO: Pat Hogan, Charles Stevens.

Kenneth Tobey
(1917–2002)
••••••••••••••••••••••••••••••

Tobey played a nominal lead as the squad commander in producer Howard Hawks's *The Thing* (1951), though cast-mate James Arness (as the title creature) went on to the coveted role of "Marshal Matt Dillon" on *Gunsmoke*. Versatile Tobey could play the big, dignified Jim Bowie on Disney's *Davy Crockett* (1955), then the following season show up as runty, rancid "Jocko," second-in-command to keel boatman Mike Fink (Jeff York), in *Davy Crockett and the River Pirates*. He starred in the contemporary Western series *Whirlybirds* (1957–1960) as "Chuck Martin," helicopter pilot who with sidekick "P. T. Moore" (Craig Hill) helped police and others do dirty jobs. Tobey's memorable roles in movie Westerns include Sheriff Bat Masterson in *Gunfight at the O.K. Corral* (1957) and the shifty Texas Ranger in the Audie Murphy oater *Seven Ways from Sundown* (1960). SEE ALSO: Fess Parker, Jeff York.

George Tobias
(1901–1980)
••••••••••••••••••••••••••••••••

This WB contract player throughout the 1930s and 1940s was often cast as the clueless sidekick of James Cagney in contemporary/period pictures. He played "Pierre Falcon," French Canadian trapper and pal to "Jonathan Banner" (Barry Nelson) on *Hudson's Bay* (1959), but is best remembered as the neighbor of the beautiful witch on *Bewitched* (1964–1971, Elizabeth Montgomery). SEE ALSO: Pedro Gonzalez-Gonzalez, Barry Nelson.

Audrey Totter
(1918–)
••••••••••••••••••••••••••••••••

A Gloria Grahame lookalike *sans* the hint of vulnerability that allowed that Oscar winner a sympathetic quality, Totter invariably found herself cast as a hardened film noir villainess. Full stardom eluded her when Robert Montgomery's "Philip Marlowe"

thriller *Lady in the Lake* (1947) ran over schedule; MGM had planned to give Totter a huge publicity buildup as the deliciously duplicitous dame in *The Killers* (1946) but had to commence shooting and recast with then-unknown Ava Gardner. Totter tried other major studios but, when nothing clicked, she ended up in B Westerns. At Republic, Totter played the female lead in *The Vanishing American* (1955), a low-budget/lowbrow version of the Zane Grey novel in no way comparable to the epic silent film. She received one last chance at stardom: TV. Totter won what seemed the most complex female character in the genre so far as "Beth Purcell," the *Cimarron City* lady who strives to turn a rough frontier settlement into a civilized community (1958–1960). The hour-long show was to be an anthology, with Totter in the lead role once every three weeks, alternating with John Smith's lawman and George Montgomery's rancher. This ambitious concept did not click, so writers scaled back, focusing on the two men, with Totter reduced to a bit part. Frustrated, she quit at midseason. She fared better on the medical shows that shortly gained popularity, as "Ella Vitnack" and "Norma Littell" on *Dr. Kildare* (1965–1966) and "Nurse Wilcox" on *Medical Center* (1972–1976). SEE ALSO: Scott Brady, Philip Carey, George Montgomery, John Smith.

Randy Travis
(1959–)

••••••••••••••••••••••••••••

Travis (real name Traywick) is one more outlaw-country star who has pursued an acting career in Westerns. His roles include Cole Younger in *Frank & Jesse* (1994), with Bill Paxton and Rob Lowe as the James boys; *Outlaws: The Legend of O. B. Taggert* (1994); "Captain Sam Garner" in *Texas* (4/16/95), from the James Michener novel; the U.S. Marshal in *Dead Man's Revenge* (4/15/94); the title role in *The Shooter* (1997); "Pecos Jim" in *The Cactus Kid* (2000); and parts in *Texas Rangers* (11/30/01) and *The Long Ride Home* (5/27/03).

Tom (Thomas) Tryon
(1926–1991)

••••••••••••••••••••••••••••

A Connecticut native, Tryon served in the U.S. Navy during World War II in the South Pacific, then moved on to acting in summer stock, Broadway, early TV, and movies. A lanky build, penetrating eyes, and an enigmatic demeanor led to strong roles in the psychological Western *Three Violent People* (1956), as Abraham Lincoln in "Springfield Incident" (2/6/57; *The 20th Century-Fox Hour* adaptation of Ford's *Young Mr. Lincoln* with Henry Fonda, 1939), and in the cult classic sci-fi film *I Married a Monster from Outer Space* (1958, opposite Gloria Talbott). Walt Disney then picked Tryon for the lead in his most expansive, ambitious "Frontierland" series, *Tales of Texas John Slaughter* (1958–1961). The actor and character were mismatched in terms of looks; the real Slaughter had been short, squat, and ugly; Ernest Borgnine would have been a perfect choice. Disney himself admitted to TV audiences he had taken a liberty here, promising that everything else would hone closer to reality than had been the case with any other TV Western, including his own. Over a three-year period of seventeen episodes (the early ones bunched in twos, as had been the case with the second season of *Crockett*), the man's life and times were gradually revealed. As for a family-hour show, certain realistic elements had to be eliminated, among them Slaughter's drinking and gambling addictions. Yet *Slaughter* qualified as the most remarkable series—truly a televised epic—since the inception of Desilu's *The Life and Legend of Wyatt Earp*. Better still, Disney made a point of including the missing element from that series: the women in the hero's life. Disney hired an upscale writer, Frank D. Gilroy (*The Only Game in Town*, 1970; *The Subject Was Roses*, 1968), a take-your-breath-away supporting cast, and veteran Western film directors Harry Keller (*Angel and the Badman*, 1947) and James Neilson (*Night Passage*, 1957).

The first season's six episodes dealt with John's joining the Texas Rangers

DISNEY'S HISTORICAL EPIC: As John Slaughter, Texas Ranger turned Arizona rancher, Tom Tryon appeared in TV's most detailed, accurate, expansive chronicle of a real-life Western hero. Courtesy Walt Disney Productions/Buena Vista Releasing.

after meeting young "Ben Jenkins" (Harry Carey, Jr.). Slaughter also planned on marrying Adeline Harris (Norma Moore) and building a ranch. Airtime was divided in each episode between Slaughter's role in capturing such notorious outlaws as Frank Davis (Robert Middleton), the Barkos (Lyle Bettger and Beverly Garland),

and Dan Trask (Dan Duryea), and his slow courtship of the reluctant Addie, who feared John's sudden outbursts of temper. At last he convinced her, and they began a family. But while John was off in New Mexico, having blazed the legendary trail that still bears his name while dealing with cattle baron John Chisholm (Harold J. Stone), Adeline passed away. John consigned his son and daughter to friends, then rode off to drink himself to death.

Season two began several years later, as John wandered into Arizona, mentored there toward redemption by friend John Scanlon (Barton MacLane) while himself teaching a naïve young Kentuckian, "Ashley Carstairs" (Darryl Hickman), the art and business of capturing wild horses. At this time, John met Viola Howell (Betty Lynn) and realized he could love again. No sooner were they married than John's children, Willie (Brian Corcoran) and Addie (Annette Gorman), came to live with them, initially despising Viola for no better reason than that she was not their biological mother. There exists no more anti-mythic image in the history of TV Westerns than the shot of Tryon as Slaughter, huge white Stetson perched high atop his head and a brace of pistols strapped around his waist, holding a screeching child in each arm while his second wife berates him. Beneath the surface of an American cowboy hero, this series (like no other) insisted, stands an ordinary man who must balance his adventurous job with the same family issues ordinary men must handle, both then and now. In time, the children calmed down, in large part due to the arrival of Batt (James Edwards), an African American ranch hand who, with John, set the pace for the integration of Texas spreads. Batt's wonderful qualities were highlighted by the return of Ashley as his foil, that once-nice young man now transformed into a trigger-happy kid who had to be taken down a peg. All the while a range war developed between Slaughter and the earlier-established rancher Ike Clanton (James Westerfield) who, along with his top gun Johnny Ringo (Allan "Rocky" Lane), resented the competition of this new arrival. Adding to John's problems was the presence of unpredictable gunman "Loco Crispin" (Gene Evans). Toward the end of the second season, hostilities broke out with neighboring Apaches, so John tried to establish a peace with Natchez (Jay Silverheels). That could not be achieved, however, until the warrior Geronimo (Pat Hogan) was captured. To this end, John agreed to help General Miles (Onslow Stevens) track down the chief while reuniting with old friend Ben, now a member of the U.S. Cavalry.

In the final season, the outfit did bring in Geronimo. But a lawless element still existed in Tombstone, so Mayor John Clum (Robert Burton) persuaded John to divide his time between maintaining the ranch and serving as a local lawman. Now he had to face off with such notorious figures as Cesario Lucero (Ross Martin), Jimmy (Behind the) Deuce (Joe Maross), and Frank Clell (Ralph Meeker). With this job finally accomplished, and with Cochise County now at peace on all fronts, John returned to his ranch and spent the rest of his life as a family man. An interesting bit of trivia: After Slaughter passed away and Viola expired, included in their estate were stocks in the Walt Disney company.

Slaughter opened up the possibility of film stardom for Tryon, but he would not achieve the heights of Steve McQueen or James Garner. First, he lost the role of "Sam Loomis" in Alfred Hitchcock's *Psycho* (1960) to John Gavin. Tryon played opposite Marilyn Monroe as one of her two loves (Dean Martin as the other) in *Something's Got to Give* (1962), but that film was never completed. Cast in Otto Preminger's immense production *The Cardinal* (1963) with an all-star supporting cast, Tryon found himself so dismayed by the self-conscious cruelty of that director that he grew insecure. His performance suffered as Tryon became stiff in front of the camera. With bad reviews and movie stardom unlikely, he headed back to TV for guest spots on Western series and the lead in one TV film, *Winchester '73* (3/4/67), playing James Stewart's role from the 1950 classic. Then he read

Ira Levin's *Rosemary's Baby* and decided to give writing a whirl. Tryon's first foray into suspense fiction, *The Other* (1972), achieved instant classic status and became a bestseller. Other books, particularly *Lady* (1974), were also met with enthusiastic response. When Tryon's health failed him, companion J. Calvin Culver (a gay porn star under the name Casey Donovan) helped to bring *Crowned Heads* (1976) to the publisher on time before passing away himself as a result of the AIDS virus. SEE ALSO: Harry Carey, Jr.; Pat Hogan; Allan "Rocky" Lane; Barton MacLane; Ross Martin.

Forrest Tucker

(1919–1986)

• •

Semi-pro football and a stint as host/comic in burlesque theater preceded Tucker's move to Hollywood. His first film was William Wyler's *The Westerner* (1940, Gary Cooper). Tucker swiftly slipped into B movies for Poverty Row's PRC, then Columbia's second-string unit, and finally Republic. Typecast as a big, cowardly Irishman, Tucker played a weak-kneed doppelganger to Duke Wayne in *Sands of Iwo Jima* (1949). With smaller films he gained bigger status, often matched as the vain villain opposite Rod Cameron's solid good guy in black-and-white oaters including *Ride the Man Down* (1952) and *San Antone* (1953). Tucker appeared

in endless B films, mostly horror (*The Abominable Snowman*, 1957) and Westerns (*Gunsmoke in Tucson*, 1958); he played the occasional good guy in major movies, such as *The Yearling* (1946) and *Auntie Mame* (1958). He seemed a natural for the lead in a TV Western, but his only series role at this time was *Crunch and Des* (1955–1956) as a fisherman, with Sandy Kenyon costarring.

He played numerous real-life Western badmen: Jim Plummer in *Last Bandit* (1949), Frank Reno in *Rage at Dawn* (1955), Bob Dalton on *Death Valley Days* (12/11/63), William Clark Quantrill on *Hondo* (11/3/67), and Lawrence Murphy in *Chisum* (1970), with Wayne in the title role. Earlier, Tucker had incarnated a thinly disguised General Custer in *Oh! Susanna* (1951) and hard-as-nails lawman "Wild Bill" Hickok in *Pony Express* (1953) with Charlton Heston as "Buffalo" Bill Cody. In the mid-1960s, he won top billing in *F Troop* (1965–1967) as "Sergeant Morgan O'Rourke," a variation on Tucker's blustery "Sergeant O'Hara" from *Warpath* (1951). Other cast members included Larry Storch as goofy "Corporal Agarn," Ken Berry as polite and well-intentioned "Captain Parmenter," Melody Patterson as sexy tomboy "Wrangler Jane," James Hampton as semi-competent young "Trooper Dobbs," Frank DeKova as caricatured "Chief Wild Eagle," and two Western vets, Bob Steele as "Trooper Duffy" and Don Diamond as "Crazy Cat."

After that show's cancellation, Tucker played the occasional role of mountain man "Joe Snag" during *Daniel Boone*'s 1967–1968 season and did some of his best acting in a Western on *Gunsmoke* in the late 1960s/early 1970s, guest-starring in six episodes. The best was "Sergeant Holly" (12/14/70), which added considerable depth and dimension to a stock part he had played numerous times. Tucker performed as "Kid Shelleen," the role that won Lee Marvin an Oscar, in the TV pilot for the *Cat Ballou* series that aired on 9/6/71 but did not sell. He also performed on *Dusty's Trail* (1973–1974) as the wagon master "Callahan"; the show offered a comedy Western redux of the beloved *Gilligan's Island* with Bob Denver reviving his old role and Tucker in the comparable part to Alan Hale, Jr.'s "Skipper." SEE ALSO: Rod Cameron, Bob Denver, Don Diamond, Charlton Heston, Robert Preston, Bob Steele, John Wayne.

Robert Urich

(1946–2002)

•••••••••••••••••••••••••••••••

This well-liked TV actor displayed abilities at comedy and drama in such shows as *Soap* (1977), *Vega$* (1978–1981), *Spenser: For Hire* (1985–1988), and *The Lazarus Man* (1996). He was cast by producer Suzanne de Passe in the pivotal role of "Jake Spoon," black sheep of the Texas cattlemen, in *Lonesome Dove* (1989), the landmark miniseries directed by movie veteran Simon Wincer. Fellow cowhands and tough characters met on the trail included Blue Duck (Frederic Forrest), "Dish Boggett" (D. B. Sweeney), "July Johnson" (Chris Cooper), "Lippy Jones" (William Sanderson), "Jasper Fant" (Barry Tubb), "Pea Eye Parker" (Tim Scott), "Needle Nelson" (David Carpenter) and, rounding out the Dickensian cast of offbeat characters from Larry McMurtry, the aptly named Southern belle "Lorena" (Diane Lane). Falling prey to bad company, Jake was executed along with outlaws by pals "Call" (Tommy Lee Jones) and "Gus" (Robert Duvall). Urich succumbed to cancer at an early age. SEE ALSO: Robert Duvall, Tommy Lee Jones.

Brenda Vaccaro

(1939–)

•••••••••••••••••••••••••••••••

The idea of an Eastern woman heading west to become "school marm" in a small town was old hat way back when Owen Wister used it in his seminal novel *The Virginian*. Invariably, the female lead played a secondary character to the male hero. Not so in *Sara* (1976), one of several attempts to take the feminist values of the *Ms.* magazine era and employ them to recreate TV Westerns. Briefly hyped as a possible new star, Vaccaro played "Sara Yarnell," dedicated to educating kids rather than becoming involved with any of the drifters who passed through this thirteen-week ratings failure. Most prominent among the townspeople were "Martha Higgins" (Louise Latham), "Claude Barstow" (William Phipps), and "Emma Higgins" (Hallie Morgan). SEE ALSO: Jane Seymour.

Jack Valentine

(19??–????)

••••••••••••••••••••••••••••••••

The least remembered of all early TV cowboys, Valentine found work as a local aspiring actor/singer in Philadelphia when he was picked without any previous TV/film experience to portray a singin' cowboy, using his own name for his character, as had been the B-movie tradition, for a local live late-afternoon show, *Action in the Afternoon*. With him were Harriss Forrest as the silly sidekick "Ozzie," Barry Cassell as "Sheriff," and Mary Ellen Watts as "Kate," editor of the newspaper in an old Western town. Rounding out the cast as "The Coroner": John Zacherle, later host of *Shock Theater* (the "Cool Ghoul") in New York City. As to *Action in the Afternoon*, there was none: Valentine sang several songs, following talk, talk, talk with the other performers

about such exciting things as stage robberies, all of which took place off-screen. On 2/2/53, the show began a national run, but kids were bored stiff and it quickly closed down.

Lee Van Cleef

(1925–1989)

••••••••••••••••••••••••••••••••

Young Van Cleef could not imagine why he wasn't making headway as an accountant. Frankly, his supervisor told him, no clients wanted to work with someone so ugly—a weird shock of black hair on his already balding pate, beady eyes (one green, the other blue), a nose that made the term *hawk-like* inadequate, and a twisted body that resembled a menacing scarecrow. Advising Van Cleef to abandon accounting, his boss suggested, "Why don't you try to break into the movies as a bad guy?" Van Cleef took him literally and won the first part he auditioned for: "Jack Colby," one of the quartet of killers in *High Noon* (1952); he then played detestable villains in scads of films and TV shows, both Western and contemporary.

Among the real-life outlaws Van Cleef enacted were Jesse James (*Stories of the Century*, 2/7/54), Cherokee Bob (*Tales of Wells Fargo*, 4/8/57), Dave Rudabaugh (*G.E. Theater*, 10/20/57), Ed Bailey (*Gunfight at the O.K. Corral*, 1957), Frank James (*Yancy Derringer*, 5/7/59), the Cherokee Kid (*The Deputy*, 5/21/60), and

Sam Bass (*The Slowest Gun in the West*, pilot for proposed series, aired 5/7/60). He is the only actor to have played each James brother in separate movies or TV shows. In the mid-1960s, when TV Westerns began to disappear, Van Cleef turned to his other love, painting. Then in 1965 Sergio Leone offered him the role of the Man in Black in *For a Few Dollars More*, the second of his spaghetti Westerns with Clint Eastwood. Van Cleef did it as a lark only to be happily surprised at the film's success and the greater popularity of follow-up *The Good, the Bad, and the Ugly* (1966). Instant celebrity opened up a new career as the star of European-lensed Westerns. Van Cleef returned to TV, now as a star, in *The Master* (1984), a contemporary martial arts action series. SEE ALSO: James (L.) Brown, Clint Eastwood, Sheb Wooley.

THE USUAL SUSPECTS: Scene-stealers (*from left to right*) Strother Martin, James Best, and Lee Van Cleef enjoy a game of poker in "The Grave," a *Twilight Zone* Western episode (10/27/61). Courtesy Carol Serling/The Rod Serling estate/CBS.

Robert Vaughn
(1932–)

• •

This cynical-looking actor always
appeared as if he had just bitten
into a notably sour lemon. Vaughn
is best known for the spy spoof *The
Man from U.N.C.L.E.* (1964–1968)
and earlier as "Lee," the cowardly
gunfighter in *The Magnificent Seven*
(1960). Nearly four decades later,
Vaughn played "Judge Oren Travis,"
presiding over the antics of a new
batch of bounty hunters on TV's *The
Magnificent Seven*. SEE ALSO: Michael
Biehn.

Mitch Vogel
(1956–)

• •

Huckleberry Finn come to life,
Vogel stole the quasi-Western *The
Reivers* (1969) from top-billed Steve
McQueen and as a result was added
to *Bonanza's* cast (9/20/70) as "Jamie
Hunter," an orphaned scam artist
who arrives in Virginia City as a self-
styled rainmaker during a drought.
He was adopted into the Cartwright
family at episode's end, allowing
"Ben" (Lorne Greene) to once more
raise a son. SEE ALSO: Lorne Greene,
Michael Landon.

James Wainwright
(1938–1999)

A former Carnegie University student, U.S. Marine, and Actors Studio member, Wainwright found himself in the right place (Hollywood) at the wrong time (1970s) to be a Western star. Effective as the heavy in his first TV appearance (*Death Valley Days*, 10/14/67), the rugged performer at once found work in menacing roles until cast as the decent pioneer "Cully" on *Daniel Boone* (1969–1970). He dared take on Clint Eastwood in *Joe Kidd* (1972), then won the lead in *Jigsaw* (1972–1973) as an unorthodox California cop modeled on "Dirty Harry." Westerns, TV and movie, were now mostly concerned with mountain men (*Jeremiah Johnson*, 1972; *Grizzly Adams*, 1974). Wainwright played the lead in the TV movie *Bridger* (9/10/76), a busted pilot about the mountain man's mountain man. He starred on the short-lived *Beyond Westworld* (1980), but without Yul Brynner as a cowboy robot, nobody cared. Or watched. SEE ALSO: Dan Haggerty, Ben Murphy, Fess Parker.

Clint Walker
(1927–)

One of the big guys (6'6") of TV Westerns, the slow-to-anger Walker proved mighty dangerous when someone pushed him too far. He worked as a carnival roustabout, a golf caddy, and even a gumshoe before taking a job as security guard for Vegas's Sands Hotel. Hollywood celebrities came by often; soon, Walker met Henry Wilcoxon, a semi-retired actor from Cecil B. DeMille's 1930s epics. Dumbstruck by the young man's remarkable physique, Wilcoxon offered to introduce Walker to his old boss. Filmographies mistakenly list Walker's brief appearance as a hulking guard in *The Ten Commandments* (1956) as his first screen appearance; two years earlier he played "Tarzan" (unbilled) in an ultra-cheap Bowery Boys movie, *Jungle Gents* (1954). A Warner Bros. exec who saw both pictures cast Walker in *Cheyenne* (1955–1962), the first of that studio's TV Westerns, setting the pace for that studio as primary supplier of this genre, for better (initially) or worse (toward the end).

Unlike *Gunsmoke* and *The Life and Legend of Wyatt Earp*, each running thirty minutes, *Cheyenne* (the first hour-long TV Western other than *Davy Crockett*) was not initially a weekly show. No one had any idea that Westerns would take off, so *Cheyenne* rotated within an anthology format featuring *Kings Row*, a soaper with Jack Kelly (later *Maverick*) and Robert Horton (*Wagon Train*), and *Casablanca*, based on the Bogart film, with Charles McGraw as "Rick Blaine." The title of the package: *Warner Brothers Presents*. Each series, *Cheyenne* included, was *not* the fifty-plus-minute TV film one might expect, but rather a forty-plus featurette, as each evening's story was followed by a "behind the scenes" segment hosted by Gig Young highlighting some Warner Bros. performer or promoting a theatrical release. The public did not appreciate being subjected to such unpaid advertise-

ments, so the approach was dropped in spring 1956. *Kings Row* quickly bit the dust at midseason; weeks later, *Casablanca* likewise became history. Meanwhile, *Cheyenne*'s ratings soared, so extra episodes were filmed; during the summer of 1956 repeats were shown on a weekly basis.

Producers Roy Huggins, William T. Orr, and Harry Foster invented the series as they went along. In early episodes, "Cheyenne Bodie" (a white man raised by Indians) accompanied "Smitty" (L. Q. Jones), an artist, as his guide, as the semi-comical Smitty sketched and mapped the West. Stories revolved around people they met and, more often than not, defended from outlaws and Indians. When that concept proved too confining, Smitty was dropped, and Cheyenne became an all-purpose Westerner with a different job in each episode: cavalry scout, wagon master, wrangler, marshal, hired hand, fur trapper, cattle drover, etc. Likely this approach was taken for no other purpose than to allow for a wide range of storytelling. Yet *Cheyenne* transformed into something no other TV Western of its era achieved: a mythological epic. Audiences accepted Bodie, whether they were conscious of it or not, as an embodiment of everything good and right in the American spirit, a man who hates violence but could turn deadly when circumstances demanded.

A quick glance at several first-season episodes reveals how Warner Bros. altered their approach, setting

TALL IN THE SADDLE: Clint Walker (*left*) was one of the first and one of the largest in stature of all TV Western heroes, seen here on *Cheyenne* with first-season sidekick "Smitty" (L. Q. Jones). Courtesy ABC/Warner Bros.

the pace for all future series. The first episode, "Mountain Fortress" (9/20/55), reveals a desire to create what appeared to be a big-scale, expensive show on a tight budget. The story was completely original: Cheyenne and Smitty happened across outlaws and honest travelers who joined forces to survive an Indian attack. This slight, serviceable tale was concocted after the writers screened an Errol Flynn Warner Bros. film, *Rocky Mountain* (1950), which told an entirely different tale. The TV approach made use of the film's settings and large-scale action sequences while creating a unique storyline with new characters, their task so seamlessly accomplished that

even people who recalled the Flynn film might not realize scenes from it were on view here. The third episode, "The Argonauts" (11/1/55), dealt with a group of disparate men, Cheyenne included, who search the mountains for gold. This episode was likewise derived from a film, this one a classic: John Huston's *The Treasure of the Sierra Madre* (1948), with Walker as the Walter Huston character. Difficult-to-shoot scenes from the original (such as the discovery of a Gila monster on top of a gold cache) were lifted intact, as was much of the dialogue. Still, some situations were altered to provide distance between the original and the TV remake. "West of the River"

(3/10/56) revealed how completely the situation had changed as the first season drew to its close. The story of a frontier "dirty dozen" (the Jailhouse Brigade, on a mission to rescue two sisters from Indians) was a shot-by-shot (though highly edited) version of *The Charge at Feather River* (1953) starring Guy Madison, TV's Wild Bill Hickok. Clearly, it's the former on view in long shots, with close-ups of Walker (wearing the same costume as Madison) repeating that other actor's lines. The writers simply gave up reinventing movies, now recycling them in the quickest, easiest, and least creative manner possible.

Cheyenne returned the following fall on a biweekly basis (episodes took eight or nine days to shoot, making a weekly series impossible), rotating with another anthology, *Conflict*. During hiatus, *Cheyenne* had been re-envisioned out of necessity. Most big Warner Bros. Western films had been pillaged for plots and action scenes for the first season's fifteen episodes. Original teleplays now appeared, most with less ambitious concepts and fewer big action scenes. During the third season, *Cheyenne* alternated with *Sugarfoot* (Will Hutchins). Ratings proved high for both, but Walker had become problematic, unhappy that Warner Bros. paid TV stars little, hiring unknowns like himself, then allowing them fame without fortune. The notion of residuals did not exist at the time, so the initial small payment was all the actors received.

Walker also hoped to employ *Cheyenne* as a springboard to movie stardom. Trying to appease him, WB put him in a B film, *Fort Dobbs* (1958), shot in black-and-white and recycling the finale of *The Charge at Feather River* for the final shootout that Walker fans had recently watched in "West of the River." Far better, *Yellowstone Kelly* (1959), in color and shot on location, with Walker playing that real-life mountain man.

Still not satisfied, Walker refused to return for a fourth season. WB retained the title *Cheyenne*, though the character now on view was, inexplicably, "Bronco Layne" (Ty Hardin). A year later, Walker begrudgingly returned, with some of his demands met. *Cheyenne* then shifted to Monday nights. The single big WB Western not previously plundered for stock footage, *They Died with Their Boots On* (1941), now provided big-scale scenes for "Gold, Glory, and Custer," a two-parter (1/4/60–1/11/60). Always on the lookout for a chance to make an extra buck, Warner Bros. edited the episodes together, marketing the piece as a feature film in Europe.

TV Westerns soon fell out of favor due to overexposure. *Sugarfoot* and *Bronco* were collapsed into Walker's series, now an anthology retitled *The Cheyenne Show*. Each star would appear alone every third week. One episode, "Duel at Judas Basin," featured the trio together (1/30/61). Clearly the genre had begun to cannibalize itself; then-current episodes lacked the craftsmanship of those produced two years earlier. During the final days, *Cheyenne* and *Bronco* rotated on a biweekly basis. The series ended in December 1962, replaced by yet another WB Western, *The Dakotas*.

Walker went on to some success in the 1960s, doing an occasional B+ Western (*The Night of the Grizzly*, 1966), also winning solid supporting roles in two big World War II films, *None But the Brave* (1965) and *The Dirty Dozen* (1967), as half-breed "Samson Posey" in the latter. With the advent of made-for-TV movies, Walker starred in four: *Yuma* (3/2/71), *Hardcase* (2/1/72), *The Bounty Man* (10/31/72), and *Scream of the Wolf* (1/16/74). He tried for a series comeback as an Alaskan patrolman in *Kodiak* (1974), so low-rated that it was canceled after a handful of episodes. One fine B feature, *Baker's Hawk* (1976), resembled Disney's *Old Yeller* (1957), with a bird in place of the dog. Walker later played a small role in *The White Buffalo* (1977, Charles Bronson). On *Centennial* (1978–1979) he played "Joe Bean," a fictional incarnation of a mountain man. Before retiring, Walker turned up as Cheyenne two more times: as a cameo in *The Gambler Returns: The Luck of the Draw* (11/3/91) and, in more fully developed form, as a guest star on *King Fu: The Legend Continues* (2/27/95). SEE ALSO: James Garner, Ty Hardin, Will Hutchins.

Larry Ward
(1924–1985)

Big, strapping, and curiously unmemorable, Ward starred in one of TV's first soap operas as "Dr. Hamilton" on *The Brighter Day* (1954–1957). He was under contract at Warner Bros., where a new show was needed on Monday evenings to replace *Cheyenne*. On the 4/23/62 episode "A Man Called Ragan," Ward was introduced as a tough marshal, patrolling the "badlands" (the original title for the series that became *The Dakotas*) with deputies Jack Elam, Chad Everett, and Mike Greene. The subsequent series lasted twenty episodes. Ward is far better recalled as the voice of "Greedo" in *Star Wars* (1977) and "Jabba the Hut" in *Return of the Jedi* (1983). SEE ALSO: Jack Elam, Chad Everett, Michael Greene, Clint Walker.

Johnny Washbrook
(1944–)

A popular child actor of the 1950s, Washbrook played "Ken McLaughlin" on *My Friend Flicka* (1955–1956), the role that had gone to Roddy McDowall in the 1943 film. This gentle, sweet-spirited series focused on life on a Montana ranch, circa 1900, from the point of view of a twelve-year-old. SEE ALSO: Gene Evans.

"HELLO, I'M JOHN WAYNE": In truth, no introduction was needed for the Duke, who appeared before the first-ever *Gunsmoke* episode. Courtesy John Wayne estate, CBS.

John Wayne
(1907–1979)

• •

This top box-office draw was too busy filming A Westerns to do a series but did pop up on two. The Duke appeared before the first-ever *Gunsmoke* (9/10/55) to give that show his blessing and ask the audience to support it, implying that young James Arness would become the John Wayne of television, which did prove true. In 1957 he performed (along with John Ford's entire stock company) in that director's single episode of *Wagon Train* (starring member Ward Bond), "The Colter Craven Story" (11/23/60). In a flashback to the Civil War, Wayne played General William Tecumseh Sherman opposite Paul Birch as Grant. He would enact Sherman again three years later in the theatrical epic *How the West Was Won* with Harry Morgan as Grant.
SEE ALSO: James Arness, Ward Bond.

Patrick Wayne

(1939–)

••••••••••••••••••••••••••••••

The most photogenic of Duke's sons,
Wayne seemed a natural for Westerns. His film premiere was in a bit
part as a kid in *Rio Grande* (1950),
with his father starring and John
Ford directing. Wayne worked again
for Ford in films starring his dad
(*The Searchers*, 1956) and as the *only*
Wayne on view in *Mister Roberts*
(1955), *The Long Gray Line* (1955),
and *Cheyenne Autumn* (1964). His
first lead was in *The Young Land*
(1959), an underrated civil rights
Western in which Wayne's young
deputy defends maligned Hispanics.
He made his TV debut in the "Black
Sheep" episode of *Have Gun—Will
Travel* (4/30/60) starring Richard
Boone, a close friend/costar of the
Duke. Wayne played historical
characters both early (James Butler
Bonham in *The Alamo*, 1960) and
late (Sheriff Pat Garrett in *Young
Guns*, 1988) in his career. Wayne
won the role that Henry Fonda had
played in *The Rounders* (1965) when
it became a series: "'Howdy' Lewis,"
an easygoing cowpoke in the contemporary West. He was also fine as a
park ranger in the Disney live-action
film *The Bears and I* (1974). Wayne
played the male lead opposite Shirley
Jones in the short-lived 1979–1980
sitcom *Shirley*, faring better as a man
of adventure in *Sinbad and the Eye
of the Tiger* (opposite Tyrone Power's

daughter Taryn) and *The People That
Time Forgot*, both in 1977. He now
runs Duke's cancer-research program.
SEE ALSO: Richard Boone, Henry
Fonda, Ron Hayes, Dennis Hopper,
Chill Wills.

Dennis Weaver

(1924–2006)

••••••••••••••••••••••••••••••

Giving deputy "Chester Goode" a
limp on TV's *Gunsmoke* was this
actor's idea after realizing he would
need some bit of business to stand out
opposite the mighty James Arness.
Weaver's scene-stealing quickly
became a beloved part of American
pop culture. With costars Milburn
Stone and Amanda Blake, he formed
a trio that played the rodeo/state-fair
circuit during the summers. Weaver
remained with *Gunsmoke* for nine
years (1955–1964), during its changeover from half-hour (1955–1961)
to hour (1961–1975) formats. The
Chester role expanded and deepened
as the series progressed. An oddity in
the violent world of TV Westerns,
Chester did not wear a pistol, perhaps
a reflection of the liberal Weaver's
own antigun sentiments. Sensing he
had done all he could with the part,
Weaver left to pursue roles in films
(*Duel at Diablo* as a villain, 1966) and
TV (*Gallegher Goes West*, 1966; Disney miniseries).

Weaver's next role was as "Tom
Wedloe" in *Gentle Giant* (1967), Ivan
Tors's nature film about a family

that adopts a huge, lovable bear. The successful venture morphed into the *Lassie*-like series *Gentle Ben* (1967–1969) with Weaver and Clint Howard as son "Mark" repeating their roles and Beth Brickell replacing Vera Miles as wife/mother "Ellen." The show proved notable as one of the 1960s quasi-Westerns that abandoned the earlier notion that a TV family must be headed by a widow or widower, never a couple. The result was pleasant family fare, but Weaver felt stymied by the realization that, despite top billing this time, he now played third fiddle to the kid and his pet.

He finally became a true star beginning with *McCloud: Who Killed Miss U.S.A.?* (2/17/70). This made-for-TV movie openly ripped off *Coogan's Bluff* (1968), a popular film with a modern-day Western marshal heading to Big Apple to solve crimes that "sophisticated" police procedures could not handle. *McCloud* returned as a series the following fall, beginning 9/16/70, and played in various formats (sixty, ninety, and 120 minutes). Sam McCloud officially moved from New Mexico to New York, joined the police force, and set to work with "Peter B. Clifford" (J. D. Cannon), "Sergeant Joe Broadhurst" (Terry Carter), and "Chris Coughlin" (Diana Muldaur), the latter a 1970s feminist who often butted heads with retro male McCloud though clearly attracted to his old-fashioned ways. Executive producer Glen A. Larson

shaped the show into a memorable metaphor for the unique 1970s battle of the sexes as well as solid entertainment; *McCloud* often appeared as an entry in NBC's Sunday night rotating *Mystery Movie* format.

Weaver appeared in several notable TV movies, including *Duel* (1971), a near-solo tour-de-force for him as a traveling businessman pursued by a crazed trucker across the American Southwest, with an early directing credit for Steven Spielberg from a script by *The Twilight Zone* veteran Richard Matheson. Weaver also played Abraham Lincoln in *The Great Man's Whiskers* (2/13/73) and later provided the voice for Robert E. Lee in *The Great Battles of the Civil War* miniseries (12/26/94). Weaver appeared as "R. J. Poteet" in *Centennial* (1978–1979) and enjoyed huge success with the TV movie *The Return of Sam McCloud* (11/12/89), which he also produced, the hero now a New Mexico senator battling for environmental causes. He had a continuing part as William Frederic "Buffalo Bill" Cody on *Lonesome Dove: The Series* (1994–1995), then essayed memorable roles in *Stolen Women, Captured Hearts* (3/16/97), *The Virginian* (1/9/00), and *High Noon* (8/20/00) as "Mart," the crippled ex-lawman played by Lon Chaney, Jr., in 1952. Weaver provided the voice of "Buck McCoy," a retired TV cowboy, on *The Simpsons*' "The Lastest Gun in the West" (2/24/02), and "Old Henry" on the modern oater *Wildfire*

(2005). He hosted Encore's Westerns Channel for ten years. SEE ALSO: James Arness, Amanda Blake, Ken Curtis, Milburn Stone.

Richard Webb

(1915–1993)

••••••••••••••••••••••••••••••

Webb starred in the single-season syndicated series *U.S. Border Patrol* (1959) as "Deputy Chief Don Jagger," who in the modern West kept illegal aliens from slipping across the border. Five years earlier, he had played the lead in *Captain Midnight* as a superhero who asked kids to drink their Ovaltine and send in proof-of-purchase for a Secret Decoder Ring.

Robin Weigert

(1969–)

••••••••••••••••••••••••••••••

Weigert graduated from Brandeis University, though you would never guess that from her raunchy role as Martha "Calamity" Jane Canary on *Deadwood* (2004–2006). Here, she provided a vivid break from the romanticized portrayals by Jean Arthur (*The Plainsman*, 1936) and Doris Day (*Calamity Jane*, 1953). The only other performance of this real-life Westerner that compares in terms of honesty and accuracy: Jane Alexander's one-woman show, broadcast on cable TV on 3/6/84. SEE ALSO: Keith Carradine.

Adam West

(1928–)

••••••••••••••••••••••••••••••

Born William West Anderson in Washington State, the boy who would become TV's *Batman* originally hoped to be a TV cowboy. After completing studies at Whitman College and spending two years in the U.S. Army, he headed for Hollywood and assumed an appropriate name. Signed by Warner Bros., the studio slated West to star in *Doc Holliday*, first portraying Doc on *Lawman* (6/7/59) and *Colt .45* (10/18/59). WB wanted a glorified version; West provided the historical man, dying from tuberculosis. Not surprisingly, the series never premiered. West played Wild Bill Hickok on *Overland Trail* (3/6/60) and a sympathetic cavalry officer in *Geronimo* (1962). After a regular role on *Robert Taylor's Detectives* (1961–1962), then on the phenomenally popular if short-lived *Batman* (1966–1968), West headed overseas for the spaghetti Western *The Relentless Four* (1965). He returned to TV with guest spots on *The Big Valley* (9/23/68) and *Alias Smith and Jones* (1/27/72).

Johnny Western

(1934–)

••••••••••••••••••••••••••••••

This appealing character actor/cowboy singer played "Private Ben Jordan" on *Boots and Saddles* (1957), a sadly neglected ensemble piece about life on a remote cavalry post. Western also costarred in *The Night Rider* (6/1/62), a busted pilot featuring several retro singin' cowboys; two theatrical Westerns, *The Dalton Girls* (1957) and *Fort Bowie* (1958); and lots of episodic TV work (*Tales of Wells Fargo*, 1958–1959; *Have Gun— Will Travel*, 1958; etc.). Western was the creator/performer of "Ballad of Paladin," which premiered during the final credits of the second-season *Have Gun* opener: "A knight without armor in a savage land." SEE ALSO: Richard Boone, John Pickard.

Stuart Whitman

(1928–)

• •

Whitman supported Broderick Crawford on *Highway Patrol* during the 1956–1957 season as "Sergeant Walters." His first movie lead cast him opposite Ethel Barrymore in *Johnny Trouble* (1957). Whitman then was hyped as a young John Wayne in two 1959 Westerns, *Hound-Dog Man* for Don Siegel and *These Thousand Hills* for Richard Fleischer. These roles were followed by second billing to Duke in *The Comancheros* (1961) and Richard Boone in *Rio Conchos* (1964). His part in the controversial contemporary drama *The Mark* (1961), as a child molester, won Whitman an Oscar nomination for Best Actor. Then the movie offers dried up. He opted for *Cimarron Strip*

(1967–1968), a big ninety-minute/color/shot-on-location oater in the wake of *The Virginian*'s success over at NBC. Whitman's CBS Thursday night outing featured him as "Marshal Jim Crown," sent to clean up the outlaw-infested area between Kansas and Oklahoma. The cast included Percy Herbert, overdoing the Scottish accent as "MacGregor"; Randy Boone as frontier photographer "Wilde"; and British blonde (for the Beatlemania-era audience) Jill Townsend as love interest "Dulcey." Cancellation sent Whitman off to Europe for violent crime dramas, the second lead (to Lee Van Cleef) in *Captain Apache* (1971), and a bit in *The White Buffalo* (1977, Charles Bronson). He later played recurring roles on *Superboy* ("Jonathan Kent," 1988–1992) and "Willis" on *Knots Landing* (1990). His last TV Western appearance to date: "Laredo Jake Boyd" on *Walker, Texas Ranger* (5/14/94). Despite a career tumble, Whitman has cried all the way to the bank: Real-estate investments had made him worth $100 million by 1998.

Peter Whitney

(1916–1972)

• •

Hulking and bear-like, with distant eyes and a perennially open mouth, this lumbering character actor was prominently cast as slow-minded villains: a brutish cavalry sergeant (*The Last Frontier*, 1955) and a crazed townsman (*Buchanan Rides Alone*, 1958). He played a heroic part on *The Rough Riders* (1958–1959) as "Sergeant Buck Sinclair," a Union veteran who heads west in the company of his former captain (Kent Taylor) and a Johnny Reb (Jan Merlin). Whitney later appeared as the loutish "Lafe Crick" on *The Beverly Hillbillies* (1964). SEE ALSO: Jan Merlin, Kent Taylor.

Richard Widmark
(1914–2008)
••••••••••••••••••••••••••••••

Nicknamed "King of the Snarlers," this former drama teacher/stage actor burst onto movie screens in 1947 as a gangster so crazy he laughs while kicking an old lady (wheelchair bound, no less) down a flight of stairs in *Kiss of Death*. In truth, Widmark was as intellectual and as restrained in life as he was wild and crazy on the screen. He found work in 1950s film noirs and Westerns *Garden of Evil* (1954), *Broken Lance* (1954), *The Last Wagon* (1956), and as Jim Bowie in *The Alamo* (1960). Widmark then brought his tough-guy persona to the small screen, first as a fictional lawman who rounds up the Dalton/Doolin gang in *The Last Day* (2/15/75). He then provided a fine supporting performance as Al Sieber, the no-nonsense scout who with Tom Horn tracked down Geronimo, in *Mr. Horn* (2/1/79). Widmark joined other TV/movie Western legends in *Once Upon a Texas Train* (1/3/88).

SEE ALSO: David Carradine, Robert Duvall, Willie Nelson.

Robert J. Wilke
(1914–1989)
••••••••••••••••••••••••••••••

Wilke's perpetual sneer, emotionless eyes, and hulking build caused him to be cast as villains in more than 250 film/TV credits. His greatest cold-blooded part: "Jim Pierce," a gunfighter shot in the back by Grace Kelly while reloading in *High Noon* (1952). Wilke then played more sympathetic roles as Ben Thompson in *Wichita* (1955) and as "Marshal Sam Corbett," the dogged but decent lawman who tracks down the title character in TV's *The Legend of Jesse James* (1965–1966). SEE ALSO: Allen Case, Chris Jones.

Bill Williams
(1915–1992)
••••••••••••••••••••••••••••••

Brooklyn may seem like an unlikely place for a cowboy star to hail from, but that's where the man born Hermann Katt was raised. In 1933 he won a bit part in the classic *King Kong*, but did not appear in another film until after completing World War II army service. Then the tall, good-looking, easygoing novice landed one role after another, mostly in B Westerns. In *The Great Missouri Raid* (1951), Williams played the outlaw Jim Younger. Later that year he

W

came to TV with *The Adventures of Kit Carson*, an early kiddie Western that lasted four seasons. The show had precious little to do with the life of the famed mountain man/scout (Christopher Carson had been notably short), though the series did at least put him in the proper setting, troubleshooting for Colonel John Fremont in Southern California following the Mexican-American War. When the show ended, Williams declared, "I hope I never hear of Kit Carson again!" Shortly he was back in B Westerns (*Pawnee*, 1957). Williams never had trouble finding work, appearing in episodic comedies and dramas and often on *Perry Mason* (1962–1965), costarring with wife Barbara Hale ("Della"). Their son, William Katt, played the Sundance Kid in *Butch and Sundance: The Early Years* (1979). SEE ALSO: Tom Berenger, Chris Connelly, Don Diamond.

Guinn "Big Boy" Williams
(1899–1962)

Beginning in 1919, this son of a Decatur, Texas, rancher/politician embarked on an acting career that would last over forty years. With a natural drawl and barrel-like frame, he seemed a natural to play none-too-bright rednecks but proved amazingly adept at giving them shadow, even subtlety, while ranging from evil to gentle and everything in between. Williams's nickname, incidentally, was

awarded him by legendary Western comic/actor Will Rogers. Williams starred in a series of low-budget oaters in the 1940s in which his continuing character had the same nickname but a different last name in each film. In addition to guest-star roles on numerous TV Westerns, he took on the continuing part of "Big Pete," a lovable rube, on *Circus Boy* (1956–1957). SEE ALSO: Noah Beery, Jr.; Micky Dolenz; Robert Lowery.

Guy Williams
(1924–1989)

If the expression tall, dark, and handsome had not already existed, it would have had to be coined to describe the man born Armando Joseph Catalano to Italian immigrants in New York City. He picked up many minor film roles, including one memorable Western, *The Man from the Alamo* (1953), before being picked by Walt Disney to star in *Zorro* (1957–1962), a delightful adaptation of the beloved adventure tales set in Spanish Los Angeles with Williams as the foppish "Don Diego de la Vega" and his alter-ego, a masked man who appeared by moonlight to right wrongs. The chief villain in early episodes was "Captain Monasterio" (Britt Lomond), aided and abetted by the rotund "Sergeant Garcia" (Henry Calvin) and the dimwitted "Corporal Reyes" (Don Diamond). "Bernardo" (Gene Sheldon) served as

Zorro's mute but not deaf (though he pretended to be) servant, "Don Alejandro" (George J. Lewis) the hero's regal father. Beautiful Latina women appeared everywhere, most notably "Anna Verdugo" (Jolene Brand) and "Moneta" (Gloria Talbott). When the half-hour series ran its course, Disney filmed four hour-long episodes for the Sunday evening anthology, then cut several first-season tales into a feature film, *The Sign of Zorro* (1958). Williams later starred in the popular *Lost in Space* (1965–1968). While visiting Argentina, he discovered that he'd become a hero to the people there for presenting one of the few positive images of Hispanics on American TV. Williams was offered his old role back in Disney's *Zorro and Son* in the mid-1980s but was too ill to take the job. He passed away near his beloved Pampas. SEE ALSO: Henry Darrow, Don Diamond, Gloria Talbott.

Chill Wills

(1903–1978)

•••••••••••••••••••••••••••••

Born Theodore, Wills received his ironic nickname from a mother who could not forget her birth pains on the hottest day of summer. His early experience included tent shows, vaudeville, and Chill Wills and His Avalon Boys, a country-cowboy band, in LA. Wills and his group sang backup in films: first, *It's a Gift*

(1934), starring W. C. Fields, an actor he idolized and imitated, playing the blustery con man who often outsmarts himself, with Wills adding a Western twang. He appeared with Laurel and Hardy in *Way out West* (1937), providing Stanley's singing voice, then achieved pop-culture immortality as the voice of "Francis the Talking Mule" in comedies during the early 1950s. Gradually he eased into "big" Westerns: the sadly forgotten *From Hell to Texas* (1958) for Henry Hathaway, and John Wayne's super-production *The Alamo* (1960) as the beekeeper, for which he received an Academy Award nomination for Best Supporting Actor. In 1962 Wills played "Colonel Casey Thompson" on *Frontier Circus*, essentially *Circus Boy* without the boy. He received the role of a lifetime as "Jim Ed Love," the crafty, self-serving rancher in *The Rounders* (1965), a Burt Kennedy Western with Glenn Ford, Henry Fonda, and the meanest strawberry roan *ever*. The film was spun off into a series with Wills, Ron Hayes, and Patrick Wayne. The cagey old country boy joined Walter Brennan, Edgar Buchanan, Andy Devine, and Jack Elam for *The Over-the-Hill Gang* (10/7/69) and *The Over-the-Hill Gang Rides Again* (11/17/70) as "Gentleman George Agnew." His last Western was Peckinpah's *Pat Garrett & Billy the Kid* (1973). SEE ALSO: John Derek, Ron Hayes, Richard Jaeckel, J. Pat O'Malley, Patrick Wayne.

W

Terry Wilson

(1923–1999)

••••••••••••••••••••••••••••••

A native Californian, Wilson joined the movie business as a stunt man/wrangler on the Raoul Walsh Western noir *Pursued* (1947), continuing in that capacity for a decade and a half. He first worked for John Ford in *Rio Grande* (1950), the last of the famed "Cavalry Trilogy," and became a regular member of the stock company, on board for *The Quiet Man* (1952) and *The Searchers* (1956), playing a Texas Ranger in the latter. His look (no one more perfectly typified the average cowboy) and pleasingly unpretentious line delivery opened up a new career; in fact, he had spoken onscreen for the first time in a 1948 B Western, *Belle Starr's Daughter*. Friends with Ward Bond in real life, Wilson won the role of "Bill Hawks," one of two lifelong pals to "Major Seth Adams" (the other, Frank McGrath, as "Charlie Wooster") in *Wagon Train*, premiering in 1957. Following Bond's death early in the fourth season, Hawks became temporary wagon master ("The Prairie Story," 2/1/61) and, when Robert Horton (as "Flint McCullough," scout) departed, he took on the guise of chief scout ("Alias Bill Hawks," 5/15/63).

John McIntire then assumed the lead as wagon master "Chris Hale." When *Train* moved to ABC in fall 1962, Wilson found himself elevated from supporting player (previously, his name had been lost in the final credits) to third-billed star (after McGrath). When the series finally reached the end of its trail in 1965, Wilson returned to small character roles in big Westerns (*The War Wagon*, 1967). Toward the end of his career, he played "The Sheriff" in the sci-fi cult classic *Westworld* (1973).

SEE ALSO: Ward Bond, Robert Horton, John McIntire, Denny (Scott) Miller, Irene Windust.

Irene Windust

(1921–1999)

••••••••••••••••••••••••••••••

Windust began a brief TV/movie career late, at age thirty-eight, in the teen flick *Roadracers* (1959), starring Alan Dinehart III (Bat Masterson on *The Life and Legend of Wyatt Earp*). During *Wagon Train*'s first season, Windust was cast as "Mrs. Hawks," wife to "Bill Hawks" (Terry Wilson), a loud-mouthed, shrewish woman who ceased heckling her husband only when in the mood to complain to "Major Seth Adams" (Ward Bond). Her part added realism, but when the writers transformed Hawks from a henpecked husband into a cowboy hero, Windust's (even her name seemed perfect) role was eliminated. The actress's career proved short-lived, concluding after appearing in the B crime movie *Ma Barker's Killer Brood* (1960) and the big-budget Warner Bros. soaper *Parrish* (1961).

SEE ALSO: Ward Bond, Terry Wilson.

Gloria Winters

(1932–)

••••••••••••••••••••••••••••

Winters played "Babs" in TV's initial (unsuccessful) *Life of Riley* (1949) with Jackie Gleason. William Bendix (who had earlier done the film) took over the following year, creating a TV sensation with a whole new cast. The young actress then moved over to *Sky King* (1952–1959), the popular juvenile Western about a modern flying cowboy (Kirby Grant) and his gorgeous niece Penny. Winters played the part (much like Gail Davis on *Annie Oakley*) as a tomboy with sex appeal. To transcend typecasting, she then portrayed femme fatales: a real-life girl outlaw in the "Little Britches" episode of *Stories of the Century* (6/17/54) and similar fictional characters on *Judge Roy Bean* (1956, precise date n.a.) and *The Life and Legend of Wyatt Earp* (12/27/60). SEE ALSO: Gale Davis, Penny Edwards, Kirby Grant.

Robert Wolders

(1936–)

••••••••••••••••••••••••••••

Wolders was added to the cast to beef up ratings on *Laredo* during its second season (1966–1967) as Texas Ranger "Erik Hunter," though his hunk appeal failed to save this floundering show. He found greater success as a real-life youthful squire to fading Hollywood legends: Merle Oberon until her death; after that, Audrey Hepburn until hers. SEE ALSO: Claude Akins, Neville Brand, Peter Brown, Philip Carey, William Smith.

Morgan Woodward

(1925–)

••••••••••••••••••••••••••••

This Texas native and University of Texas grad started law school (1951) but received the call to serve in the U.S. Air Force during the Korean War. To this day, he remains an aviation buff. Woodward lost interest in his studies after returning stateside and drifted to LA to try acting. His first role was in Disney's Civil War epic *The Great Locomotive Chase* (1956). Endless if often obscure TV work followed, including nineteen *Gunsmoke*s during its two-decade run. He played "Shotgun Gibbs" on *The Life and Legend of Wyatt Earp* (1958–1961); at the beginning of the fourth season, Woodward was added to the cast to fill the void left by the departure of Alan Dinehart as Bat Masterson. Shotgun emerged as a hard-bitten, sullen, silent codger who wore a buckskin jacket, smoked a huge pipe, and carried a weapon that lent him his nickname. For casual viewers, Woodward's ripe performance allowed the series a new lease on life. For those who appreciated historicity, such a conventional sidekick seemed a major disappointment. When Earp moved to Tombstone at the beginning of the fifth (and next-to-last)

W

season, the focus appeared to be shifting to the manner in which the Earp brothers actually operated in Arizona. Suddenly Morgan and Virgil were gone, without explanation; Shotgun returned for the next one-and-a-half years. Then, as the gunfight at the O.K. Corral neared, toward the sixth season's close, "Gibbs" disappeared (again, without justification) as Wyatt's brothers rematerialized.

Newsweek eventually honored Woodward as one of the six most-wanted bad guys in TV Westerns. He received the "Golden Lariat," "Golden Boot" (1988), and "Cowboy Spirit" (2006) awards. In later years, he played "Marvin 'Punk' Anderson," the most Western of the characters on *Dallas* (1980–1987). His final appearance on a TV Western before retirement came as the bounty hunter "Sam Travis" on *The Adventures of Brisco County Jr.* (1/7/94). SEE ALSO: John Anderson, Bruce Campbell, Jim Davis, Alan Dinehart, Hugh O'Brian.

Sheb Wooley

(1921–2003)

●●●●●●●●●●●●●●●●●●●●●●●●●●●●●●

One day in 1958, this cowboy actor/country-western performer mused about the sad demise of the singing cowboy (he had journeyed to Hollywood from Oklahoma to become one) due to teens' interest in monsters from space and rock 'n' roll. In a silly mood, Wooley composed "The Purple People Eater" as a parody of both trends. To his own surprise, the record hit number one on the charts and sold more than three million copies. Wooley received an invitation to appear on *The Dick Clark Show*, though the middle-aged Westerner looked lost while standing next to Dick Clark's teen stars.

Wooley's first part had been in *Rocky Mountain* (1950), a later Errol Flynn Western at Warner Bros. He showed up at Custer's Last Stand twice, as a fictional trooper trying to warn the general of upcoming annihilation in *Little Big Horn* (1951), then as George Armstrong himself in *Bugles in the Afternoon* (1952). He played Jim Younger in the "Younger Brothers" episode of *Stories of the Century* (4/2/54), and nearly a dozen fictional badmen in episodes of *The Lone Ranger* and *Kit Carson*. He appeared in two bona fide classics, *High Noon* (1952) as one of four outlaws stalking Gary Cooper (he is the first killed by "Will Kane"), and next as part of a lynch mob out to string up Joan Crawford in *Johnny Guitar* (1954). He delivered a memorable performance as "Lassater," an authentic top hand, opposite Kirk Douglas in *Man Without a Star* (1955). This led to the role of "Pete Nolan," another rugged drover, in *Rawhide*. Wooley was third-billed (below Eric Fleming and Clint Eastwood) during the first three seasons, but his earlier experiences as a working cowboy brought realism to *Rawhide*. After several seasons he left; without him, the show

THREE FACES WEST: Amid the many dozens of TV Westerns, precious few actually dealt with the daily work of cowboys; the most authentic to do so was *Rawhide,* starring, from left to right, Sheb Wooley, Clint Eastwood, and Eric Fleming. Courtesy CBS.

never felt quite the same. Wooley returned on occasion, Pete turning up as an army scout. As the TV Western faded, Wooley concentrated on country-western music, often performing parodies of other artists' serious songs ("Sunday Morning Fallin' Down") under the name Ben Colder. He premiered as a member of the original *Hee Haw* cast in 1969 but left after the first thirteen episodes. Wooley showed up in Eastwood's *The Outlaw Josey Wales* (1976) and Lawrence Kasdan's *Silverado* (1985), his presence referencing the entire TV Western genre. His final film was *Purple People Eater* (1988), a mild spoof of his own hit from thirty years earlier. SEE ALSO: Lloyd Bridges, Clint Eastwood, John Ireland.

Clare Wren

(19??–????)

• •

As "Rachel Dunne," the frontierswoman who helped maintain a post in Sweetwater, Kansas, for Pony Express riders, Wren acted as mother figure beginning with second season of *The Young Riders* (1990–1992). SEE ALSO: Stephen Baldwin, Josh Brolin, Melissa Leo.

WHEN THE EAST WAS THE WEST: Though most TV Westerns dealt with the post–Civil War era and our final frontier, a few chronicled an earlier period. Jeff York played real-life boatman Mike Fink in two Disney episodes. Courtesy Walt Disney Productions/Buena Vista.

Bruce Yarnell

(1935–1973)

A brilliant baritone, Yarnell was shoehorned into a Western role as "Deputy Chalk Breeson" on *Outlaws* (1961–1962). He felt far more comfortable playing "Hippolyte" in *Irma La Douce* (1963, Jack Lemmon) but returned to oaters as "Muley Jones" on *Bonanza* (1964–1965). A star of the San Francisco Opera, Yarnell died in a plane crash. SEE ALSO: Barton MacLane, Slim Pickens.

Jeff York

(1912–1995)

Born Granville Owen Schofield in LA, this big (6'4"), burly character actor worked mostly in low-budgeters as everything from heroes ("Pat Ryan" in *Terry and the Pirates*) to comedic country bumpkins (title role in *Li'l Abner*), both in 1940. A whole new career opened up when

Disney hired him to play real-life river boatman Mike Fink on TV. Before the cameras could roll, *Davy Crockett* beat him to the punch. To accommodate the unexpected craze, writers combined the two in a pair of tall tales set on the Ohio River; these were later edited into a feature film, *Davy Crockett and the River Pirates* (1956). Fess Parker and York played hero/sidekick in three other films: *The Great Locomotive Chase* (1956), *Westward Ho the Wagons!* (1956), and *Old Yeller* (1957). York became a regular as "Joe Crane," a fictional though authentically portayed mountain man, in *The Saga of Andy Burnett* (1957–1958), later recreating that role on *Zorro* in spring 1959. He moved further north in a similar role, "Reno McKee," for Warner Bros.' *The Alaskans* (1959–1960). York would have seemed a natural for "Yadkin" on Fess Parker's *Daniel Boone*, but the role went to Albert Salmi. On 10/6/66, York and Parker were reunited in a *Boone* episode that had York playing frontier braggart "Big Zack." SEE ALSO: Buddy Ebsen, Brian Keith, Fess Parker.

Otis Young

(1932–2001)

••••••••••••••••••••••••••••

A Korean War vet and New York University drama student, Young found himself in the right place at the right time for TV stardom. In 1965, Bill Cosby received second billing alongside Robert Culp in the James Bond–like caper *I Spy*. That show's enormous popularity convinced TV producers that civil rights was now "in." Other series popped up with similar white/black heroic teams, with *The Outcasts* (1968–1969) the most significant Western version. The premise had Southerner/former plantation owner Earl Corey (Don Murray) wandering in the company of former slave "Jemal David" (Young). Their uneasy alliance created unique tensions, the two uniting to fight off villains only to turn on each other the moment outside enemies had been defeated. Young's finest single performance came as Jack Nicholson's friend "Mule Mulhall" in *The Last Detail* (1973). Later in life he left Hollywood to work as both a college professor and an ordained minister. SEE ALSO: James Edwards, Don Murray, Raymond St. Jacques.

Tony Young

(1937–2002)

••••••••••••••••••••••••••••

Brooding, alienated, vulnerable, yet tough: That was the self-image of 1950s youth, embodied by Marlon Brando on the big screen and by Tony Young on the small. From Young's first TV appearances, this emerged as his stock role, on *Tombstone Territory* (10/23/59), *Lawman* (11/22/59), and *Overland Trail* (2/14/60). The series *Gunslinger* (1961) was produced for CBS by some members of the team that had created *Rawhide* two years earlier, with all of that previous show's stylistic elements intact right down to a Dimitri Tiomkin title song performed by Frankie Laine. Young played "Cord," a one-name loner. The title character hooked up with the cavalry to redeem his dark past. Meanwhile, back at the fort, pretty Amby (Midge Ware) waited for her bad boy with a heart of gold to return. Charles D. Gray ("Pico") and Dee Pollock ("Billy Urchin") lightened things up. Opposite *The Untouchables*, this show lasted half a year. Young played Cord-like characters in low-budget oaters for R. G. Springsteen, dedicated to keeping the B Western alive during the 1960s: *He Rides Tall* (1964) and *Taggart* (1964), both costarring the venerable Dan Duryea. SEE ALSO: Preston Foster, Charles D. Gray, John Pickard.

Chief Yowlachie

(1891–1966)

••••••••••••••••••••••••••••••••

A Washington State native of the Yakima tribe, Yowlachie originally intended to become an opera singer under the Anglo name Daniel Simmons. Hollywood offered him Indian roles, best of all "Quo" in *Red River* (1948), the helper to "Groot" Walter Brennan, a cook on the cattle drive. Yowlachie played Geronimo twice: in the serial *Son of Geronimo: Apache Avenger* (1952) and on *Stories of the Century* (2/14/54). SEE ALSO: Mary Castle, Jim Davis, Rodd Redwing.

Gareth Yuen

(1978–)

••••••••••••••••••••••••••••••••

Yuen played "Hop Sing," houseboy/cook, on *Ponderosa* (2001–2002), the prequel to *Bonanza*. Every attempt was made to keep the role from becoming an Asian stereotype as in the original. He later portrayed "Dax Lo" on *Power Rangers: Operation Overdrive* (2007). SEE ALSO: Matt Carmody, Jared Daperis, Daniel Hugh Kelly, Drew Powell.

Anthony Zerbe

(1936–)

••••••••••••••••••••••••••••••••

A smug smile caused Zerbe to be typecast for TV/films as the villain. This was *not* true of his first Western, the classic *Will Penny* (1968), in which he played "Dutchy," Charlton Heston's long-suffering sidekick. He showed up as nasty types opposite Paul Newman (*The Life and Times of Judge Roy Bean*, 1972), John Wayne (*Rooster Cogburn*, 1975), and Richard Chamberlain (as John Charles Fremont), as a mean-spirited Big Bill Williams (*Dream West*, 1986). Zerbe received an Emmy award (Best Supporting Actor) for the suave police lieutenant "K. C." in *Harry O* (1975–1976, David Janssen). Then came the role of a lifetime: "Teaspoon Hunter," the rascally but humane overseer of teenage heroes in *The Young Riders* (1989–1992). Most recently he appeared as "The Councillor" in the *Matrix* movies. SEE ALSO: Stephen Baldwin, Josh Brolin, Ty Miller.

INDEX OF NAMES

Names in **boldface** indicate main
encyclopedia entries. Page numbers
in **boldface** indicate photographs.

G

Howard, Ronald, 91
Hoy, Robert F., 88
Huffaker, Clair, 284
Huggins, Roy, 109, 326
Hull, Henry, 84
Hunnicutt, Arthur, 156, 176, 239
Hunter, Evan, 264
Hunter, Jeff(rey), 71, 84, 102, 130, 176–179
Huston, Anjelica, 122, 133
Hutchins, Will, 9, 23, 178, 282, 328

7

Ireland, Jill, 60, 74, 179
Ireland, John, 54, 68, 118, 179–180
Ivers, Robert, 95

J

Jackman, Hugh, 261
Jaeckel, Richard, 118, 135, 162, 181
Jaffe, Taliesin, 301
Jennings, Waylon, 80, 181–182, 194, 238–239
Johnson, Ben, 71, 132, 182
Johnson, Brad, 106, 107, 116, 166, 183
Johnson, Brad, 183–184
Johnson, Chubby, 177
Johnson, Rafer, 255–256
Johnson, Russell, 23, 53, 184, 233, 250
Jolley, Norman, 230
Jones, Buck, 68, 218
Jones, Chris(topher), 184
Jones, Dick(ie), 30, 82, 95, 184–185, 208, 246
Jones, L. Q., 132, 185–186, 326, 327
Jones, Stan, 186–187
Jones, Tommy Lee, 13, 58, 77, 150, 187, 288, 321
Jory, Victor, 101

K

Kamm, Kris, 280
Kane, Joseph, 70
Kavovit, Andrew, 40
Keim, Betty Lou, 189
Keith, Brian, 112, 115, 136, 188, 189–190, 253, 280, 311
Keller, Harry, 316
Kelley, DeForest, 190
Kelly, Daniel Hugh, 190
Kelly, Jack, 9, 35, 87, 148, 191, 266, 280, 326
Kelly, Sean, 160
Kennedy, Adam, 191
Kennedy, Arthur, 189, 192
Kennedy, Burt, 284
Kennedy, Douglas, 192, 230, 278
Kenyon, Sandy, 285, 319
Kern, Roger, 267
Kershner, Irvin, 18
Kerwin, Brian, 264
Kimmell, Leslie, 141
King, Wright, 193, 266
Knight, John Forrest "Fuzzy," 30, 32, 68, 193
Knight, Shirley, 240
Kook, Guich, 301
Kozak, Harley Jane, 54
Kristofferson, Kris, 2, 31, 80, 182, 193–194, 201, 238–239, 246
Kruschen, Jack, 89

L

Lacher, Taylor, 143
Ladd, Alan, 17, 67, 74, 94, 115, 179, 182, 234, 251, 264, 274
Ladd, Diane, 293
Laine, Frankie, 344
Lake, Stuart N., 244–245
Lambert, Jack, 35
L'Amour, Louis, 14, 49, 73, 132, 184, 295

Sullivan, Grant, 95
Summers, Hope, 89
Swain, Jack, 256
Swam, Robert, 35
Sweeney, D. B., 321
Swift, Susan, 264

7

Taeger, Ralph, 260, 300, 309
Talbot(t), Gloria, 247, 309–310, 316,
   337
Tannen, William, 246, 310
Taylor, Buck, 217, 310–311
Taylor, Cliff, 201
Taylor, Dub, 238, 280, 311
Taylor, Forrest, 273
Taylor, Joan, 40
Taylor, Kent, 227, 312, 335
Taylor, Robert, 135, 154, 163, 253, 264,
   272–273, 312, 333
Taylor, Robert Lewis, 285
Taylor, Rod, 237, 313–315
Teal, Ray, 314
Tenorio, John, Jr., 143
Thompson, Peter M., 247
Thornton, Sigrid, 174, 314
Thorpe, Jerry, 74
Thundercloud, Chief, 314
Thurston, Carol, 247
Tibbles, George, 296
Tiomkin, Dimitri, 344
Tobey, Kenneth, 314–315
Tobias, George, 314
Tong, Kam, 47
Toovey, Shawn, 293
Torn, Rip, 20, 88
Torrey, Roger, 279
Tors, Ivan, 91, 331–332
Totter, Audrey, 202, 230, 315
Townsend, Jill, 334
Tracey, Ray, 24
Travis, Randy, 316

Tritt, Travis, 182, 239, 280
Tryon, (Thomas) Tom, 171, 310, 316,
   317–319
Tubb, Barry, 289, 321
Tucker, Forrest, 55, 68, 107, 113, 235,
   313, 319–320
Tully, Tom, 74
Turner, Frederic Jackson, 12

U

Urecal, Minerva, 140
Urich, Robert, 321

V

Vaccaro, Brenda, 321
Valentine, Jack, 322
Van Cleef, Lee, 47, 71, 322–323, 334
Van Patten, James, 264
Vaughn, Robert, 324
Verdugo, Elena, 130
Vic, Federick W., 34
Victor, James, 274
Vidal, Gore, 287
Vinson, Gary, 296
Vogel, Mitch, 324
Voight, Jon, 150, 187, 289

W

Waggner, George, 284
Wainwright, James, 52, 325
Wakely, Jimmy, 105, 311
Walker, Clint, 136, 148, 163, 169, 173,
   185, 232, 265, 280, 325–326, 327–329
Wall, Bree Seanna, 259
Wallace, George, 247
Waller, Eddy, 192, 211
Walter, Tracy, 171
Walters, Jamie, 261
Ward, Larry, 157, 329
Ware, Midge, 344

INDEX OF SHOWS

Titles of TV series are indicated by boldface; titles of made-for-TV movies are
italicized; titles of TV mini-series are en-
closed in quotation marks. Page numbers
in **boldface** indicate photographs.